ISLAMIC HISTORY
OF THE MIDDLE EAST

ISLAMIC HISTORY
OF THE MIDDLE EAST

backgrounds, development, and fall
of the Arab Empire

WILSON B. BISHAI
Harvard University

Allyn and Bacon, Inc., Boston

To William, David, and Linda

Library of Congress Card Catalog Number: 68-12977

Printed in the United States of America

Second printing . . . May, 1969

FOREWORD

There is no abundance of books on the history of the medieval Near East, so Dr. Bishai's work is most welcome. One might divide books on history into those which are concerned primarily with facts and give one many details, and others which eschew happenings to discuss the philosophical implications of the movement of nomads, the decline of a culture, or speculations on "it might have been." Dr. Bishai's book, which was written mainly for college students, steers a middle course. He describes the chronological sequence of events but more is added to the bare bones of events and dates. Reasons for the fall of a dynasty or a change in outlook are given to the reader who is invited to consider further implications of the great periods of Islamic history.

Islam brought a profound change to the Near East and permanently altered the course of history. The extensive conquests of the Arabs seem almost miraculous, and it is only proper that the history of the Near East after the seventh century should concentrate on the Arabs. After the Arab conquests the Arabic language became the vehicle of culture as well as communication throughout the Islamic world, much as Latin in western Europe in the Middle Ages. While it may be true that the message of the Arabs—that history began with Muhammad—caused the Egyptians, Syrians and people of Mesopotamia to forget their own ancient and tradition-filled histories, this same attitude did not overwhelm the Iranian peoples, the Turks and others who accepted Islam. Islam may have been the national culture of the Arab people in the first two centuries of Islam, but it soon became universal or oecumenical. Arab or Arabic and Islam ceased to be synonyms, if they ever were, and Islam became a world culture and civilization vying with the Christian culture of Europe. The architects of this oecumenical civilization of Islam were, for the most part, the Iranian peoples, and their contributions in all fields of learning to the Islamic edifice are legion.

Just as the unity of the Christian world was broken, so the realm of Islam split into various kingdoms and principalities after the decline of the Abbasid Caliphate. Yet an underlying unity, based on religion, continued. It was only with the development of national states in the 15th and 16th centuries that the Near East became stabilized between the two poles of the Ottoman Empire and the Safavid state of Persia, opposed in religion as well as politics. The background of the present Near East must be studied in order to understand the rivalries and tensions which still beset that part of the world. And since our world is now so small the Near East is almost in everyone's back yard.

The present book provides a general basis for further investigations. The glossaries of terms and unfamiliar words, following each chapter, are commendable, especially for students, and the bibliographies are well balanced for more reading. It is hoped that many readers will be stimulated to greater interest in a fascinating part of the world by Dr. Bishai's volume.

Richard N. Frye
Aga Khan Professor of Iranian
Harvard University

PREFACE

The term "Arab Empire" occurring frequently in this book is used mainly in its linguistic connotation rather than its original, or ethnic meaning. Besides its limited reference to the Arabs of Arabia, known to have migrated into various regions of the Middle East after the rise of Islam, it also refers to the vast majority of the original inhabitants of these regions who became Arabicized by conversion to Islam as well as by adoption of Arabic as a mother tongue. The Arabic language is known to have followed wherever Islam went. In the peripheral regions of the Islamic domain, it constituted a noticeable substratum in many languages; in the interior (the Fertile Crescent, Egypt, and North Africa), however, it gradually displaced the native languages and became the mother tongue of the bulk of the population, both Muslim and non-Muslim. It may well be said that the ethnic prestige of the Arabs during the Umayyad regime was generally replaced during the Abbasid regime by the linguistic and literary superiority of the Arabic language. As a matter of fact, a number of writers during the classical period belonged to the non-Muslim, but Arabicized, segment of the population—an indication that although Islam was a major factor in shaping the features of the Arab Empire, Arabic was the main expression of its cultural and literary heritage. Accordingly, in spite of the fact that during the Abbasid regime the original Arabs of Arabia did not exercise as much political authority as the Arabicized Muslims of other ethnic backgrounds, the empire was, for all practical purposes, Arabic in speech, literature, and orientation—a situation which well justifies the use of the term "Arab Empire" to refer to the whole period from the Arab conquest of the Middle East until the fall of Baghdad in 1258. An analogous situation may be found in the history of the Roman Empire; after the rule of Hadrian, Romanized citizens rather than native Romans ruled over the empire.

Referring to history as literature, G.M. Trevelyan has said, "History, is in its unchangeable essence, 'a tale.' " As a "tale," the history of the Arab Empire was recorded by Arab historians in minute detail. In fact, their annals abound with intriguing stories of the public and private lives of many Arab caliphs, as well as reports of numerous other events that took place within the Islamic domain. Some historians have recently cast doubt upon the veracity of a number of these tales and reports; nevertheless, these writings still constitute the main source for reconstructing the Islamic history of the Middle East—especially during the empire period.

This book is not intended to be a reference history of the Islamic period of the Middle East; it is designed rather to furnish readers (especially those exposed to the history of the area for the first time) with the fundamentals of Middle East history during the Arab Empire, without making it necessary for them to read through so many of the intricate details supplied by Arab historians. It is not by any means merely a compilation of selected "tales" of the Islamic history of the Middle East; it also includes some analytical and interpretational material for the purpose of exploring, even if in a limited way, the various factors (religious, social, and political) that led to the rise, development, and fall of the Arab Empire. The Islamic religion as a way of life, tribalism, and Arab dual allegiance, for instance, are discussed as prime factors that greatly influenced the course of history in the Islamic Middle East.

Furthermore, since the Islamic period serves to a certain extent as a link between ancient and modern history, an attempt has also been made to indicate briefly the major links between Islam and the ancient Semitic cultures, and between Islam and medieval Europe.

Each part of this book begins with a short introduction and ends with two lists—one of important terms, the other of suggested supplementary readings. The Appendices include lists of important dynasties as well as translations of excerpts from Arabic literary sources; these are given to acquaint the reader with some features of the reports of Arab historians. At the end of the book a table of important dates is supplied to help the reader obtain a chronological picture of the various major events of the Arab Empire.

There remains a brief remark about the transliteration system of Arabic names. For reasons concerned mainly with printing difficulties, no diacritical marks appear with transliterated Arabic names. In other words, these names are spelled according to their Arabic pronounciation but without any diacritical marks. The *hamza* sign is ' and the *ayn* sign is ' ; however, they do not appear in an initial position. There should be no serious difficulties arising from this unavoidable system of transliteration.

I am deeply grateful to Professor Edwin Wright, Professor D.M. Dunlop, Dr. Lawrence Marwick, Dr. William Spencer, and Dr. Phebe Ann Marr for reading the manuscript of this book in advance and offering helpful remarks that contributed effectively toward the improvement of its final format.

Wilson B. Bishai
Harvard University
Cambridge, Massachusetts

CONTENTS

PART V
BEGINNING OF THE ISLAMIC STATE

PART VI
THE ORTHODOX CALIPHATE, 632-661

PART VII
THE UMAYYAD DYNASTY, 661-750

PART VIII
THE EARLY ABBASID PERIOD, 750-861

MAPS

PART I

GEOGRAPHY OF THE MIDDLE EAST

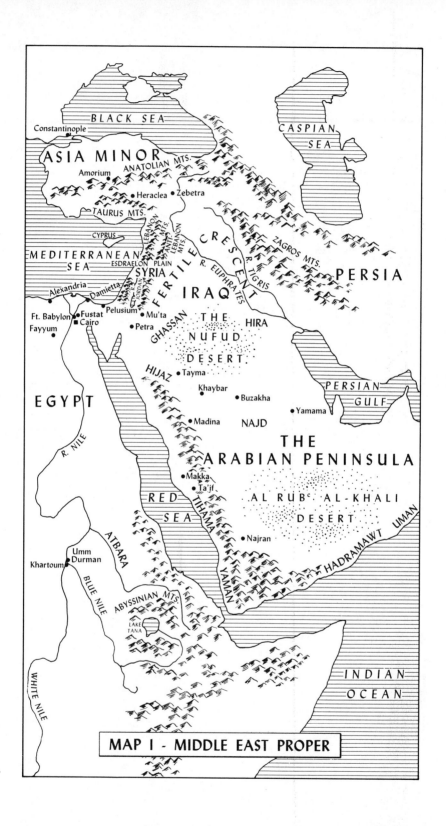

MAP I - MIDDLE EAST PROPER

CHAPTER 1

INTRODUCTION

The "Middle East" is a geographical term frequently used to refer to various territories around the Mediterranean Sea, but excluding Western Europe. This vast area extends from Morocco in the west to Persia and Afghanistan in the east, and from the Balkan peninsula in the north to the Sudan and the Indian Ocean in the south. Reasons for the amorphous nature of the boundaries of the Middle East go back perhaps to the period before World War I when, in relation to Western Europe, the territories of the Ottoman Empire were called "the Near East," India and its neighboring territories "the Middle East," and China and Japan "the Far East." During World War II, however, the British were forced to move their Middle East Command from India to Cairo in Egypt, an area commonly included in the Near East. Consequently, the terms "Middle East" and "Near East" came to be used interchangeably to refer to various territories in Europe, Asia, and Africa, especially around the eastern Mediterranean. Since military communications during the war frequently used the term "Middle East," the use of "Near East" gradually diminished. At present it is used only by a few writers who insist on using the terms Near, Middle, and Far East in their original geographical meaning.

Many writers now use the term "Middle East" to refer roughly to the non-European areas around the Mediterranean, together with the European portion of Turkey. In any case, it has become customary procedure among writers and historians to define the boundaries of the term "Middle East" to fit their particular purposes. In this book, the term "Middle

East Proper" is used in a narrow sense to refer to the territories where Semitic cultures rose and developed in the ancient world. It includes the regions of the Fertile Crescent, Arabia, and the valley of the Nile. In modern terms it includes Iraq, Syria, Lebanon, Israel (Palestine), Jordan, the Arabian Peninsula, and Egypt.

In a broader sense, the term "Middle East" is used to refer to a larger area including the Middle East Proper *plus* the rest of the Arabic-speaking countries in North Africa, together with Turkey and Iran in Asia. Although the latter are non-Arab Muslim countries, their Islamic history ties them inseparably to the Arab world.

The Middle East Proper may be divided into three main areas: the Fertile Crescent, the Nile Valley, and the Arabian Desert. The Fertile Crescent was the location of ancient Mesopotamia and Canaan, the Nile Valley was the center of ancient Egyptian civilization, and the Arabian Desert was primarily responsible for the early waves of nomadic migrants generally believed to have directly or indirectly triggered the birth of civilization in both Egypt and Mesopotamia. On the other hand, it is very probable that the early settlers of the Nile and the Fertile Crescent Valleys could have never succeeded in initiating any cultural revolutions had the geography of the two regions not made it possible for man to make the most remarkable transition in all history—namely, the transition from food gatherer to food producer.

In a very broad sense, Islamic civilization may be considered a continuation of the ancient Semitic cultures of the Middle East. In fact, some patterns of these ancient cultures have survived more or less till the present time, constituting, as it were, a visible link between the ancient and the modern eras. In the Middle East today a traveler may observe certain patterns of culture established much earlier than the Islamic period existing side by side and in sharp contrast with those of the twentieth century.

The Middle East Proper is commonly known as the cradle of civilization. From the chronological point of view, it represents about seven millennia of sedentary life, of which the first five and a half belong to the ancient cultures that flourished in Mesopotamia, Egypt, and Canaan. The last fifteen hundred years are marked mainly by the rise and fall of the Arab Empire and the spread of Islamic civilization throughout the whole Middle East.

The Middle East Proper is also the home of the Semites who are credited with introducing to the world its three monotheistic religions – Judaism, Christianity, and Islam, of which the latter alone claims about half a billion adherents. Besides their spiritual contributions, the Semites are credited with developing civilization and maintaining the cultural lead in Western Asia for over two thousand years before the Persians defeated the New Babylonians in 539 B.C. For about a millennium afterwards, non-Semites were dominant until the Arabs established their empire shortly after 622 A.D.

CHAPTER 2

THE FERTILE CRESCENT

The Fertile Crescent is a huge, sickle-shaped curve of cultivable soil that begins north of the Persian Gulf and follows the path of the Tigris and Euphrates Rivers in a northwesterly direction until it reaches the mountains of Anatolia, then bends down in a southwesterly direction toward the Sea of Galilee where it begins to straighten in a southerly direction following the course of the Jordan River to the Dead Sea. This is supposed to be the route followed by the patriarch Abraham as he traveled from Ur of the Chaldees in Mesopotamia to Canaan, the Promised Land. It is a route which runs through two river valleys—the Tigris-Euphrates Valley and the Jordan Valley—marking an extensive alluvial plain which separates the vast Arabian Desert from the Anatolian Mountains in Asia Minor and the Zagros Mountains in Persia.

THE TIGRIS-EUPHRATES VALLEY

The Tigris-Euphrates Valley is by far the largest valley in the Mediterranean region. Its two rivers are supplied by numerous streams that flow from the Anatolian Mountains. The larger river, the Euphrates, follows a southeasterly course across Syria, where it is augmented by the Khabur River before winding its way into Iraq. There it carves its path through extensive marshlands until it reaches its confluence with the Tigris at Shatt-al-Arab.

The Tigris also starts in the Anatolian Mountains of

5

southeast Turkey, but it flows directly into Iraq. There it is augmented by the Greater Zab and the Lesser Zab, by the Uzaym River (whose
basin averages 4,000 square miles), and by the Diyala River, which
joins it only twenty miles below Baghdad. Like the Euphrates, the Tigris passes through extensive marshlands before both rivers join at
Shatt-al-Arab into one stream that flows into the Persian Gulf.

These two rivers spring from areas with abundant rainfall that
yearly fills their streams to overflowing. As they approach the middle
of Mesopotamia, they enter dry country with negligible rainfall; there
they overflow their basins for several weeks during the flood season
before they recede to their main streams. Southern Mesopotamia is
fairly dry with little or no rainfall; however, due to the regular flooding of its two main arteries the soil is naturally watered, supplied
with silt, and then left to dry during the low season. The regularity of
this cycle apparently challenged the ancient dwellers of Mesopotamia
not only to discover agriculture, but also to dig canals in strategic
locations in order to control the yearly flow of water. Otherwise, these
floods would have become a continuous threat to human life in the
whole region.

THE JORDAN VALLEY

The western side of the Fertile Crescent is formed in one of
nature's most amazing molds on the earth's surface. It starts in the
north at an elevation of 3770 feet in the Biqa' Valley,which lies between two chains of mountains –the Lebanon to the west and the Anti-
Lebanon to the east. It then drops down to 685 feet below sea level at
Lake Tiberias and follows the sharp and steep windings of the River
Jordan to a depression 1292 feet below sea level in the region of the
Dead Sea. The Jordan Valley is about sixty-five miles long and varies
in width from three to fourteen miles. The Jordan River is the main
stream, and drains the mountain watersheds on both sides. This great
depression extends beyond the Dead Sea into Wadi al-Araba, which
continues southward through desert land toward the Gulf of Aqaba.

From the Lebanon Mountains to the north of the Jordan Valley flow
two main streams, the Orontes and the Litani, which supply the
fertile Biqa' Valley with water before they pour into the Mediterranean.
East of, and parallel to, the Lebanon Mountains extends another chain
of mountains called the Anti-Lebanon from which a few small streams
flow eastward, chief of which is the Barada, which supplies the city of
Damascus with water, and causes the area around it to be a fertile
oasis in the midst of the desert.

In brief, the terrain of Syria and Palestine may be described as a
series of alternating highlands and lowlands. First comes the coastal
strip, about twenty-five miles wide in Palestine but narrowing considerably in Lebanon to a width of about four miles near Beirut; in
fact, in some locations the mountains rise directly from the water. To

the east of this coastal strip, running north to south, tower the Lebanon Mountains, breaking their guard only to allow entrance to the Plain of Esdraelon and then resuming with the highlands of western Palestine, whose own altitude accents the great depression of the Jordan Valley. East of these mountains lie the Biqa' Valley in the north and its counterpart the Jordan Valley in the south. East of these valleys rise the Anti-Lebanon Mountains in the north and the highlands of Eastern Palestine and Jordan, holding back the Arabian Desert before it claims domain over a vast area below the Fertile Crescent from the Red Sea to the Persian Gulf.

CLIMATE OF THE FERTILE CRESCENT

The entire Fertile Crescent enjoys a typically Mediterranean climate – hot dry summers and mild damp winters. Only along the northeast border of the Crescent, as it reaches its highest latitude and begins to curve southward again in Iraq, does more continental weather with severe extremes prevail. The peaks of the Lebanon and Zagros Mountains remain snow covered all the year round, forming a majestic backdrop for the fertile valley below.

During the winter, rainfall varies from abundant to scarce in many areas of the Fertile Crescent. Torrents of water overflow rivers and creeks while snow accumulates on the mountain tops. During the summer, however, creeks dry up and rivers become the main supply of water in the valleys. On the mountains, especially in Lebanon, melting snow forms beautiful running streams that descend the mountain slopes, winding their courses through the rocks. Many springs gush to form rapidly running creeks that decorate the mountainside. On the other hand, where the landscape is flat, especially in southern Iraq, the summer sun dries up much of the moisture in the air, causing heat and dust to be the daily order. At night, however, a cool breeze refreshes the atmosphere and partially compensates for the parching heat of the day.

CHAPTER 3

THE NILE VALLEY

THE RIVER NILE

The Nile is the longest single river in the world and is the dominating feature of the northeastern quarter of Africa. It stretches from Kenya and Tanganyika in central Africa to Egypt on the Mediterranean in a course 4160 miles long. The only waterway that exceeds it in length is the Mississippi River together with its tributary, the Missouri. The Nile, however, has unique features. Its waters are derived mainly from the mountains of Ethiopia, Kenya, and Tanganyika where there is considerable rainfall. After these waters meet at the juncture of the White and Blue Niles, they travel a distance of almost 2000 miles in an area of little or no rainfall in northern Sudan and Egypt. Yet the amount of water carried by the Nile is so tremendous that the river floods its banks in these two countries, covering a basin of about one million square miles for over a month each year before it recedes. Without the phenomenon of this annual flood, all Egypt and northern Sudan would be part of the great Sahara Desert that extends across North Africa.

Among the main tributaries that feed the Nile is the White Nile. It supplies the main stream with a steady flow of water all the year aound. The White Nile flows with a regular and steady flow because the vast lakes, Victoria and Albert, serve as huge reservoirs in times of drought. The White Nile is also supplied by other smaller tributaries that flow from as far away as the Congo in West Africa. The Blue Nile joins the White Nile between Khartoum and Umm Durman, and several miles to the north the Atbara joins the main stream. The White Nile has a steady supply of water throughout the year. However, during the flooding period between July and September, first the Atbara and then the Blue Nile, with strong descending currents from the Ethiopian mountains, almost cut off the White Nile's flow as they flood their own banks as well as the banks of the main stream until the latter reaches the shores of the Mediterranean. The Atbara is the last tributary to feed the Nile; the main stream flows through otherwise barren land until it branches at the Delta and pours into the sea.

GEOGRAPHY OF EGYPT

The geography of Egypt, therefore, may be summarized as "the Nile." Nothing describes Egypt better than the famous statement made by Herodotus about four centuries B.C., which simply says, "Egypt is the gift of the Nile." Without the Nile there would have been no inhabitable Egypt; it is no wonder then that the ancient Egyptians deified and worshiped it.

Egypt is a large segment of northeast Africa totaling 386,198 square miles, or almost as much territory as the combined states of Texas and New Mexico. Most of the country is desert, but curiously enough many Egyptians live and die without ever catching a glimpse of its sands. At present about 30 million Egyptians live in a narrow strip of land totaling only 13,500 square miles, which the Nile irrigates yearly. This strip is among the most densely populated areas of the world, averaging more than 2000 persons per square mile.

The terrain of Egypt is flat, with some low hills separating the Nile Valley from the desert on both sides of the river. Efforts have been made recently to tap the subterranean waters of large areas in the western desert; so far, sweet water wells have allowed about six oases to thrive west of the Nile Valley. If subterranean waters prove to be plentiful, there is great hope of cultivating millions of acres in certain low areas in the western desert. The climate of Egypt is hot and dry during the summer, and mild with negligible rain in winter; the autumn and spring are ideally moderate.

A little study reveals the unique strategic location of Egypt. It is almost at the center of the three continents of Africa, Asia, and Europe, and enjoys natural protection on four sides. The Mediterranean and Red Seas shield it from the north and east, the desert affords a nearly impenetrable frontier on the west, and the cataracts of the Nile in the Sudan make navigation from the south very difficult. It is generally believed that Egypt's natural fortifications have been the main reason for the long duration of its independence in ancient times, and the survival of the Egyptian people for almost 5000 years of recorded history.

THE EGYPTIAN SYSTEM OF IRRIGATION

Since ancient times the Egyptians have depended on the flooding of the Nile to irrigate their lands; as floods receded, the peasants planted their seeds and waited for the harvest. In some instances the ancient Egyptians are believed to have dug irrigation canals and developed techniques to lift water to higher levels. The water wheel and a native instrument called the *shaduf* are two ancient inventions that are still used. In the nineteenth century the Egyptians embarked on a large-scale project to control the flood waters in a network of canals in order to till as many acres as possible. Thus, instead of cultivating the soil only once a year after the receding flood, they are able to plant up to three times a year by drawing water from these canals whenever needed.

Although the Nile is Egypt's life, it is also its main source of trouble. If it is generous and brings more water than expected, it floods its banks, submerging thousands of villages scattered along its main course. If it is miserly, the crops fail and Egypt suffers famine. The Egyptians, both blessed and plagued by the Nile, must continually build dams and reinforce its banks to control its ravaging floods. In spite of these problems, the mighty Nile continues to be the greatest and most precious possession of the Egyptians.

CHAPTER 4

THE ARABIAN PENINSULA

Of all the countries of the Middle East Proper, Arabia is by far the largest. Unfortunately, most of it is uninhabitable desert; only a narrow coastal strip sustains some cultivation. The Arabian Desert extends beyond the northern borders of Arabia itself and penetrates deeply into Jordan, Syria, and Iraq to be checked only by the Fertile Crescent. Were it not for the Red Sea and the Nile Valley to the west, the Arabian Desert might be considered an extension of the great Sahara of North Africa. As it is, the Arabian Desert is almost surrounded by major bodies of water. The Red Sea borders it to the west, the Indian Ocean lies south, the Persian Gulf stretches along its eastern side, and the waterways of the Fertile Crescent close in on it from the north. It is no wonder that the Arabs themselves call their land *Jazirat al-Arab*, "the Island of the Arabs."

THE COASTLINE OF ARABIA

The Arabian Peninsula is inhabited mainly along its coastal areas, the western and southern sides being the chief centers of population. There, in a coastal strip about thirty miles wide, which the Arabs call Tihama in the north and Yaman in the south, enough rain falls to sustain some vegetation. The limited rainfall in these areas collects in short creeks that flow rapidly into the sea, leaving dry narrow plains called *wadis* scattered along the coastal line.

11

To conserve the water drained into the sea, the Arabs of the south built dams across these creeks to store water to cultivate the scattered *wadis* that would have been otherwise swallowed up by the encroaching desert.

HIJAZ, NAJD, AND THE EASTERN SHORES

Next to Tihama in the north, a chain of mountains borders the coastal strip and separates it from the desert interior. These mountains are called the *Hijaz,* "separation," a term used also to refer to the whole area of northwest Arabia. The heart of Arabia east of the Hijaz and west of the Persian Gulf may be divided into three main regions. In the north lies the Nufud Desert, whose numerous sand dunes are difficult to traverse. Through the center extends a semi-desert plateau called Najd, known for its scattered wells and oasis-like centers that serve as outposts along the caravan route crossing the interior of Arabia from east to west. South of the Najd stretches the most rugged and uninhabitable desert in the whole world. It is known as *al-Rub' al-Khali,* "the empty quarter," and was crossed in 1931 for the first time by the daring explorer Bertram Thomas.

The eastern coastal region along the shores of the Persian Gulf sustains some vegetation, especially around the sheikdom of Uman. Had it not been for the rich deposits of oil that were discovered there at the turn of the nineteenth century, however, that portion of eastern Arabia would have remained an almost uninhabitable part of the desert.

AGRICULTURE AND TRADE ROUTES IN ARABIA

The climate of the Arabian Peninsula changes from north to south. South Arabia enjoys more rainfall and a better climate, especially near the mountains of Yaman, while North Arabia has meager rainfall on the coast and no rain at all in the interior. The weather is continental, with extreme temperatures in both winter and summer, especially inland where the desert is almost untraversable.

Due to its climate, South Arabia became the main center of agriculture in the peninsula, producing herbs, spices, and coffee. The rest of Arabia, otherwise a wasteland, prospered from its trade routes which joined South Arabia to the Fertile Crescent, and also eastern Arabia to the western coastal line. From ancient times, North Arabia practically monopolized trade routes not only to South Arabia, but also to the Persian Gulf and the Indian shores. Accordingly, the coast of Arabia is dotted with numerous towns which evolved from earlier settlements that once served as commercial centers where merchants traded commodities between the Orient and the Middle East.

IMPORTANT TERMS

Al-Rub' al-Khali: ''The empty quarter,'' a non-traversable rough desert located in the southern Arabian Peninsula.

The Biqa' Valley: A valley northeast of Lebanon watered by small rivers flowing from the Lebanon Mountains.

The Fertile Crescent: A sickle-shaped valley north of the Arabian Desert formed by the Tigris and Euphrates Rivers in the east and the Jordan in the west.

Hijaz: A low mountain ridge separating Tihama from Najd in Arabia. It also refers to the northwestern region of Arabia.

Jordan River: A narrow, winding river in Palestine flowing from the Sea of Galilee into the Dead Sea, forming a part of the western arm of the Fertile Crescent.

Middle East: A term used in this book to refer to the area occupied by all Arab countries in both North Africa and Asia with the addition of Turkey and Iran.

Middle East Proper: A term used in this book to refer to the area now occupied by Egypt, the Arabian Peninsula, Iraq, Syria, Lebanon, Israel, and Jordan.

Najd: A central plateau east of Tihama in Arabia.

Nile River: A vital stream of water in northeast Africa, whose yearly overflow is Egypt's chief source of wealth.

Nufud: A rugged desert in the north of the Arabian Peninsula.

Tigris and Euphrates Rivers: Two rivers in Iraq fed by the Anatolian Mountains that form the eastern arm of the Fertile Crescent.

Tihama: The coastal strip of western Arabia south of Hijaz.

Yaman: The coastal strip of southwest Arabia below Tihama.

SUPPLEMENTARY READINGS

Atlas of the Arab World and the Middle East (London, 1960). Introduction by C.F. Beckingham.

GRANT, CHRISTINA, *The Syrian Desert* (London, 1937).

HAZARD, HARRY W., *Atlas of Islamic History* (Princeton, 1951).

HURST, H.E., *The Nile* (London, 1952).

FISHER, W.G. *The Middle East: A Physical, Social, and Regional Geography* (London, 1956).

PEARCY, GEORGE E., *The Middle East an Indefinable Region* (Washington, 1959).

PHILBY, H. ST. JOHN, *Arabian Highlands* (Ithaca, 1952).

——, *The Empty Quarter* (London, 1933).

POUNDS, NORMAN, and KINGSBURY, ROBERT, *An Atlas of Middle Eastern Affairs* (New York, 1963).

ROOLVINK, R., *Historical Atlas of the Muslim Peoples* (Amsterdam, 1961).

SEMPLE, ELLEN C., *The Geography of the Mediterranean Region* (London, 1932).

TWITCHELL, K.S., *Saudi Arabia* (Princeton, 1958).

PART ii

SEMITIC BACKGROUNDS OF THE ARAB WORLD

This part sketches the ancient history of Mesopotamia, Egypt, and Canaan for the purpose of outlining the development of early Semitic cultures. Emphasis is laid on the transition from tribalism to city-states, and from city-states to national existence and empire.

When the Persians occupied the Middle East Proper about 539 B.C., the Semites began a period of decline that lasted for many centuries. The rise of the Arabs in 622 A.D. may therefore be considered a "revival" of the ancient Semitic cultures that rose in Egypt, Mesopotamia, and Canaan as early as the third millennium B.C. and continued till the Persian occupation.

In discussing high points of the ancient history of the Semites in the following chapters, an effort will be made to point out the role of religion in establishing civil authority. It may be observed that even as the ancient kings who ruled in the Middle East Proper claimed divine sanction for their authority, so also the Islamic state was guided by "revealed" legislation at its inception. This clearly indicates that patterns of culture which characterized the ancient Semitic world were also functioning in the establishment of the Arab Empire.

CHAPTER 5

HOME OF THE SEMITES

SEMITIC MIGRATIONS: THE EARLY SEMITES

Anthropologists may disagree on when and how man originated, but there is a general agreement that the original home of the Caucasian race was the Caucasus plateau between the Caspian and Black Seas. It is generally assumed that early in prehistoric times when man emerged, Europe was still covered by a receding glacier; the Fertile Crescent was in a marshy state, having just shed its ice cap; and Arabia enjoyed an ideal climate in which man could make his first home. Accordingly, the early migrations of some groups of the Caucasian race were most probably directed toward the south through the Fertile Crescent into the Arabian Peninsula. Later on, however, perhaps due to the favorably changing climate in the river valleys, the direction of migration was reversed back to the Fertile Crescent ushering in the beginning of historic times in the area.

The early migrants who came to settle in the Arabian Peninsula apparently spoke languages related both to each other and to the Arabic language of today. From a linguistic point of view, these languages have been classified into a group frequently called the Semitic family of languages; the people who populated Arabia and its neighboring territories and who spoke these languages therefore have been called "Semites." They inhabited the coastal areas east of the Red Sea and west of the Persian Gulf; some of them may even have reached the southern strip of the peninsula along the Indian Ocean. Thus, Arabia cannot be considered the place where the Semites originated; at best, it was the place to which the Semites first migrated early in prehistoric times.

Archaeological objects abound in written and unwritten forms, testifying that the peoples of the Middle East Proper had made considerable progress toward establishing permanent settlements and distinctive cultures and civilizations by the dawn of the historical period about 3000 B.C. Egypt, for example, had a king who governed a unified realm; in Mesopotamia, aggregates of city-states were grouping together to form what may be called coalitions of cities. In Canaan and Arabia, nomadic and semi-nomadic tribes were still moving over hills and mountains and across plains and desert places. What we know of events of prehistoric times is gleaned from the archaeological evidence that has survived over the years.

NATURE'S CHALLENGE AND MAN'S RESPONSE

Rise of City-states

If civilization is in reality the result of "nature's challenge and man's response," then Mesopotamia and Egypt were ideal places for the rise of civilized communities and advanced cultures. There in the remote past man discovered agriculture and made the revolutionary transition from food-gathering to food-producing. The regular floods of the Tigris-Euphrates Rivers in Mesopotamia and the Nile in Egypt almost forced man to devise means to check the overflow of waters which threatened his dwelling –tasks that could never have been accomplished without joint action on the part of the whole community. When primitive societies found that cooperation was essential to their welfare and prosperity, a cornerstone of human civilization was laid. This cooperation, which was encouraged by the recurrent challenge of the annual flood, led to the aggregation of communities into villages, and later on into cities that developed into centers of trade. The rise of cities in the ancient Middle East may be considered a turning point in human social organization. Not only did these early peoples have to change their nomadic tribal customs in favor of communities not based simply on blood relations, but they also had to form political units and systems of government to safeguard the society against foreign invaders and domestic lawbreakers.

Arabia proper, whose meager resources could not maintain an expanding population for any length of time, became a home base from which Semitic tribes continually raided the settled communities in the Fertile Crescent and, to a lesser extent, Egypt. These systematic raids from Arabia acted as the main stimulus for establishing coalitions of cities. Such coalitions presumably started as defensive blocks to become later on nuclei for cooperative settlements and centralized governments.

Impetus for Religion

In observing various natural phenomena ancient man found many that defied his reason and perplexed the innermost depths of his soul. The systematic flow of water into canals giving life to buried seeds, the sunshine and warmth, the wind and thunderstorms—all these created in man deep concerns that led to myths and legends which attempted to explain the supernatural powers that governed his universe and to belief in numerous gods that supposedly had control over natural phenomena. Evidently the early settlers of the Middle East Proper became awed by the whims and moods of these various gods as interpreted to them by the priests and sorcerers of each god. With the passage of time, formal beliefs and rituals emerged and became vital features of the daily life of ancient man.

Development of Writing

The development of local trade and city governments created a need for keeping records of agricultural products and evidently compelled the early settlers of both Egypt and Mesopotamia to develop signs and symbols for recording business transactions. By the middle of the third millennium B.C., there existed highly developed systems, introducing what was to be perhaps the greatest invention in man's history—writing. In Mesopotamia the writing system called "cuneiform" developed consisting of wedge-shaped characters incised on soft clay tablets, while Egyptian writing took the form of hieroglyphics, a combination of pictures and symbols. The Canaanites, about a millennium later, developed the Semitic alphabet, whose symbols in different forms were later on introduced in the non-Semitic world, including Europe.

BEGINNING OF CIVILIZATION

Three Ancient Institutions

About 3000 B.C., there was laid in the Middle East the foundation for three institutions destined to revolutionize the social structure of the whole area: (1) trade, (2) government, and (3) religion. The city, as it was developing in the Fertile Crescent and the Nile Valley, was the nucleus and center for these three institutions. It was a market place for business transactions, a headquarters for emerging systems of government, and a meeting place for pilgrimage and worship. The Semitic nomads of Arabia, who periodically raided the settled areas in the Fertile Crescent, supplied the challenge that ultimately forced the sedentary population to form coalitions and establish unified political authorities. Archaeological records have revealed that as Semites from the desert raided or migrated to settled areas of the Fertile Crescent, political as well as cultural progress occurred.

These nomadic tribes were presumably surplus population of Arabia whose ancestors had settled in its coastal plains in prehistoric times after finding a few running creeks that sustained some agriculture. But periodically they were forced—possibly by drought or some other calamity—to abandon their settlements and find refuge elsewhere. Since Arabia had no exit except toward the Fertile Crescent, its inhabitants had to migrate first toward the north, and then turn eastward to Mesopotamia or westward to the Jordan Valley. Egypt was also within their reach, and they are believed to have crossed the Sinai Peninsula and entered Egypt either directly from the north or migrated southward along the coastal line of the Red Sea and reached Egypt through Wadi Hammamat.

The Millennial Theory

Although Semitic infiltration into the Fertile Crescent and the Nile Valley continued almost without interruption throughout ancient history, some historians have noticed that Arabia has experienced a large-scale population explosion roughly once every thousand years. This millennial theory is based on the hypothesis that the climate in Arabia has been adversely changing through the years and that the Arabs have been periodically forced to flee the encroachment of the desert upon arable lands. It is very difficult, however, to substantiate any drastic changes in the earth's weather pattern over the past five thousand years; and, therefore the periodic outbursts of the population of Arabia during this period of time must rest on some other grounds. In the absence of definite archaeological evidence, these outbursts may be attributed to temporary local calamities that forced mass emigration.

Be this as it may, according to the millennial theory the first of these Semitic outbursts was directed against Egypt in the middle of the fourth millennium B.C., and resulted in the mixing of Semites with native Egyptians and in the blossoming of the predynastic civilization in the Nile Valley. In the third millenium B.C., the Semitic Akkadians imposed their power upon the Sumerians of southern Mesopotamia and the Canaanite population of Syria and Palestine. Toward the middle of the second millennium B.C. the Hyksos (Semitic warriors) invaded Egypt. A few centuries later the Hebrews made their way toward Palestine, and the Arameans settled in the northern part of Syria known as the Biqa' Valley. About the middle of the first millennium B.C., some Arabs known as the Nabateans established themselves south of the Jordan Valley and founded a civilization that flourished till the Christian era. Under the banner of Islam, in the first millennium A.D. the Arabs spread their influence and sometimes power as far as Africa and China; this expansion is the main theme of this book. Finally, in our own millennium, only a few centuries ago, the Wahhabi movement took place in Arabia itself. Indeed, it was a movement of internal reform; but it might have expanded its influence to other regions outside the peninsula.

CHAPTER 6

THE SEMITES IN MESOPOTAMIA

BABYLONIAN SUPREMACY

Sumerians and Semites

Early documents from southern Mesopotamia reveal that a certain stock of people called Sumerians settled there first and established agricultural units that developed later into villages, towns, and cities. Early Semitic migration into these Sumerian settlements is generally believed to have taken place around the beginning of the third millennium B.C., that crucial period when cities were emerging and a Sumerian system of writing was ushering in the dawn of literacy. This Semitic infiltration into southern Mesopotamia is believed to have taken place peacefully. The urbanized Sumerians must have been as much in need of manpower for their growing settlements as the immigrating Semites were in need of food and products of technology. The incoming Semites were easily assimilated into their new environment, and they adopted the Sumerian customs and religion; however, they evidently kept their own Semitic dialects.

This was not by any means the end of nomadic infiltrations into Mesopotamia. Toward the end of the third millennium a group of Semitic tribes called Akkadians may have invaded Mesopotamia, and by the end of the same millennium another Semitic group called Amorites spread themselves, whether by conquest or peaceful infiltration, almost everywhere in the Fertile Crescent. Moreover, other scattered nomadic tribes, such as the Khaneans, the Benjaminites, and the Sutians, time and again beleaguered the growing settlements of the Fertile Crescent.

Babylonian Supremacy

The story of ancient Mesopotamia consists of the history of its southern regions, generally referred to as Babylonia,[1] whose beginning goes back to the third millennium B.C., and the history of Assyria in the north, which emerged about a millennium later. Babylonian history may be divided into the following periods.

1. The early dynastic, 2800-2340 B.C.

2. The Old Empire, 2340-2008 B.C.

3. The first period of decline, 2008-1750 B.C.

4. The Middle Empire, 1750-1595 B.C.

5. The second period of decline, 1595-612 B.C.

6. The New Empire, 612-539 B.C.

The Early Dynastic Period, 2800-2340 B.C.

During the early dynastic period coalitions of cities emerged, resulting in the establishment of regional confederations each ruled by a local dynasty of kings; among these confederations Uruk, Lagash, and Nippur were prominent. However, the main feature of the early dynastic period was the gradual transition from tribal to local territorial units. Continuous blows against Mesopotamian settlements from Arabia produced among the early sedentary population of Babylonia an urgent need for defense and security—a need that could not be met without the cooperation of various tribes on a level above tribal ties. However, at this point, individual loyalties still followed tribal lines, as each tribe continued to act independently as its own source of authority.

The transition from tribal to regional loyalties was perhaps achieved when the intertribal influence of religious institutions assumed a political role. Fortunately, Babylonian mythology had envisioned some celestial cooperation among the various gods of these tribes. Ancient Babylonian documents frequently mention assemblies

---

[1] The city of Babylon itself became politically prominent during the Middle Empire period; however, for the sake of convenience, the term Babylonia is used to refer to southern Mesopotamia throughout its ancient history.

of gods to discuss their problems and act collectively in any emergency affecting their domain. The most prominent gods in early
Babylonia were An, Enlil, and Ninhursag, presumably of Sumerian
origin. Enlil became especially important and was called "the father
of the gods" and "the king of all the lands." Since Enlil "resided"
at Nippur, which according to Sumerian mythology became the city
of the assembly of the gods, it gradually emerged as the chief religious
center in southern Mesopotamia. It is generally believed that other less
important religious centers emerged in various regions of Babylonia,
and later joined some political confederations in which the religious
allegiance of the tribes coincided more or less with their regional
loyalty to the confederation. In other words, the individual's allegiance
to the chief god of his own center became at the same time a duty
of loyalty to the larger political unit formed by a confederation of
cities. Among such confederations, the Nippur League was dominant,
being the center of the chief god Enlil himself.

The Old Empire, 2340-2008 B.C.

The movement toward unity progressed in the Old Empire with
the transition from various regional loyalties to one "national"
loyalty brought about by the force of religious allegiance. As the
Nippur League expanded and gained prestige, it gave the Babylonians
a sense of unity and religious solidarity far beyond their tribal or
regional differences, which increased as Enlil gained supremacy
and became a "national" god. It can be fairly assumed that shortly
before the Old Empire period there was an opportunity for a leader
to capitalize on the growing religious sentiments of the Babylonians,
both Sumerians and Akkadians. This opportunity was successfully
seized by Sargon of Akkad, who claimed a divine appointment (by
authority of the god Enlil) to unite all Babylonians. His title was
"the great governor of Enlil"; his justification for expansion was
a "divine" command to dismantle the walls of all the cities as far
as the shores of the sea. Under Sargon of Akkad the Babylonians
may be said to have reached a stage of "national existence" in which
tribal and regional loyalties were sublimated to one national loyalty
to the king, who ruled by order of the national god. This pattern of
transformation of loyalties was repeated in other regions of the Middle
East Proper down to the time of Islam, and in each case religion
played a very important role.

With the momentum gained by claiming divine guidance, Sargon
expanded his domain far beyond Babylonia proper; when he died he
left to his successors the first empire in the Fertile Crescent. Things
went well with Sargon's first two successors. However, troubles
began when the fourth king, Naram-Sin, apparently ignored the strong
religious sentiment of the people. He not only neglected to perform
the various religious rituals, but also dared to desecrate the temple
at Nippur itself, causing what the Babylonians later called "the

curse of Akkad." This unholy act of Naram-Sin struck at the very roots of Babylonian national sentiment, namely, religious allegiance. Dissatisfaction arose and rebellions flared up in almost all the cities of Babylonia. Internal troubles weakened the empire so that it fell an easy prey to certain desert warriors known as the Gutians who raided Babylonia and brought about the downfall of Sargon's empire.

The First Period of Decline, 2008-1750 B.C.

After a brief revival during the rule of the third dynasty of Ur, the Old Babylonian Empire came to an end. Political authority collapsed as several city states competed for supremacy. Chief of these cities were Isin and Larsa. They continued to maintain the lead among other Babylonian cities during the first period of decline until Babylonian "nationalism" flared up again, giving rise to the kingdom of the great Hammurabi and the Middle Empire.

The Middle Empire, 1750-1595 B.C.

Before Hammurabi came to power, an important development in Babylonian mythology is believed to have taken place. According to religious texts, a celestial war arose between the goddess Tiamat and Marduk, god of the city of Babylon, resulting in Marduk's triumph. Supposedly Enlil then summoned an assembly of the gods, in which Marduk was chosen to be their chief with a new title, "Enlil of the gods." The allegiance of the Babylonians was therefore directed to Marduk, their new national god, and to the city of Babylon as a center of worship. The Babylonians are believed to have rallied around Hammurabi, a strong leader who apparently captured their religio-national allegiance. In a lightning campaign of conquests in the name of the new chief god Marduk, Hammurabi was able not only to achieve political unity but also to establish an empire encompassing the whole of the Fertile Crescent. Non-Babylonian peoples became subject nationalities within the empire, which was destined to last for almost two centuries. Hammurabi is known in ancient history as the chief lawgiver of the Middle East Proper. Archaeologists have recovered his famous code of laws, and its importance has been acknowledged not only for its revelation of the nature of justice in Babylonia itself, but also for its presentation of many concepts found also in the Hebrew laws of the Old Testament, especially those of the patriarchal period.

The Second Period of Decline, 1595-612 B.C.

Unlike Hammurabi, the last kings of the Middle Empire were weak. The empire fell apart around the middle of the second millennium, and Babylonia itself was invaded by tribesmen of uncertain

origin known as the Kassites. Soon after this, Assyria gained supremacy in Mesopotamia and blocked Babylonian attempts to recover
throughout the second period of decline, which lasted for almost
a thousand years. While Assyria was at the peak of its glory, the
Babylonians and the non-Semitic Medes – in a hasty alliance – brought
about the sudden collapse of the Assyrian Empire in 612 B.C. and
burned its great capital, Nineveh.

The New Babylonian Empire, 612-539 B.C.

The year 612 B.C. marks the beginning of the New Babylonian
Empire under Nabopolassar and his famous son Nebuchadnezzar,
whose name is frequently mentioned in the book of Daniel of the
Old Testament. The strength of the New Babylonian Empire lay in
the hands of the Chaldean segment of the population. These Chaldeans
had apparently migrated to Babylonia from Arabia during the period
of Assyrian supremacy, mingled with the native population, and considered themselves Babylonians and followers of the great god Marduk.
Recent archaeological discoveries have revealed a link between these
Chaldeans and the Arabs of southern and eastern Arabia. Moreover,
Nabonidus, one of the kings of the New Babylonian Empire, is known
to have built a resort city for himself in Arabia named Tayma – an
indication of a strong Arabian-Chaldean relationship.

Nebuchadnezzar, with the help of the Medes, brought about the
final defeat of the Assyrians and captured their territories in Syria
and Palestine. This New Babylonian Empire was short-lived. Not
long after Nebuchadnezzar's death, the Persians under Cyrus in
539 B.C. captured Babylon itself from its king, Nabonidus, and his
co-regent son, Belshazzar. This fall of Babylon marked the beginning of an era in which Semites were defeated by non-Semites, and
lost political leadership to the Persians.

ASSYRIAN SUPREMACY

As mentioned previously, during the second period of Babylonian
decline, Assyria, which occupied the northern portion of Mesopotamia, gradually rose to supremacy. Assyrian cities achieved a
national identity around 2000 B.C. but soon fell victims to Hammurabi's empire around 1750 B.C. The chief god of the Assyrians was
Ashur, and the main center of worship was the city of Ashur itself.
When the Kassites brought about the fall of Hammurabi's empire
(the Middle Babylonian Empire), Assyria failed to achieve independence and fell under the rule of the Mitanians of Asia minor until 1365
B.C., when it became independent. Between 1365 and 811 B.C., Assyria
and Babylonia were engaged in almost continuous warfare which finally
resulted in the capture of Babylon by Shamshi-Adad V of Assyria.

From that time on, the Assyrians expanded their rule in the Middle East Proper, going beyond Palestine and conquering Egypt around 669 B.C. under the leadership of Esarhaddon, son of Sennacherib. The Assyrians are known to have taken drastic measures to kill national sentiments among conquered peoples; however, all their efforts were in vain. When they believed their conquests to be secure, sudden rebellions flared everywhere allowing the New Babylonians, with the help of the Medes, to capture their capital city, Nineveh, and reduce it to ashes in 612 B.C.

CHAPTER 7

THE SEMITES IN EGYPT

THE PREDYNASTIC PERIOD

Early Egyptian Cultures

Egypt's prehistory is still shrouded with mystery; in the earliest documents, Egypt already appears to be enjoying a well-developed civilization with a king, a government, and a standing army. However, some information about the predynastic period may be found in clues from the tomb remains. It is generally believed that the original inhabitants of Egypt belonged to a stock quite similar to the Nubians of today. Their remains, as revealed by the early Tasian and Badarian cultures, indicate that they lived in villages and practiced primitive agriculture. However, remains found in tombs belonging to the Amratian and Gerzean cultures, which followed chronologically the Tasian and Badarian, indicate that a new stock of people must have infiltrated into Egypt and driven the original inhabitants south to the borders of Nubia. Since certain aspects of the Gerzean culture resembled the prehistoric Babylonian culture, it is believed that these new settlers were Semites of the Fertile Crescent. Semitic nomads are believed to have crossed the Sinai Peninsula; some of them entered Egypt from the north, and others traveled southward in the eastern desert and entered from the south. The amalgamation of the Semitic and the original Egyptian stocks is generally considered the main stimulus to the rise of the Egyptian civilization.

Coalitions of Cities

No records exist revealing the existence of city-states or coalitions of city-states in prehistoric Egypt, but such a state could easily be inferred from analyzing some predynastic carvings. Some of these carvings show banners of certain confederations that fought against each other and supply some evidence of city-states and coalitions of city-states. Other indications of the existence of cities may be deduced from Egyptian mythological stories which mention many cases of mergers of various gods into one deity. These mythological experiences may be interpreted as parallels to actual terrestial events of predynastic times. It is believed that as the early settlers of Egypt developed religious concepts, they divided into numerous cults and worshiped several local deities. When coalitions of cities were formed, several centers of worship evidently developed, each having a chief god ruling over the whole coalition. The transition from tribal to regional loyalties apparently came about as religious allegiance shifted from a local god to a regional chief deity. When members of several tribes owed allegiance to a central god, it may be said that the tribal unit of government based upon blood ties gave way to a larger unit of government in which people unrelated by kinship were willing to support one regional leader.

Egypt United in One Kingdom

Apparently the merger of gods continued in Egypt till the dawn of the dynastic period when Egypt was divided into two regions: Upper Egypt in the south and Lower Egypt in the north. Again Egyptian mythology is perhaps the only source by which Egyptian national unity can be explained. The Osiris legend mentions that he (Osiris) was the chief deity in Lower Egypt as Seth was in Upper Egypt; however, Seth is said to have fought with Osiris and caused him to drown in the Nile. Horus, the son of Osiris, sought to avenge his father's murder, and the issue was brought before an assembly of the gods. This assembly ruled in favor of giving Horus his father's domain in Lower Egypt and allowing Seth pre-eminence in Upper Egypt. Apparently Horus did not accept this verdict and continued his campaign to displace Seth completely from Upper Egypt. A war between the two followed, the result of which was the vindication of Horus' authority over all Egypt. Horus then made his headquarters in Upper Egypt, where his father, Osiris, was buried, and Seth moved to Lower Egypt where he managed to claim a few followers. Later on, another conflict between Horus and Seth resulted in the final victory of Horus over all Egypt. The end result of these mythological struggles was that Horus became a national god and, accordingly, his followers in the two parts of Egypt apparently tried to reconcile the political situation with religious conditions. Greek historians mention Menes as the king who united the two Egypts, but archaeology has produced an engraved palette of a king of Upper Egypt called Narmer which reveals that the national god Horus helped Narmer to subdue his opponents in Lower Egypt and unify the land. In the name of Horus, the falcon god and descendant of the sun god, the Egyptian pharaohs of the first few dynasties ruled over a united Egypt and served as ministers of the gods. Later on, each Egyptian pharaoh proclaimed himself "a Horus" and assumed the title "Son of Ra"; the pharaoh himself was considered a god. Egyptian unity evidently was based on centralized religious allegiance and the doctrine of divine kingship. In both Egypt and Mesopotamia the first kings to rule over a united nation had to resort first to divine appointment and celestial authorization before they could bring under control previously scattered and diverse tribal groups.

Ancient Egyptian history may be divided as follows:

1. The Old Kingdom, 2700-2200 B.C.

2. The First Intermediate Period, 2200-2050 B.C.

3. The Middle Kingdom, 2050-1800 B.C.

4. The Second Intermediate Period, 1800-1550 B.C.

5. The New Kingdom, 1550-1165 B.C.

6. The Late Dynastic Period, 1165-525 B.C.

THE OLD KINGDOM, 2700-2200 B.C.

Manetho, an Egyptian of the fourth century B.C. who wrote in Greek, divided Egyptian history into thirty-one dynasties.[1] The Old Kingdom consists of the first five dynasties during which Egypt developed a complete governmental apparatus including kings, ministers, provincial governors, a standing army, and a judiciary. The chief relics of this period are the huge Great Pyramids of Egypt whose remains today testify to the glory and majesty of ancient Egypt. The largest of these pyramids covers over thirteen acres and rises to a height of 480 feet. It is supposed to be the largest tomb ever erected by man. The kings of Egypt presumably could not afford to go on building such mammoth pyramids indefinitely; later Egyptian kings were satisfied with less-imposing tombs scattered around these huge pyramids.

By the end of the Fifth Dynasty, waves of Semitic nomads from Asia are believed to have infiltrated into Egypt and weakened the

---

[1] Although many inaccuracies have been found in Manetho's list, Egypt's chronology is still generally referred to in dynastic terms.

central government, until authority eventually reverted to the provinces. Independent provincial rulers governed in Egypt from the Sixth Dynasty through the Tenth Dynasty. This period witnessed the breakdown of law and order. Relations between the provinces were often hostile leading to warfare and bloodshed.

THE MIDDLE KINGDOM, 2050-1800 B.C.

The founders of the Eleventh Dynasty were rulers of the province of Thebes in Upper Egypt before they started a campaign to reunite Egypt in the name of Ra, the sun god and father of the gods. By the end of the Eleventh Dynasty, as Egypt was on its way to unity and order, an army commander named Amenemhet successfully proclaimed himself pharaoh, thus ushering in the Twelfth Dynasty. Amenemhet elevated the rank of his god Amon in Thebes to that of Ra. The chief god of Egypt from that time on was called "Amon-Ra," a merger of the two deities. The kings of the Twelfth Dynasty were agricultural reformers; they are known to have entrusted the land to agricultural overseers who eventually became feudal masters over the land of Egypt. This development weakened the central government and gradually led to the second intermediate period, which lasted until the end of the Seventeenth Dynasty, when Egypt was again victim of various Semitic raiders from the East.

The most noteworthy of these Semitic invaders were the Hyksos, who apparently infiltrated the Nile Valley during the sixteenth century B.C., and to a large extent adopted most features of Egyptian culture. They ruled the country for about two centuries, assuming Egyptian names and worshiping Egyptian gods. During their rule, Lower Egypt was infiltrated by more Semites from Western Asia—a condition which led to the belief that Joseph's famous biblical journey to Egypt, which started the Hebrew sojourn in the country, might have taken place during that period.

THE NEW KINGDOM, 1550-1165 B.C.

The Upper Egyptians maintained a stubborn resistance to the alien Hyksos regime. Meanwhile the torch of what may be called Egyptian "nationalism" once more was kindled at Thebes. Seknenre of the Seventeenth Dynasty of Thebes sacrificed his life to save Egypt from foreign domination. His struggle was continued by his son Kamose, who succeeded in driving the Hyksos completely out of Egypt, bringing an end to the second intermediate period and ushering in the Egyptian Empire. Kamose was followed by the famous kings of the Eighteenth and Nineteenth Dynasties, who made the power of Egypt felt from Somaliland in Africa to the Euphrates River in Mesopotamia. Thutmoses II and Thutmoses III of the Eighteenth Dynasty and Seti I and Ramses II of the Nineteenth Dynasty were great leaders at whose commands many peoples of the then-known world trembled. The mummies of these kings, even to this day provoke in their viewers a sense of awe and respect.

Among the kings of the Eighteenth Dynasty, Akhenaton has received special attention for the religious reforms which he tried to impose on the Egyptians. He conceived of one presumably impersonal god whose symbol was the sun disk, "Aton," and repudiated pharaoh's divine claim to be Horus, the son of Ra himself, to become only a servant of Aton. This religious "innovation" is considered by some writers as the first historical record of monotheistic worship; however, it was not destined to last very long in conservative Egypt. The priests of Amon-Ra at Thebes succeeded in arousing Egyptian religio-national sentiments against the "heretic king," and when Akhenaton died, his successors gradually reverted to traditional Egyptian worship. A son-in-law of Akhenaton—and his third successor— was Tutankhamon, who became world famous following the discovery of his gold-laden tomb in 1923.

THE LATE DYNASTIC PERIOD, 1165-525 B.C.

With the passing of the Nineteenth Dynasty of Egypt, the period of its decline began. The Twentieth Dynasty included a number of kings who ruled only through the momentum created by past successes. The Twenty-first Dynasty consisted mainly of priests who devoted themselves to the glory of the temple at Thebes. This allowed the Libyan community that had already infiltrated into the delta from the west to assume rule over Egypt, giving rise to the Twenty-second, Twenty-third, and Twenty-fourth Dynasties, whose kings, in the main, were not native Egyptians. The Libyan dynasties were followed by Ethiopian kings who conquered Egypt from the south and ruled as the Twenty-fifth Dynasty. For some time, Egyptian "nationalism" appeared to have been quenched, but apparently it was only dormant. The Assyrians invaded Egypt and drove out the Ethiopians, thus giving rise to the Twenty-sixth Dynasty, whose kings were native Egyptians. Rekindling the torch of Egyptian "nationalism," these kings not only drove the Assyrians out of Egypt, but recaptured for Egypt most of its lost empire in Palestine and Syria. Pharaoh Necho of this dynasty brought the kings of Judah and Syria under his command for some time, but he was defeated at the battle of Charchemish in 605 B.C. by Nebuchadnezzar. Egypt lost its Syrian empire for the last time; however, it maintained its independence during the rule of the last kings of the Twenty-sixth Dynasty until conquered by Cambyses of Persia in 525 B.C. The Twenty-seventh Dynasty kings were Persians; however, the Twenty-eighth, Twenty-ninth, and Thirtieth Dynasties include names of some local Egyptian kings who tried several times in vain to liberate Egypt from foreign rule. The Thirty-first Dynasty included a few Persian kings under whom Egypt was governed till 332 B.C., when Alexander the Great defeated the Persians and imposed Greek rule on Egypt.

CHAPTER 8

THE SEMITES IN CANAAN

A LATE START

As a geographical term, Canaan refers to the territories east of the Mediterranean Sea now often called the Levant. It consists of Syria, Lebanon, and Palestine, and comprises the western curve of the Fertile Crescent from the Biqa' Valley to the Negev Desert. Because of its strategic location, Canaan served for a long period as a bridge between Egypt and Mesopotamia. The Canaanites, who were mainly nomads, acted as unwitting carriers of culture between the two major civilizations of the ancient world. Unfortunately, Canaan was not blessed with rivers given to regular inundations; and therefore, the development of its cultural patterns was quite different from that of the river civilizations. Furthermore, the expansionist policies of the ancient empires of both Egypt and Mesopotamia did not afford the Canaanites a chance to establish permanent political regimes; on the contrary, the Canaanites were victims of frequent invasions, and their emerging cities were targets for war and destruction for many centuries. It is not surprising, therefore, that the Canaanites remained nomads or semi-nomads for a long period of time – throughout the entire third millenium B.C. and more than half of the second. Nevertheless, the Canaanites managed to build and rebuild their settlements, maintaining their identity until the end of the second millennium B.C., when the power of both Egypt and Mesopotamia was ebbing, thereby allowing Canaan to establish a group of independent states.

The Early Canaanites

Early in the second millennium B.C., the Amorites, who had infiltrated Mesopotamia, also migrated to Canaan, where they became a major element of the Canaanite population and established a few Canaanite cities, chief of which was Ugarit, whose ruins have recently been excavated in Syria. Later on, around the middle of the millennium, the Arameans occupied the Biqa' Valley and the Israelites settled in Palestine. These were nomadic peoples with a tribal system of government. A few scattered cities such as Jericho, Gezer, and Megiddo continued to exist, each maintaining its own local government. Archaeological excavations have revealed that these cities were frequently destroyed and rebuilt; it is believed that they attacked each other and were also attacked by Egyptian and Babylonian armies marching back and forth in the Fertile Crescent. Around the twelfth century B.C., sea travelers known as the Philistines invaded the shores of both Egypt and Canaan. Rebuffed by Ramses III of Egypt, the Philistines settled in the southern coastal strip of Palestine and posed a real threat to the Hebrew peoples who had just settled there. Their territory, Philistia (Palestine), was named after them.

Canaan's National Period, 1200-722 B.C.

Prospects for an independent Canaan were greatly enhanced at the turn of the twelfth century when both Egypt and Babylonia went through a period of relative decline and Assyria had not yet become a major power. A brief look at the political progress of both Egypt and Babylonia reveals that throughout the history of the ancient Middle East, when Egypt was strong, Babylonia was weak, and when Babylonia was gaining in strength, Egypt was passing through a period of decline. Only when this polarization of power was temporarily halted between the latter part of the twelfth century and the early part of the eighth century B.C., did Canaan have its opportunity to establish independent states.

Religious and Political Forces in Canaan

As was the case with Egypt and Mesopotamia, so it was with Canaan—strong forces of religion and mythology were chiefly responsible for crystallizing national sentiments and uniting various tribes into states. During the eleventh century, the Canaanites may be said to have gradually taken form as four local groups, each worshiping a chief deity. For instance, the Sidonians, known also as Phoenicians, were distinguished by their worship of the god Baal, whose authority was mainly confined to the region around Tyre and Sidon. North and east of the Sidonians, the Arameans constituted another nationality and acknowledged the divine rule of the god Haddad-Rimmon in the region roughly corresponding to modern Syria. South of the Sidonians, the Philistines worshiped their god Dagon and occupied the territory now known as western Palestine (modern Israel). In the eastern part of Palestine or in the territory represented now by the western side of Jordan lived the Israelites, who worshiped a nonpersonal god without image or human representation named Jehovah, known today as the God of the Judeo-Christian tradition. South of Palestine lived the Midianites, the Edomites, the Moabites, and the Ammonites, who formed semi-independent states before becoming part of the Israelite kingdom. They worshiped various gods, chief of whom was Kemosh, god of the Moabites.

THE CANAANITE NATIONS

The Kingdom of Israel

It appears that whenever a community of tribes became distinguished as worshipers of a certain god, a divine oracle usually followed appointing a king over the whole community.

In Israel, for example, the Old Testament records the story of the prophet Samuel, who was directed by Jehovah to anoint Saul as king of Israel. The biblical record asserts that when Saul was in the fields searching for his father's lost asses, he went to consult with Samuel and was immediately annointed as the first king of Israel. Later on when Saul disobeyed the word of God, he was rejected as king, and David was anointed in his place, again by divine order. When David became king he is reported to have fulfilled the laws of Jehovah. He was able to expand the borders of his kingdom by defeating the emerging nations around him, mainly, the Philistines, the Moabites, the Ammonites, and all the other nations south of Palestine. When he died, his son Solomon inherited his father's domain in the land of Canaan. Unfortunately, Solomon's son Rehoboam was not prudent enough to win the loyalty of his people; after a rash statement on his part, ten tribes of the Israelites rebelled against him and followed an antagonist of Solomon named Jeroboam. Only two tribes remained with Rehoboam, who continued to rule as king of Judah. This action divided the Davidic monarchy into Israel and Judah, and it stayed divided till Israel was finally overrun by Shalmaneser V and his successor Sargon II of Assyria in 722 B.C., and Judah by Nebuchadnezzar of Babylonia shortly after 605 B.C. When the Persians defeated the Babylonians in 539 B.C., the whole land of Palestine became a Persian province.

The Aramean Kingdom

The rivalry between the kingdoms of Israel and Judah weakened both states and gave three nationalities a chance to establish independent monarchies. First to free itself from Israel was the nation of Aram, with its capital in Damascus. Its god Haddad-Rimmon posed a serious challenge to the kingdom of Israel as his followers, the Arameans, established a coalition with nearby nations and defeated an Assyrian army at the battle of Qarqar in 853 B.C. This battle kept the Assyrians away from the Mediterranean coast for almost seventy years, a period during which the kingdom of Aram was the most significant power in Canaan. The Assyrians, however, returned to Canaan and captured the whole region soon after 722 B.C. Aram then became a part of the Assyrian Empire, changing masters from Assyrians to Babylonians to Persians to Greeks, who presumably referred to it as Syria –a name by which it is known till the present time.

The Sidonians (Phoenicians)

The Sidonians were descendants of the ancient Canaanites who established cities such as Byblos, Tyre, and Sidon along the shores of the Mediterranean. Since they were harassed by the invading armies passing through their territory, they found an outlet on the sea. They became seafarers and established Phoenician settlements in various islands in the Mediterranean and at Carthage. Some records mention Phoenician settlements as far as Spain. However, by the ninth century B.C. Greek seafarers posed a real challenge to the Phoenician sea traffic, forcing the Sidonians to strengthen their own home base. When the kingdom of Israel was divided, and while the Arameans were still recuperating from the Israelite occupation, favorable circumstances enabled the Sidonians to establish their national existence. Their two chief cities, Tyre and Sidon, with other small cities, united into one nation, giving rise around 950 B.C. to the Sidonian kingdom, under the religious leadership of Baal. Between 900 and 850 B.C. the borders of the Sidonian kingdom reached as far as Mount Carmel in the south and Tripoli in the north. However, after the great victory of Aram over the Assyrians in 853 B.C., Aramean pressure against the Sidonians increased, forcing withdrawal to the main cities of Tyre and Sidon, which remained independent till Assyria took over the whole area soon after 722 B.C.

OTHER CANAANITES

East and south of the kingdom of Israel, the Ammonites, the Moabites, the Edomites, and the Midianites continued to be ruled by the kingdom of Israel; however, during the reign of some weak Israelite kings, rebellions, especially of the Moabites, are reported to have taken place. Records reveal that in Moab a king called Mesha rallied the Moabites behind him and, under the religious leadership of their god Kemosh, freed his nation from Israel. The victory stele in which he recorded his successful campaign against Israel has been recently recovered by archaeologists; it reveals the existence of strong national sentiments among peoples destined to remain under foreign domination through most of their history. The Assyrians, and later on the Babylonians, are reported to have deported many of the dwellers of southern and eastern Palestine to distant places, resulting among many of these Canaanite nations in the loss of their identity. In any case, the peoples who were not deported are believed to have fled into the desert and become a part of the Arab Nabatean kingdom that rose a few centuries later.

IMPORTANT TERMS

Amenemhat: Founder of the Twelfth Dynasty of the Middle Kingdom of ancient Egypt, under whose leadership Egypt was reunited.

Arameans: A Semitic people that spread along the Fertile Crescent about the twelfth century B.C. Those who settled in Canaan established the Aramean kingdom, which flourished about the eighth century B.C. with its capital in Damascus.

Assyrians: Settlers of northern Mesopotamia. Their empire reached its height after the ninth century B.C. Their capital was Nineveh, which was destroyed in 612 B.C.

Cuneiform: A script, used mainly by the Babylonians, consisting of wedge-shaped characters impressed by a stylus on clay tablets.

Esarhaddon: The Assyrian king under whose rule Assyria reached its maximum expansion about 669 B.C.

Hammurabi: Founder of the Middle Babylonian Empire, 1750-1895 B.C.

Hieroglyphics: Ancient Egyptian writing. Its characters are composed of various pictographic signs engraved on stone or written on papyrus.

Hyksos: Semitic peoples from Western Asia who occupied Egypt during the second intermediate period. They are believed to have established an empire that extended beyond the borders of Egypt.

Israelites: A Semitic group of people that settled in southern Canaan around the twelfth century B.C. They established their kingdom two centuries later in what is known as Palestine.

Menes: The first king of Egypt, probably legendary, traditionally believed to have first united Upper and Lower Egypt into one kingdom about 2700 B.C.

Moabites: A Semitic group of people related to the Israelites that settled in the southern region of Palestine. They established a short-lived regime during the decline of the kingdom of Israel shortly after the ninth century B.C.

Nebuchadnezzar: A great conqueror during the New Babylonian Empire, 612-539 B.C.

Philistines: Sea peoples from the islands of the Mediterranean who attacked the shores of Canaan about the twelfth century B.C. Later they were assimilated by the kingdom of Israel.

Phoenicians: See Sidonians.

Sargon of Akkad: Founder of the Old Babylonian (Akkadian) Empire, 2340-2008 B.C.

Seknenre: A patriotic Egyptian ruler who reputedly united Egypt against the Hyksos at the beginning of the New Egyptian Empire, 1550-1165.

Sidonians: A Semitic people descended from the original Canaanites who settled along the eastern shore of the Mediterranean. They established a short-lived regime about the eighth century B.C. They are also known as Phoenicians.

SUPPLEMENTARY READINGS

ALBRIGHT, W.F., *From Stone Age to Christianity* (New York, 1957).
——, "The Role of the Canaanites" in G.E. Wright *The Bible and the Ancient Near East* (New York, 1961).
ANATI, E., *Palestine Before the Hebrews* (Leiden, 1963).
DIRINGER, DAVID, *The Alphabet* (New York, 1953).
DRIVER, GODFREY, *Semitic Writing* (London, 1945).
GARDINER, ALLAN H., *Egypt of the Pharaohs* (Oxford, 1961).
GRAY, JOHN, *The Legacy of Canaan* (Leiden, 1957).
HALL, H.R., *The Ancient History of the Near East* (Edinburgh, 1957).
MOSCATI, SABATINO, *Ancient Semite Civilizations* (London, 1957).
——, *The Face of the Ancient Orient* (London, 1960).
OLMSTEAD, ALBERT T., *History of Assyria* (Chicago, 1960).
PRITCHARD, JAMES, *The Ancient Near East in Pictures* (Princeton, 1954).
SAGGS, H.A.J., *The Greatness that was Babylon* (New York, 1962).
WILSON, JOHN A., *The Burden of Egypt* (Chicago, 1951).

PART **iii**

PRE-ISLAMIC ARABIA

The emergence of Islam both as a religion and a state (political organization) cannot be fully understood without a clear picture of the historical, religious, and socio-economical backgrounds of pre-Islamic Arabia. In this part, the chapter about historical backgrounds includes a short survey of the history of South Arabia, the Northern Fringes, and North Arabia (the Hijaz), furnishing a brief sketch of the political situation of the Arabian Peninsula. It summarizes the development of various Arab kingdoms which emerged in these areas and explains their relations with other countries of the non-Semitic world.

The chapter on religious backgrounds deals mainly with the development of religious trends in Arabia and their relations with other Semitic religions. In this chapter an attempt is also made to show how religions and political authorities usually went hand in hand throughout the history of Semitic civilizations, including that of pre-Islamic Arabia.

Several nonreligious factors prompted the rise of Islam as a state, chief of which was the importance of Arabia as the center of caravan trade routes binding both the Orient and Europe to the Middle East. This caused the Arab merchants to become very rich while the nomads languished in poverty. In their effort to obtain some of the wealth of the merchants, even at resort to force, the nomads mastered the art of raiding and surprise attack. This situation led to several tragic intertribal wars which made the rise of a unifying political institution almost essential for the survival of the Arabs.

In brief, the situation in pre-Islamic Arabia presented

three roles in search of leaders to cope with the various needs of the restless Arabs: (1) a role for a political leader, (2) a role for a religious leader, and (3) a role for a military leader. It would be very difficult indeed for three leaders to rise at the same time and together assume these roles; however, one man emerged who took up the heavy duties of the three roles simultaneously and brought about the emancipation of the Arabs from the bondage of their own land. This leader was Muhammad, the Prophet of Islam.

CHAPTER 9

HISTORICAL BACKGROUNDS

THE KINGDOMS OF SOUTH ARABIA

Pre-Islamic Arabia in Islamic Annals

Muslim historians have divided the history of pre-Islamic Arabia into three parts: (1) history of the extinct Arabs, *al-Arab al-Ba'ida* – believed to refer to the ancient Semitic civilizations of the Fertile Crescent – who, in their estimation, have long since disappeared; (2) history of the ancient Arabs, *al-Arab al-Ariba,* referring to the Arab dynasties in South Arabia and on the fringes of the Fertile Crescent; and (3) history of the Arabicized Arabs, *al-Arab al-Musta'riba,* believed to have settled in Tihama, Hijaz, and Najd, the regions generally known as North Arabia and often referred to as the home of the Islamic religion. These historians trace the ancient Arabs of South Arabia to a certain Ya'rab ibn Qahtan – hence the origin of the word "Arab"; and the Arabicized Arabs to a certain "Adnan," a descendant of Ishmael, the son of Abraham of the Old Testament. Although there is no historical evidence to substantiate the authenticity of these two names, Arabic traditions stress this point rather strongly. It is unlikely, however, that the word "Arabs" originated from the assumed progenitor of the South Arabians since it had occurred earlier in Assyrian documents, referring to nomadic tribes in the Syrian Desert.

The Kingdoms of Saba, Ma'in, Qataban, and Hadramawt

Greek historians who wrote during the early Christian centuries mention four kingdoms in South Arabia, whose beginnings can be traced back to the tenth century B.C. These kingdoms, according to classical history, were Saba, Ma'in, Qataban, and Hadramawt, whose chronology has been a matter of dispute for some time. Archaeological evidence, however, has revealed that Saba must have preceded Ma'in and not *vice versa*. A reconstruction of the history of the whole area based on the evidence of both classical history and archaeology reveals that agricultural settlements began in the western side of South Arabia during the fifteenth century B.C. By the tenth century B.C. the kingdom of Saba rose when several Arab tribes merged into one state. The Sabaean kingdom is mentioned in the Old Testament in connection with King Solomon of Israel, whose fame is supposed to have induced the Queen of Saba (Sheba) to make her famous trip to Jerusalem in order to hear Solomon's wisdom. Saba is also mentioned in Assyrian documents around the seventh century B.C., an indication that it was still independent at that time. Soon after the rise of Saba, Ma'in is believed to have established itself as an independent kingdom and posed a threat to Saba's supremacy. It is also believed that during the few centuries preceding the Christian Era, Saba and Ma'in merged into one kingdom with Marib as its capital. East of the Saba-Ma'in federation, the kingdoms of Qataban and Hadramawt made their appearance a few centuries before the Christian Era. These two kingdoms are believed to have merged; however, this merger did not pose any threat to the supremacy of the greater kingdom of Saba.

Union under the Himyarites

By 115 B.C. a powerful family in South Arabia known as the Himyarites succeeded in holding the reins of the kingdom of Saba. Under their rule a new greater federation was established in which the two opposing federations merged into one kingdom known as the "Kingdom of Saba, Raydan (formerly Ma'in), Hadramawt, and Yaman." This glorious period of unity for South Arabia under the sons of Himyar lasted nearly 400 years—well into the Christian Era. In A.D. 275 the Himyarite Sabaean kingdom was attacked by the Abyssinian Christians, whose missionaries had already won some converts there. Rivalry between the Jews and Christians in South Arabia is believed to have triggered the Abyssinian occupation of the land of Himyar, which, from that time on was called Yaman. The foreign domination of Yaman lasted till A.D. 374 when the Himyarites threw off the Abyssinian yoke and restored the independence of their kingdom.

The Abyssinian Occupation

During the Abyssinian occupation, Christian communities multiplied in South Arabia especially around Najran. These communities were composed of monophysite Copts (believing in the single nature of Christ) of Egypt and Abyssinia, and of Nestorians (believing in two distinct natures—human and divine—of Christ) as well as Arians (denying the divine essence of Christ); the latter are believed to have fled to Arabia when the Christian Council of Nicaea declared them heretics in A.D. 325. Soon after 374 the famous Marib Dam, which helped to maintain the agricultural wealth of Yaman, collapsed; this hastened the region's economic decline and the emigration of many Himyarites to North Arabia and the fringe areas. In 525 the Abyssinians reoccupied Yaman and remained there till 571, when the Himyarites invoked the help of the Persians against them. The Abyssinians then retired to their homeland. However, the Abyssinians brought elephants with their army, so impressing the people of South Arabia that they called the year A.D. 571, "the year of the elephant." It coincided with the birth of the Prophet Muhammad.

After the defeat of the Abyssinians, the Persians briefly occupied South Arabia. They soon became engaged in bloody battles with the Byzantines and withdrew from Yaman.

THE SEMITIC INTERMEDIATE PERIOD

The Nabateans

The years between the fall of the Neo-Babylonian Empire in 539 B.C. and the rise of the Arab Empire after A.D. 622 may be considered a period in which political leadership passed to non-Semites. During this millennium, however, the Semites were not altogether dormant; on the northern fringes of Arabia along the southern border of the Fertile Crescent a few Arab kingdoms arose—some of which made considerable progress. These Arab kingdoms in chronological order were (1) the Nabatean kingdom, (2) the kingdom of Palmyra, and (3) the kingdoms of Hira and Ghassan. The Nabateans migrated to Mesopotamia around the middle of the first millennium B.C. and then to the southeastern side of Palestine, where the Edomites and several non-Jewish nations lived during the Jewish exile. By the middle of the fourth century B.C. the Nabateans had absorbed those peoples that survived the Assyrian and Babylonian invasions, and established a strong kingdom in the Negev Desert, where wealth was based on trade. Their capital, known from Roman times as Petra, was carved indelibly in cliffs of red rock, and its remains still stand today as a great monument to their civilization. Their power was so great that they stood firm before the Greek armies of Alexander the Great and his generals.

The Nabateans probably spoke an Arabic vernacular although their documents were recorded in Aramaic. Their kings were divided into a number of dynasties, chief of which was the dynasty of Aretas, mentioned in the New Testament in connection with the journey which the apostle Paul made to Arabia. The Nabatean kingdom expanded eastward across the Syrian Desert till it reached the borders of Najd. However, the Roman Emperor Trajan directed a campaign against the Nabateans in A.D. 106, and conquered them.

The Kingdom of Palmyra

Trade routes which once passed by Petra soon shifted to another Arab city called Tadmur, the capital of the kingdom of Palmyra, located about 140 miles northeast of Damascus. The Palmyrene kingdom had been a Roman province since A.D. 130; however, when Tadmur's importance increased, it secured its independence from Rome and became an important power in the middle of the Syrian Desert. The war between the Romans and the Persians which started in A.D., 258 permitted the kingdom of Palmyra to expand swiftly; it reached the peak of its strength during the rule of Udhayna (Greek: Odenathus), whose neutral role between East and West allowed him to control an empire extending over all Syria and most of the Fertile Crescent. Udhayna's rule was carried on after his death by his famous wife Zenobia, who maintained the strength of Palmyra in behalf of her young son and extended its influence as far as Egypt in the south and Asia Minor in the north. However, in A.D. 272, toward the end of her rule, the Roman armies besieged Tadmur under Aurelian and captured the city, bringing an end to the Palmyrene kingdom. Zenobia herself ended her days in exile.

Hira and Ghassan

In the course of their fighting, Rome and Persia helped two Arab satellite states to develop along their borders on both sides of the Syrian Desert. To the east, the Persians supported an Arab dynasty called Lakhm to rule independently over the kingdom of Hira from A.D. 268 to 628. Almost simultaneously, the Romans, and later on the Byzantines, supported a rival dynasty to rule in the west over another independent kingdom called Ghassan. These two Arab kingdoms were enemies and carried on the feud between their patrons to a great extreme. The bitter fighting that arose between them became legendary in Arabic literature in the centuries that followed. By the turn of the sixth century, and within a few years of each other, both Byzantium and Persia restricted the independence of Ghassan and Hira respectively. The two Arab states remained under the influence of their respective masters until Islamic armies liberated them and they became a part of the Islamic community. It may be noteworthy to mention

here that the Ghassanian state was mostly Christian, while the Lakh-
mids of Hira were pagans at first but later on embraced Christianity.
Among the kings of Hira was the famous Umru' al-Qays, who may be
considered the first Arab "Nationalist " as a result of the effort he
exerted toward the unification of all Arabs. On his recently discovered
tombstone there is an Arabic inscription dated about A.D. 328 in which
Umru' al-Qays recorded his title as "king of all the Arabs," perhaps
on the ground that his influence had extended as far as Najran in the
south.

NORTH ARABIA

The Nomadic Way of Life

Between South Arabia and the Northern Fringes extended the main
bulk of the Arabian Desert, a wide expanse of no man's land. Most of
its inhabitants were nomadic tribesmen who lived in Najd and also
along the coastal strip known as Tihama. The history of North Arabia
before Islam was transmitted by word of mouth till Arab historians
recorded it as late as the ninth century A.D. These historians did not
mention very much about the early history of North Arabia, considering
it a period of "ignorance," jahiliyya, a term that may refer also to
paganism and ignorance of the knowledge of God.

A second look at the history of North Arabia reveals that, although
the bulk of its population was nomadic or semi-nomadic, a few cities
did emerge and prosper, such as Makka and Madina, which began as
trading posts along the extended caravan route between South Arabia
and the Fertile Crescent. The political authority in these cities, however, continued to center around the tribe itself.

Roman Invasion of North Arabia

After his great victory over Anthony and Cleopatra of Egypt at the
battle of Actium in 31 B.C., the Roman Emperor, Augustus Caesar,
dispatched the governor of Egypt, Aelius Gallus, in 25 B.C. to invade
Arabia. Gallus enlisted in his force of about 10,000 soldiers, a
Nabatean commander from Petra called Syllaeus (Arabic Salih) together with 1000 Nabatean soldiers. This force advanced toward Yaman
and penetrated deeply into the Hijaz of North Arabia. Some reports
mention that it reached the borders of Najran in South Arabia; however,
sickness spread among the soldiers, who were not trained for desert
warfare, and the whole force retreated with great losses in supplies
and manpower. Thus ended in failure the first and last effort by a
European power to invade the Arabian Peninsula.

The Kinda Dynasty

Mention should be made here of the people of Kinda in Najd, who migrated from South Arabia and, upon settling in the Najd Plateau, established a local dynasty from A.D. 450 to 560. Its last ruler was the poet-king Umru' al-Qays (unrelated to Umru' al-Qays of Hira), whose father died while the young prince was enjoying a night of wine and poetical mirth. Apparently he could not muster enough power to assume his father's place, and shortly after his father's death, Kinda slipped into the tribal system that prevailed over most of the desert.

CHAPTER 10

RELIGIOUS BACKGROUNDS

EARLY RELIGIONS

Religion in South Arabia

With the exception of the Northern Fringes, the main feature of pre-Islamic Arabian religions may be described as paganism, resembling in some ways the characteristics of older Semitic religions in the ancient Middle East. In South Arabia, religion developed along the same pattern as it did in Mesopotamia, Egypt, and many smaller Canaanite states—starting with polytheism, then developing into henotheism as one of the gods assumed leadership over the others. Such development must have encouraged the scattered tribes to merge into larger communities; and as several tribes paid allegiance to one chief deity, a king emerged claiming theocratic authority for the purpose of uniting the whole community in a single nation-state. Fragmentary records from South Arabia reveal that a temple dedicated to the moon-god Sin was constructed during the early stages of the Sabaean kingdom. Moreover, Islamic annals reveal that another temple dedicated to a sun-god also existed along with other shrines for a number of lesser gods. However, as the Saba-Ma'in federation was developing, a priest became ruler over a united dynasty, adopting the religious title, *Mukarrib*, meaning "nearest" or "mediator." A number of *Mukarribs* ruled in South Arabia until the federation of Saba, Ma'in, Qataban, and Hadramawt was accomplished and the main center of religion moved from

Sirwah to Marib, which became the capital of the united kingdom. Marib was the center of the god al-Umuqu under whose auspices the kings of the new kingdom ruled. Its inhabitants attributed their unity and prosperity to their god al-Umuqu. The king himself was considered the servant of the god and on many occasions was pictured presenting thank offerings to al-Umuqu for his protection and support. This further indicates that as societies grew and developed in the Middle East Proper, religious allegiance was usually the backbone of political authority.

Religion in the Northern Fringes

The fringe states of Arabia —namely the Nabatean and the Palmyrene kingdoms and the two kingdoms of Hira and Ghassan—had been influenced by Hellenism and the Judeo-Christian tradition. Hira and Ghassan were mostly Christian; the Nabateans and Palmyrenes followed, to a certain extent, in the footsteps of the Greeks, whose culture began to spread into the Middle East Proper even before the conquests of Alexander the Great.

Religion in North Arabia

In the regions of Tihama, Najd, and Hijaz, generally known as North Arabia, the ancient Semitic pattern of religio-political development was still in progress when Muhammad was born. The chief feature of Arab worship may be said to have been its tangibility. This tangibility can be traced back to ancient Semitic times when the gods were represented by various forms and shapes such as the falcon-Horus, the jackal-Seth, and the bull-Ibis in Egypt, and a host of statues in Babylonia and Assyria. Furthermore these gods were worshiped by tangible means, as represented by the Akito ritual in Babylonia and the Sed festival in Egypt, consisting of standardized ceremonies and numerous rituals combined with gifts and sometimes sacrifices.

Akhenaton's short-lived religious revolution may be considered a deviation from this norm. Historians have not agreed on the significance of Akhenaton's concepts, but it is generally believed that he tried to introduce to Egyptian society the concept of a nontangible god whose symbol was the sun-disk Aton. *Maat,* meaning "truth" or "justice," was the king's concept of satisfying the desires of this god. If these concepts were truly formulated by Akhenaton, he may be considered as having lived more than a millennium before his time, since nontangibility in religious concepts was a feature of Neoplatonism and Hellenistic Christianity.

Judaism's contribution to the development of religions may be considered as the introduction of a nontangible God, Jehovah by name, who was not represented by any form or image. However, Jewish means of worshiping Jehovah continued for a long time to be tangible, consisting of various offerings and sacrifices. Evidently the Jewish religious concept of worshiping a nontangible God failed to impress surrounding cultures, which continued to maintain their tangible gods till Christianity spread its spiritual concepts in the area.

The Judeo-Christian Tradition

In Yaman the South Arabians practiced tangible rituals and ordinances consisting of animal sacrifices and other types of offerings until Christianity reached them from Abyssinia, bringing a host of metaphysical concepts. In fact, the entire community of Najran in South Arabia was Christian before the Muslims claimed it, along with the whole Arabian Peninsula, for Islam. In the Northern Fringes, Christianity was introduced relatively early to the kingdom of Ghassan. Hira hesitated at first to accept its teachings, but later on King al-Nu'man ibn al-Mundhir became Christian and introduced Christianity to his kingdom. Several Arab tribes in the northern region of Arabia, such as Tanukh, Taghlib, and Kalb, are also believed to have been converted to Christianity.

Judaism

After the destruction of the Jewish Temple by the Romans in A.D. 70, the Jews scattered in all directions. Many of them went to Arabia and established Jewish communities in several Arabian cities and trade centers. Yathrib (known later as Madina), located about 250 miles northeast of Makka, was inhabited by a large Jewish community; Jews in great numbers also settled in Khaybar, Fadak, and Wadi al-Qura; a few other Jewish tribes spread across Arabia as nomads. Apparently these Jews did not have a chance to practice the rituals of their religion, so their influence was limited mainly to the nontangible concepts of their God, Jehovah, or Elohim. Thus, during the centuries immediately preceding Islam, both paganism and the Judeo-Christian tradition existed side by side in the Arabian Peninsula. Paganism drew the Arabs toward tangibility of worship and concreteness of devotional duties, while the Judeo-Christian tradition drew them in the opposite direction, toward nontangibility and abstraction. By the time of Muhammad, the religious life of the Arabs was in a state of confusion, and the only answer seemed to be in the hope of a suitable compromise.

PAGAN IDOLS AND BELIEFS

Paganism in North Arabia

Most of the North Arabians, who were neither Jews nor Christians, worshiped a number of gods housed in a shrine called Ka'ba inside

Makka, the greatest trade center on the main caravan route from Yaman to Petra. Chief among the Arabian deities were Allat, goddess consort of the sun; Uzza, the personification of Venus; Manat, the goddess of fate; and Hubal, who may have been the god of fertility. It may be of interest to note here that Allah, whose name is believed to have been a borrowing from Hebrew Elohim through Aramaic Eloah, and who later on became the God of Islam, was also included among the Arabian gods in Ka'ba. According to some traditions, shortly before Muhammad's lifetime, Allah was gaining prestige in Ka'ba and many Arabs worshiped him as a chief deity. In fact, the same traditions consider Allat, Manat, and Uzza as daughters of Allah and inferior to him in rank.

The Arabs' main religious ritual consisted of a yearly pilgrimage to Makka during the month of Dhu al-Hijja, at which time they presented various gifts to their gods. The rest of the time, as they wandered from place to place, they erected temporary shrines for simple rituals in order to please their gods. Makka became a meeting place for the vast majority of the tribes, and it is fair to presume that a number of religious arguments among the Jews, Christians, and pagans must have taken place periodically in and around Makka, resulting perhaps in more confusion to the Arabs, who apparently were not ready to accept many of the nontangible concepts of a religion such as Christianity. In spite of their rejection of the metaphysical Judeo-Christian concepts, the desert dwellers must have felt some resentment toward their own pagan gods, who, failing time and again to protect them, proved themselves to be unreliable.

The Arabs and the Jinn

Besides their disillusionment in the protective powers of their pagan gods, the Arabs were plagued by a belief in the existence of numerous spirits known as *jinn,* whose main function was to bring harm and bad fortune. Therefore, they resorted to securing the services of magicians called *kahins,* whose job was to prevent the *jinn* from tormenting the people. Supposedly the *kahins* were not possessed by *jinn* themselves; but as the *jinns'* friends, they were capable of mediating in behalf of potential victims of the *jinn.* The *kahins* wrote certain magic formulas in rhyming prose that were pleasing to the Arab ear. These magic rhymes were carried by many Arabs as good-luck amulets to protect them in their everyday life. In spite of these measures, the Arabs appear to have been greatly disappointed by the ineffectiveness of their pagan gods and were undoubtedly looking for a change that would bring them dignity as well as security. Perhaps they wanted to worship an impersonal god as did other peoples around them, but at the same time continue to practice some of the traditions of their ancient heritage.

An Attempt at Reformation: The Hanif Religion

Only a few years before Muhammad's time, a compromise religion was in the making; some of the more sophisticated Arabs accepted Allah of the Ka'ba as a nontangible God without a form or representation; however, they worshiped him according to their old pagan customs. In other words, they accepted the element of nontangibility only as it applied to the person of God but not to the means of his worship. This group of Arabs were called the Hanifs, many of whom later on became followers of Muhammad due, perhaps, to the great similarity between Islam and their beliefs. Muhammad's cousin-in-law is known to have been a Hanif, and many scholars assert that Muhammad himself had been greatly influenced by Hanif concepts before he introduced the Islamic religion to Arabia. This Hanif religion was gradually spreading among the Arabs; however, due perhaps to its failure to supply a political framework that would uphold and maintain its religious beliefs, it was soon absorbed by the Islamic religio-political structure.

CHAPTER 11

SOCIO-ECONOMIC BACKGROUNDS

TRADE IN ARABIA

Main Trade Routes

It is obvious that North Arabia could not be self-supporting economically since its agricultural capacity fell far short of the demands of its population. Fortunately, its geographical location – South Arabia leading the way to India and the borders of China on one side, and the Fertile Crescent, Egypt and the Mediterranean on the other side – made it almost the only channel through which merchants could transport their wares. Since only the Bedouins of the desert were familiar with the routes which wound their way across the peninsula, they had a natural monopoly on the lucrative trade. Many of them became traders traveling back and forth between East and West, transporting herbs, spices, silk, incense, and other raw materials to the Mediterranean region, and bringing back corn, oil, silver, wine, and manufactured goods to South Arabia and Asia.

The main trade route passed along the coastal line of the Red Sea, joining the South Arabian cities with Petra on the fringes of the Fertile Crescent. Another route traversed the Najd Plateau directly from the Persian Gulf to Makka and then turned north toward the Mediterranean. A third route, beginning at the coast of the Persian Gulf on the eastern side of the peninsula, stretched directly northward toward Hira and Iraq, which were also connected to Makka, on the western side of the peninsula, by still another route extending across the northern desert and Najd.

Whenever the overland traffic was dangerous and insecure, ships carried merchandise through the Red Sea waterway, but the problems of building ships and supplying them from ports along the shore made the desert caravan an indispensable means of transporting goods. Trading depots presumably developed into market places and then into prosperous cities, chief of which were Makka and Yathrib in the Hijaz off the coast of the Red Sea.

Arabian trade with Canaan in ancient times has been archaeologically substantiated by the discovery of incense pottery jars in both South Arabia and the southern region of Canaan. The potsherds in these widely separated regions obviously had been broken and discarded along the way. However, the amazing resemblance these fragments of jars bear to one another proves that trade routes traversed North Arabia at least from north to south.

Merchants Versus Nomads

At the dawn of Islam, the dwellers of North Arabia became divided into two social groups: (1) the city dwellers, al-hadar, meaning "urbanized," who controlled the trade routes and lived rather luxuriously, and (2) the desert nomads known as al-badw or Bedouins, who continued to wander from place to place in search of pasture and food. Nevertheless, whether they were city dwellers or nomads, the Arabs before Islam lived in the main under the tribal system of government; developed city-states had not yet emerged. Chief among the Arab tribes were the Quraysh in Makka and the Aws and Khazraj in Yathrib. According to ancient Arab traditions, Makka was the city where the patriarch Abraham visited his son Ishmael and drank from the waters of the well Zamzam on its outskirts. Since the pagan Arabs were used to making annual pilgrimages to their gods in Makka, members of the Quraysh tribe, besides being rich merchants, also became the guardians of the holy shrine and recipients of all the gifts and offerings brought to the various Arab dieties.

THE NOMADIC WAY OF LIFE

North Arabian Ancestors

According to their own traditions, the Arabs of North Arabia descended from three main tribes: (1) Quda'a, (2) Rabi'a, and (3) Mudar. As members of these tribes multiplied, they divided into clans and sub-clans, which in turn grew and constituted new tribes fully independent of each other. For instance, Quda'a split into a number of lesser tribes, such as Asad, Kalb, and Tanukh, who settled in the area north of Najd and who were instrumental in the expansionist campaigns directed by the Muslims against the Fertile Crescent. Around Makka lived many other tribes descended from Rabi'a and Mudar who were engaged in intertribal warfare shortly before the rise of Islam. Chief among the Rabi'a tribes were Bakr and Taghlib, who frequently fought against each other and against the tribe of Tamim, a descendant of the Mudar line. From Mudar descended other warring tribes, chief of which were Abs and Dhubyan, who feuded with each other for a long time as well as with Kinana and Quraysh (the Prophet's own tribe in Makka). Furthermore, both of the latter tribes participated in a lengthy war against Qays called the Fijar, witnessed by Muhammad himself.

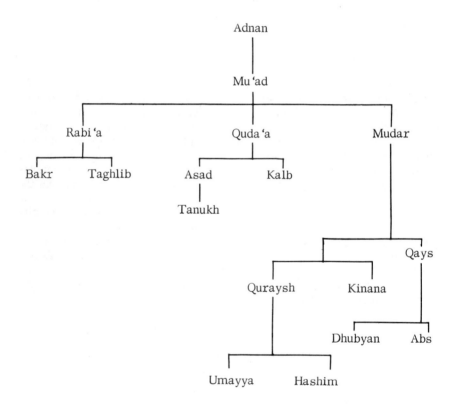

Genealogy of the Major Arab Tribes in Pre-Islamic Times
According to Islamic Historians

Nomads – Not by Choice

The Arab Bedouins did not become wandering nomads by choice; this life of hardship and instability was forced upon them by the severity of their desert environment. Since rain was scant and irregular, they were forced to move from place to place in search of pasturage. Their homes were tents and their furniture was whatever they could carry along with them. The camel became their chief companion; it was their vehicle of transportation and their main supply of hair to make clothes and tents. They drank its milk, ate its flesh, and used it as currency to exchange goods and pay dowry demands and "blood fees." Their main food consisted of milk and dates; when the climate was clement and some rain fell, a few goats could be raised and used as meat. Otherwise, the desert Bedouins lived on spoils acquired by raids. They looked for caravans on the desert routes and, having the advantage of surprise attack, could usually overcome the caravan guards and carry off their goods as booty. Less fortunate Bedouins who found no caravans on the road would attack other, more successful tribes.

Thus, while the city dwellers, or the *hadar*, of North Arabia lived on trade, the nomadic *badw* lived on raids. Their very existence depended on frequent attacks; yet this means of existence often brought early death to male members of the tribes. Security, therefore, became the responsibility of each individual household. Arab homes considered it a great blessing when boys were born into the family since the males were indispensable for the defense and sustenance of the home. On the other hand, girls, besides their need to be fed, had also to be protected and sheltered against attacks. It is no wonder, therefore, that the desert Arabs resorted to the practice of infanticide of girls in order to relieve themselves of the heavy responsibilities that went with the protection of females. In spite of this, losses among the men were so great that widows multiplied and became a serious problem among the nomads. This situation led to the practice of unlimited polygamy and the inevitable degradation of the woman's lot in the Bedouin's home.

THE TRIBAL SYSTEM OF GOVERNMENT

The Tribe as a Unit of Authority

An Arab tribe consisted usually of one unit of government under the leadership of a *shaykh,* "sheik" –also called *sayyid* –elected by the council of elders of the tribe and supported by an oath of allegiance pledged by all heads of households. The *shaykh* was the legislator (articulator of customary law) of the tribe; and in a time of emergency his command was law —a situation analogous to the patriarchal system of the Old Testament. According to the *shaykh's* command (after consulting with his elders), the tribe moved from place to place, attacked certain settlements, or engaged in warfare against raiders. A tribe might consist of several clans which could be divided into subclans and further divided into households. Filial devotion was the main feature of each household, in which the father had almost complete authority. In many cases when the father died at an early age leaving behind a number of children, the mother would take over and rule the household till her eldest son grew up and assumed his father's responsibilities.

Blood Revenge and Arbitration Among the Arabs

An important institution adopted by the nomadic tribes as a means of implementing justice and equality was the system of blood revenge, which, curiously enough, became a main deterrent against unchecked spilling of blood. A soul for a soul, a tooth for a tooth, and an eye for an eye became the basis of the tribal system of justice. According to the desert rules, the next of kin of any murdered individual was entitled to retaliate in kind by taking the life of the murderer or any other member of his tribe. However, since individual prestige counted highly among members of each tribe, revenge was sought by murdering a more prominent member of the opposite tribe. Such an action could lead to further retaliatory acts of revenge, causing attacks and counter-attacks to continue for extended periods of time. In such cases, the only means of settling the problem would be arbitration. Members of a neutral tribe would be chosen to discuss the whole feud and issue a final judgment consisting usually of certain blood fees (usually payable in camels) to be paid to the family of the last-murdered individual. Arbitration became a desert institution of great importance to the feuding Arabs. Once arbitration was agreed upon by the feuding parties, its verdict became mandatory and both sides were expected to abide by it —a procedure which the Arabs usually followed throughout their nomadic history.

Hospitality Among the Arabs

Perhaps the scarcity of resources and the fierce competition to acquire them caused the Arabs to develop temperaments of extreme hostility; however, the opposite is also true. When the Arabs were not troubled with want or danger, they were disposed to generous hospitality. In fact they had an unwritten law called the law of *dakhala*, meaning "hospitality," which stipulated that whenever a stranger set foot within the tent of an Arab, he was automatically eligible for the full hospitality of the household. Even if an enemy became lost in the desert and unknowingly entered the tent of his opponent, hostilities would be deferred as long as the enemy was within the gates of his host. When he departed hostilities would be resumed; on many occasions an Arab would attack an enemy whom he had entertained inside his tent a few days before.

Hilf al-Fudul and the Forbidden Months

In spite of all these measures, tribal wars and raids continued and reached alarming proportions in the years before the rise of Islam. In an effort to deter constant raids and bloodshed among the various tribes, the leaders of certain Arab tribes formulated what could be termed an intertribal league, called *hilf al-fudul*. One of the rules of this league banned all kinds of violence and hostility in and around the vicinity of Makka during the pilgrimage season. The purpose of such an agreement was to preserve the sanctity of the holy place during the sacred pilgrimage season, which had been frequently desecrated by fighting and bloodshed.

Through another intertribal agreement, the Arabs designated five nonconsecutive months of the year during which fighting and revenge were outlawed. These months were called *haram*, meaning "forbidden," and murder or violence committed during any of them would be investigated by an arbitration council. Both the *hilf al-fudul* and the *haram* months were noteworthy institutions introduced into the pre-Islamic society. They should be considered a credit to a community that tried hard to adapt itself to a harsh environment.

Arabic and the Arabs

Among all the regions of the Middle East Proper, only North Arabia failed to leave behind any significant ancient documents or archaeological objects, perhaps due to the harsh environment which prevented a settled existence. Although thousands of inscribed tablets have been found in the Fertile Crescent, Egypt, and South Arabia, not a single one has ever turned up in the areas of Tihama, Najd, or Hijaz; it is not even known whether an Arabic script had ever been developed before Islam. In any case, post-Islamic records reveal that the Arabs before Muhammad possessed a highly sophisticated and greatly embellished oral heritage. Pre-Islamic poetry and prose (orally transmitted till they were recorded around the ninth century) are still considered among the classics of Arabic literature, in spite of the fact that they were recorded over three hundred years after their composition. Apparently the Arabs developed keen memories and lively imagination and frequently debated in verse. Since they were fairly isolated from foreign languages, they preserved their speech from any significant linguistic interference. Arabic (from a purely philological point of view) is, therefore, the closest of all Semitic languages to what is frequently referred to as

Proto-Semitic, i.e., the language hypothetically considered the ancestor of all Semitic tongues. The rhyming patterns of the Arabic language, augmented by an elaborate system of affixation, contributed greatly to the poetic inclination of the wandering Arabs, who used to meet together periodically during the pilgrimage season in market places such as the one called Ukaz (near Makka) and compete in verse. During these poetic debates, hundreds of verses were recited and most probably committed to memory by the hearers, who transmitted them orally from generation to generation until they were finally recorded during the Arabic classical period.

CHAPTER 12

THREE ROLES OF LEADERSHIP

ARAB INTERTRIBAL WARS

Arabia Sealed Off

The rise of the Arab kingdom of Palmyra in pre-Islamic times, followed by the establishment of the two buffer states of Hira and Ghassan, all but sealed off Arabia from its northern fringes and thus blocked the free movements of the Arab nomads to the north. Almost simultaneously, South Arabia was occupied by the Abyssinians, to be followed by the Persians about A.D. 570. These occupations formed another barrier against any southward migration of the Bedouins of North Arabia. In brief, the desert nomads were completely trapped within their own barren land, checked by the Persian Gulf and the Red Sea from east and west, and by strong foreign powers from the north and south. In the event of a population overflow, these nomads had no way out; they had to resign themselves either to starvation or raids. Accordingly, Arab life during the few decades before Muhammad consisted of continuous intertribal wars augmented by vicious blood feuds that continued till the early years of the Prophet's life. These wars, known as *ayyam al-Arab,* may be divided into three phases: (1) wars between the two major tribes of Rabi'a and Mudar, (2) wars among the various sub-tribes of Rabi'a, and (3) wars among the various sub-tribes of Mudar.

The Basus War

As mentioned above, Rabi'a's main tribes were Bakr and Taghlib, and those of Mudar were Tamim, Kinana, Quraysh, and Qays. The first phase of the Arabian intertribal wars took place between Bakr of Rabi'a and Tamim of Mudar. According to Arab records, Tamim defeated Bakr in at least six battles, while Bakr won against Tamim in at least six other battles, some of which continued till the early years of Islam. Wars among the sub-tribes of Rabi'a itself took place between Bakr and Taghlib, chief of which was the Basus war summarized here from Arabic pre-Islamic traditions for the purpose of illustrating some features of Arab intertribal feuds.

A man of Taghlib named Kulayb married a woman from Bakr called Jalila, whose cousin once entertained a guest. A camel belonging to this guest ran into the household of Kulayb and was hit by an arrow. This was considered a great insult to Jalila's family since the guest was still staying within the gates of her cousin's home. To avenge this great humiliation, Jalila's brother Jassas killed Kulayb, who was considered a chief of his tribe. This act aroused Taghlib against Bakr —especially since a chief had been murdered for the sake of a camel. The two tribes began a series of battles that lasted for over forty years, during which many of the great men of both sides were killed. These battles ended only when Kulayb's brother, a famous poet named Muhalhal, reportedly appealed in verse to all the descendants of Rabi'a to close ranks and refrain from shedding more blood.

Other Wars

There were two main wars within the tribe of Mudar; the first between the Abs and Dhubyan called the war of Dahis and Ghabra', and the second between Quraysh and Kinana on one side and Qays on the other. The first war started presumably as a result of foul play in a horse race in which Dahis, a horse belonging to a man from Abs, was purposely detained during a certain race so that Ghabra', a mare belonging to a man from Dhubyan might win. Dahis' owner took revenge by murdering the son of his opponent; this started a war that lasted several years. Finally arbitration settled the feud, but not without the appeals of an eloquent poet named Antara.

War of the Fijar

The Fijar war started with an exchange of insults between a man of Kinana and another of Qays that ended with the murder of the man from Qays, whose people rallied to take revenge upon Kinana. Quraysh came to the help of the latter, and, during the first round of battles, took refuge in Makka's forbidden grounds. The following year, the battle took place in the market place of Ukaz with no clear victory for either side. Muhammad was twenty years old when this battle took place; some reports mention that he even played a role in it. The whole feud ended after arbitration had been requested by both sides. The verdict was to match the fallen men on both sides one for one; the families of those left unmatched from one side were paid blood fees by the other.

ANSWER TO THE ARABS' NEEDS

Three Roles in Search of a Leader

These prolonged intertribal wars among the Arabs left them in desperate need of unity and stability. However, what the Arabs needed more than anything else was a strong leader to transform their warring energies into an effective force for the common interest.

Furthermore, the Arabs' exposure to the Judeo-Christian tradition left them somewhat dissatisfied with their own pagan customs. They were perhaps willing to give up idol worship, but apparently they could not accept the abstract theology inherent in monotheistic religions. This left the Arabs' spiritual life in a sort of vacuum as the need for a new ideology that would satisfy their monotheistic desires as well as their traditional system of worship was strongly felt.

Besides unity and a new ideology, the Arabs also needed food and sustenance. Any leader who would be able to unite their ranks and satisfy their minds must also be able to bring them bread and prosperity. Being trapped in their own "island," the only way for the Arabs to obtain the treasures of the non-Arab states around them was to launch offensive warfare against them. This required organization and military discipline; thus the Arabs also needed a military leader who would be able to organize them into an army under one banner and expand their borders in order to obtain the riches of their neighbors.

To solve these serious and complicated problems, the Arabs of pre-Islamic times were in need of a hero capable of assuming a tripartite role. First, he should be a political leader in order to establish a united Arab nation; second, he should be a religious leader with divine authority to receive support beyond tribal boundaries; and third, he should be a military leader to transform the Arab raiding capacity into a fighting force capable of bringing advantage to the Arabs as a whole.

Muhammad and His Mission

This tripartite role found a leader in the person of Muhammad, son of Abd-Allah of the tribe of Quraysh, a quiet, lonely but determined and efficient man. Under his leadership the scattered feuding Arabs were destined to emerge from utter insignificance to rule one of the world's largest empires. Muhammad was a statesman, prophet, and military commander. He supplied his people with an awareness of unity, a religion, and a military organization. The Arab Empire was destined to reach from the Atlantic Ocean in the west to the borders of China in the east, and from Central Europe in the north to Central Africa in the south. The religion of Islam itself was destined to become the second-largest religion in the world. As the history of the Arab Empire is related on the pages of this book, it is worthwhile to note how Muhammad's personality was stamped on the Islamic movement so strongly that it continued after his death to bear the tripartite characteristic of his own life. Islam, therefore, may be considered in a broad sense a political, religious, and military movement. Throughout Islamic history, these three aspects became, in one way or another, the dominant features of Islamic civilizations that continued to shape the destinies of millions of Arab and non-Arab Muslims until the present time.

IMPORTANT TERMS

Adnan: Traditional ancestor of the Arabs of North Arabia.

Allah: The proper name of God in Islamic religion. It is believed to be a borrowing from Hebrew Elohim through Aramaic Eloah.

Ghassan: An Arab buffer kingdom supported by the Byzantines during the sixth century A.D. on the southern border of Syria.

Hadramawt: A kingdom in South Arabia which later on united with Qataban before both became a part of the Himyarite territory.

Hanif: A sort of monotheistic religion that was starting in Arabia during the early part of Muhammad's life.

Himyarites: A dynasty that unified all the earlier kingdoms of South Arabia about 115 B.C. This federation lasted till A.D. 275.

Hira: A buffer Arab kingdom supported by the Persians during the sixth century A.D. on the southern borders of Iraq.

Ka'ba: The holy shrine of Makka that houses the "Black Stone."

Kinda: A small kingdom in North Arabia which flourished a few decades before the rise of Islam.

Ma'in: One of the old South Arabian kingdoms which flourished around the sixth century B.C.

Mukarrib: A title given to the priests of ancient South Arabia. It later became a royal title.

Nabateans: A Semitic people who settled south of Palestine. They established a flourishing civilization during the third century B.C.

Najran: A city in South Arabia which later on became the chief center of Christianity in the peninsula.

Palmyra: An Arab kingdom which flourished around the fourth century A.D. between Syria and Iraq with its capital at Tadmur.

Qahtan: Traditional progenitor of the South Arabians.

Qataban: One of the early kingdoms in South Arabia.

Quraysh: An Arab tribe in Makka whose members were supervising the Ka'ba. Muhammad belonged to the tribe of Quraysh.

Saba: One of the kingdoms of ancient South Arabia. Under Saba's leadership, the South Arabian federation was established about 115 B.C.

Yathrib: A city located about 250 miles northeast of Makka to which Muhammad immigrated in A.D. 622. It is known in Islamic history as Madina.

SUPPLEMENTARY READINGS

BOWEN, R., *Archaeological Discoveries in South Arabia* (Baltimore, 1958).

HOGARTH, D.G., *Arabia* (Oxford, 1922).

HOURANI, G.F., *Arab Seafaring in the Indian Ocean* (Princeton, 1951).

JAMME, A., *Mahram Balqis* (Baltimore, 1963).

LAMMENS, H., *L'Arabie occidentale avant l'hegire* (Beirut, 1928).

LEVI DELLA VIDA, G., "Pre-Islamic Arabia," in Nabih A. Faris, *The Arab Heritage* (Princeton, 1946).

NOLDEKE, Th., "Arabs (ancient)" in Hastings *Encyclopedia of Religion and Ethics,* Vol. I.

O'LEARY, DE LACY, *Arabia before Muhammad* (London, 1927).

ROSTOVTZEFF, M., *Caravan Cities* (Oxford, 1932).

RYCKMANS, G., *Les Religions arabes preislamiques* (Louvain, 1951).

THOMAS, BERTRAM, *The Arabs* (New York, 1937).

VASILIEV, A.A., *Notes on Some Episodes Concerning the Relations between the Arabs and the Byzantine Empire from the Fourth to the Sixth Century* (Cambridge, 1956).

PART iv

THE ISLAMIC RELIGION

The main topic around which any discussion of Islam as a religion usually revolves is the personal life of the Prophet Muhammad, its founder and first preacher. Although Muhammad was born at a time when the world around him was relatively civilized and recording its own history, his biography was orally transmitted over a period of approximately 200 years before it was reduced to writing about A.D. 828. This lapse of time between the real man and his recorded image presents the modern historian with both bewilderment and confusion – bewilderment, because the historian finds in the transmitted tradition a legendary image of the real man; and confusion, because it is extremely difficult to reject the whole tradition as myth and sheer invention. Muslim historians produce a life history of Muhammad shrouded with supernatural manifestations parallel to those of earlier prophets in the Judeo-Christian tradition; while others attempt to strip Muhammad's biography of all superhuman embellishments, presenting him only as a human being possessing insight, imagination, and a will to achieve his goals. In the following chapters, the two approaches to this controversial subject of the enigmatic personality of Muhammad are presented together with a digest of the main Islamic beliefs and devotional duties.

CHAPTER 13

MUHAMMAD, THE PROPHET OF ISLAM

MUHAMMAD THE MAN

His Birth and Early Childhood

It is generally believed that Muhammad was born in A.D. 571, traditionally known as the year of the elephant, the year during which the Abyssinians invaded Arabia. He was born into the important Quraysh tribe whose members served as the custodians of the holy shrine, Ka'ba, which housed most of the pagan gods of the Arabs. However, Muhammad's clan, known as Hashim, was second in prestige to its sister clan Umayya, which had traditionally supplied the leadership of the whole tribe. The Quraysh tribe as a whole drew sizable revenues from the yearly gifts that the Arabs poured into the Ka'ba; thus paganism was to them a source of income as well as a religion. Hashim, the great-grandfather of Muhammad, although the eldest son and rightful leader of the tribe, became engaged in a lucrative caravan business that earned him more wealth than the revenues of the Ka'ba; therefore, the actual leadership of Quraysh was vested in his brother Abd-Shams, the father of the Umayyad clan. Abd al-Muttalib, Muhammad's own grandfather, made a great effort to reclaim the leadership from Abd-Shams but failed, and thus the Umayyad clan continued to rule Quraysh until Muhammad was born.

Muhammad's father was named Abd-Allah, "servant of Allah"—an indication that Allah was among the chief gods

of Quraysh. His mother was named Amina and is said to have descended from one of the best families of her tribe. However, Muhammad's
father died before his birth, and his mother died when he was six
years old. Muhammad then was cared for by his grandfather, who
died two years later. From that time on, Muhammad was under the
charge of his uncle Abu Talib. These conditions made the early
years of Muhammad rather difficult, but he apparently held up well
under them, not withstanding some reports which described him
as lonely and of quiet disposition. He developed a reputation for
honesty and was therefore called *al-Amin*, "the faithful." At the
age of twelve, he accompanied his uncle on a trade caravan to Syria,
where he is reported to have met a monk in one of the monasteries,
who held Muhammad in his arms and predicted that he would be a
leader of his people.

His Attitude Toward Intertribal Wars

Muhammad grew up in Makka, where he had ample opportunity
to listen to religious arguments among Arabs, Jews, and Christians,
as they frequently debated in the market place of Ukaz. He is known
to have witnessed the Fijar war between Quraysh and Qays, and to
have participated in convincing the two feuding parties to accept
arbitration. Muslim annals report that he abhorred intertribal wars;
on one occasion he intervened to prevent a major war in Makka
at the time the Ka'ba was being rebuilt about 590. The chiefs of
Quraysh disagreed among themselves as to which clan should have
the honor of putting the precious Black Stone (a stone—possibly a
meteorite—with traditional religious value) back in its place. The
dispute might have resulted in a blood feud, had it not been for Muhammad's intervention and proposal of a peace plan. He threw his garment
on the floor of the Ka'ba, placed the Black Stone on it, and asked
the chiefs of each clan to hold a corner of the garment; thus all of
Quraysh participated in the act and peace was preserved.

MUHAMMAD THE PROPHET

Muhammad's Prophetic Call

When Muhammad was twenty-five years old, a rich widow named
Khadija asked him to take care of her business and lead a trade
caravan to Syria. Seeing that he discharged his responsibilities so
faithfully, Khadija, fifteen years his senior, took a liking to him,
and they were married shortly afterward. This marriage solved
Muhammad's financial problems and supplied him with wealth and
security. Nevertheless, he reportedly did not use his newly acquired

wealth in worldly pleasures or luxurious living; on the contrary, he used to repair to a cave a few miles away from Makka in a mountain called Hira' and spend long periods in meditation and retreat. At the age of forty, while he was praying in that cave during the month of Ramadan, he reportedly heard a voice commanding him to read. He replied, "I am not a reader." The voice commanded him again:

> Read in the name of thy Lord who created –
> He created man from a clot.
> Read and thy Lord is Most Generous,
> Who taught (to write) with the pen,
> He taught man what he knew not.
>
> Qur'an 96:1-5 [1]

Islamic annals mention that Muhammad rushed home trembling and asked his wife Khadija to cover him with a cloak. When she did, he heard the same voice saying:

> O thou who art clothed!
> Arise and warn,
> And thy Lord do magnify,
> And thy garments keep purified,
> And uncleanness do shun,
> And bestow not favours that thou mayest receive again with increase,
> And for the sake of thy Lord, be patient.
>
> Qur'an 74:1-7

When he told his wife about this unusual experience, she consulted her cousin Waraqa ibn Nawfal, who had been reportedly influenced by Christian as well as Hanif doctrines. When Waraqa indicated that Muhammad could be a true messenger of Allah, Khadija believed her husband's claims and became his first convert. Muhammad's message at that time was limited to calling the attention of the people to three main items of doctrine: (1) the oneness of God, (2) Muhammad's appointment as the messenger of God, and (3) the belief in the day of judgment.

Rejection of Muhammad's Message in Makka

Muhammad immediately began his mission of warning, preaching first to his own tribe Quraysh from which he won a few noted con-

---

[1] All Qur'anic texts are taken from the *Translation of the Holy Qur'an* by Muhammad Ali, Lahore, W. Pakistan. There are several translations of the Qur'an in English. A well-known paperback edition is M. M. Pickthall, *The Meaning of the Glorious Koran,* a Mentor Book publication.

verts, such as Abu Bakr, a rich and respected merchant; Ali, Muhammad's own cousin; Uthman and Talha, two rich members of Quraysh; and later on Umar, a wise and greatly talented leader. As he continued to win converts, the leaders of Quraysh, who drew large revenues from their services as custodians of the gods at Ka'ba, began to realize that Muhammad's message would prove ruinous to their lucrative business. Accordingly they opposed him, ordering him to abstain from telling the people about the uselessness of their traditional gods. Nevertheless, Muhammad persisted in his mission and continued to preach publicly in market places and in the midst of Makka's public square, denouncing idol worship and calling on all Arabs to abandon polytheism and to worship Allah alone. Due to the high prestige of the Qurayshis among the Arabs, their opposition to the Prophet succeeded in turning many away from listening to Muhammad; after three years of constant preaching, his converts numbered only fifty—a small but faithful group whose faith survived great persecution and ridicule.

Muhammad and the Christians

When he met with preliminary failure in trying to convert his own people, Muhammad turned his attention to the Christians and the Jews. He sent some of his oppressed followers to find refuge in Abyssinia with a message to its Christian king, the Negus, which indicated that they had been persecuted because of worshiping God, the creator of all things. When the Negus inquired about their belief in Jesus Christ, they added Muhammad's own instructions that Jesus Christ, the son of Mary, was a word from God made incarnate through the Virgin Mary. (Compare Qur'an 3:45, 19:19, 21, and 66:12) Hearing this, the Negus is reported to have responded by saying that Muhammad's beliefs and the Christian doctrines apparently originated from the same source, and therefore granted the Muslim refugees asylum. Muslim annals report that afterwards a few Christians went to Makka and, in the light of what they had heard about Christ, accepted Muhammad as a messenger of God. To the Christians in and around Makka, Muhammad sent the following appeal:

> Certainly they disbelieve who say: Allah is the third (person) of the three. And there is no god but the One God. And if they desist not from what they say, a painful chastisement will befall those among them who disbelieve.
> Will they not then turn to Allah and ask His forgiveness? And Allah is Forgiving, Merciful.
>
> Qur'an 5:73,74

Apparently these Christians treated Muhammad kindly but did not make any move toward recognizing his claim to prophecy. He therefore continued his appeals to them as follows:

> The Messiah, son of Mary, was but a messenger—messengers before him have indeed passed away. And his mother was a truthful woman; they both used to eat food. See how We make the communications clear to them, then behold, how they are turned away.
>
> Say: O People of the Book! Be not unduly immoderate in your religion, and follow not the low desires of people who went astray before and led many astray, and went astray from the right path.
>
> Qur'an 5:75,77

Obviously, some heated arguments took place between Muhammad and the Christians of both Makka and Madina, who refused to abandon their own ways and follow him. At last, when he lost hope of converting them, he apparently reversed his original esteem for Jesus Christ as a word from God, and announced that he was nothing but dust, created no better than Adam (Qur'an 3:59).

Muhammad and the Jews

Disappointed with the Christians, but not indignant, Muhammad next turned his attention to the Jews. To attract their attention he announced his famous nocturnal trip to Jerusalem during the night of *Mi'raj* (Qur'an 10:16) and his almost instantaneous return, announcing his choice of the holy city as *qibla*, "the direction of prayer." Furthermore, he incorporated as an Islamic fast day the Jewish feast of the day of atonement usually celebrated on the tenth day of the first month each year, and called it *Ashura*, meaning "the tenth." These measures not only failed to impress the Jews into recognizing him as a prophet, but apparently caused them also to ridicule him for his attempts at converting them. Finally, he changed the *qibla*, "direction of prayer," from Jerusalem to Makka (Qur'an 2:144), replaced the fast of *Ashura* with the fast of the Muslim month Ramadan, and denounced the unbelieving Jews in these words:

> From among the Jews are those who alter words from their places and say: We have heard and we disobey; and: Hear, mayest thou not be made to hear! and: Listen to us—distorting (the word) with their tongues and taunting about religion. And if they had said (instead): We have heard and we obey, and hearken, and grant us a little delay, it would have been better for them and more upright; but Allah has cursed them on account of their unbelief, so little is it that they believe.
>
> Qur'an 4:46 (compare Qur'an 5:41)

Furthermore he added:

> The likeness of those who were charged with the Torah,
> then they did not observe it, is as the likeness of the ass
> carrying books. Evil is the likeness of the people who reject
> the communications of Allah. And Allah guides not the unjust
> people.

Qur'an 62:5

Comparing the Jews with the seemingly less adamant Christians,
Muhammad says:

> Thou wilt find the most violent people in enmity to those
> who believe (to be) the Jews and the idolaters. And thou wilt
> find the nearest in friendship to those who believe (to be)
> those who say, We are Christians. This is because there are
> priests and monks among them, and because they do not behave
> proudly.

Qur'an 5:82

Muhammad and His Own People

While still in Makka, trying in vain to win the Christians and
the Jews, Muhammad made a desperate effort to win his own people
of Quraysh. They had already announced a boycott against him and
his followers, pledging that none of them should buy, sell, marry,
or give a wife in marriage to any of the adherents of the Islamic
religion who became known as Muslims. Muhammad himself was
threatened, but his uncle Abu Talib announced his personal protection of his nephew, declaring that if Muhammad were murdered
a war within Quraysh would surely follow. In his anxiety to win his
own people, Muhammad stood one day in the midst of the Ka'ba and
asked his kinsmen to listen to Allah's message. He said:

> By the star when it sets.
> Your companion does not err, nor does he deviate;
> Nor does he speak out of desire.
> It is naught but revelation that is revealed –
> The Lord of Mighty Power has taught him,
> The Lord of Strength. So he attained perfection,
> And he is in the highest part of the horizon.
> Then he drew near, and drew nearer,
> So that he was the measure of two bows or closer still.
> So He revealed to His servant what He revealed.
> The heart lied not in what he saw.
> Do you dispute with him as to what he saw?
> And certainly he saw Him in another descent,
> At the farthest lote-tree,

> Near which is the garden of Refuge,
> When that which covers covered the lote-tree;
> The eye turned not aside, nor exceeded the limit.
> Certainly he saw of the greatest signs of his Lord.
> Have you considered Lat and 'Uzza
> And Manat, the third, the last?
>
> Qur'an 53:1-20

At this point of his recitation, Muhammad's own biographer, Ibn Ishaq, asserts that Satan put upon his tongue the following statement: "These are the exalted Gharaniq (possibly demigods) whose mediation is accepted."

Upon hearing the last statement, the people of Quraysh rejoiced and spread the rumor everywhere that Muhammad had attributed the power of intercession to the gods of the Ka'ba. This led them to continue worshiping these gods with greater zeal, especially since Muhammad himself recognized their merit. This episode was doubly damaging to the Prophet's cause; not only did the Qurayshis persist in worshiping their own idols, but the Muslims themselves became greatly grieved and dismayed. To save the situation Muhammad later recited to his followers this statement:

> And those who strive to frustrate Our communications, they are inmates of the flaming fire.
>
> And We did not send before thee any messenger or prophet, but when he desired, the devil made a suggestion (of opposition) respecting his desire; but Allah annuls that which the devil suggests; then Allah establishes His communications. And Allah is Knowing, Wise.
>
> Qur'an 22:51,52

It should be noted that the verses attributing intercessory powers to the pagan gods, known in Islamic history as "the Satanic Verses," are recorded in Muhammad's biography but omitted in the Qur'an. They reveal beyond doubt Muhammad's fallibility as well as his personal desire to convert his own people by any means.

Apparently this last effort to win the Makkans was in vain, and, therefore, to hold the faltering faith of his already-won followers, he made the following announcement:

> Say: O unbelievers!
> I serve not that which you serve,
> Nor are you servers of Him whom I serve:
> Nor was I (ever) a server of that which you
>   served.
> Nor are you servers of Him whom I serve.
> You will have your recompense and I shall have
>   my recompense.
>
> Qur'an 109:1-6

Period of Despair

To add to his woes, his beloved wife and companion Khadija, on whom he relied heavily for counsel and encouragement, died about 619. Muhammad's devotion to his first wife is considered beyond compare according to Arab standards; as long as she lived he kept himself only unto her. After her death he married no less than seven wives, including a Copt called Mariya, who bore him his only son, Ibrahim, who died in infancy. Khadija had born Muhammad a girl named Fatima, who was the only daughter to bring grand-children to the Prophet. Fatima was married to Ali, the Prophet's cousin; her two sons, Hasan and Husayn, were the progenitors of the *sharifs* and *sayyids,* those who claimed direct descent from Muhammad.

Shortly after Khadija's death, Muhammad lost his uncle and pro-tector, Abu Talib. His other uncle, Abu Lahab, who assumed leadership of the clan of Hashim, persecuted Muhammad mercilessly—to the extent that he reportedly once asked his wife to put thorns in the path of the Prophet. To comfort Muhammad the angel Gabriel is supposed to have given him the following revelation about Abu Lahab whose name, incidentally, means "father of the flame":

> Perdition overtake both hands of the father of the
>   flame, and he will perish.
> His wealth and what he earns will not avail him.
> He will burn in fire that flames,
> And his wife, the bearer of slander,
> Upon her neck a halter of strongly twisted rope.
>
> Qur'an 111:1-5

The Prophet was thus left alone in utter grief and discouragement during the hardest years of his mission. He tried to win some con-verts in a city about fifty miles southeast of Makka called Ta'if, but apparently the influence of Quraysh's opposition to the Prophet was so great that he was unable even to begin preaching. In the next two years Muhammad experienced great anguish and temptation as his faith was tested severely; however he maintained extreme devotion and loyalty to what he believed was the call of God.

Divine Endorsement of the Prophet's Acts

It appears from this brief analysis of the early life of Muhammad that the divine revelations which he claimed to have received from Allah corresponded rather well with his own personal experiences as he continued to preach his message. Even in his private life, revelations seemed to coincide quite well with his own personal desires, allowing him to do several things from which he would otherwise have been forced to abstain. For instance, after Khadija's death when he wanted to marry his daughter-in-law Zaynab, wife of his adopted son Zayd, he hesitated at first because it was not customary among the Arabs to marry a daughter-in-law, even if she were divorced. But Muhammad quoted a divine sanction when he recited the following Qur'anic revelation allowing him to do so:

> And when thou didst say to him to whom Allah had shown favour and to whom thou hadst shown a favour: Keep thy wife to thyself and keep (thy duty to) Allah, and thou dost conceal in thy soul what Allah would bring to light, and thou dost fear men, and Allah has a greater right that thou shouldst fear Him. But when Zaid divorced her, We gave her to thee as a wife, so that there should be no difficulty for the believers in respect of the wives of their adopted sons, when they have divorced them; and Allah's command must be performed.
>
> Qur'an 33:37

The obvious correlation between Muhammad's revelations and his actual experiences is a striking phenomenon in the development of the religion of Islam that has caused some historians to accuse Muhammad of insincerity. However, other historians find it very difficult to believe that any man could stick by fancy-framed ideas for so long under such trying circumstances as Muhammad did, especially during the two years before 622. In any case, it can be fairly stated about Muhammad that he had set a goal for himself and his people, and he was completely dedicated to the accomplishment of this goal.

CHAPTER 14

ISLAMIC BELIEFS AND DEVOTIONAL DUTIES

ISLAMIC BELIEFS

The will of God is supposed to have been revealed to Muhammad through the ministry of the angel Gabriel at various intervals. Accordingly, the beliefs and duties of the religion of Islam (sometimes incorrectly called Muhammadanism) were not instituted by the Prophet at any one phase or period of his ministry. During his entire life after he received his first revelation, Muhammad claimed to be receiving revelations from God; Islam as a religion therefore continued to develop till the time of his death, when inspiration stopped and the Islamic religion was sealed.

Definition of Islam

Islam in the Arabic language means "submission," a term that best describes the main feature of the religion. A Muslim is an adherent to Islam and is, therefore, an individual who submits his own will to the will of God. Shortly before his death, Muhammad performed his last pilgrimage to Makka and is reported to have said:

> Forbidden to you is that which dies of itself, and blood, and flesh of swine, and that on which any other name than that of Allah has been invoked, and the strangled (animal) and that beaten to death, and that killed by a fall and that killed by being smitten with

the horn, and that which wild beasts have eaten, except what you slaughter, and what is sacrificed on stones set up (for idols) and that you divine by the arrows, that is a transgression. This day have those who disbelieve despaired of your religion, so fear them not, and fear Me. This day have I perfected for you your religion and completed My favour on you and chosen for you Islam as a religion. But whoever is compelled by hunger, not inclining wilfully to sin, then Allah is surely Forgiving, Merciful.

Qur'an 5:3

Although Muhammad directed his message primarily to his own kinsmen, he never hesitated to bring out the universal nature of Islam. According to Muslim orthodox theologians, Islam calls on people of all nations to adhere to its three basic aspects: (1) *iman,* meaning "faith," (2) *ibadat,* meaning "devotional duties," and (3) *mu'amalat,* meaning "interpersonal relations." The first one consists of a set of Islamic theological beliefs, the second concerns relations between man and God, and the third regulates relations between man and his fellow men.

Belief in One God

The faith aspect of Islam is dogmatically binding upon all Muslims, requiring them first to believe in the oneness of God whose will is absolute and without whose permission nothing can happen, either good or bad. The second item of faith requires the Muslims to believe in Muhammad as the messenger and prophet of God. The third requires them to believe in the day of judgment on which God will usher believers into a paradise under which rivers flow. Any individual professing these three items of faith becomes a Muslim in essence and, therefore, is considered a believer worthy of Muhammad's mediation for admission to eternal bliss.

As Islamic theology developed, the Muslim belief in God was further embellished and is now commonly accepted to consist of three main concepts: (1) the essence of Allah, (2) his attributes, and (3) his works. The essence of God, *dhat Allah,* includes concepts such as his oneness, his formlessness, and his omnipotence. His attributes, *sifat Allah,* include such characteristics as life, knowledge, power, will, speech, and activity. His works, *a'mal Allah,* include several capabilities such as creation, preservation, revelation, and predestination. The Qur'an itself speaks about Allah as follows:

Allah is He besides Whom there is no god, the Everliving, the Self-subsisting by whom all subsist. Slumber does not overtake Him nor sleep. To Him belongs whatever is in the heavens and whatever is in the earth. Who is he that can intercede with Him but by His permission? He knows what is before them

and what is behind them, and they cannot comprehend anything
out of his knowledge except what He pleases. His knowledge
extends over the heavens and the earth, and the preservation of
them both tires Him not, and He is the Most High, the Great.

Qur'an 2:255

Besides the above three concepts of God, Muslims attach to him
ninety-nine names, generally known as *al-asma' al-husna*, "the most
beautiful names," which include qualities such as the first, the last,
the enduring, the truthful, the mighty, the gentle, the just, and many
others. Perhaps the most striking feature of Allah, according to
Muslim beliefs, is his absoluteness. By virtue of this belief a Muslim
is usually fatalistic, believing in God's predestination of both good
and bad events in man's life.

DEVOTIONAL DUTIES

Islamic devotional duties, *ibadat*, or as they are sometimes
called "the pillars of Islam," consist of five obligations whose fulfillment is morally and sometimes legally obligatory, but not dogmatically required for reaching paradise as that of the belief in Allah
and his Prophet. The degree of earnestness in fulfilling these duties
distinguishes the piety of individual Muslims and brings them that much
nearer to God in paradise. These duties are: (1) testimony, (2) prayer,
(3) fasting, (4) alms, and (5) pilgrimage. Some Muslims list *jihad*,
"holy war," as a sixth duty under *ibadat*, but others consider it one
of the mandatory requirements of *mu'amalat*, "interpersonal relations," described below.

Testimony

The first devotional duty is known as the *shahada*, "testimony,"
which may be compared in a very broad sense to the Christian creed.
It was initiated especially for converts from non-Muslim communities
to Islam. Such converts are required, as a first step toward prac-
ticing their new religion, to recite before at least two witnesses the
Muslim testimony, which goes as follows:

I testify that there is no God but Allah, and I testify that
Muhammad is the messenger of Allah.

Of course they are supposed to believe fully in this part of faith under
the branch of *iman*. But reciting the testimony audibly before witnesses is deemed a duty of worship that confirms them as Muslims.
Born Muslims are not obligated to go through the formality of the
testimony before witnesses, but they should be willing to recite it
whenever an occasion arises to announce their faith.

Prayer

The second devotional duty is prayer. A pious Muslim prays five times a day—at dawn, at noon, in the mid-afternoon, at sundown, and late in the evening. To remind the Muslims of the approaching time of prayer, a loud call for prayer called *adhan* is made from tops of minarets in every Muslim community. The *adhan* usually consists of several chantings in a loud, slow-paced voice, of the *shahada*, "testimony," which reiterates the belief of the Muslims in the oneness of God and the message of his prophet Muhammad. When a Muslim hears the *adhan*, he is supposed to go through the ritual of cleansing, called *wudu'*, which stipulates washing the face, hands, and feet with water—or sand in case water is not available. Then the Muslim, wherever he may be—in his field or in the office, at home or visiting friends—stretches a prayer rug, turns his face to the *qibla*, "direction toward Makka," and prays.

His prayer usually begins with the recitation of the *takbir*, which repeats "God is greatest" several times; then he recites the *Fatiha*, the first chapter of the Qur'an, which may be compared to the Christian Lord's Prayer; then he bows down until his chest makes a right angle with his hips. He then lifts his head up and kneels down prostrating himself till his forehead touches the ground. After this he sits on his heels for awhile, then prostrates himself forward once more to touch the ground with his forehead. As he proceeds from one position to another he repeats the *takbir* and the *shahada* several times.

The second prostration marks the end of one round of prayer, called *rak'a*, which may be repeated as many as four times during the late evening prayer or twice during other prayers. When the required *rak'as* are completed, the Muslim sits on his feet, turns his face from one side to the other, and pronounces the salutation, *"al-salamu alaykum,"* which means "the peace (of God) be upon you"; he then resumes his normal daily routine.

Besides these daily prayers, Muslims meet once a week at noon on Friday for a congregational prayer that usually takes place at the mosque. In Islam, Friday is not a day of rest comparable to the Judeo-Christian Sabbath; it is a day of congregation when all Muslims of any community meet together for worship. An *imam*, "leader," usually leads the congregational prayer so that all the various movements of the *rak'as* are performed simultaneously. Either before or at the close of the prayer ritual, the congregation usually listens to the Friday sermon, ordinarily delivered by a noted Islamic scholar. Besides words of faith and encouragement and the inclusion of a petition to bless believers in all lands, the sermon is made in the name of the local head of state as a sign of allegiance and obedience. Women are usually allowed to attend congregational prayers, but they must wear a headdress and are separated from the men.

In addition to Friday meetings, Muslims congregate for prayer twice a year during their two main feasts. The first feast falls at the end of the fasting month of Ramadan; the second is on the tenth day of the month of Dhu al-Hijja, during which Muslims perform the pilgrimage duties. As a whole, Muslims are supposed to perform their prayer duties regularly; only sickness or travel may prevent them from participating in these rituals.

Fasting

The third devotional duty is fasting. Through the whole month of Ramadan Muslims abstain from eating, drinking, and marital relations during daylight. At night, however, they are allowed to eat as many times as they may desire. Accordingly, during the fasting month, sleep, weariness, and fatigue are apparent during the day while nights are usually bustling with signs of life, feasting, and entertainment. By fulfilling this duty, Muslims show their recognition of God's grace in sending to them, through the Prophet Muhammad, his divine revelations –the first of which is supposed to have been inspired during the month of Ramadan.

Alms

The fourth devotional duty requires the capable members of the community to pay what is known as zakat, "alms," to help support their poor neighbors. The Islamic religion ordains that alms be paid first to the poor of one's own clan, and then to any of the unfortunate people of the whole community. Later on, however, zakat was instituted by the state as a religious tax. Muslims were usually asked to pay about 2 1/2% of their income to the state treasury. This arrangement did not continue long; modern Islamic states (outside of Arabia) apply no force upon the Muslims to pay specified amounts of their income as a religious tax. Nevertheless, charitable donations and subsidies are officially administered by the state for promoting national welfare projects such as building hospitals and schools. This sacred duty of sharing one's own benefits is incumbent upon the well-to-do persons of the society –supposedly without any external force or pressure applied; the only motive for paying zakat is supposed to be a religious conviction that the payment of alms by believers is in harmony with Allah's divine will.

Pilgrimage

The fifth devotional duty is that of pilgrimage, which is in essence a yearly congregational prayer conducted on the mountain of Arafat near Makka during the first half of the month of Dhu al-Hijja of the

Muslim calendar. Muslims of all countries are urged to visit Makka during the pilgrimage season at least once in their lifetime. Many poor Muslims spend a major portion of their life savings to perform this sacred duty. It is considered a very joyous occasion, on which devout Muslims of all nationalities and backgrounds gather together without distinction of rank or wealth, wearing seamless white robes, to perform the pilgrimage duty. Before the congregational prayer at Arafat, the pilgrims usually tour the holy shrine of Ka'ba seven times and throw a kiss at the Black Stone. They also visit the famous well of Zamzam, traditionally associated with the patriarch Abraham; the more fortunate of them might get a drink from its holy water and take a bottle or two home for relatives and friends. After the congregational prayer, they usually make a trip to Madina in order to visit the mosque in which the Prophet was buried. The pilgrims then begin their trip back to their respective countries, each holding the new title *Hajj,* "pilgrim," which they esteem very highly. There is a widespread but unsupported belief among the Muslims that if a poor man spends all his money to visit the tomb of the Prophet, all his impious actions will be forgiven. It is no wonder, therefore, that so many Muslims go through extreme difficulties in order to perform the pilgrimage duty and receive the honorable title of *Hajj.*

INTERPERSONAL RELATIONS

Five Levels

The third aspect of Islamic religion is *mu'amalat,* "interpersonal relations;" it regulates duties and obligations among believers, involving most family affairs and matters of inheritance. There are five levels of *mu'amalat* requirements which range from what is mandatory to what is forbidden. The five levels are: (1) *wajib,* "mandatory," (2) *mandub,* "recommended," (3) *mubah,* "permitted," (4) *makruh,* "reprobated," and (5) *haram,* "forbidden."

The mandatory level *"wajib,"* may be either universally or individually binding upon Muslims. In the first case, if a section of the community fulfills the duty, the whole group receives credit; in the second case, each individual is required to carry out the mandatory duty on his own. The holy war, *jihad,* is a mandatory universal duty upon Muslims. It is among the most important duties of the *mu'amalat* —to the extent that some schools of thought consider it among the pillars of Islam usually known as *ibadat,* discussed above. *Jihad* is the duty upon the household of Islam to fight unbelievers whenever the Muslim caliph announces a holy war. Those who die in such a war are guaranteed heaven without precondition; and the victory of the combat group is usually counted for the whole community. Individual mandatory duties include requirements such as the conclusion

of a marriage contract before two witnesses and the husband's support
of his family.

The recommended level, *mandub,* includes such duties as setting
slaves free and supplying a separate home for each wife of the four
a Muslim is permitted to have at any one time. On the other hand,
the permitted level, *mubah,* allows, for example, the Muslim male to
marry up to four wives and to divorce any of his wives simply by
stating three times "I divorce you," on condition that these statements
be pronounced while the person is fully sober, not outraged, and not
mentally disturbed. Under this category Muslim males are permitted
to marry Christian or Jewish wives.

The reprobated level, *makruh,* includes such acts as gambling,
charging usuary on personal loans, which are considered hateful. The
last duty of the *mu'amalat* consists of the forbidden items, *haram,*
which include murdering believers, stealing their goods, mistreating
their wives, and the infanticide of girls. Under this category it may
be mentioned that Muslim males are forbidden to marry idolaters or
polytheists and Muslim females are forbidden to marry any except
believers.

Some of the *mu'amalat* requirements are enforced by the state,
which has the right to condemn violators; however, others are left
to the discretion of the individual Muslim. For instance, it is considered *mandub,* "recommended," that a Muslim give a dowry to the
father of his bride; yet, the state does not enforce duties of this kind
in spite of their inclusion in the *mu'amalat* branch of Islamic religion.

OTHER MUSLIM BELIEFS

Other Beings

Muslims believe also in the existence of angels, the devil, and a
third group called the *jinn,* "spirits."[1] The angels are believed to be
creations made of fire who function as messengers to carry out God's
errands. Gabriel is supposed to have given Muhammad his divine
revelations; other angels are believed to have been assigned the task
of keeping records for the day of judgment (Qur'an 82:10-12); others
are charged with strengthening believers when fear strikes them;
and still others are believed to be angels of death to gather the believers to God (Qur'an 32:11). The Qur'an pictures the angels as
having wings, some two, some three, and some four, with which
they fly wherever they desire. (Qur'an 35:1).

One of these angels, known as the devil *(shaytan),* is believed to
have become proud and rebelled against God's will. When Adam was
created, this angel refused to obey God's command to worship man;

---

[1]The singular of *jinn* is *jinniyy,* from which English "genie" is derived.

and, therefore, Allah cursed him and changed him into a devil called *Iblis,* who began to ambush believers, tempting them to disobedience (Qur'an 7:11-16). It was the devil who is believed to have seduced Adam and Eve to eat of the forbidden tree in paradise (Qur'an 7:20-22).

The *jinn,* on the other hand, are spirits that may be either good or bad. Like human beings, the *jinn,* according to Islamic beliefs, are required to obey God and his prophets. Some of these spirits are reported to have been sent to listen to Muhammad's revelations (Qur'an 46:29-31). The good *jinn* are considered by Muslims to be friendly to humans, while the bad ones attempt to frighten them on occasions. Probably this Islamic belief in the *jinn* is a continuation of the pre-Islamic concept of evil spirits against which pagan Arabs used to wear magical amulets.

Islam and the Judeo-Christian Tradition

It may be noted here that a number of the Judeo-Christian stories of the Old and New Testaments of the Bible are repeated in the Qur'an almost without change. Accordingly, Muslims believe also in many prophets before Muhammad, such as Noah, Abraham, Joseph, Moses, John the Baptist, and Jesus Christ. However, according to Islamic beliefs, Muhammad is the seal (last) of all prophets; this precludes the rise of any possible claimants to prophecy after him. Muslims believe that all the prophets before Muhammad possessed the power of mediation even though God never promised to fulfill their intercessions in behalf of their followers. On the other hand, Muhammad is believed to have received an assurance from Allah that all his mediations will be accepted on the day of judgment (Qur'an 66:8). This belief, together with the general belief that Muhammad had already promised to mediate for all those who would follow him, gives Muslims almost an unqualified assurance of entering paradise.

This brief analysis of Islam as a religion indicates that Muhammad introduced the Arabs to a system of beliefs and concepts derived mainly from pre-Islamic customs, the Judeo-Christian traditions, and the Arab Hanif doctrines. In other words, realizing that the Arabs were not ready to accept nontangible concepts, the Prophet of Islam brought to them a religion which allowed them to worship a nontangible God, but through tangible means. To this end he stripped the biblical tradition of its metaphysical concepts, accepted only some of its tangible ordinances and rituals, and concentrated heavily on one main belief—namely, the oneness of God and his absolute rule.

CHAPTER 15

THE QUR'AN

THE QUR'AN AS SCRIPTURE

Origin of the Qur'an

The Qur'an, meaning "recitation" or "reading," is the scripture of Islam just as the Bible is the scripture of the Judeo-Christian tradition. It contains all the divine revelations supposed to have been given by the angel Gabriel to Muhammad, from the time of his call to prophecy till his death. Muslims call it "the noble Qur'an" or sometimes "the glorious Qur'an," but never "the Holy Qur'an" as some translators have erroneously called it.

According to orthodox Islamic beliefs the Qur'an is the uncreated word of God – the original words of Allah revealed to the Prophet Muhammad, who acted only as a recipient and a messenger. Some Muslims believe that *Umm al-Kitab,* "the original archetype" of the Qur'an, is eternally preserved in heaven in the presence of God. This belief clearly reveals the high esteem that the Muslims attach to their own scripture, placing it above any criticism of either text or substance.

Style of the Qur'an

The Qur'an is written in Arabic in a style commonly known as rhymed prose which consists of short rhyming statements that follow each other in rhythmic succession. The rhymes are so numerous that it often appears that more emphasis is laid on sound than sense—a feature that has posed extremely difficult problems to Qur'anic interpretation. This particular rhyming style of Arabic is known to have been used by the pagan *kahins*, "sooth-sayers," as they wrote magical formulas on leaves or bits of skin to be used as amulets against evil spirits. When some of Muhammad's Qur'anic utterances were criticized by the Makkans, who apparently considered them similar to the *kahins'* divine formulas, the Prophet had this to say:

> But nay, I call to witness that which you see,
> And that which you do not see;
> Surely it is the word of an honoured Messenger.
> And it is not the word of a poet; little is it
>   that you believe;
> Nor the word of a soothsayer; little is it that
>   you mind.
> It is a revelation from the Lord of the worlds.
>
> Qur'an 69:38-43

The flowing style of the Qur'an together with its beautiful sounds —especially appealing to the Arab ear—make it a unique piece of literature that is hard to duplicate. Accordingly, Muslims consider it the miracle of miracles and the greatest evidence that Muhammad was the messenger of God. The book itself mentions this:

> Say: If men and jinn should combine together to bring the like of this Qur'an, they could not bring the like of it, though some of them were aiders of others.
>
> Qur'an 17:88

In view of the general belief among Muslims that Muhammad was illiterate, and by himself could not produce anything similar to the Qur'an, such texts have allowed the doctrine known as *i'jaz*, "the miraculous aspect of the Qur'an," to emerge in Islamic theology and become one of the strongest arguments used to support the Islamic religion.

REVELATION OF THE QUR'AN

Muhammad During Revelation

Muhammad maintained that during the last twenty years of his life, with the exception of a few intervals of no more than two years, the angel Gabriel revealed to him the Qur'an piecemeal.

When once asked about the manner in which the angel appeared to him, he answered that he would first hear a loud voice and then feel as if someone had struck him a blow. His youngest wife, A'isha, testified that during an instance of revelation she had seen the Prophet's brow soaked with perspiration even though it had been a very cold day. It is therefore very hard to dismiss Muhammad's claim to revelation as sheer invention; he must have been used to going through some sort of psychological or spiritual experiences which he interpreted as appearances of the angel Gabriel.

Expediency of the Revelations

On many occasions as he was asked certain questions, Muhammad would defer answering till he had consulted with the voice or revelation. A few days later, the "revealed" answers to these questions would be announced and found to be in harmony with Muhammad's own desires —a feature which caused some historians to accuse him of dishonesty. However, since Muhammad believed in God's special interest in him personally, as he pondered on any particular problem it is quite possible that a certain relaxing impulse caused him to feel that God was in full agreement with his own ideas.

RECORDING OF THE QUR'AN

The Qur'an Memorized

Muhammad recited all Qur'anic texts immediately after they were "revealed" to him. Sometimes he would ask certain scribes to record them for him; other times he was satisfied when his hearers had committed the whole recitation to memory. The Arabs were reputed to have keen memories, which often enabled them to remember a short text after hearing it once. They would inscribe a few words of certain passages on stones, palm leaves, or bones, perhaps to remind themselves of the beginnings of these passages. In fact, the Arabs are known to have preserved a part of their most important pre-Islamic legacy, namely, poetry, by the talent of memorization and transmission from father to son throughout the centuries. Likewise, Muhammad's utterances must have been preserved and transmitted by numerous reciters until they were recorded shortly after his death.

The Qur'an Recorded

Muhammad is reported to have used personal secretaries during the latter years of his life when community legislation was being formulated under divine sanctions. Muslim annals mention the following story about one of the Prophet's secretaries, Abu Sarh. Muhammad was dictating to him the passage recorded now in Qur'an 23:12 ff. about the creative power of God. When the Prophet reached the end of verse 14, which says, ". . . and We clothe the bones with flesh, then We cause it to grow into another creation," he paused for lack of further words. At this point, Abu Sarh reportedly interjected a clause rhyming with the above statement, which went like this, "So blessed be Allah the best of the creators." Immediately Muhammad accepted it and ordered it recorded in the text. Abu Sarh later on became doubtful as to the authenticity of Muhammad's claims to revelation, denied the Muslim faith, and returned to his people in Makka.

Another scribe employed by Muhammad to record the Qur'an was Zayd ibn Thabit, a scholar well versed in many languages, including Syriac and Greek. The script in which the early parts of the Qur'anic texts were written poses a problem, since the Arabic script known today developed long after Muhammad's time. Since Zayd was well versed in the writing systems of several languages, it is very probable that he used a modified form of the Syriac script, which developed later on into the Arabic script, to record the early Qur'anic texts.

Hafsa's Recension

Muhammad died before Zayd could complete the recording of the Qur'an under his direct supervision. Whatever Zayd could not write down was preserved, according to Islamic traditions, in the memories of believers. The traditional story of the collection of the Qur'an asserts that after Muhammad's death, his successor, Abu Bakr, was engaged in wars with apostate Arab tribes. At a battle called Yamama, a number of Qur'an reciters were killed, and, therefore, Umar, who became second successor to the Prophet, insisted that Abu Bakr should order Zayd to continue the work that had been interrupted by the Prophet's death.

After some hesitation, Abu Bakr agreed and Zayd began to collect the scattered texts of the Qur'an from the memories of reciters, who reportedly had written portions of them on stones, palm leaves, bones, ribs, and bits of leather. After recording all the texts that he could collect, he is believed to have kept the first Qur'anic copy at the house of Umar's daughter Hafsa. This copy, known as the Recension of Hafsa, later served as a guide to standardizing the Qur'anic text. Apparently other Muslims outside Arabia had also attempted to record the text of the Qur'an from the memories of some reciters, and no less than four other recensions are mentioned in Islamic annals.

Uthman's Recension

During the time of Uthman, the third successor to the Prophet, Muslims apparently were reading the Qur'an according to different recensions, and some variations in pronunciation and content were easily observed, causing strife and anxiety within the household of Islam. Uthman is reported to have ordered Zayd to undertake the task of standardizing the text of the Qur'an according to Hafsa's Recension, and to destroy all other copies. Zayd then revised Hafsa's Recension and made four identical copies of the revised edition, one of which was to be sent to each of the cities Kufa, Basra, and Damascus, and the fourth to be kept in Madina. Uthman's Recension, as it was called later on, became the source of all future Qur'anic texts.

About two hundred years later during the Abbasid period, an Arabic script known as Kufic emerged as a fully developed writing system in which the Qur'an was recopied. The oldest copies of the Qur'an existing today go back only to this Kufic script. No earlier copies have survived to reveal which script was first used in recording the Qur'an. However, there is no cause to suppose that the Qur'anic text of today differs significantly from what Muhammad originally recited or dictated to his scribes.

THE QUR'AN AS A BOOK

Contents of the Qur'an

The Qur'an contains 114 *suras,* "chapters," arranged according to their length, with the longer ones placed first and the shorter last, without attention to their chronological order. The only exception to this is the *Fatiha* chapter, commonly recited during prayers, which has been placed as the opening passage in spite of its brief contents. It reads as follows:

The Opening

In the name of Allah, the Beneficent, the Merciful.
(All) Praise is due to Allah, the Lord of the worlds,
The Beneficent, the Merciful,
Master of the day of requital.
Thee do we serve and Thee do we ask for help.
Guide us on the right path,
The path of those upon whom Thou hast bestowed favours,
Not of those upon whom wrath is brought down, nor of
    those who go astray.

Each *sura,* or chapter, is introduced by the following statement, which is very frequent in the Islamic religion, "In the name of Allah, the Beneficent, the Merciful." This is generally known as the *basmala.* Before the *basmala* of each *sura,* the place of its revelation is usually given—whether in Makka or in Madina—together with a brief title such as "The Cow," "The Cave," "The Bee," etc. These titles have no particular significance; they are words picked almost at random from the body of each chapter to distinguish one *sura* from another.

In twenty-nine *suras,* just before the text of the chapter begins, some mysterious letters are recorded that do not have any known meaning. The connotation of these letters is very hard to determine, and, therefore, their significance remains unknown in spite of several suggestions that have been made to reveal their mystery.

Chronology of the Qur'an

Long *suras* in the Qur'an usually include numerous ideas without necessarily concentrating on particular themes. On the other hand, Qur'anic messages and legislations that logically belong together are scattered throughout several *suras.* Evidently the compilation of the Qur'an did not follow a system or plan and this poses an extremely difficult problem in determining the chronology of its text. However, certain scholars have worked on this problem and, on the grounds of internal evidence only, have rearranged the *suras* of the Qur'an in a very broad chronological order according to the following categories: (1) early Makkan *suras,* (2) late Makkan *suras,* and (3) Madinan *suras.*

The early Makkan *suras* deal mostly with matters of faith and belief in Allah, the day of judgment, and the ministry of Muhammad as a warning to his people. The late Makkan *suras* generally tell of the Prophet's dealings with his opponents, who ridiculed his warnings and efforts to strengthen the faith of his followers. These two categories include religious instructions containing items of faith, various stories about earlier prophets, and certain Islamic devotional duties. The third category, known as the Madinan *suras,* contains mostly legislation especially designed to organize social relations in the new Islamic state. Its acts deal with family laws, commercial laws, and social laws in regard to the Islamic community and its relations with non-Muslims.

DOCTRINE OF ABROGATION

It may be noted here that certain Qur'anic texts appear to contradict each other, causing some critics to accuse Muhammad of fabricating the whole text. However, the Qur'an as scripture includes a unique doctrine known as *al-nasikh wa al-mansukh,* meaning "abrogation," by which a later utterance by the Prophet may abrogate and make void any previous utterance that contradicts it. This doctrine of abrogation is based on certain Qur'anic texts such as those quoted below:

Whatever communication We abrogate or cause it to be forgotten, We bring one better than it or one like it. Dost thou
not know that Allah is the Possessor of power over all things?

Qur'an 2:106

and

Allah blots out what He pleases and establishes (what He
pleases), and with Him is the basis of the Book.

Qur'an 13:39

Thus, by claiming divine authority, Muhammad was able to account
for any contradictory statements that may be found in the Qur'an,
thereby thwarting in advance any attack or criticism regarding this
matter.

THE QUR'AN IN EVERYDAY LIFE

Muslims of all nations approach the Qur'anic text with extreme
reverence. Whenever they meet on solemn occasions they begin
their celebrations with the recitation of portions of the Qur'an by
trained readers, who usually chant it in protracted semi-musical
tones. Written in Arabic, which is known for its poetic structure, it
received from the language beauty and effectiveness, and in turn
gave the Arabic language prestige and importance. Due to this single
book, Arabic rose from almost complete insignificance to be the
holy tongue of the second largest religious community in the world,
numbering about half a billion adherents. Today, in many countries in
Africa, Southeast Asia, as well as the Middle East, the chantings of
the Qur'an in Arabic are heard daily in homes, over loud-speakers,
and in official gatherings – a clear evidence of the profound impression
this single book from Arabia has left upon millions of the world's
inhabitants.

CHAPTER 16

THE TRADITIONS

ORIGIN OF THE TRADITIONS

Need for Traditions

As the Arabs were passing through the transitional period from tribalism to what may be called "national existence" during the early stages of the Islamic state, the need developed for laws binding upon the whole community. Since tribes obeyed only the orders of their own chiefs, Muhammad had to use laws supported by divine revelations and authority in order to maintain discipline within the Islamic community. It may be recalled that almost throughout Semitic history, as nations emerged, all laws were instituted with the authority of local gods in each community. The Islamic pattern, therefore, may be considered in a broad sense a continuation of the ancient Semitic pattern, the main difference being the monotheistic nature of Islam. During the later years of Muhammad's life, Qur'anic revelations consisted mostly of communal legislation. When Muhammad died unexpectedly in 632, the authoritative source of laws came to an end and no leader from the Muslim community – regardless of his rank or prestige – could have effectively legislated for the Arab tribes as a unit. Due to the sudden halt in divine revelations, the Qur'an did not include laws applicable to an expanding empire; Muslim jurists, therefore, had to resort to the traditions of Muhammad's life, commonly known as *sunna (t) al-Rasul,* for guidance and direction.

Collections of the Traditions

Several years after Muhammad's death, numerous stories about him began to circulate, picturing him not only as a leader and a prophet, but also as an exemplar among the Arabs. A wide search was made for individuals who had memorized conversations of the Prophet or remembered any actions which he might have taken before his death. Thousands of stories were collected; some of them were valid and others were undoubtedly either fabricated or exaggerated. Muslim scholars then began to scrutinize these numerous stories, and several collections of traditions were made. At the present time, the collections listed below are considered canonical and acceptable by the majority of Muslims throughout the world:

1. *al-Sahih* by al-Bukhari (d. 870 A.D.)
2. *al-Sahih* by Muslim (d. 875 A.D.)
3. *al-Sunan* by Ibn Maja (d. 887 A.D.)
4. *al-Sunan* by Abu Dawud (d. 888 A.D.)
5. *al-Jami'* by al-Tirmidhi (d. 892 A.D.)
6. *al-Sunan* by al-Nasa'i (d. 915 A.D.)

The first one, collected by al-Bukhari, is the most important of them all since its compiler is reported to have traveled far and wide in search for the *sunna,* "traditions," of the Prophet, collecting, according to Arab historians, about six hundred thousand items of information. After examining each one of them, he accepted only seven thousand three hundred and ninety-seven, which he incorporated in his famous book, *al-Sahih.*

AUTHENTICITY OF THE TRADITIONS

Method of Tracing Traditions

Each item of the *sunna* is called a *hadith,* meaning "saying," because it usually involved a piece of information received by oral transmission. Muhammadan Traditions are sometimes called the books of *hadith,* which together with the Qur'an constitute the main source of Islamic theology and jurisprudence. Each *hadith* usually includes two parts: (1) the *isnad,* consisting of the chain of transmission through which the information was reached, and (2) the *matn,* which is the substance of the information received. A sample of *hadith* with a relatively short line of transmission is quoted below to illustrate what is meant by transmission of information and by substance of information:

Muhammad, son of Bashshar, and Uthman, son of Umar, and Ali, son of Mubarak, told me that they heard from Yahya, son of Abu Kathir, who heard from Abu Salma, who heard from Abu Hurayra, who said: "The people of the book (Jews) were reading the scripture in Hebrew and interpreting (translating) it into Arabic to the Muslim believers; then the Prophet of God —may Allah bless him and give him peace—said, 'Do not believe the people of the book and do not disbelieve them, but tell them that you believe in God and in the books which He revealed to you and to them as a sign'"

al-Sahih by al-Bukhari, vol. 9, p. 111

The succession of names at the beginning of this *hadith* is the *isnad*, revealing the amount of reliability that could be attached to its *matn*, the substance which followed. In this particular *hadith*, the *isnad* is given by only six transmitters and, therefore, their information is considered fairly reliable. In other *hadiths* when the line of transmitters includes fifteen or more names, the *hadith* may be considered dubious or even void. Muslim scholars sometimes attach more importance to the *isnad* than the *matn;* and while some accept certain doubtful Traditions, others reject them, giving rise to debate among the Muslim scholars themselves.

Legality of Traditions

Muhammad's *sunna,* "Tradition," derives its authenticity from the Qur'an itself, which urges all the Muslims to obey the judgments of the Prophet and submit to his decisions (Qur'an 4:65). Muslims maintain that God had always corrected the Prophet whenever the latter erred, and, therefore, the argument of Muhammad's fallibility does not seem to affect the binding claims of his traditions.

Muslims also believe that since Allah favored Muhammad so much, he automatically sanctioned and endorsed all Muhammad's actions and practices as well as his religious interpretations. Therefore, in the absence of an explicit divine correction, Islamic Traditions are considered as authoritative and as equally binding upon the Islamic community as the Qur'an itself.

USE OF THE TRADITIONS

Many embellishments in the three aspects of Islamic religion —belief, worship, and interpersonal relations as explained above— have been supplied from Muhammadan Traditions, which contain many precedents not mentioned in the Qur'an. For instance, regarding the doctrine of belief, *iman,* Traditions reveal the existence of seven heavens in each of which one of the ancient prophets dwells. They also reveal the existence of an angel of hell named Malik, who never smiles, and who stands guard before the gates of eternal fire that consumes unbelievers.

Regarding worship, *ibadat,* the Traditions supply most of the details for the rites of prayer, fasting, pilgrimage, and alms. In prayers, for example, the exact times during the day as well as the exact number of kneelings per prayer have been mainly prescribed from the Traditions. In matters of interpersonal relations, *mu'amalat,* Traditions, for instance, forbid the marriage of any pair who nursed from the same breast, as well as numerous other instructions about trade and agricultural rules not specified in the Qur'an.

In the light of this brief analysis of Islamic traditions, it becomes clear that orthodox Muslims are not allowed to innovate in either their religious beliefs or practices, and, therefore, Islam is to them a guide regulating their spiritual as well as their secular patterns of life. It is utterly forbidden for them to introduce into the Islamic society any patterns of foreign culture that contradict or do not follow the explicit words of the Qur'an or the Traditions of the Prophet. Accordingly, the religion of Islam becomes to them, in essence, a religion of imitation, *taqlid.* An orthodox Muslim, by virtue of his religion, is an imitator, *muqallid,* imitating Muhammad's pattern and emulating his character in spite of the expanse of time that separates him from the Prophet.

IMPORTANT TERMS

Abu Talib: An uncle who cared for Muhammad when the latter was a boy eight years old. Abu Talib continued to protect Muhammad until he died in 619.

Gabriel: Name of the angel reportedly instrumental in bringing passages of the Qur'an to Muhammad.

Hadith: An item of information related to Muhammad containing either something he did or something he said.

Hafsa's Recension: The first collection of the Qur'anic chapters recorded by Zayd and kept at the house of Hafsa, Umar's daughter.

Hashim: A clan of Quraysh to which Muhammad belonged.

Ibadat: A branch of Islamic religion relating to the duties of worshiping God.

I'jaz: The doctrine of the miraculous nature of the Qur'an, stipulating that the Qur'an could not be duplicated.

Iman: A branch of the Islamic religion that deals with beliefs. The chief item of faith among Muslims is the belief in the oneness of God.

Islam: Name of the religion introduced by Muhammad. It means "submission" to the will of God.

Jinn: Besides the belief in the existence of devils, Muslims also believe in the existence of another group of spirits called *jinn,* who may be either bad or good depending on their obedience to God.

Khadija: Muhammad's first wife. She was a rich widow fifteen years older than he. Khadija's marriage to Muhammad gave him security and encouragement.

Mu'amalat: A branch of the Islamic religion that deals with interpersonal relations among believers.

Muslim: An adherent to the religion of Islam. It means "one who submits his will to the will of God."

Pillars of Islam: Duties incumbent upon Muslim believers as part of the *ibadat* branch. These duties are the testimony (profession of faith), prayer, fasting, alms, and pilgrimage.

Qibla: Direction of prayer for Muslim worshipers. At first it was toward Jerusalem, but shortly after 622 it was changed to Makka.

Qur'an: Collection of revelations claimed by Muhammad to have been transmitted to him by the angel Gabriel directly from God.

Quraysh: The chief tribe dwelling in Makka during Muhammad's life. Members of the Quraysh tribe were custodians of the Ka'ba, the holy shrine of the Arabs.

Sunna: Traditions of Muhammad.

Sura: One chapter of the Qur'an.

Uthman's Recension: The second collection of the Qur'an based on Hafsa's Recension. It was recorded also by Zayd, and is the origin of the Qur'an in its present form.

Zayd ibn Thabit: Muhammad's chief secretary. He is credited with having collected and recorded the earliest recensions of the Qur'an.

SUPPLEMENTARY READINGS

ALI, MAWLANA MUHAMMAD, *Muhammad the Prophet* (Lahore, 1951).
ANDRAE, TOR, *Muhammad: The Man and His Faith* (New York, 1957).
ARBERRY, A.J., *The Koran Interpreted I and II* (New York, 1955).
BELL, RICHARD, *Introduction to the Qur'an* (Edinburgh, 1953).
CALVERLY, EDWIN E., *Islam: An Introduction* (Cairo, 1958).
DERMENGHEM, EMILE, *Muhammad and the Islamic Traditions* (New York, 1961).
GIBB, H.A.R., *Muhammadanism* (Oxford, 1960).
GUILLAUME, A., *The Life of Muhammad—A Translation of Ishaq's Sirat Rasul Allah* (Oxford, 1955).
———, *The Traditions of Islam, an Introduction to the Study of the Hadith Literature* (Oxford, 1924).
JEFFREY, ARTHUR, *The Qur'an as Scripture* (New York, 1952).
———, *Islam—Muhammad and his Religion* (New York, 1958).
MARGOLIOUTH, D.S., *Muhammad and the Rise of Islam* (New York, 1905).
MORGAN, KENNETH W., *Islam—the Straight Path* (New York, 1958).
MUIR, W., *The Life of Muhammad* (Edinburgh, 1923).
ROSENTHAL, ERWIN, *Judaism and Islam* (London, 1961).
SWEETMAN, JAMES W., *Islam and Christian Theology* (London, 1955).

WATT, W.M., *Muhammad at Mecca* (Oxford, 1953).
_____, *Islamic Philosophy and Theology* (Edinburgh, 1962).
WENSINCK, A.J., *A Handbook of Early Muhammadan Tradition*(Leiden, 1960).

PART V

BEGINNING OF
THE ISLAMIC STATE

This part will trace the development of Arab unity under Islam from the time of Muhammad's migration to Madina in 622 till his death in 632.

Details of the Prophet's contacts with the two leading Arab tribes in Madina are first discussed with emphasis on the reasons why these two feuding tribes of the neighboring city were willing to accept Islam as a religion and Muhammad as a leader. When the Islamic state was inaugurated in Madina in 622, fighting broke out between Madina and Makka and continued till the Muslims finally captured Makka in 630. Muhammad's efforts to establish his rule over all Arabia are discussed with a brief description of the final expulsion of the Jews and some of the Christians from the Arabian Peninsula. Mention is also made of the personal messages sent by Muhammad as head of the Islamic state to four non-Arab heads of state – the King of Persia, the Emperor of Byzantium, the Negus of Ethiopia, and the Governor of Egypt – with a brief note about their authenticity and significance.

This part also describes the religio-political features of the Islamic state as outlined in the Constitution of Madina, which was proclaimed in 622 immediately after Muhammad's migration to the city. It was then that Muhammad may be said to have fully assumed the three roles of leadership mentioned in previous chapters. The following chapters show how he performed the duties of these three roles in such a way that he not only established the Arabs as a unified community for the first time, but also gave the newly established Arab state enough momentum to expand into an empire within only a decade of his death.

CHAPTER 17

MIGRATION TO MADINA

FIRST CONTACTS WITH THE ARABS OF MADINA

Arabs and Jews at Yathrib

Madina, known as Yathrib in pre-Islamic times, is located about 250 miles northeast of Makka. It was the center of a large Jewish community that settled there as early as the reign of the Roman Emperor Hadrian. By the time of Muhammad, three Jewish tribes – Qaynuqa', Quraydha, and Nadir – controlled most of the trade passing through Yathrib from the east and south. Besides the Jewish community, two important Arab tribes, the Aws and the Khazraj, settled in Yathrib together with other lesser tribes and clans. Although they were cousins, the Aws and the Khazraj engaged in lengthy intertribal wars that continued till the time of the Prophet. The feud between them not only weakened Arab prestige in Yathrib, but also helped the Jews to secure and maintain economic superiority in the city. As long as the Arabs were feuding among themselves, the Jewish community continued to flourish and prosper; by the time of Muhammad, the two fighting Arab tribes apparently reached a point of exhaustion, causing them to search for a neutral arbitrator who could settle their feuds without loss of face.

The First Aqaba Conference

Muhammad was not a total stranger to the Arabs of Yathrib; his mother, Amina, was a daughter of a well-known member of a sub-clan of the Khazraj tribe, who, together with their cousins the Aws, considered the Prophet a fair arbitrator. During the pilgrimage season of 620, only one year after the Khazraj tribe had been defeated by the Aws, six leaders of the former sought Muhammad at a valley called Aqaba on the outskirts of Makka. During this meeting, the six Khazra-jites reportedly related their troubles to Muhammad, who must have indicated to them that by the rules of the Islamic religion tribal boundaries would completely disappear, allowing Muslims of every tribe to become one community. When the Khazrajites asked him about the necessary steps to become Muslims, Muhammad taught them how to recite the *shahada*, "testimony," emphasizing Islam's chief doctrine of belief in Allah as God and Muhammad as his prophet. According to Islamic annals, these members of the Khazraj tribe immediately ac-cepted Islam and announced their belief in Allah, promising to go home and promote the new religion among their own leaders and the leaders of the Aws tribe also.

When they returned to Yathrib, they told their leaders about Muhammad's message, which, to be sure, also included a promising solution of their immediate problems. As one Muslim community, they would be in a position to close ranks easily and end their bitter feud.

The Second Aqaba Conference

Muslim annals report that many of the members of the two tribes (Aws and Khazraj) welcomed the idea of conversion to Islam and announced their faith in God and his Prophet Muhammad. Others who were not immediately converted are reported to have sought further instructions about the new religion. Accordingly, during the pilgrimage season of the following year, 621, twelve prominent men representing most of the Arab clans in Yathrib met with Muhammad at the valley of Aqaba and inquired about details of Islam. Muhammad is believed to have told them, among other things, that Allah expected his people to abstain from wrongdoing such as murder, adultery, and stealing, adding that if they fulfilled the will of God, he would lead them to paradise; if they would follow their own ways, their destiny would be in God's hands—he might forgive them or punish them as he wished. It is reported that upon hearing this message, the delegation from Yathrib declared their belief in Allah, pledged their allegiance to Muhammad his Prophet, and vowed unanimously to fulfill their duties as Muslims.

Preaching Islam in Yathrib

The twelve men returned to Yathrib as apostles of the new religion and preached the simple message of Islam to the Arabs of that city. Furthermore, the Prophet dispatched Mus'ab, one of his trusted followers who had memorized large portions of the Qur'an, to Yathrib to encourage the new converts and recite to them the words of Allah. This movement proved to be an unprecedented triumph for Muhammad's cause, since within a short period most of the Arabs in Yathrib were converted to Islam. It is reported that the number of converts in that one year surpassed the number of all converts that Muhammad had won elsewhere during the preceding thirteen years of his ministry. This outstanding success was more than adequate compensation to the persevering and ambitious Prophet for the persecution and anguish he had endured. At last a door was opened for the cause of Islam, and no one could shut it.

DECISION TO EMIGRATE

Mus'ab's Report to Muhammad

During the pilgrimage season of 622, Mus'ab returned to Makka with a delegation of seventy-three Muslims, representing all the Arab clans in Yathrib, to meet the Prophet and report to him about the spread of Islam in the neighboring city. The chief item in this report was the story of the conversion of the two chief leaders in Yathrib, Ibn Mu'adh and Ibn Khudayr. It is reported that while Mus'ab was visiting one of the new converts, Ibn Mu'adh approached them and ordered them with ridicule to stop converting other members of the peaceful community. Shortly after, Ibn Khudayr arrived with his spear in hand and threatened to kill Mus'ab, who earnestly appealed to Ibn Khudayr to listen to him. Ibn Khudayr then stuck his spear in the ground and sat down to listen to the words of the Qur'an. Mus'ab had recited only a few portions before Ibn Khudayr inquired about the requirements for conversion to Islam. When told about the Muslim testimony, *shahada,* he is reported to have immediately testified, "There is no God but Allah, and Muhammad is his Prophet," adding that if Ibn Mu'adh also became converted the whole community would follow them.

Upon the departure of Ibn Khudayr, Ibn Mu'adh returned reportedly raging and accusing Mus'ab of converting many of his people to Islam. Mus'ab appealed to him not to judge the new religion without exploring its teachings. As Ibn Mu'adh listened to Mus'ab's explanation of the doctrines of Islam, he reportedly believed and immediately recited the testimony. He then went to the other leaders of his clan and said to them: "O people of Ashkal, you are naught till you believe in Allah and his Prophet." Shortly after this episode, the whole community is said to have been converted, urging Ibn Mu'adh himself to become their temporary leader.

Invitation to Immigrate

Muhammad listened to these encouraging reports, and, as he was praising Allah for the splendid success of his message at Yathrib, he was urged by the seventy-three man delegation to migrate to their city and become their leader. While the Prophet was considering the consequences of accepting this invitation, his uncle Abbas (still an unbeliever) reportedly stood up and said:

> O people of Khazraj, Muhammad is our man; and although we have prevented him from pursuing that upon which we disagreed with him, he is still safe and secure among his people. However, he decided to join you. If you think that you can fulfill your pledge of allegiance to him and defend him against his enemies, you must then bear the responsibility of your pledge. But if you think you cannot protect him, I urge you to leave him alone, because he is secure only in his own hometown and among his own people. [1]

The Prophet then stood and said to the representatives of Yathrib, "I pledge you myself, if you promise to protect me as you do your own children and wives." One of the delegation responded, "We pledge to protect you as we do our own household." Muhammad then replied, "For blood or for war, I am yours and you are mine. I shall fight whomsoever you fight, and make peace with whomsoever you make peace." [2]

At this point, Muhammad decided to emigrate from Makka and settle at Yathrib. Assuming the temporal leadership of the Muslim community, he ordered the delegation to divide into twelve groups, each headed by a local leader, to make the journey back. He commanded his own followers from Makka also to make the trip to Yathrib in small groups in order not to arouse the suspicion of the Makkans. When all the believers departed, Muhammad and a few followers were left behind to emigrate at an opportune time.

[1] Al-Tabari, *Tarikh al-Umam wa al-Muluk* (Cairo, 1908), Volume 2, pp. 238, 239. This work will be referred to henceforth as al-Tabari, *Tarikh*. See also Ibn Hisham, *Sirat Rasul Allah* (Cairo, 1918), Volume 2, pp. 49-55.

[2] Al-Tabari, *loc. cit.*

THE PROPHET'S EMIGRATION

Makka Threatens Muhammad

Meanwhile the news of Yathrib's alliance with Muhammad reached the Makkan leaders, who saw in it a potential threat to their security. They decided to kill the Prophet on the spot, and, in order to prevent an intertribal war, they asked each clan to designate one of its members to participate in the act of murder so that Muhammad's blood would be spilled by the whole community.

Muhammad consulted with Abu Bakr, his eldest counselor, who invited him to stay in his own home while Ali, the Prophet's cousin, temporarily lodged in Muhammad's home. Soon thereafter, the Prophet, together with Abu Bakr, escaped through a window in the rear of Abu Bakr's home. They decided to avoid the straight route to Yathrib and instead took a lonely and deserted path. Meanwhile, the Makkans reportedly offered a reward of one hundred camels for anyone who would tell them the whereabouts of Muhammad, but no one was able to locate him. When Ali received word that the Prophet and Abu Bakr were safe in one of the caves, he secretly departed from Makka and joined them about halfway to Yathrib.

Arrival at Yathrib

Muhammad's trip from Makka to Yathrib is believed to have lasted almost six months during which the Prophet and his companions must have climbed several hills and crossed numerous valleys until they reached their destination on September 20, 622. This fateful year became known in Islamic history as the year of emigration or *Hijra*. It marks the beginning of the Muslim calendar, which includes twelve lunar months rotating around the seasons. Yathrib then became the center of all Islamic activities, and its name was changed to *Madinat al-Nabiy*, "the city of the Prophet," which was gradually shortened to Madina — the name it bears today.

In Madina, Muhammad was warmly received by its Arab inhabitants, who, with very few exceptions, had already been converted to Islam. He came to Madina as a prophet, but soon became a political leader, giving Islam the characteristic of being a state as well as a religion. As a neutral person from another tribe, Muhammad was accepted as a compromise leader to rule the tribes of Aws and Khazraj; and as a prophet, he could legislate in the name of Allah and expect his followers to obey. Although they retained their tribal affiliations, the Muslims of Madina became one community or *umma* known as the *umma* of Muhammad, or the *umma* of Islam.

MUHAMMAD'S IMMEDIATE PROBLEMS

Supporters and Emigrants

As Muhammad embarked on his political career, he faced many internal as well as external problems. Internally, the population of Madina was divided into three distinct groups: (1) the supporters of the Prophet, *ansar*, who had invited him to Madina and who constituted the majority of the Muslim population, (2) the emigrants, *muhajirun*, who made the trip from Makka to Madina with Muhammad and who constituted a privileged elite, and (3) the Jewish community, which now became a group of non-believers in the midst of Muslims and posed considerable problems to the Prophet. Externally, Muhammad faced possible attack by the Makkans, who had already decided to get rid of the Muslim threat in Madina before it could spread.

As Muhammad became a chief of state, he had to assume two more roles of leadership in addition to being a prophet; he became both a political and military leader.

Order to Raid Caravans

The transfer to Madina was undoubtedly a marked triumph for the cause of Islam, yet it was not without its serious problems. Muhammad was suddenly faced with the responsibility of providing material support for his emigrant followers, who had abandoned their wealth and property at Makka. In Madina the Aws and Khazraj tribes had just emerged from a lengthy war with each other during which the Jews had gained control of the city's economy. The Madinan Muslims, therefore, found themselves hard put to eke out their own living, much less support an added population. Moreover, Muhammad could not at this early stage of his activity afford to attack or even antagonize his rich Jewish neighbors, who were strong enough to deal a fatal blow to his emerging movement. The material needs of his followers must be met without creating premature problems within Madina. The most natural solution, therefore, was to raid the caravans passing near the city on the route between Yaman and Syria; so the command was given to raid.

CHAPTER 18

BETWEEN MAKKA AND MADINA

BEGINNING OF HOSTILITIES

Islam and Militarism

Muhammad had been preaching piety, godliness, and meekness to the Muslims as religious virtues. However, since he was forced to order his followers to raid and fight, he had to support his new tactics with divine endorsement. Therefore, he claimed several revelations from God which urged the believers to fight the unbelievers wherever and whenever the latter were found, promising paradise without delay to those who died in battle.

The following are some Qur'anic verses to this effect:

> And fight in the way of Allah with those who fight with you, and do not exceed (this limit). Allah does not love those who exceed (the limits).
> And kill them wherever you find them, and drive them out from whence they drove you out, and persecution is severer than slaughter. And do not fight with them at the Sacred Mosque until they fight with you in it; if they fight you, then slay them; such is the recompense of the unbelievers.
>
> Qur'an 2:190,191

And also:

O you who believe! When you meet those who disbelieve
marching for war, turn not your backs to them.

And whoever turns his back to them on that day —unless
he turn aside for the sake of fighting or withdraw to a company —
he, indeed, becomes deserving of Allah's displeasure, and his
refuge is hell —an evil destination!

Qur'an 8:15,16

Although the Qur'an discourages unprovoked aggression, it con-
siders religious persecution a valid pretext for war. Encouraged by a
divine sanction, the Muslims engaged in numerous battles against the
Makkan unbelievers; only the most important ones are discussed here
as samples of the struggle between the two main cities of Arabia.

The Battle of Badr, March, 624

In 623, one year after the *Hijra*, and during one of the *haram* months
(in which wars were forbidden), Muslims are reported to have ambushed
a certain caravan, murdering its leaders and taking its goods as booty.
This action greatly aroused the Makkans, who immediately accused
Muhammad of disregarding Arab traditions by desecrating the sacred
months. To justify his actions before his own followers, Muhammad
produced the following text:

They ask thee concerning the sacred month —about fighting in
it. Say: Fighting in it is a grave matter, and hindering (men)
from Allah's way, and denying Him, and (hindering from) the
Sacred Mosque and turning its people out of it, are still graver
with Allah; and persecution is graver than slaughter. And they
will not cease fighting with you until they turn you back from
your religion, if they can. And whoever of you turns back from his
religion, then he dies while an unbeliever —these it is whose works
go for nothing in this world and the Hereafter; and they are the
inmates of the fire: therein they shall abide.

Qur'an 2:217

During the same year, Abu Sufyan, a leader of Quraysh, was escorting
his caravan to Syria. Knowing in advance of a Muslim ambush, he veered
from the main route detouring his caravan toward the sea. On his way
back, he heard that Muslim raiders were still waiting for him. He
therefore requested the Makkans to send men to protect the caravan as
it passed near Madina. In the meantime, he changed his course and
followed a deserted route close to the sea and far from Madina. The
caravan arrived home safely, but the Makkans who had already advanced
northward met the Muslims, who were hiding near the wells of Badr,
north of Makka and west of Madina. A battle followed. It is reported
that when the fighting was over, the Makkans counted seventy dead while

the Muslims lost only fourteen. This skirmish was considered a victory for the Madinans, who began to boast that Allah helped them against a superior enemy.

The Muslims gained considerable booty from the battle of Badr, capturing numerous prisoners among whom was Abbas, the uncle of the Prophet himself. To gain more wealth, Muhammad agreed to free the prisoners for redemption fees that were paid according to the prestige of each individual prisoner. When individual Muslims began to disagree among themselves on the distribution of the booty, Muhammad, through revelation, asked them to surrender everything to him personally, and he later distributed portions of the booty among his followers at his own discretion.

The Battle of Uhud, March, 625

The Makkans were so distressed by their defeat at Badr that they reportedly allotted all the profits from Abu Sufyan's caravan to take revenge against the Muslims. Three thousand Quraysh warriors and their allies rallied around Abu Sufyan, who acted as their commander. They marched toward Madina early in 625 (the third year of the *Hijra)*. Some reports mention that Muhammad's uncle Abbas, who had previously been taken prisoner at Badr and released by the Prophet, sent a secret message of warning to his nephew. Immediately, the Prophet began consultations with his chief advisors, who counseled him to meet the Makkans inside the city where supplies would be adequate and where women could help by throwing stones from the roof tops. However, the bulk of the fighters, composed of young people, decided to go outside the city. Muhammad is reported to have followed the advice of his younger warriors and led one thousand of his men to the foot of the mountain of Uhud where for several days they camped facing the direction from which the Makkans would appear.

The Prophet ordered his warriors to stand firm with their backs to the mountain and their faces toward the enemy, and to fight until the Qurayshis fled. However, three hundred of them, seeing that they would be hopelessly cornered at the foot of the mountain, withdrew and refused to fight. In order to prevent the rest of the army from defecting, the Prophet is reported to have received the following revelation:

> And Allah did certainly assist you at Badr when you were weak; keep your duty to Allah then, that you may give thanks.
>
> When thou didst say to the believers: Does it not suffice you that your Lord should assist you with three thousand of the angels sent down?
>
> Yea! if you remain patient and keep your duty, and they come upon you in a headlong manner, your Lord will assist you with five thousand of havoc-making angels.
>
> Qur'an 3:123-125

The battle of Uhud started with isolated combats, followed by a massive attack by the Muslims. The Makkans suddenly retreated, giving an impression of defeat; however, while the Muslims were busy gathering booty, the Makkans took them by surprise, killing a considerable number of them. Muhammad himself was seriously wounded and lay motionless and bloody while the Makkans shouted victory in the belief that their archenemy was dead. Some Muslims clustered around Muhammad and protected him with their bodies, while others wailed and lamented their sudden defeat. When the Makkans left, the Muslims carried the Prophet into their city, where he soon recovered and ordered his followers to gather the dead bodies of the martyred Muslims for burial.

VICTORY FOR THE MUSLIMS

Skirmishes After Uhud

As soon as the Muslims recuperated from their defeat at Uhud, they began to engage more actively in raiding against other tribes in Hijaz and Najd, especially those on friendly terms with Quraysh. The Muslims also worked to isolate the Makkans from their neighbors, while the Makkans, in spite of their victory, remained passive and took no decisive action to consolidate their victory. Moreover, the Muslims had only one leader vested with complete authority, in contrast to the Makkans, whose clannish subloyalties undoubtedly weakened their strength.

Once Muhammad consolidated his forces, he challenged the Makkans to another fight, which Abu Sufyan, the Makkan leader, accepted. The following year, 626, the two sides agreed to meet again for battle near the wells of Badr. The Muslims reportedly arrived with fifteen hundred men only to discover that the Makkans had stayed home. After camping for eight days, the Muslims returned to Madina claiming a bloodless victory that greatly boosted their morale. The Makkan embarrassment was very great; and they feared intensely the increasing Muslim influence over other tribes around Madina. Abu Sufyan, therefore, gathered about ten thousand warriors from Makka and several other Bedouin allies to deal Muhammad and his supporters a final and fatal blow. Early in 627 the Makkan troops began to move northward; as the news of their progress reached Muhammad, he planned defenses to protect his city.

Expedition of the Trench, March, 627

Madina is surrounded by mountains on three sides and open to attack only from the north. One of Muhammad's advisors, a Persian

Muslim, counseled him to dig a trench at the open side of the city to keep the invaders away. The Muslim warriors, numbering no more than four thousand, remained inside the city waiting for the expected attack. When the Makkans approached Madina and learned of the trench, they were indignant and called it foul play according to Arab customs. Four horsemen from the Makkans crossed the trench and challenged the Muslims to a duel. Ali, Muhammad's cousin, reportedly rushed to one of the Makkan leaders and fatally stabbed him, driving the remaining three back to their camp.

Siege of Madina

The Makkans had no alternative but to besiege Madina. This siege lasted about twenty days during which the Makkans quarreled among themselves, while the Muslims stood firm behind the trench unmoved by hunger or cold. However, some of the Muslims are reported to have murmured among themselves, wondering in despair how Muhammad could fulfill his earlier promises to give them the treasures of Persia and Byzantium while they appeared to be hopelessly trapped inside their own city.[1]

In spite of these mild complaints, the Muslims held firm until open dissension plagued the Makkan camp. Some of the lesser leaders of the various clans criticized Abu Sufyan and accused him of mishandling the whole affair. Abu Sufyan gave up his leadership and consented to let it rotate among other leaders, allowing each to take command of the entire camp for one day. This idea proved to be fatal to the Makkan army since it further encouraged factionalism and confusion, nearly immobilizing the whole army.

On the twentieth day of the siege, things became intolerable for Abu Sufyan, who suddenly decided to go home. In his absence the other leaders could not agree on a unified plan to attack Madina, and one by one they returned to Makka, each with his troops.

Increase of Muhammad's Prestige

After the Makkans retreated from Madina in 627, it became clear to all the Arabs of the peninsula that Muhammad as a prophet and chief of state was a formidable power. Several tribes, therefore, became conciliatory and extended their friendship, expressing their willingness to accept Islam. The following story is included here as a sample of many others recorded in Muslim annals. It was reported that a messenger from a certain tribe from the line of Bakr once came to the place of Muslim worship (mosque) in Madina and asked about Muhammad. When the Prophet identified himself, the man said, "Did God

[1]See Ibn Hisham, *Sirat Rasul Allah* (Cairo, 1918), Volume 2, p. 238; and al-Ya'qubi, *Tarikh al-Ya'qubi* (Leiden, 1883), Volume 2, p. 51.

really send you as a messenger to us?" Muhammad answered, "Yes, he did." When the man inquired and was told about the duties and ordinances of Islam, he is reported to have proclaimed his faith and recited the *shahada*, "testimony," on the spot. Upon returning to his home, he told of his encounter with the Prophet and the result was the conversion of the whole of his tribe to Islam.

OTHER IMPORTANT EVENTS

The Raid Against Mustaliq

Numerous raids were directed against several tribes which had rejected Muhammad's friendly gestures. From the military point of view, the raid against Mustaliq was not among the most significant ones; however, it is considered one of the important battles in Islamic history because on the way back, after defeating the Mustaliqs, two important incidents occurred within the Muslim camp that threatened to tear it apart. The first incident was an open fight between the emigrants or *muhajirun* and their fellow Muslims, the supporters or *ansar*. A leader of the *ansar* named Sinan quarreled with a leader of the *muhajirun* called Ghifari. During the quarrel the latter reportedly beat the former on the face. Sinan called upon his people to support him against Ghifari, who in turn called upon his people to rally around him. An interfactional battle within Islam was impending, and was prevented only by Muhammad's persuasion of both factions to call off the feud.

Incident of the Slander

The second incident after the raid against Mustaliq touched upon the honor of Muhammad's youngest wife, A'isha, daughter of Abu Bakr, the Prophet's senior advisor. When Muhammad was on a trip or a raid outside Madina, he cast lots among his wives to choose the one who would accompany him. The lot fell on A'isha to go with the Prophet on the raid against Mustaliq. On the way back, just before the group reached Madina, A'isha is reported to have lost her necklace and gone back a short distance to look for it. She found it and hurried to the camp only to discover that the caravan had left without her. A young man named Safwan passed by and invited her to mount his camel, which he led till they reached Madina. Many of Muhammad's followers, especially his cousin Ali, accused A'isha of infidelity and requested the Prophet to divorce her. Apparently the Prophet was not convinced that A'isha was guilty and refused to yield to the request for divorce. Finally, the whole problem was solved when the following verse was revealed to the Prophet:

Those who concocted the lie are a party from among you. Do not regard it an evil for you; nay, it is good for you. Every man of them will have what he has earned of sin; and he who took upon himself the main part thereof will have a grievous chastisement.

Qur'an 24:11

Muhammad's Claim to the Ka'ba

For the two years following 627, Muhammad's prestige continued to increase as the Makkans' authority over the Arabs sharply decreased. Confident in his political advantage, the Prophet apparently decided that the only way to win the Arabs was to eliminate the Makkan opposition. Obviously, the general trend in Arabia would be favorable to Islam only if the traditional holy place of Ka'ba were to be a part of the Islamic religion. As a preliminary measure toward gaining the allegiance of all the Arabs and consequently capturing Makka itself, he shrewdly announced that the Ka'ba was also the sacred shrine of the Muslims and ordered his followers to change the *qibla*, ''direction of prayer,'' from Jerusalem to Makka. With this skillful maneuver Muhammad achieved two important goals: besides winning the esteem of his countrymen, he obtained a lawful excuse to seek religious rights within Makka itself in preparation for its eventual capture.

CHAPTER 19

CAPTURE OF MAKKA

A TRUCE AGREEMENT

First Attempt to Visit Makka

Having proclaimed the Ka'ba a Muslim holy place, Muhammad advised his followers to visit Makka whenever possible and perform the duty of *hajj,* "pilgrimage." As leader of the Muslim community, Muhammad initiated this sacred duty himself by accompanying fourteen hundred of his followers on their way toward Makka early in 628. Skeptical of the Prophet's intentions, the Makkans obstructed the pilgrim's way into the city. Muhammad immediately dispatched his distant cousin Uthman, who later became the third caliph, to convince the Makkans of the purely religious purpose of the trip and to assure them that the Prophet had no intentions of making war.

When the Makkans detained Uthman for some time, rumors of his murder spread to the Muslim camp. Enraged by the report, the Prophet declared war against the Makkans and requested the support of his followers. It is reported that all but one of the fourteen hundred men pledged their lives to Uthman's revenge and promised never to retreat until victory was theirs.

The Muslims, therefore, marched against Makka and, in order to avoid its eastern defensive lines, circled around toward the sea to approach it from the west. They halted at Hudaybiyya, about half a day's journey from Makka, when news of Uthman's safety reached their camp.

Negotiations Between the Muslims and the Makkans

Waiting patiently to learn the official Makkan reaction to Uthman's message, Muhammad made it clear that he would force his way in if obstructions to the pilgrims' entering were not eventually removed. The Makkans, therefore, dispatched an official delegation headed by an eloquent speaker named Suhayl to negotiate with the Muslims. The two sides first agreed to release all emissaries that had been detained as prisoners. Upon the release of Uthman, the two parties began serious negotiations and drafted an agreement for ratification.

While formalizing the treaty, Muhammad asked his cousin Ali (acting as his secretary) to write, "In the name of God (Allah) the merciful, the compassionate." Suhayl refused to accept this purely Islamic introduction and insisted on writing only, "In thy name, O Allah." After some hesitation, Muhammad accepted Suhayl's brief introduction, but another sharp disagreement arose in respect to the Prophet's title. Muhammad asked Ali to write "the Apostle of God," but Suhayl remarked that if he could sign such a statement on behalf of the Makkans there would be no need for strife or negotiations between the two camps since all would be Muslims. Muhammad accepted Suhayl's opinion, and, contrary to the advice of his closest companions, agreed to a compromise formula in which no titles appeared. Accordingly, the treaty reportedly began as follows, "This is what Muhammad, son of Abd-Allah; and Suhayl, son of Amr, have agreed upon." Apparently Muhammad realized that any agreement with the Makkans, regardless of its contents, could be interpreted as a formal recognition by the Makkans of the political status of the Muslim community. Consequently, having so much to gain and nothing to lose, Muhammad was willing to accept any conditions or reservations raised by Suhayl.

The Treaty of Hudaybiyya

After the preamble, the treaty, which later on became known as the truce of Hudaybiyya, consisted of seven articles:

1. Both parties would refrain from all hostilities against one another for ten years.
2. The Muslims promised to return to Makka young people who might accept Islam against the will of their parents.
3. Quraysh was not under obligation to return apostate Muslims to Madina.
4. Heads of households who wished to change sides would not be prevented from doing so.
5. The Muslims who came on pilgrimage during the signing of the treaty would return to Madina without entering Makka that year.

6. Muslims who desired to perform the duty of pilgrimage could do so beginning with the following year.

7. The Makkans promised to vacate the Ka'ba three full days for the Muslim pilgrims, on the condition that the latter should come unarmed. Swords carried for defensive purposes during the trip were to be kept in leather bags during the three-day stay in Makka.

The second, third, and fifth articles of this treaty may appear somewhat slanted against the Muslims in favor of the Makkans. But one must not forget that actually the Muslims did not stand to lose anything by the concessions they made. If they could not enter Makka the same year, provision was made for them to do so the following year. In fact, this may be considered a great victory for the Muslim cause, since they would have an excellent opportunity to demonstrate, without opposition, the advantages of their faith. The fact that Muslims were obliged to return Qurayshi youths to Makka, while the Makkans were not obligated to reciprocate, may appear to be an unwarranted injustice to the Muslims. However, from a practical point of view, the Muslims lost no converts since no backsliders were ever reported among their ranks. On the other hand, the Makkans faced the serious problem of many young people defecting to Madina.

Islam, as a monotheistic religion ingeniously tailored to fit the Arab environment, was preached at a very opportune time when most pagan Arabs were ready for a new faith that would provide them with a nonpagan religion on a par with the monotheistic tradition of the Jews and Christians. The main deterrent to the Arabs' acceptance of Islam presumably had been the opposition of the tribe of Quraysh to Muhammad, based chiefly on material considerations since the Qurayshis acted as custodians of the Ka'ba. Nevertheless, as soon as the prestige of Quraysh suffered a serious blow after their retreat from the expedition of the Trench, Arab conversions to Islam sharply increased, especially among the young people of Makka, posing a serious problem to the pagan Makkans.

The Treaty Put to Test

Apparently Muhammad had already envisioned the final overthrow of Makka when he agreed to the article of the treaty emphasizing the Muslims' obligation to return converted young people to Makka. This aim is indicated by a significant incident which occurred after the ratification of the treaty and which severely tested the Muslims' intentions to abide by their promises. Muslim annals report that when Muhammad and Suhayl, together with several witnesses, had just finished signing the treaty, Suhayl's own son Abu Jandal came running to Muhammad announcing his conversion to Islam and seeking asylum. As soon as his father saw him, he reportedly turned to the Prophet requesting him to honor the treaty. The report goes on to say that

Muhammad looked at the youth and remarked, "Abu Jandal I be patient and submit (to the will of God). Truly God will soon provide for you and for anyone who is like you an outlet and a way of deliverance."

On their way home, a number of Muhammad's companions sounded their complete dissatisfaction with the Treaty of Hudaybiyya. Umar, who later became the second caliph, expressed his great disappointment to the quiet and elderly Abu Bakr, who calmed him down and advised him to conform to whatever the Prophet had approved. It was indeed hard for the Muslims to return without having either entered Makka or fought a battle to save face. But finally they yielded to the Prophet's judgment, not without at least three times disobeying his explicit orders to prepare themselves for the trip back.

The First Muslim Pilgrimage

Although Muhammad and his followers returned to Madina without fulfilling their ultimate goal of pilgrimage, the balance of power had shifted to them. Heads of households, as well as independent individuals, continued to come to the Prophet in Madina, announcing their adherence to the new religion, while strife and disagreement shattered the Makkans' ranks. As stipulated in the Treaty of Hudaybiyya, early in 629 Muhammad gathered about two thousand Muslims, claiming the right to visit the holy Ka'ba for pilgrimage. The Qurayshis fulfilled their part of the agreement and withdrew to the mountains while the Muslims made their way toward the Ka'ba. At the head of the Muslim army of pilgrims rode the Prophet himself, flanked by his closest companions, leading the Muslim pilgrims as they circled the holy place seven times. Muhammad is reported to have touched and kissed the Black Stone —a custom obviously derived from pre-Islamic traditions and adapted to Islam. To be sure, many pagan observers must have watched with great curiosity as the Muslims showed extreme devotion to the most revered place of all Arabia; indeed, to the pagans the spectacle must have been impressive.

In addition to all the prescribed ritual of the pilgrimage, Muhammad led his followers in a solemn congregational prayer under the watchful eyes of the curious Makkans. Undoubtedly during those fateful moments many pagan Arabs were greatly impressed with the earnest zeal of the Muslims. They were convinced that Muhammad's religion not only included doctrines superior to the outmoded beliefs of their ancestors, but also showed great devotion and respect to their cherished sanctuary in Makka.

Famous Converts to Islam

During this first pilgrimage to Makka, the Muslims did not carry their swords for battle, yet they won the hearts of many unbelievers and captured their deepest sympathies. This peaceful demonstration of some of the practices of Islam won for the Muslims more good will and respect than all the battles they had fought. As the Muslims marched back to their own city, it was clear that pagan strength was ebbing. Hundreds of converts joined the Muslim ranks as the bewildered leaders of Quraysh became aware of their final decline.

Among the famous Makkans to announce their conversion were Khalid ibn al-Walid, a great commander who was later known as "the Sword of Islam," and Amr ibn al-As, who was to be the conqueror of Egypt and Palestine. It is reported that when Khalid made up his mind to accept Islam, he stood before many Qurayshi dignitaries saying, "It is quite clear to any rational individual that Muhammad is not a magician or a composer of rhymes; his words emanate indeed from the words of the Lord of all creation; and therefore I have decided to follow him." By that time the Makkan resistance to Muslim converts had apparently lost its effect, since no Makkans attempted to threaten Khalid or oppose his decision.

As Khalid was about to leave Makka for Madina, he reportedly met Amr, another noted warrior, who asked him of his destination. Muslim annals mention that when Khalid told Amr his decision, the latter said, "I have also made up my mind to follow Muhammad." Thus both warriors proceeded together toward Madina to announce their new faith to the Prophet and join the ever-increasing community of Muslim believers.

CAPTURE OF MAKKA

The Expedition of Mu'ta

Toward the end of 629, the year of the Muslims' greatest peaceful victory over the Makkans, Muhammad could easily recognize that Makka itself would soon fall into his fold. Feeling secure against any possible threats from Quraysh, Muhammad turned his attention for awhile toward the northern fringes of Arabia. So far, the support of the Muslims in Madina had depended mainly on the booty obtained from raids on unbelievers. As conversions to Islam increased, the Muslims found it more difficult to locate enemy caravans; the resulting shortage of booty caused a sharp decline in their economy. This situation posed a serious problem to Muhammad, who evidently had promised his followers not only to obtain Allah's material blessings at home, but also gain the treasures of Persia and Byzantium abroad.[1] When the economic situation became serious and a number of Muslims voiced their dissatisfaction, Muhammad thought of dispatching an expedition to Syria for two purposes. First, it would report about the political conditions there, and secondly, it would bring back booty to help support the growing population of Madina.

[1] See Chapter 18, footnote 1, p. 113.

Reports mention that Muhammad first sent an emissary to the Prince of Ghassan, the Byzantine buffer state south of Syria, inviting him to accept Islam. When the emissary did not return and rumors of his assassination reached Madina, Muhammad mobilized his followers for war. Three thousand anxious Muslims rallied behind Muhammad, ready to conquer Ghassan in the name of Allah. The expedition was entrusted to the leadership of Zayd ibn Harith, Muhammad's freed slave and adopted son. The news of the Muslims' approach soon reached the Prince of Ghassan, who immediately sought and received assistance from Byzantium. Unaware of the preparations against them, the Muslims proceeded toward southeastern Palestine. When they arrived at a place called Mu'ta, they heard that a force about three times their size had been mobilized by the Byzantines to fight them. The Muslims deliberated for two days and finally decided to go into battle.

In the plain of Mu'ta, near the hills of Moab, the two armies met for battle. The Muslims were badly defeated and forced to flee leaving behind many fallen warriors, including Zayd, their commander. Khalid ibn al-Walid took over the command and led the remaining Muslims back to Madina, arriving early the following year, 630. This defeat must have been a severe blow to Muhammad's personal prestige. Failing to gain the wealth of unbelievers to the north, the Muslims must have felt especially disappointed as they began to realize that the desert would continue to be their home for some time to come.

The Capture of Makka, January, 630

After Mu'ta, the Prophet was in a desperate position, requiring a quick victory to turn the attention of his followers away from their defeat. In spite of a truce with the Makkans outlawing hostilities for ten years, the Prophet could not resist the temptation to capture Makka, which, from a military point of view, became an easy target. As a pretext, he used an appeal for help against Quraysh sent to him by an allied tribe; he therefore mobilized all Muslims capable of fighting for a final attack against Makka. Ten thousand fighters are reported to have been gathered for the battle which won all Arabia for the Muslims.

When the Makkan leaders heard of Muhammad's sweeping preparations to attack their city, terror filled their ranks. Abu Sufyan, Makka's chief leader, rushed to Madina seeking an audience with the Prophet, who adamantly refused to see him. Denied an audience with even one of the lesser personalities of Madina, Abu Sufyan returned to Makka in great humiliation and indignation. There was actually nothing that he could do except to surrender unconditionally to Muhammad and his commanders, who had already begun their historic march.

Abu Sufyan, accompanied by Abbas, the Prophet's uncle, led a delegation to negotiate the terms of surrender. While in the presence of Muhammad, Abbas is reported to have announced his conversion to Islam and asked Abu Sufyan to do the same. When he hesitated, Abu Sufyan was told that in view of the grave situation the only alternative to Islam would be death. He therefore announced his conversion and requested the Prophet to refrain from shedding blood. Being in a position to dictate his conditions of surrender, the Prophet insisted that all Makkans should stay inside their homes as the Muslims entered the city; anyone who strayed outside would be killed. Upon his return, Abu Sufyan is reported to have asked his fellow Makkans to honor his agreement with Muhammad and stay indoors.

Accordingly, when the Muslim troops arrived, the city was almost evacuated; they went directly to the Ka'ba and destroyed all idols and statues of pagan Arabia, proclaiming Islam the only religion of the Arabs. It was a moment of great victory for Muhammad, who, in a single bloodless and triumphant move, became ruler of the most revered city in Arabia.

MUHAMMAD'S LAST YEAR

Muhammad, Ruler of Arabia

Muhammad summoned the Makkans to swear allegiance to him as their leader and prophet. He sat in the midst of the Ka'ba while numerous Arab leaders filed past him to shake his hand and announce their loyalty. According to Arab historians, when some women came to pledge their allegiance to the Prophet, he asked Umar to shake hands with them in his behalf – it was his custom not to touch the hands of any woman except those of his wives.

Having received the allegiance of the Makkans, he declared a general amnesty for all Arabs who would announce their acceptance of Islam. He remained in Makka to receive Arab delegations that came to profess their conversion to Islam and pledge their allegiance to the Prophet. Muslim annals report that during the year 630 delegations representing most of the tribes of Arabia came to pay homage to Muhammad.

Two tribes south of Makka continued to defy the Prophet's authority. He therefore dispatched an expedition to discipline them and set them as examples for other tribes contemplating disobedience. The first tribe, known as Hawazin, was defeated at the battle of Hunayn, which yielded abundant booty to the Muslims, one fifth of which was given to Muhammad personally. The second tribe, known as Thaqif, was defeated after a long siege at Ta'if, a town that had rejected Muhammad about ten years earlier during his years of misery and dejection.

Muhammad's Death

Thus, in a quick succession of events, the Prophet became a statesman with supreme authority over almost all the tribes of Arabia. The Arabs, who had lived for centuries as scattered nomads roaming the vast desert, made their first move toward national existence under Muhammad's leadership. During the pilgrimage season of 631, the Ka'ba was visited only by Muslims for the first time in its history. During that pilgrimage, Muhammad announced that none but Muslim believers should be allowed to visit Makka, a rule that has continued to be observed until the present time.

By the end of 631, Muhammad had reached the height of his career, as Arab deputations announcing their allegiance came to him from as far as Yaman and Bahrayn in the south. He spent the last few months of that year establishing the legal foundations of Islam as a state. Most of the Qur'anic relevations of this period contained numerous laws regulating relations between Muslims and non-Muslims and between Muslims and other Muslims.

Early in 632, as the Prophet was still strengthening the foundations of his newly established state, he visited Makka during the pilgrimage season and preached his last sermon, confirming Allah's intentions to make Islam the religion of all Arabia. When he returned to Madina his health rapidly deteriorated until fever forced him to remain in bed. Before his companions could comprehend the seriousness of his condition, he died. At a time when the hopes of all the Arabs were focused upon him, it was extremely difficult for many of his followers to accept the fact of his death. Dazed and bewildered, they began to consider what they should do.

CHAPTER 20

THE ISLAMIC STATE

THE CONSTITUTION OF MADINA

Birth of the Islamic State

In assessing Muhammad's role as a statesman it is very hard to pinpoint the exact time when he began to envision the existence of an Islamic state. It is certain, however, that at the start of his mission as a prophet, he confined his activities to his own people, Quraysh, whose leaders not only rejected his message, but also persecuted and threatened him and his few followers. Perhaps his great disappointment in failing to win his own tribe caused him to expand the boundaries of his mission to include other tribes in Arabia that might be receptive to his message.

When the delegations from Madina (at that time still called Yathrib) discussed with him their immediate problems as Arabs beset by rivalries and tribal feuds, and requested him to become their leader and arbitrator, Muhammad must have envisioned a political structure in which Arab tribes could unite and form a great Arab state. To Muhammad, the unifying factor that could cut across tribal boundaries was the force of Islam as a religion. Therefore, he must have envisioned an Arab state whose citizens would not only be Arabs but also Muslims.

The Islamic Umma

When Muhammad arrived in Madina in 622, he drew up a document generally known as the Constitution of Madina in which he announced that Muslims of all tribes constituted one *umma*, "community." The word *umma*, as the Prophet used it, referred to a community whose individual members became joined together by bonds of religion. In other words, the new political structure which Muhammad established in Madina was based on the concept that the main distinguishing mark of its members was not Arab ethnic origin, but Islam as a religion. Accordingly, the new Islamic state established in Madina in 622 may be defined as a political structure with a religious core, or, in other words, an Arab state with an Islamic identity. As a prophet, Muhammad enacted laws emanating from the will of God, and as a statesman he enforced His laws without opposition since Muslims were essentially believers who had already submitted their wills to the will of God.

Other Articles in the Constitution of Madina

Besides establishing the Muslim believers as one *umma*, the Constitution of Madina contained other articles regulating relations between the two main components of the *umma*, namely the Makkan emigrants and the Madinan supporters. One article, for example, required each group to be responsible for paying redemption fees to free its members. Another prohibited a believer from murdering another believer or helping an unbeliever against a believer. In case of war against a common enemy, the Constitution of Madina explicitly required the whole *umma* to be united. Disputes arising among believers within the *umma* were to be referred to Muhammad personally, whose judgment was considered final, reflecting the will of God.

As a whole, the Constitution of Madina was a revolutionary development in the social structure of Arabia. Although it allowed some tribal institutions to continue within the *umma*, it affirmed that tribal subloyalties should be subordinate to the more commanding religio-national loyalty, which individual believers owed to the whole *umma*, "community of believers." Later on, during the empire period when Muslims indulged in luxury and when religious faith lost its early intensity, it may be said that tribal factionalism reappeared allowing old subloyalties to pose a serious threat to the very existence of the Islamic state.

Jews and Muslims in Madina

When the Muslim state was initiated in 622, the Muslim community was rather small and flanked on all sides by unbelievers. The Jews of Madina were influential and, if antagonized, also capable of destroying the Muslims. Muhammad therefore thought to tolerate them, and seek their good will. Concerning religion, he tried on many occasions to demonstrate his willingness to incorporate many Jewish traditions into Islam if the Jews would only accept him as prophet. In politics, an article in the Constitution of Madina stipulated that the Jews constituted another *umma*. Between the Jewish *umma* and the Muslim *umma* there should be mutual friendship and cooperation. In times of peace the Jews were allowed to pursue their own affairs without Muslim interference, but in case of war or an attack against Madina, the Jews were asked to defray part of the expenses while the Muslims engaged in fighting. Another article of the Constitution of Madina explicitly asserted that in case of war, the Jews should take the side of the Muslims with sincere friendship and honorable dealing; otherwise, they would be considered traitors.

EXPULSION OF THE JEWS FROM ARABIA

The Break with the Jews

During the few years following 622, as the Makkans and Madinans engaged in continuous raids and battles, the balance of power shifted gradually in favor of the Muslims. The Jews persisted in rejecting Muhammad's appeals to accept his claim to prophecy, and he gradually changed his tactics. Instead of instituting religious rituals in harmony with Jewish traditions, he began to discredit Jewish customs and dissociate Islamic duties from those of the Jews. He changed the *qibla*, "direction of prayer," toward Makka instead of Jerusalem. He also declared the fast of *Ashura*, a Jewish day, to be no longer obligatory, and instead, he instituted the fast of Ramadan, an Arab month. Muhammad seemed to have lost hope of converting the Jews and therefore directed most of his efforts to win his fellow Arabs. Perhaps at this time, Muhammad decided to establish an Islamic state whose population would be uniformly Muslim. Accordingly, as he was winning the Arabs to Islam, he turned his attention to the struggle against the Jewish tribes living in and around Madina.

Expulsion of the Qaynuqa' Tribe

After their victory at Badr in 624, the Muslims felt strong enough to turn overtly against their Jewish neighbors. Muhammad is reported to have sent a warning to the leaders of the Jewish tribe of Qaynuqa' inviting them to accept him as a prophet or to fight. Ridiculing the Prophet's invitation and minimizing his victory against the Makkans, the Jews chose to fight. Consequently, the Muslims besieged the Jewish quarters of the tribe of Qaynuqa' in Madina for several days during which Jewish leaders began seriously to count the cost of combat. Convinced that they were doomed to a losing battle, they reportedly surrendered unconditionally; after some hesitation the Prophet consented to let them migrate to Syria, while their homes and properties were taken by Muslims as welcome booty.

Expulsion of the Nadir Tribe

The following year, 625, the Muslims suffered a defeat at the battle of Uhud in which the Prophet himself was seriously wounded. This defeat was perhaps the main cause behind Muhammad's desire to secure a quick victory against one of the Jewish tribes in order to boost Muslim morale. Muslim annals report that Muhammad went to the leaders of Nadir and requested them to help pay redemption fees for two persons mistakenly murdered by Muslims. The Nadir leaders consented to make a contribution and entered their homes to bring the money. While they were gone, something never explained must have happened, after which Muhammad slipped away into the Muslim quarters and accused the Jews of plotting to murder him. The Muslims, therefore, besieged the Nadir Jews for six days, burning their palm trees and threatening to burn their homes. The Nadir tribe capitulated and accepted Muhammad's terms to leave their homes and property and migrate to Syria. By sending the Nadir tribe into exile, the Muslims secured two victories; they considerably weakened their non-Muslim neighbors in Madina, and they gained more land and property to provide for their ever-increasing numbers.

Extermination of the Quraydha Tribe

During the battle of the Trench in 627, when Madina was besieged by about ten thousand Makkan troops, some Jews apparently engaged in intelligence activities against the Muslims. When the siege ended in failure, Muhammad commanded his warriors to turn immediately on the Jews, especially the tribe of Quraydha. The Muslims surrounded their enemies for twenty-five days before the leaders of Quraydha surrendered with an appeal for mercy. Muhammad reportedly asked one of the elders of the tribe of Aws to pass a judgment against the Jews. According to Arab historians, the Arab elder stood up and said, "I rule that the men be killed, the properties be divided, and the women and children be taken captives."

The Prophet accepted this verdict and ordered it to be executed immediately. Almost seven hundred men of Quraydha were reported beheaded as their women, children, and property were divided among the Muslims. According to the law concerning booty, Muhammad received one fifth of the wealth of the Jews.

After this devastating campaign against the tribe of Quraydha, the remaining Jews gradually left Madina, which eventually became totally Muslim. After the Treaty of Hudaybiyya the Jews living north of Madina in places such as Khaybar, Fadak, and Wadi al-Qura recognized the growing danger and migrated north to Syria, leaving behind their lands and property to be confiscated by the Muslims.

As soon as the Muslims captured Makka in 630, scattered Arab tribes from all over the peninsula sent delegations to Muhammad professing Islam as their religion and claiming the Prophet as their leader. During the pilgrimage season of 631, Muhammad stood up in the midst of an all-Muslim crowd announcing Makka as a religious center to be visited only by Muslims. Religion now officially became a part of the political structure of the emerging Islamic state, and the Arabian peninsula became formally recognized as the territory of that state.

MUSLIMS AND CHRISTIANS IN ARABIA

The Christians of Najran

The chief center of the Christian population in the fast-growing Islamic state was Najran in South Arabia. A considerable distance from Makka and Madina, it was practically inaccessible to any military force that Muhammad could dispatch. According to some reports, the Prophet made an agreement with its people by which they would continue to live in their own quarters under the protection of the Muslims on condition that they pay a tax called *jizya*. The Christians of Najran lived peacefully with their Muslim neighbors for a few years, but during the rule of Umar, the second caliph, they were asked to evacuate the peninsula in an effort to make Arabia purely Muslim.

The Christians of the Northern Fringes

In a wide area north of Makka and Madina lived a few Arab Christian tribes – Kalb, Quda'a, Lakhm, and others, who, for all practical purposes, controlled the desert borders near the Fertile Crescent. Following the Muslim defeat at Mu'ta, Muhammad was evidently convinced that some of them had served as intelligence agents, passing the news of the Muslim march to their northern neighbors of Ghassan. After capturing Makka and receiving the allegiance of most of the Arab tribes, he felt strong enough to send a force against these Christian tribes. By the end of 630, Muslim forces had subdued the Christians in the northern fringes of Arabia, and claimed complete control over the whole territory.

When Muhammad was asked about the fate of the subdued tribes, he ruled that since they were believers in a scripture, they could be tolerated within the Muslim community if they paid the *jizya*, "poll tax." The Christians agreed to pay this tax and remain in their lands; but when Umar, the second caliph, announced Arabia to be a Muslim territory, these Christians together with the inhabitants of Najran, were forced to leave their homes and migrate to Syria.

MUHAMMAD AND THE NON-ARAB WORLD

The first encounter between Muslims and the non-Arab world took place when the early followers of Muhammad in Makka went to Abyssinia with a message from the Prophet to the Negus (king of Abyssinia). This encounter is known to have been between individual Muslims and a state. However, certain reports of several contacts between Muhammad, as head of a state, and other heads of state are explicitly mentioned in Islamic annals. Some western historians cast doubt upon the authenticity of such reports, yet their contents cannot be ignored as pure inventions. Islamic annals report that upon his return to Madina from Hudaybiyya, Muhammad dispatched messengers to the Negus of Abyssinia, the emperor of Byzantium, the governor of Egypt, and the king of Persia with written messages, in which he invited them to accept him as a prophet and accept Islam as a religion. However, it may be safely assumed that these messages referred to other political matters that were not fully known to Islamic historians.

At any rate, these reports mention that only the king of Persia tore up the message, while the others gave various polite responses. Regardless of the truth of these reports it is quite certain that Muhammad was not willing to confine his religio-political claims to Arabia. He could easily recognize that his desert homeland did not have enough resources to support its population, and, therefore, he must have envisioned an Islamic state extending beyond the peninsula. As mentioned above, he had already promised his followers during the Makka-Madina battles that Allah would not only subdue Makka, but that he would also allow the Muslims to inherit the treasures of Persia and Byzantium. This clearly indicates that in laying the foundations of Islam, Muhammad had in mind a state in which both the Arabs of the peninsula and the non-Arabs of the adjacent lands would be ruled according to Islamic laws. Although Muhammad died before realizing his dreams, the Islamic state which he launched contained so much momentum that within one decade of the Prophet's death the Arabs were in full control of the adjacent civilized world.

IMPORTANT TERMS

Abbas: An uncle who assumed the responsibility of protecting Muhammad after the death of Abu Talib. Abbas is reported to have greatly sympathized with the Prophet's message although he delayed his conversion till the capture of Makka.

Abu Sufyan: Leader of the Quraysh tribe during the skirmishes between Makka and Madina. He resisted Muhammad's rise to power until the capture of Makka.

A'isha: Muhammad's youngest wife and the daughter of Abu Bakr.

Amr ibn al-As: One of the Quraysh warriors who announced his conversion to Islam after the truce of Hudaybiyya.

Ansar: The followers of Muhammad from Madina. They were also called "supporters."

Aws: One of the Arab tribes of Madina that invited Muhammad to its city.

Badr: The first significant battle between the Muslims and the Makkans in 624, in which the Muslims were victorious.

Constitution of Madina: A set of laws announced by Muhammad upon his arrival in Madina in 622, intended to regulate relations within the newly established Islamic community.

Hijra: The emigration of Muhammad and his Makkan followers from Makka in 622. It marks the beginning of the Muslim calendar.

Hudaybiyya Treaty: An agreement reached in 628 between Muhammad and the Makkans, in which both sides promised not to renew hostilities for ten years.

Khalid ibn al-Walid: A great warrior who joined the Muslim ranks after the Treaty of Hudaybiyya. Muhammad is reported to have called him "the Sword of Islam."

Khazraj: One of the two Arab tribes of Madina that invited the Prophet to immigrate to their city.

Madina: A city about 250 miles northeast of Makka, known in pre-Islamic times as Yathrib. The emigration of Muhammad from Makka to Madina in 622 marks the beginning of the Islamic community.

Muhajirun: The group of Muslims who emigrated with Muhammad from Makka to Madina in 622. They are also known as the "emigrants."

Mu'la Expedition: A Muslim contingent sent by the Prophet to the territory of Ghassan in 629. It was defeated by Byzantine forces at Mu'ta.

Nadir: See Qaynuqa'.

Qaynuqa', Nadir, and Quraydha: The three chief Jewish tribes forced to evacuate their homes and immigrate to Syria. The men of Quraydha were sentenced to death on charges of spying.

Quraydha: See Qaynuqa'.

Scriptuaries: A term used by Muslims to refer to the Jews, Christians, and other non-Muslim sects who believe in a revealed book.

Trench, Expedition of: An expedition sent from Makka to inflict a final defeat upon the Muslims in 627. The Muslims dug a trench around the open part of their city, forcing the Makkans to retreat after a siege of twenty-one days.

Uhud: A battle fought outside of Madina in 625, in which the Muslims were defeated and the Prophet seriously wounded.

Umma: An Arabic term referring to the Muslims as a community, first used in 622 in Madina.

SUPPLEMENTARY READINGS

BROCKELMANN, CARL, *History of the Islamic Peoples* (New York, 1947).

GABRIELI, F., *The Arabs—A Compact History* (New York, 1963).

GLUBB, SIR JOHN BAGOT, *The Great Arab Conquests* (Englewood Cliffs, N.J., 1963).

GOITEIN, S.D., *Jews and Arabs* (New York, 1955).

GUILLAUME, ALFRED, *The Life of Muhammad—A Translation of Ishaq's Sirat Rasul Allah* (Oxford, 1955).

————, *Islam* (Oxford, 1954).

HITTI, PHILIP K., *History of the Arabs* (New York, 1960).

LEWIS, BERNARD, *The Arabs in History* (London, 1954).

MARGOLIOUTH, D.S., *Muhammad and the Rise of Islam* (New York, 1905).

WATT, W.M., *Muhammad at Madina* (Oxford, 1956).

――――, *Muhammad, Prophet and Statesman* (Oxford, 1961).

WILLIAMS, J.A., *Islam* (New York, 1961).

PART VI

THE ORTHODOX CALIPHATE, 632-661

The following chapters deal mainly with the development of Islam as a state immediately after the sudden death of Muhammad in 632. During this period, commonly known as that of the orthodox caliphate, Muhammad's successors (caliphs) were selected as political, religious, and military leaders of the Islamic community.

The first two caliphs, Abu Bakr and Umar, were chiefly responsible for suppressing apostasy at home and for establishing the Arab Empire, which within only ten years of the Prophet's death expanded to encompass the whole of the Middle East Proper. The military situation outside Arabia around the year 632 afforded the Arabs a unique opportunity to expand northward at the expense of two great empires, Persia and Byzantium. It so happened that for almost ten years prior to 629, these two leading powers of the then-civilized world had engaged in a costly war that rendered them militarily weak. At last they concluded a peace agreement, chiefly because both armies were completely exhausted and utterly unprepared for new military adventures. In 634, less than five years after the Persian and Byzantine troops had been demobilized, the Arabs launched their offensive in the Middle East. It is no wonder, therefore, that their troops, sometimes referred to as the wolves of the desert, won unprecedented victories over the Persians and the Byzantines.

CHAPTER 21

ABU BAKR, 632-634

SELECTION OF ABU BAKR

Shock After Muhammad's Death

Muhammad died unexpectedly at a time when the hopes of Arabia were focused upon him; however, the foundations of Islam were already laid before his death. Nevertheless, Muhammad's emerging religio-political structure needed further authoritative guidance to lead it safely toward consolidation and stability. In other words, at the time of Muhammad's death, Islam as a religion and state lacked the final touches of its founder, which would have enabled it to cope with problems of expansion and security.

Umar was the first of the Prophet's close companions to see him on his deathbed. He is reported to have been so greatly shocked at the thought of the Prophet's death, that he stood before the crowd gathering outside Muhammad's home, excitedly repeating that the Prophet had not died and that soon he would stand up and punish those who thought so. At this point Abu Bakr is reported to have arrived and entered Muhammad's chamber. He reportedly kissed the cheeks of the dead Prophet and covered his face with a sheet; then he came out to the crowd and gave his short, now famous, speech: "O people, if anyone (of you) worshiped Muhammad, surely Muhammad has died. But whosoever worships God, (let him know) that God lives and cannot die."

These words seemed to sober the excited crowds, allowing the Prophet's companions to begin deliberations for the choice of a successor. Since Muhammad left no instructions regarding the choice of a successor, there was indecision in Madina. However, in harmony with the tribal tradition of selecting a *shaykh*, "leader of a tribe," the Prophet's companions decided to meet together and discuss the problem.

The Saqifa Meeting

The Muslim community of Madina was composed of two main groups: the *ansar*, "supporters," and the *muhajirun*, "emigrants." The former group constituted the original dwellers of Madina who had earlier invited the Prophet to move to their city and become their leader. Accordingly, they were the group justly credited with the establishment of the Islamic state. The emigrants, however, were the closest companions to the Prophet, having stood by his side during the period of oppression and persecution. When they migrated with the Prophet to Madina, they continued to be his nearest friends and most trusted consultants. The supporters, therefore, found themselves treated as subordinates in their own town and no doubt were unhappy.

When the Prophet died, the supporters saw an opportunity to make a bid for leadership. Without delay, their leaders gathered in the *saqifa*, "guest room," of one of their members and began deliberations to choose a leader from among themselves while the body of the Prophet was still lying in state. They had almost agreed upon a Khazrajite leader, when word of their independent meeting reached the emigrants. Abu Bakr immediately gathered his companions and went to the *saqifa*. The sharp difference of opinion between the supporters and the emigrants that ensued threatened to split the ranks of the Islamic state in its infancy. However, the wisdom and prestige of Abu Bakr finally prevailed, and the problem was quickly solved.

Abu Bakr Chosen

Upon the arrival of the emigrants' delegation to the supporters' *saqifa*, Abu Bakr argued that a leader from the Khazraj tribe would probably be unacceptable to the Arabs. Moreover, he insisted that the Aws themselves, who supported the selection of a Khazrajite leader, might soon turn against that leader, and the old feud between the two tribes would be renewed. The only solution to the problem, he said, would be to select a successor from Quraysh, whose prestige was high among all the Arabs. This argument was convincing, particularly as presented by so dignified a man as Abu Bakr. As soon as the supporters showed signs of approving Abu Bakr's argument, he asked the whole group to select either Umar or al-Jarrah, two prominent leaders of Quraysh. Seeing that the vote might be split between himself and al-Jarrah, Umar rose up and reportedly approached Abu Bakr saying, "Didn't the Prophet delegate you to lead the Muslims in prayer? You are then his successor and we give you our allegiance." Islamic annals record that al-Jarrah and all the leaders in the guest room followed suit in giving allegiance to Abu Bakr.

While the body of Muhammad was still lying in state, the Muslim leaders left the *saqifa* and announced their selection of Abu Bakr as successor of the Prophet. The Arabic word for "successor" is *khalifa* from which the word "caliph," used throughout this book, is derived. Abu Bakr became the first caliph of Islam at a very critical period of its development. The youthful Muslim state was faced with grave internal problems that threatened its very existence, and upon Abu Bakr fell the responsibility of diverting the growing restlessness of the Arabs from possible internal wars and destruction to the path of foreign expansion and survival. Abu Bakr, who possessed great prudence and fortitude, proved himself capable of the task. During the two years of his caliphate, he was able not only to put down a strong anti-Islamic movement that rose in Arabia soon after Muhammad's death, but also to organize the Arab military potential and dispatch troops toward Syria and Iraq for conquest. Abu Bakr's success was due to four main factors: (1) his personal prestige, (2) his wise selection of capable army commanders, (3) the religious motivation that stimulated Muslim warriors to fight sacrificially, and (4) the deterioration of military prowess in the two main rival powers outside Arabia, namely, Persia and Byzantium.

FALSE PROPHETS

Arab Apostasy

Upon the capture of Makka in 630, delegations from almost all Arab tribes had come to the Prophet and pledged their allegiance to Islam. By that time, many Jewish tribes had left Arabia for Syria as all Arabia became the home of the Islamic community. Since Muslims were not permitted to raid other Muslims, the newly established state had to be financed by other means. The only logical way, followed in almost every national state, was to levy taxes. Muhammad sent emissaries to the scattered tribes around Makka and Madina asking for the religious tax, called *zakat*. Dissatisfaction began to brew among the scattered Arab tribes, who had never been subjected to taxes. Muslim annals mention that some of Muhammad's tax collectors were beaten and others killed as several tribes, used to freedom and independence, persisted in defying Muhammad's orders. Anti-Islamic religious movements began to appear secretly in various sections of Arabia, supported by prophets claiming revelations and repeating rhymed utterances that denied Muhammad's sole authority. After the Prophet's death, these secret movements came to the open, protesting Islam's right to levy taxes.

There were three main centers of apostasy and rebellion against the authority of Abu Bakr. The first was north of Makka among the tribes of Asad led by their prophet Talha, whose name was changed by Muslim historians to its diminutive form, Tulayha. The second rebellion flared up east of Makka among the Tamim tribes under the leadership of a prophetess called Sajah. The third, and most notorious, was at Yamama among the Hanifa tribes under the leadership of a prophet called Maslama (diminutive Musaylama), who claimed to have had visions and recited Arabic rhymes similar to Qur'anic utterances.

War Against the Apostates

Before his death, Muhammad had given permission to Usama, son of Zayd, the murdered commander of the defeated expedition to Mu'ta, to lead a raid against the borders of Syria and avenge the murder of his father. Although Usama was only twenty-four years old, Abu Bakr allowed him to proceed with his raid as ordered by the Prophet.

Abu Bakr is reported to have given to the troops departing under Usama the following famous admonition frequently quoted by Muslims to indicate the good will of their armies:

> Deceive none and betray none. Do not misbehave or act un-seemingly. Do not kill a child or an old man, and do not kill a woman. Do not cut down or burn palm trees, or any fruitful tree. Do not slaughter a sheep, a cow, or a camel. You will meet some people retiring in monasteries—leave them alone. You will pass by people with plenty of food—mention the name of the Lord upon the food you eat. You will meet men who shave the center of their heads leaving hair to grow around the sides —destroy them completely by the edge of the sword. March in the name of Allah.[1]

Upon Usama's return from his mission, Abu Bakr appointed Khalid ibn al-Walid as supreme commander of the Muslim troops with full authority to suppress apostasy and rebellion in the various sections of Arabia. The Muslim army is reported to have been divided into eleven columns, each under the command of a capable warrior. These columns spread out of Madina in every direction with zeal and courage to fight the apostates in the name of Allah. Khalid himself led the Muslim contingent against the Asad tribes and defeated Talha's fol-lowers at the battle of Buzakha, after which most of the northern tribes returned to the fold of Islam. Talha was captured and sent to Madina where, reportedly, he repented and was reconverted to Islam.

[1]Ibn al-Athir, *Al-Kamil fi al-Tarikh* (Bulaq, 1858), Volume 2, p. 139.

After Buzakha, Khalid turned south to the Tamim tribes and defeated their leader, Malik ibn Nuwayra, whom he killed and whose widow he married. During Khalid's skirmish with Tamim, the Muslim column sent under Ikrima to the rebellious Hanifa tribes was being defeated by a sizable army organized by Maslama. Wasting no time, Khalid ordered his army to proceed toward Yamama where he met Maslama's troops. A vicious battle followed in which several thousands from both sides were killed, making the battle of Yamama the most destructive of all wars in Arabia. Maslama himself was killed and his army badly defeated while the Muslims lost a great number of their troops, including many reciters of unrecorded Qur'anic utterances.

Soon after his glorious but costly victory at Yamama, Khalid allowed Ikrima to continue his campaign toward the south while he himself began a campaign in the northern border areas of Arabia. Ikrima followed the coastal line of the Persian Gulf, reached Uman, and continued along the southern shores to Hadramawt and Yaman. Khalid, meanwhile, proceeded toward the Northern Fringes, where he won numerous victories over the border tribes; and thus, in less than two years, all Arabia was brought back within the fold of Islam.

BEGINNING OF EXPANSION

The Military Situation Outside Arabia

The political rivalry between the Byzantines and Sassanians can be traced back to the power struggle between the Roman Empire and the Parthians in Persia which continued almost without interruption till the beginning of the third century A.D. While the center of power in the Roman Empire was being gradually transferred to Constantinople, a very strong regime had been established in Persia under the rule of the Sassanian dynasty. Accordingly, when Byzantium inherited the legacy of the Roman Empire, the old quarrel between Rome and the Parthians was resumed – this time carried on between Byzantium and the Sassanians.

Shortly after the Byzantine Emperor Heraclius was crowned in 610, Chosroes, the Sassanian king of Persia, marched swiftly against Byzantine territories in the Middle East Proper. In 614 the Persians occupied Syria, captured Jerusalem, and carried away the Holy Cross from the city. In 616 they occupied Egypt and expelled the Byzantine forces from the whole region. Heraclius was so discouraged that he thought for a while of abandoning his own capital and fleeing to Africa. His generals, however, advised him instead to call upon his people for a holy war to liberate the cross.

Backed by the senate, Heraclius was successful in marshaling the forces of his empire and, in 619, resumed his campaigns to liberate Jerusalem and retrieve the cross. He gained partial success as he defeated the Persian troops at Cappadocia in 622, the year in which Muhammad migrated to Madina. Heraclius continued to inflict defeats upon the Persians in Cilicia and around the Black Sea. However, due to an alliance between the barbarian Avars and the Sassanians, he returned to Constantinople in 626. In 627 the Byzantine armies launched a strong offensive against the Persians, liberated Egypt, and reached the vicinity of ancient Nineveh. Chosroes was assassinated in 628 by his own son. By 629 both camps were militarily exhausted and ready to make peace. A treaty was signed restoring the frontiers of 602, thus leaving Byzantium in charge of protecting the Holy Land. This year, 629, was hailed in the Christian world as the year of the liberation of the cross, and many celebrations were held in the Byzantine Empire to honor the occasion.

When Muhammad sent a Muslim expedition to Mu'ta in late 629, the Byzantines had just concluded their peace treaty with the Persians; their troops, still in Palestine, easily defeated the three thousand Muslims, already worn out by their march across the desert. However, in 632 when Abu Bakr was ready to send more troops to the borders of the Fertile Crescent, Persian as well as Byzantine troops had just been demobilized and all military activities between the two camps had ceased. The timing of the Islamic expansion may be considered one of the rarest phenomena of coincidence in all history. In less than a decade the Arabs of the desert became rulers of an empire.

On the Road to Conquest

Khalid, hero of the battle of Yamama, not only distinguished himself as a warrior, but also as a great military organizer. Seldom in the history of the Middle East could a head of state and a military organizer see eye to eye on vital matters of the state so well as Abu Bakr and Khalid. Both must have been thoroughly convinced that the only way to avoid disruption in the Islamic state was to organize the Arabs into military contingents and send them into foreign lands. Religion was, of course, a very strong motivation for encouraging the Arab tribes to venture outside their own land.

Accordingly, as a last glorious achievement, Abu Bakr mobilized the Muslims of Makka and Madina into an army under the leadership of Ibn al-As, Shurahbil, and al-Jarrah. He ordered Khalid to proceed toward Syria, Ibn al-As to follow the coastal line, and Shurahbil to advance along the overland route. As Shurahbil met with some initial difficulties on his way, Abu Bakr sent al-Jarrah to take over the command from him. Abu Bakr, however, died in 634 before seeing the final results of his calculated adventures. Nevertheless, the preparations which he made toward insuring the success of his campaigns were so effective that his successor, Umar, suddenly found himself ruler over a large empire instead of a nation-state. Abu Bakr has been remembered in Islamic history as the leader whose administration witnessed the change in Islam from tribalism to national consciousness and political unity.

CHAPTER 22

UMAR, 634-644

Abu Bakr died in August, 634, as Muslim armies were advancing to the north under the able leadership of Khalid ibn al-Walid, al-Jarrah, and Ibn al-As. In order to avoid another factional fight within the Muslim ranks, Abu Bakr had designated Umar as his successor. It may be recalled that Umar was the first one to nominate Abu Bakr during the *saqifa* meeting in 632, and undoubtedly the latter remembered this action and was convinced that Umar would be the best leader for the Muslims.

When Umar assumed the caliphate, he was called "Successor of the Successor of the Messenger of God." However, this title soon became discarded, and he was addressed only as "the Successor," i.e., caliph. Umar is known to have adopted also the title "Commander of the Faithful," which continued to be used for many generations after him.

CONQUEST OF SYRIA

Battle of Ajnadayn, 634

While Arab columns led by al-Jarrah and Ibn al-As slowly progressed toward Syria and Palestine, Khalid's division advanced rather swiftly against Iraq.[1] Khalid had already

[1] Iraq had been part of the Persian Empire until the Arabs captured and separated it from Persia.

141

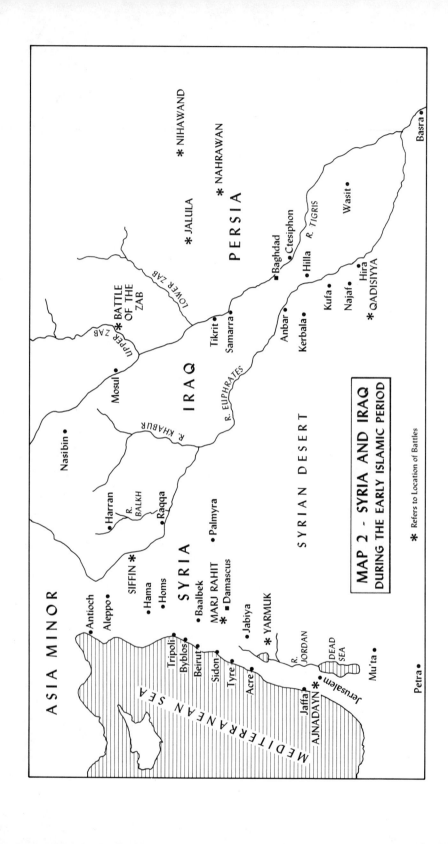

MAP 2 - SYRIA AND IRAQ
DURING THE EARLY ISLAMIC PERIOD

* Refers to Location of Battles

captured Hira and the southern region of the Tigris-Euphrates Valley when Abu Bakr ordered him to move to Syria and help al-Jarrah, whose army was slowed down by Byzantine forces at the Yarmuk River. Khalid reached Syria early in 634, and, having seen the concentration of Byzantine forces around the Sea of Galilee, advised the Arabs to move their forces toward Palestine and to help Ibn al-As, who was fighting in the area between the Mediterranean and the Dead Seas. In July, 634, during the battle of Ajnadayn, Khalid once more distinguished himself as a great warrior and army commander.

Khalid's Deposition

The good news of the victory at Ajnadayn reached Abu Bakr as Khalid was returning toward southern Syria and the Yarmuk River. However, the elderly caliph died soon after hearing the news, and Umar assumed office almost immediately. Umar's first act upon assuming the caliphate was to remove Khalid from his command in Syria and appoint al-Jarrah in his place. Many reasons have been given to explain this surprising move by Umar, but the most plausible one may be Umar's fear lest Khalid's victories would lead him to disobey the caliph. It is true that Khalid's prestige in Hira and southern Iraq caused him to dictate capitulation terms and receive booty on his own initiative without referring matters to higher authorities in Madina.

In any case, Khalid received Umar's letter of deposition while the battle of Yarmuk was raging; however, he kept it a secret till victory was assured. At the moment of his highest glory, instead of arousing the Arabs against their caliph, he withdrew quietly from his high command and continued to fight as a simple soldier till he died in 642.

Battle of the Yarmuk, 636

Heraclius' army, encamped in the Yarmuk Valley in northern Palestine, was greatly dismayed by the Muslim victory at Ajnadayn. Nevertheless, the Byzantines continued to hold their fortifications on one side of the Yarmuk River as the Arabs gathered on the other side. The Byzantine commander hesitated to attack first and began to lure the Arabs to surrender by offering them money and generous gifts. The Arabs, who needed time to reinforce their positions at Yarmuk, bargained at length with the Byzantines. Finally, when enough equipment and supplies arrived from Madina to assure victory, the Arabs cut short their bargaining and attacked.

Muslim annals mention that on a windy day, as the blowing sands were darkening the skies, Arab armies took the Byzantines by surprise and dashed to their fortifications from all directions. Confusion reportedly filled the Byzantine camp as many soldiers were killed, and the rest fled northward in complete disarray. Their losses were so

great that they could not regroup and take up defensive positions
elsewhere. Heraclius, therefore, ordered the remnant of his army to
evacuate the interior of Syria and Palestine and retreat to the coastal
region, leaving the way open for the Arabs to occupy Syrian cities with
a minimum of fighting. Many cities surrendered to the Arabs with almost no resistance. Damascus, destined to be a great Muslim capital
between 661 and 750, surrendered after a siege of six months.

Capitulation of Jerusalem

As al-Jarrah, with the help of Khalid, continued to subjugate the
Syrian cities, Ibn al-As and Shurahbil marched against the cities of
Palestine. When Ibn al-As reached Jerusalem, the patriarch of the
Holy City, Sophronius, insisted that Umar himself should come and
accept its capitulation. Umar accepted the proposal and started his
trip to Jerusalem. On his way, Umar stopped at Jabiya in Ghassan,
where the caliph met with his commanders in 637 to discuss the new
strategy for expanding the empire and defeating the Persians in Iraq.
Umar then rode to Jerusalem, where he concluded with the patriarch an
agreement for the surrender of the city in 638. The terms of this
agreement included the following:

1. The Muslims were to be responsible for the defense of Jeru-
    salem and the protection of its inhabitants.
2. Non-Muslim scriptuaries were to pay *jizya,* "poll tax," to the
    Muslims, who became their protectors.
3. Christians were guaranteed freedom of worship on condition
    that their practices should not interfere with Muslim worship.
4. Converts to Islam were to be exempted from paying tax.

Upon concluding this agreement, Umar entered Jerusalem as a
conqueror and, refusing to pray in any of the holy shrines, he reportedly went to the holy rock of the Jewish temple and performed his
prayer. As a consequence, a mosque revered by all Muslims and held
second only to the Mosque of the Prophet in Madina, was built on the
temple compound where Umar prayed.

At that time, Umar decreed that Arabia proper should be the homeland of Muslims only. Therefore, he asked the Christians of Najran
and the Jews of Khaybar to evacuate Arabia for Syria and Iraq, thus
ending the formal agreements which the Prophet himself had previously
concluded with them.

CONQUEST OF PERSIA

Rustum and the Arabs

During Khalid's absence from Iraq, his successor, Muthanna, was
forced to abandon certain positions already captured by the Arabs.

Accordingly, Umar dispatched new forces under the leadership of Ibn Abi Waqqas to complete the conquest of Iraq and Persia. The new Muslim troops advanced in Iraqi territory to Qadisiyya. There, Rustum, the Persian commander, is reported to have asked for an Arab representative to explain to him why the Muslims were fighting; Ibn Abi Waqqas therefore sent to him one of his chief commanders called Mughira. Rustum reportedly said to the Arab messenger, "I understand that poverty and deprivation caused you to come here. We shall give you sufficient food and supplies if you evacuate our land." Muslim annals mention that Mughira answered saying, "God has sent to us his Prophet. . . , and we are happy to follow him. He ordered us to conduct a holy war against the adversaries of our religion. . . . We invite you to worship Allah alone and to believe in his Prophet; otherwise the sword will decide matters between you and us."[2]

Battle of Qadisiyya, 637

Having failed to convince the Arabs to retreat peacefully, Rustum ordered his army to prepare for combat. A few days passed during which only minor skirmishes took place. Meanwhile, in response to earlier orders from Umar, the Arab troops who had been at Yarmuk advanced on their way to strengthen their fellow warriors at Qadisiyya. As this greatly needed help began to arrive, the Arabs suddenly decided to take the offensive. According to Arab historians, on a dark night the desert-trained soldiers of Arabia, who proudly called themselves the wolves of the desert, took the Persian army by surprise. Relentless fighting continued through the night; by daybreak such severe winds reportedly blew against the Persian forces that the Muslims were able to claim a decisive victory. Struck by havoc and confusion, the Persian troops fled while the Arabs rushed to Rustum's headquarters and slew him in front of his throne.

The Muslim victory at Qadisiyya opened the way for the Arab capture of the cities in Iraq. One year later, in April, 638, Ctesiphon, the Persian capital, was captured as the Sassanian King Yezdegird fled to the northeastern borders of his country, leaving his daughter behind as a prisoner of the Arabs. Ibn Abi Waqqas requested Umar to give him permission to proceed eastward, but, cautious lest the rapid Arab expansion get out of control, Umar ordered him to first consolidate his positions in captured territories.

Battle of Nihawand, 642

The Arabs followed the fleeing Persian troops to the north and east defeating them again at Jalula. Yezdegird crossed the Zagros

[2] Al-Baladhuri, *Futuh al-Buldan* (Cairo, 1900), p. 265.

Mountains and took refuge at Hamadan. According to Umar's order, after capturing Hulwan the Muslim armies halted, allowing Yezdegird and his commanders to consolidate their forces at Hamadan.

Three years later, Yezdegird mustered about 60,000 troops, and, as he was preparing for battle, Umar gave permission to his commander in Kufa to move two-thirds of his armies in Iraq eastward and meet the Persian forces on their own soil. When the two armies met at Nihawand in 642, a violent battle followed, and, although the Persians fought desperately for their land, the Arabs inflicted a costly defeat after which most of the Persian cities lay open to Arab occupation. Because of the great significance of the battle of Nihawand, Muslim historians refer to it as "the battle of battles." Indeed, it brought into Arab hands all the wealth of the Sassanians. Yezdegird himself was hunted from city to city until he was finally captured and killed ten years later, bringing to an inglorious end the line of the great Sassanian monarchs.

Non-Muslims and the Jizya

As the Arabs were consolidating their hold over the vast Persian possessions, many cities capitulated without war, while others surrendered after some resistance. Those cities which peacefully agreed to pay the *jizya*, were assured protection of their lives and property, while the cities which offered resistance were considered spoils of war. This meant that they lay at the disposal of the Arab governor; if he desired he could sell their inhabitants as slaves and capture their properties as booty; or if he liked, he could tolerate them after they payed the *jizya*. In any case, at this early stage of Islamic development, converts to Islam were always exempted from paying the poll tax. As it developed, many non-Arabs were converted to Islam, and, within a few generations, Muslims became the major sector of the population in the Middle East.

CONQUEST OF EGYPT

Religious Struggle in Egypt

While the Arab armies were fighting east of the Mediterranean, the Egyptians had their own internal problems. The Coptic Orthodox Church of Egypt, whose adherents were essentially monophysite in doctrine, faced its bitterest opposition at the hands of another Christian church, namely the Church of Byzantium, whose main orientation was dyophysite. [3] In 451 the Council of Chalcedon declared the dy-

[3] Monophysites believe in the doctrine of the one nature of Christ, while the dyophysites maintain that Christ has two natures.

ophysite doctrines to be correct, a decision the Egyptians stubbornly rejected in spite of threats of persecution and oppression by the Byzantines. In 610 Heraclius ascended the throne of Byzantium, and in 627 he liberated Egypt from Persian occupation. He then devised a monothelite compromise, by which he emphasized the one will of Christ instead of the one nature, and sent an archbishop-governor called Cyrus (Arabic, al-Muqawqas) to impose it upon the Egyptians. The latter rejected Heraclius' compromise; the result was a reign of terror under which the Egyptians suffered greatly. Thus when the Arabs appeared on the Egyptian frontiers as conquerors, some of the Copts of Egypt welcomed them as liberators from Byzantine oppression.

Muslim historians mention that when Muhammad sent a message to al-Muqawqas of Egypt inviting him to accept Islam, the latter responded politely and sent to him a Christian maid, Mariya, whom the Prophet later married. Muhammad is reported to have said to his companions, "God will help you conquer Egypt; therefore, be kind to its Coptic inhabitants for you have there a trust and a brother-in-law." Regardless of the authenticity of this statement, the time to conquer Egypt was ripe when Ibn al-As completed the subjugation of most of the cities in Palestine. Ibn al-As is believed to have visited Egypt in pre-Islamic times and to have seen its wealth and prosperity. He therefore requested Umar in 639 to give him permission to proceed toward the Nile Valley. Before Umar's reply reached Ibn al-As, the latter had already crossed the Egyptian borders south of Palestine. Umar's letter is reported to have asked Ibn al-As to leave Egypt alone if he had not yet gone within its borders; otherwise, he wished him Godspeed.

The Battle of Egypt

Ibn al-As and his troops reached the Egyptian border city of al-Arish in December, 639, and continued their march westward toward Pelusium. There a battle lasting two months took place, after which the Arabs advanced southward. Assured that their line of supplies from Palestine was secure, they captured Balbis and reached the outskirts of Heliopolis, where they were faced with some resistance. Ibn al-As requested Umar to send him reinforcements; meanwhile the Muslim troops maneuvered on the eastern side of the delta for four months waiting for help.

About four thousand fresh troops under the leadership of Zubayr finally arrived from Madina, and almost immediately the Arabs resumed their march and captured Heliopolis. They then besieged a stronghold of the Byzantine forces called the Fort of Babylon. After a month of siege, al-Muqawqas requested negotiations with the Arabs, who gave him three alternatives: (1) Islam, (2) *jizya*, or (3) war. Al-Muqawqas, who in the first place had alienated the Egyptians from rallying around the Byzantine forces, was the first to seek peaceful surrender when the time of trouble approached. He advised Emperor Heraclius to accept the Muslim peace terms requiring the Egyptians to pay tribute; but Heraclius is reported to have refused capitulation and bitterly rebuked al-Muqawqas. However, the Byzantine Emperor died early in 641 as the battle of Babylon was in progress. In April, 641, the Arabs captured the famous fort and moved toward Alexandria.

While the Muslim troops were waiting for Heraclius' response to their terms, they campaigned in the Fayyum and along the western side of the delta. By this time the Egyptians, who apparently thought of gaining supremacy as a result of Arab-Byzantine wars, became disillusioned and began to fight the Arab invaders; but it was too late. Alexandria surrendered in September, 642, and the terms of a renewed agreement between the Arabs and al-Muqawqas went into effect. These terms are summarized as follows:

1. Non-Muslim scriptuaries were each asked to pay two dinars per year as *jizya*.
2. Hostilities were to cease for eleven months.
3. The Muslims agreed to guarantee the safety of the Christian churches, and promised not to interfere in Christian affairs.
4. The Byzantine garrison in Alexandria promised to depart.
5. Jews were allowed to remain in Alexandria as scriptuaries.

Relations Between Arabs and Egyptians

Although the Arabs fought several battles in Egypt, they considered its conquest as peaceful surrender. Therefore, they did not regard its people as slaves or its wealth as booty. On the contrary, the Arabs treated the Egyptians very kindly; they restored their deposed Patriarch Benjamin, whom the Byzantines had exiled. The Egyptians were free to administer local affairs without Muslim interference. To ensure the freedom of the Egyptians, the Arabs built their own city, Fustat, near Heliopolis and ordered all immigrating Arab tribes to settle there. However, as the Muslim community increased through conversions and the Coptic community gradually decreased, the Arabs spread throughout Egypt and became its dominant group.

UMAR'S REIGN

Administration of the Provinces

Ibn al-As is known to have sent two military campaigns from Egypt, one to Libya in North Africa, and the other to Nubia in Central Africa. The main purpose of these campaigns was to impress Egypt's neighbors that its new conquerors were there to stay and repel any possible attacks from either side. Having accomplished his main purpose, Ibn al-As fulfilled Umar's orders and abstained from expansion beyond Barqa on Egypt's western border.

The last years of Umar's caliphate were spent in organizing the affairs of the Arab Empire. Undoubtedly the Arabs realized that the various peoples whose lands they had captured possessed different and also higher material cultures than their own. Therefore, according to Umar's commands, they built special settlements in the conquered territories, where for the first few decades they lived by themselves without having to mix with their subject populations. Chief of these Arab settlements, which later developed into major cities, were Kufa and Basra in Iraq, Jabiya in Syria, and Fustat in Egypt. Meanwhile, subject peoples, at least during Umar's time, were left free to conduct their business and cultivate their land on condition they paid the *jizya*. Another tax, the *kharaj* (property tax), was supposed to be collected from those who owned taxable property regardless of whether they were Muslims or not. However, during the early period of the Arab Empire, many Muslims who owned property did not pay taxes and the burden of financing the state rested almost completely upon non-Muslims.

Umar's Assassination

With the conquest of Egypt completed in 642, the Arabs had established an empire that comprised a significant part of the civilized world. Expansion was so swift that Umar himself was afraid lest the Arabs would misuse the great wealth which they suddenly acquired. He therefore issued explicit orders to Ibn al-As not to cross the boundaries of Egypt toward North Africa and to Ibn Abi Waqqas not to go eastward beyond the Persian borders.

Umar possessed perhaps the greatest authority of any head of state during his time, yet he lived an extremely modest life. He refused to be escorted by bodyguards or accompanied by any sort of entourage. On several occasions he reportedly slipped away alone to inspect the conditions of his people and to give help to the needy.

A Persian slave named Abu Lu'lu'a, who had come to Madina with his master, Mughira,[4] wanted to complain to the caliph about some injustice. The caliph apparently did not give him the attention he wanted. One morning early in November, 644, as Umar was getting ready to lead his companions in prayer, Abu Lu'lu'a stabbed him six times and then stabbed himself. The caliph was carried to his own chamber seriously wounded. Knowing that he had but a few hours to live, he invited an old companion of the Prophet named Ibn Awf to be his successor. When the latter declined, Umar named seven of the Prophet's companions to act as a committee to select his successor. The next morning, after requesting to be buried beside the Prophet and Abu Bakr, he quietly passed away. Umar goes down in Islamic history as a great administrator; his greatness was immensely enhanced by his modesty.

[4] This is the same person who met with Rustum before the battle of Qadisiyya. See p. 145.

CHAPTER 23

UTHMAN, 644-656

THE HOUSEHOLD OF ISLAM

Levying of Taxes

Laws regulating relations between Muslims and non-Muslims in conquered lands were based mainly on the provisions in (1) the Constitution of Madina instituted by Muhammad himself in 622, (2) the Constitution of Umar prepared during the surrender of Jerusalem in 638, and (3) the terms of the capitulation of Alexandria in 642.

According to these laws, territories captured by Muslim armies were considered part of *dar al-Islam*, "the household of Islam," to which numerous tribes immigrated and lived in newly built Arab settlements. The Arabs were in charge of protecting the frontiers of the household of Islam against attacks; accordingly, they were not expected to engage in domestic duties such as farming. They were, however, supported by subsidies known as *ata'at*, periodically distributed to them by the governors of the provinces.

Next in rank to the Arabs were the non-Arab Muslims. These were converts to Islam who had abandoned their own communities and attached themselves to Arab tribes as clients or *mawali*. Since the *mawali* were exempted from paying *jizya*, "poll tax" (imposed only on non-Muslims), their numbers continued to increase. It is believed that by the middle of the twelfth century, conversions had made the Muslims the majority of the inhabitants of the Middle East. Muslim converts, however, were required to pay an annual property tax known as *kharaj* on whatever taxable property they possessed.

Third in rank were the scriptuaries or *dhimmis* consisting of Jews, Christians, and other sects who believed in a revealed book. During the early stages of the Arab Empire, *dhimmis* composed the majority of the household of Islam and were required to pay poll tax as well as property tax. As time went on, many of the *dhimmis* were converted to Islam and became exempted from the poll tax. Pagans and infidels were not allowed (at least theoretically) to live in *dar al-Islam* since Muhammad had asked the Muslims to fight them.

Distribution of Taxes

Taxes levied from the *dhimmis* (non-Arab non-Muslims) and from the *mawali* (non-Arab Muslims) were deposited in the treasury of each province. One-fifth of these taxes was to go to Madina for the support of the inhabitants of the homeland. A major portion of the taxes was distributed as *ata'at,* "gifts," to the Arab warriors living in the provinces; the remainder was divided among the governor and his army commanders. Levying taxes was the responsibility of the governors of provinces, but rules were not enforced with equal rigor by each governor. Depending on varying circumstances, certain governors exempted the *mawalis* from property taxes and instead increased the poll taxes paid by the *dhimmis*. Other governors insisted that the *mawalis* continue to pay not only property taxes but also poll taxes. On occasion, some governors considered the property of the *dhimmis* who surrendered after fighting as *ghanima,* "booty," and felt free to seize it. As a result, the Arab elite, whether living in the provinces or in Arabia proper, built houses, wore silk garments, and enjoyed a life of luxury and prosperity.

Under such circumstances, Uthman became caliph, and in contrast to the modest Umar, he embarked on a course of extreme luxury, the like of which the Arabs had never seen. During Uthman's reign the Arabs began to enjoy the fabulous wealth of the Persians and Byzantines, but also fell prey to bitterness and disruption within the Islamic state. From Uthman's election till the fall of the Arab Empire, strife and factionalism never departed from the household of Islam.

UTHMAN'S ADMINISTRATION

Uthman's Election

Before his death, Umar assigned seven of the most trusted companions of the Prophet to the task of selecting his successor. The seven included Ali (the Prophet's cousin), Uthman, Ibn Abi Waqqas,

Ibn Awf, Zubayr, Talha, and Umar's own son, Abd-Allah. The dying
caliph is reported to have told them to deliberate for three days, and to
select the "Commander of the Faithful" by the fourth day. However,
the committee failed to agree, perhaps because each wished to be
caliph himself. Ibn Awf, the eldest, reportedly withdrew from nomination and asked others to follow, but none did so. He therefore asked
Ali to name the person whom he would nominate if he were not involved
in the matter. Ali suggested Uthman. Ibn Awf then asked Uthman the
same question, and Uthman recommended Ali. When Ibn Awf requested
the remaining four members for their votes, they split between Ali
and Uthman, placing the deciding vote in the hands of Ibn Awf.

Beginning of Disruption

Ibn Awf reportedly went to the people and asked their opinion. Since
Ali represented the Hashim line of Quraysh, and Uthman the Umayyad
line, the Muslims split into two groups. Muslim historians report
that a leader of Hashim, called Ammar, nominated Ali, while an
Umayyad leader named Ibn Abi Sarh nominated Uthman. Followers of
each group began to shout as they called out the name of their candidate. Skirmishes between the two factions took place in which Ibn Abi
Sarh reportedly insulted Ammar saying, "When did you become a
counselor to the Muslims?" A riot threatened, but Ibn Awf took matters
into his own hands and, according to Muslim reports, asked Ali what
he would do if entrusted with the caliphate. Ali responded by saying that
he would follow the tradition of the Prophet and his successors as well
as his own judgment. When Uthman was faced with the same question,
he responded by indicating his willingness to follow only the traditions
of his predecessors. Accordingly, Ibn Awf cast his deciding vote for
Uthman, who was immediately proclaimed caliph. Although the Muslims
pledged their allegiance to Uthman according to Arab customs, their
ranks were split between Hashim and Umayya.

Uthman and the Governors of the Provinces

Having deposed Khalid from his command in Syria in 636, Umar
appointed al-Jarrah not only as commander-in-chief of the Arab armies
but also as governor of Syria. However, al-Jarrah died of bubonic
plague in 639 and was followed by Mu'awiya, a leader destined to
establish the strong Umayyad dynasty in 661 with its capital in Damascus. Being a cousin of Uthman, Mu'awiya was retained as governor
of Syria after Umar's death.

Ibn al-As, the conqueror of Egypt, also became its governor. Surrounded by the wealth of Egypt, Ibn al-As neglected to send enough food
and support to Madina and was therefore deposed from the governorship
of Upper Egypt, retaining Lower Egypt only. Ibn Abi Sarh, a milk
brother of Uthman (having nursed from the same woman), was appointed to share with Ibn al-As the responsibilities of governing Egypt and

sending supplies to Arabia. When Uthman became caliph he completely removed Ibn al-As from Egypt and appointed Ibn Abi Sarh in his place.

On the Iraqi-Persian front, Ibn Abi Waqqas was appointed supreme governor after the surrender of Ctesiphon in 638. He made his capital in Kufa, and was assisted by Mughira in Basra and Ash'ari in Khuzistan. However, Mughira was accused of adultery and recalled to Madina while Ash'ari became governor of both Khuzistan and Basra. Meanwhile complaints reached Umar against Ibn Abi Waqqas, who was therefore removed from his post. His immediate replacement proved to be very weak, and finally in 642 Umar announced Mughira's innocence and reappointed him governor of Iraq, while Ash'ari continued to be governor of Persia. When Uthman became caliph, he recalled Mughira and replaced him with two of his own relatives, one in Kufa and the other in Basra.

In Hijaz itself, Uthman appointed his cousin Marwan to be governor of Madina and allowed him to receive one-fifth of some booty captured in North Africa. Since Marwan was reportedly once dismissed from the presence of the Prophet, the Muslims in Hijaz never forgave Uthman for this appointment.

Conquests During Uthman's Caliphate

Having imprudently appointed most of his relatives as governors of the provinces, Uthman apparently decided to relax in Madina and enjoy a comfortable life of luxury and prosperity. The governors were able to rule almost independently, especially since the caliph in Madina sanctioned their acts and decisions without reservation.

No sooner had Ibn Abi Sarh settled in his new position as governor in Egypt, than the Byzantines under Manuel recaptured Alexandria with a naval contingent. Muslim annals mention that the Copts themselves requested Uthman to send back Ibn al-As because of his previous experience with the Byzantines. The caliph reportedly agreed and ordered Ibn al-As to take over the command in 645. The Arabs and the Byzantines met in battle south of Alexandria, and once more the Arabs won. The defeated troops were pursued until they completely evacuated the shores of Egypt. This victory made the Arabs' position in Egypt secure. With the ensuing immigration of many Arab tribes to Egypt, the ancient land of the pharaohs became a stronghold of the Arabs and Islam.

After the defeat of the Byzantines at Alexandria, Ibn Abi Sarh — still governor — felt secure enough to attempt the conquest of North Africa. He crossed the borders at Barqa, where Ibn al-As had been previously ordered to stop, and penetrated deep into African territories. However, since no information about the progress of the war was received in Madina, Uthman dispatched Zubayr, who had come to the help of Ibn al-As during the siege of the Fort of Babylon in 640, to help Ibn Abi Sarh in Africa. Zubayr's tactics helped the Arabs to win a victory after which they returned to Egypt. In 654 Ibn Abi Sarh sent a campaign against Nubia, resulting in a trade agreement by which the Nubians would sell slaves to the Arabs in exchange for grains.

In Syria, Mu'awiya pressed the Byzantines driving them deep into Anatolia. However, the main Byzantine threat was from the sea, and therefore Mu'awiya decided to build a navy and attack them at the threshold of their own home. In 649 about two hundred ships were built in Egypt and Syria for the transport of a whole army. While these ships were being built, the Muslims continued to make regular raids on the Byzantine troops along the Mediterranean coast north of Syria. As the Byzantine navy once more advanced against Alexandria, the Arab navy, by that time ready for combat, moved in the opposite direction and the two navies met in a severe battle called *Dhat al-Sawari* "battle of the masts." Apparently huge losses were incurred on both sides, since only a few ships returned to their respective ports.

As the news of Umar's murder by a Persian slave reached Persian cities beyond the Zagros Mountains, rebellion erupted. However, Uthman's relatives in Kufa and Basra dispatched Arab troops and quickly put down these revolts. While doing so, they captured more cities lying both on the eastern borders toward India and on the northern borders as far as Marv and Adharbayjan.

UTHMAN'S ASSASSINATION

Arab Dissatisfaction With Uthman

The life of luxury which Uthman led in Madina was considered by many of his companions as an innovation to the Arab way of life. It has been reported by Islamic historians that Uthman used to order meals of huge amounts of lean meat as well as white bread baked of the finest flour sifted especially for him. He reportedly wore gorgeous silk brocade garments and covered his teeth with gold plates. Since the desert Arabs were not used to such luxury, criticism of the caliph began, first secretly and then in the open. One of the Prophet's companions, al-Ghifari by name, volunteered to travel to several places in the Arab Empire calling attention to the luxury of Uthman, branding riches and prosperity as anti-Islamic innovations. In an attempt to get rid of al-Ghifari and his criticism, Uthman sent him to Damascus to his cousin Mu'awiya. Al-Ghifari thereupon began a campaign against Mu'awiya himself, who was forced to send him back to Madina; eventually only death relieved Uthman of the severe criticism of the old companion.

The Arab warriors living in the several Arab settlements and border towns throughout the Islamic Empire fought fewer battles during Uthman's reign than they had during Umar's. Since they were not allowed to mix with the population and participate in domestic affairs, and because revenue was regularly delivered to them by the governors, they became idle. Leading such a life of ease and comfort, they drifted into gossip and open criticism. Uthman's imprudent behavior offered an opportunity not only to talk and criticize, but also to take sides in a conflict.

Umayya Versus Hashim

It should be remembered that when Ibn Awf cast his deciding vote against Ali in favor of Uthman, he in fact bypassed the Prophet's clan, Hashim, and allowed its rival, Umayya, to take power. This action split the Arab tribes into two factions, the pro-Hashims and the pro-Umayyads. The prestige of Ibn Awf prevented an open split immediately after Umar's death, but when Ibn Awf died and Uthman began to indulge in nepotism and luxury, dissatisfaction became intense. The rift between the supporters of Hashim and those of Umayya continued to widen as time went by.

Growing Dissatisfaction With Uthman

As disputes increased and murmuring spread among the Arabs, who had become sharply split over the behavior of Uthman, delegates from the provinces came to Madina to discuss matters with the aging caliph. Uthman reportedly promised to look carefully into their complaints and do his best toward reform. However, when they left Madina, Uthman told his associates that the delegates confessed that all the unfavorable rumors had been erroneous and grossly exaggerated. This misleading report by the caliph was counted against him, and many accused him of lying.

Uthman and the Egyptian Delegation

Shortly after this episode, the Egyptian Arabs sent a delegation to Uthman complaining against Ibn Abi Sarh, governor of Egypt. Uthman promised them to take action concerning Ibn Abi Sarh, but instead sent a message to his governor in Egypt asking him to punish the rebels. This letter was intercepted by the delegation on the way back to Egypt. Upon reading it, they returned to Madina and besieged the caliph's house. They asked him about the contents of the intercepted letter, but he denied any knowledge of it. Accordingly, the Egyptian Arabs informed him that either he knew about the letter or he did not; if he did know, he was a liar to deny the fact. In case he did not know, it would follow that his secretary was writing messages stamped with the caliph's seal without authorization. Either of these possibilities, they told Uthman, was enough to disqualify him as caliph. They officially requested him to resign, but he refused, instead sending a plea for help to his cousin Mu'awiya. Curiously enough, Arab leaders in Madina are reported to have left the city and Uthman was left alone to face his fate.

When the rebels found out about Uthman's plea to Mu'awiya, they broke into his house and began assaulting the old man, who was silently reading the Qur'an. This seems to have aroused the rebels' anger for they then stabbed and clubbed him to death. As his wife tried to shield him in her bosom, a sword severed two of her fingers. The rebels left the house and called upon the Arabs to choose another caliph. Meanwhile, the Arab chiefs who had left Madina returned, and the consensus of Arab opinion favored Ali, who was invited to assume the caliphate. Ali accepted the office he had sought since the Prophet's death and dispatched letters to all the provinces informing the governors of his appointment. In the meantime, Uthman's wife sent the dead caliph's coat and her two severed fingers to Mu'awiya in Syria, who displayed them in the mosque and called upon loyal Umayyads to seek revenge. By then, the split in the Muslim camp became more polarized as some Arabs sided with Ali supporting Hashim, and others sided with Mu'awiya supporting Umayya. As Uthman's wife arranged for the burial of her husband, the Muslim world moved toward civil war.

CHAPTER 24

ALI, 656-661

CIVIL WAR

Forces Against Ali

Those who offered the caliphate to Ali in Madina were mostly Arabs from the provinces, strengthened by the support of some dissatisfied companions of the Prophet. However, a few companions who sympathized with the murdered caliph refused to pledge their allegiance to Ali, allowing several young Arabs to follow suit. In Syria, where Mu'awiya had exhibited the blood-stained garment of Uthman and the severed fingers of his wife, many outraged Arabs rallied behind their governor seeking revenge for the spilled Umayyad blood. In Iraq, however, the Arabs were split between the two camps; those in Basra supported Ali while their opponents in Kufa called for his deposition.

In Madina, two old companions of the Prophet, Talha and Zubayr, allied themselves against Ali and were greatly encouraged by the support of the Prophet's most beloved widow, A'isha. It may be remembered that Ali had once requested Muhammad to divorce her after the incident of the slander,[1] but the Prophet refused Ali's request and produced a revelation exonerating her. It appears that A'isha had suppressed resentment against Ali since the incident; when the opportunity availed itself, she aligned herself against her husband's cousin.

[1] See p. 114.

Battle of the Camel, 656

Since most of the followers of the tripartite alliance of Talha, Zubayr, and A'isha were in Kufa, the three leaders left Madina for Iraq. They sent a contingent of warriors to discipline Ali's supporters in Basra in an effort to claim supremacy over all Iraq. However, Ali gathered his supporters and marched toward Kufa to put down the revolt. Assuming the leadership of the tripartite alliance, A'isha ordered Talha and Zubayr to meet Ali in battle. Encouraging her followers to fight, she rode out before them on a camel in an effort to incite them against the Prophet's own cousin and son-in-law. Ali's efforts to avoid conflict collapsed, and a severe battle between fellow Muslims followed. Talha and Zubayr were killed and A'isha's camel was seriously wounded as Ali claimed a victory that at least assured him of the loyalty of Iraqi Arabs. He reportedly treated A'isha with due respect and sent her back to Makka, where she lived quietly until her death in 678.

Battle of Siffin, 657

Most of the Arabs living in Syria were strong supporters of Uthman, who was also related to them by marriage. According to tribal customs, many of them vowed not to bathe or sleep on comfortable beds till Uthman's blood was avenged. Mu'awiya was thereby able to muster an army of strong Umayyad supporters willing to sacrifice themselves to redeem the reputation of their clan.' Early in 657 Mu'awiya marched at the head of his troops toward Iraq as Ali and his supporters marched from Kufa. The two Muslim armies met at Siffin, a small village west of the Euphrates on the Syrian-Iraqi border. It may be recalled that a few decades before, the Arabs of Hira had engaged in numerous feuds against the Arabs of Ghassan in support of their respective superiors, Persia and Byzantium. In fact, the battle of Siffin may be considered a revival of the old struggle between the rulers of Iraq and those of Syria, whose roots can be traced back not only to the Persian-Byzantine wars, but also to the Parthian-Roman conflicts in classical history, and to the Babylonian-Egyptian quarrels in ancient history.

The battle of Siffin was actually a series of quarrels interrupted by rhetorical debates and personal duels between members of the two Muslim camps. During these quarrels, Ali and Mu'awiya exchanged several messages in which the caliph requested the disobedient governor to recognize his caliphate and avoid further bloodshed. Mu'awiya refused to submit to Ali unless the latter would surrender the murderers of Uthman. Ali's troops refused and sent a message to Mu'awiya telling him that all soldiers in Ali's camp were Uthman's murderers. Relentless fighting resumed as hundreds of Muslim warriors on both sides sacrificed their lives for the sake of their respective leaders.

RESORT TO ARBITRATION

Agreement to Arbitrate

As fighting continued during the battle of Siffin, disgust and resentment at the slaughter of fellow Muslim believers spread throughout the two camps. Considered a rebellious governor, Mu'awiya received most of the blame for the strife and bloodshed within the household of Islam. As Ali's troops were on the verge of victory, Ibn al-As, now fighting on Mu'awiya's side, resorted to a tactful trick to thwart the caliph's triumph. Ibn al-As requested Mu'awiya to lift up on several spears the copy of the Qur'an that had been sent to Damascus during Uthman's time. This action was calculated to halt hostilities. When Ali's troops saw the Qur'an lifted up, they reportedly stopped fighting, and Mu'awiya took advantage of the lull to seek arbitration. In harmony with Arab customs as well as the general consensus within his own camp, Ali agreed to arbitration and signed a temporary pact with Mu'awiya to halt all hostilities between the two camps. Ali delegated Ash'ari as his chief representative to negotiate a final agreement with Ibn al-As, who was sent by Mu'awiya as his chief advisor.

Failure of Arbitration

During the month of Ramadan, 658, Ibn al-As and Ash'ari, with their respective delegations, met at Adhruh. A firm believer in the Islamic tradition that Muslims should not murder Muslims, Ash'ari was willing to accept any formula that would stop fighting and bloodshed. Ibn al-As, on the contrary, being a tactful military commander who wanted victory for his side at all costs, threatened Ash'ari with continued warfare until the sword decided the fate of the Arab Empire. Ash'ari agreed to a proposal which included deposing both Ali and Mu'awiya and referring the whole matter to the Muslim people. Since that was the original request of Mu'awiya, who actually had never been acclaimed as caliph, Ibn al-As accepted the compromise proposal. Accordingly, both chief delegates agreed to stand before the Muslim peoples and announce the deposition of their respective superiors.

Before a huge crowd of anxious Muslims, Ash'ari and Ibn al-As stood up to announce their verdict. Ash'ari was the first to speak and announced the deposition of Ali. Ibn al-As followed him and shrewdly announced that since his opponent agreed to depose his master, he would like to nominate Mu'awiya for the caliphate. Immediately Ash'ari denounced Ibn al-As's nomination as a deceitful betrayal. Arbitration collapsed as Ali decided to resume fighting till the sword would decide matters between him and Mu'awiya.

ISLAMIC SECTS

Further Rifts in the Household of Islam

As soon as Ali accepted arbitration to decide the fate of his office, his own supporters split into two groups: the Kharijites, meaning "outlaws," and the Shi'ites, meaning "adherents." The Kharijites sharply criticized Ali for disregarding his divinely vouchsafed office and subjecting it to human negotiations and deliberations. They contrasted him to his predecessor, Uthman, who accepted the fate of a martyr's death rather than renounce his divine right to the caliphate. By his shameful behavior, the Kharijites argued, Ali had actually renounced his rights to the caliphate and, therefore, supporting him was contrary to the spirit of Islam. They promoted among themselves the doctrine of choosing for the office of the caliphate the best-qualified Muslim —regardless of his clan, tribe, race, or color. As arbitration collapsed, allowing Ali to reclaim his prerogatives as caliph, the Kharijites rebelled and began to spread sedition and discord among the Muslims of Iraq.

In their stubborn opposition to Ali's caliphate, the Kharijites actually became his bitter opponents, causing the Shi'ites (Ali's adherents) to react to the other extreme and support Ali's caliphate by all means at their disposal. The Shi'ites circulated a saying attributed to Muhammad during his last pilgrimage to Makka: "Whomsoever I am his lord, Ali is his lord also. May Allah support his supporters and fight his opponents." Accordingly, the Shi'ites announced the disqualification of the three preceding caliphs — Abu Bakr, Umar, and Uthman —maintaining that Ali had been the Prophet's choice as leader of the Islamic community. Furthermore, they announced Ali to be their imam as well as their caliph. An imam, according to the Shi'ite doctrines, was a religious leader capable of introducing laws having the same binding force as the Qur'an and Traditions. In their stubborn support of Ali, the Shi'ites went as far as to declare the imamate a divine and hereditary office restricted to the household of Ali.

Ali and the Kharijites

Muslim annals report that Ali tried several times to pacify the Kharijites insisting repeatedly that arbitration did not mean his abandonment of the caliphate. However, all his efforts were in vain; the Kharijites withdrew from the battleground and began to concentrate in Harura, near Kufa (for this reason, they are sometimes called the Harurites). Taking advantage of Ali's absence on the Syrian front, they spread their rebellious doctrines among the peoples of Kufa and Ctesiphon, who became greatly confused by the new Kharijite doctrines and especially by their call to open rebellion. Ali was obliged to leave Siffin and return to Kufa in order to put down the Kharijite rebellion. Toward the end of 658, Ali defeated the Kharijites near Nahrawan; their remnants went underground and were a serious threat to the stability of the Islamic state for a long time.

CESSATION OF HOSTILITIES

Agreement Between Ali and Mu'awiya

While Ali was occupied in fighting the Kharijites at home, Mu'awiya had an opportunity to consolidate his position in Syria and the western portion of the Arab Empire. Ali had appointed Muhammad, son of Abu Bakr, as governor of Egypt to replace Ibn Abi Sarh, Uthman's protégé. But before Muhammad could become familiar with the situation there, Mu'awiya dispatched Ibn al-As, an old hand in Egypt, to capture the Nile Valley. Ibn al-As took Muhammad by surprise, inflicted a quick defeat on him, and claimed Egypt as Mu'awiya's domain. This was a tremendous boost to the Umayyad rule in Syria and a serious blow to Ali's cause.

By the time Ali was ready to resume fighting with Mu'awiya, the latter had strengthened his position and was capable of bringing about the final downfall of the Hashimite caliphate. Accordingly, the leaders of the two Islamic camps, Ali and Mu'awiya, made a gentleman's agreement by which all hostilities would cease on condition that Ali would leave the western part of the Arab Empire fully under Mu'awiya's control.

Death of Ali

The great concession which Ali was forced to make to Mu'awiya aroused bitter indignation among the Kharijite group, who decided to take matters into their own hands. They blamed Ali for his failure to maintain the authority of his office and blamed Mu'awiya for his personal greed and complete disregard for the dignity of the caliphate. They decided to rid the Islamic community of the two "ill-fitted" leaders and to give the Muslims an opportunity to select a new caliph. Two of their adherents were assigned to murder the rival leaders on a designated day. When that day arrived, the person in charge of murdering Mu'awiya failed, but the assassination of Ali was accomplished. Ali's murderer, Ibn Muljam, met him at the mosque on January 20, 661, and stabbed him, reportedly saying, "Authority belongs to Allah not you, Ali!" The fourth caliph died and was buried at Najaf near Kufa, which became a sacred shrine for all Shi'ite adherents.

IMPORTANT TERMS

Abu Lu'lu'a: A Persian slave brought to Madina by Mughira. He assassinated Umar in 644.

Al-Ghifari: A companion of the Prophet who criticized the luxury of both Uthman and Mu'awiya.

Ali: Muhammad's cousin and son-in-law. He was among the early believers in Islam. He became a caliph in 656, after the murder of Uthman. During his reign, the Islamic community was torn by civil war between his followers and those of Mu'awiya.

Al-Jarrah: Arab commander in the wars against Syria. He became its governor and died of bubonic plague in 639.

Al-Muqawqas: Bishop and governor of Egypt during the rule of the Byzantine emperor Heraclius. He surrendered Egypt to the Arabs in 642.

Ash'ari: A warrior in Persia, who also became its governor. He represented Ali during the arbitration between Ali and Mu'awiya in 658.

Fustat: An Arab town in Egypt built near the Fort of Babylon shortly after the Arab conquest.

Heraclius: The Byzantine emperor faced with Arab expansion into Egypt and Syria. He died in 641 during the siege of Alexandria.

Ibn Abi Waqqas: An Arab commander sent to help in the conquest of Iraq; he fought at the battle of Qadisiyya in 637, became governor of Iraq, and was later deposed by Umar.

Ibn al-As: A great warrior and politician. He conquered Egypt in 640, became its governor, and was deposed by Umar. He supported Mu'awiya in his wars against Ali.

Ibn Muljam: A member of the Kharijite sect who assassinated Ali in 661 as a part of a plot to eliminate the claimants to the caliphate.

Kharijites: A group of Ali's followers who rebelled against him when he accepted arbitration with Mu'awiya. The Kharijites became among the strongest enemies of Ali and finally plotted his murder.

Mu'awiya: A cousin of Uthman who opposed Ali's caliphate and sought to revenge the murder of his cousin. As governor of Syria, he rebelled against Ali and continued to fight him until Ali's death. Mu'awiya founded the Umayyad dynasty.

Mughira: An Arab warrior in Iraq. He became governor of Kufa after the Arab conquest but was recalled to Madina by Umar on charges of adultery. He was acquitted and sent back to Kufa.

Nihawand: The second major battle against the Persians. After the Arab victory at Nihawand in 642, Persia surrendered and the Sassanian kingdom ended.

Qadisiyya: A major battle between the Arabs and Persians in 637, after which Iraq became Arab territory.

Shi'ites: The followers of Ali who supported him against the Kharijites. The Shi'ites became a sect in Islam calling for restriction of leadership in the Islamic community to the household of Ali.

Siffin: A battle between Ali and Mu'awiya in 657, after which both sides agreed on arbitration.

Uthman: A distant cousin of the Prophet from the Umayyad clan. He served as one of Muhammad's secretaries and became caliph in 644. His murder in 656 touched off a feud between the Hashimite and the Umayyad clans of the Quraysh tribe.

Yamama: A stronghold of apostasy in Arabia that erupted after the Prophet's death. Khalid fought and defeated the apostates at the battle of Yamama in 633.

Yarmuk: Important battle between the Arab and Byzantine forces in Syria fought in 636.

SUPPLEMENTARY READINGS

ARNOLD, THOMAS W., *The Caliphate* (Oxford, 1924).

BROCKELMANN, CARL, *History of the Islamic Peoples* (New York, 1947).

BUTLER, ALFRED, *The Arab Conquest of Egypt* (Oxford, 1902).

DENNET, D.C., *Conversion and Poll Tax in Early Islam* (Cambridge, 1950).

GABRIELI, F., *The Arabs — a Compact History* (New York, 1963).

GLUBB, SIR JOHN BAGOT, *The Great Arab Conquests* (Englewood Cliffs, N.J., 1963).

HITTI, PHILIP K., *History of the Arabs* (New York, 1960).

_____, *The Origins of the Islamic State* [a translation of al-Baladhuri's *Futuh al-Buldan*] (Beirut, 1966).

LEWIS, BERNARD, *The Arabs in History* (London, 1954).

MUIR, WILLIAM, *The Caliphate* (Edinburgh, 1924).

RUSTUM, A.J. and C.F. ZURAYK, *History of the Arabs and Arabic Culture* (Beirut, 1940).

SPULER, B., *The Muslim World, The Age of the Caliphs* (Leiden, 1960).

TRITTON, A., *The Caliphs and Their Non-Muslim Subjects* (Oxford, 1930).

PART Vii

THE UMAYYAD DYNASTY, 661-750

Although all four orthodox caliphs belonged to the tribe of Quraysh, they were not closely related to each other nor descended from each other. Their rule may be roughly called a republican form of government, in which the caliph usually reigned supreme.

The first Umayyad caliph, Mu'awiya I (661-680), changed the succession from an informal type of selection to dynastic rule. The chief weakness of this dynastic rule, as the Umayyads inaugurated it, was the fact that each reigning caliph assumed the responsibility of choosing his successor (or sometimes successors) from among his own sons, or, under certain circumstances, from among his close relatives, leading to long periods of uncertainty regarding the exact identity of the succeeding caliph. The Umayyad regime became characterized by numerous quarrels and disputes among the Umayyad factions on the one hand, and between Umayyads and Hashimites on the other.

Although Mu'awiya I was almost unanimously acclaimed as caliph immediately after Ali's assassination in 661, his successors found it difficult to consolidate their power. Before the Umayyads finally held authority over the entire Arab Empire, they murdered the Prophet's own grandson, Husayn ibn Ali, and twice bombarded Makka itself, causing considerable damage to the Muslim holy city and to its sacred shrine, the Ka'ba.

During the Umayyad regime, the Arab Empire extended its frontiers to the borders of France in the west and the borders of China in the east. Arabs ruled most of Spain, all of North Africa, the Middle East Proper, Persia, Transoxiana, and northern India. Nevertheless, chronic factional disputes among the Umayyads themselves (such as between the Yamanites and the Qaysites) greatly contributed to the eventual decline and fall of the Umayyad regime.

CHAPTER 25

UMAYYA VERSUS HASHIM

The twenty-five years between the capture of Makka in 631 and the assassination of Uthman in 656 was a period of intense religious devotion, strengthened by enthusiasm for political expansion. Many zealous believers sacrificed themselves to promote the cause of their religion. Personal relations between Muslims were based mainly on principles of religious equality and mutual cooperation; the worst crime a believer could commit was to spill the blood of another believer.

However, as Islam entered a period of material luxury, religious zeal waned, piety was abandoned, and fraternity forgotten. The brutal murder of Uthman at the hands of fellow believers marked a transformation in the behavior of Muslim believers. Personal gain appears to have become more important than religious principles; to achieve certain political goals, believers not only attempted to murder fellow believers, but dared to spill the blood of the Prophet's closest relatives and bombard the most sacred of all Islamic shrines, the Ka'ba.

MU'AWIYA I, 661-680

Mu'awiya Proclaimed Caliph

After the murder of Ali, Mu'awiya was proclaimed caliph in both Syria and Egypt while Hasan, son of Ali, called upon the people of Kufa to support his claim to the caliphate. Recognizing that Mu'awiya was better equipped militarily, the Arabs of Iraq hesitated to pledge allegiance to Hasan. When Mu'awiya sent representatives to negotiate with Hasan, the latter was willing to renounce his claim in return for a generous pension Mu'awiya offered.

Mu'awiya went to Kufa, where he gained the allegiance of its citizens, thereby uniting the Arab ranks for the first time since Uthman's assassination. Islamic annals refer to the year 661 as *am al-jama'a*, "the year of unity." At that time, open opposition to the Umayyad caliphate ceased. Its opponents went temporarily underground in preparation for the next round of strife and contention, which began immediately after Mu'awiya's death. To ensure tranquility in Iraq, Mu'awiya appointed his ruthless foster brother Ziyad as governor of Kufa.[1] Ziyad ruled Iraq with an iron hand; as long as he was governor the Arabs of Kufa and Basra remained under firm control.

Beginning of the Umayyad Dynasty

Some of Mu'awiya's advisors reportedly counseled him to designate his son Yazid as his successor. Mu'awiya, however, sought the advice of his foster brother Ziyad. Fearing renewal of hostilities among Muslims, Ziyad advised the caliph to wait a little longer. When Ziyad died, Mu'awiya discussed designating his son as heir with his cousin Marwan at Madina, who also advised him against it for fear of possible opposition on the part of the Hashimites. Nevertheless, Mu'awiya named Yazid as his successor. The Arabs of Syria, Egypt, and Iraq supported him; however, as expected, leaders of the Hashim clan in Madina strongly opposed Mu'awiya's appointment and refused to pledge their allegiance to Yazid. The chief Hashimite leaders were Husayn ibn (son of) Ali, Abd-Allah ibn Abi Bakr, and Ibn Zubayr. Mu'awiya went to Madina, met first with the Prophet's widow A'isha to gain her support, and then met with his three Hashimite opponents, who continued to reject his plans. As a last resort, he reportedly ordered two soldiers to stand behind each of the three opponents as he made his final request for their support of his designation. Under this threat, the three Hashim leaders gave their approval to Mu'awiya's plan and, at least outwardly, supported Yazid as his successor.

In so doing, Mu'awiya succeeded not only in transferring the caliphate to the Umayyad clan, but also in transforming it to a hereditary monarchial institution. Mu'awiya himself emulated many features of Byzantine royal life; he initiated a palace court, surrounded himself with a royal entourage, and established the caliph's bodyguard. During the Umayyad period, Damascus was a royal city, capital of the Arab Empire, and residence of its sovereign "Commander of the Faithful" with all the pomp and show that accompanied the caliph's court.

[1]According to Arab historians, Ziyad was the illegitimate son of Mu'awiya's father by a harlot named Sumayya.

YAZID I, 680-683

Opposition to Yazid's Rule

Mu'awiya died in 680 after a rule of almost twenty years. His shrewd tactics and wise selection of subordinates had kept the empire secure from internal rifts. However, as soon as Yazid assumed the caliphate, resistance to the Umayyad rule was resumed. Supporters of the Hashim clan in Kufa refused to accept Yazid, while in Madina, Husayn, Ibn Zubayr, and Ibn Abi Bakr vehemently opposed his caliphate. To the detriment of the Hashimite cause, these three opponents did not act with unity against Yazid. Husayn and Ibn Zubayr each claimed the caliphate for himself while Ibn Abi Bakr withdrew from the race. When Yazid began his rule, two main trouble spots emerged – Kufa and Madina. Yazid acted swiftly and firmly; the result was the resumption of civil war with more tragic consequences than those of any of the preceding wars between Ali and Mu'awiya.

Massacre at Karbala in 680

Fearful of the vengeance of the Umayyad governor in Madina, both Husayn and Ibn Zubayr fled to Makka, where they took refuge near the sacred shrine. Meanwhile, Husayn received messages from Kufa inviting him to Iraq, where many Hashim supporters had promised to fight for him against Yazid. Husayn hesitated, but many of his followers encouraged him to trust the Kufans in spite of the fact that once before they had failed to support his father Ali. On the other hand, Ibn Zubayr knew very well that as long as Husayn was in Hijaz, his own chances of becoming caliph were slim. He therefore urged Husayn to trust the Kufans and leave for Iraq. Despite the encouragement to go to Kufa, Husayn was still reluctant. Instead of going himself, he sent his cousin Muslim to assess the situation and report to him. Muslim found most of Kufa's inhabitants very enthusiastic about Husayn with almost no opposition to his rule. Accordingly, he sent a message to his cousin in Hijaz encouraging him to come to Iraq and reclaim his father's domain.

In the meantime, Yazid had been consulting with his advisors regarding steps to crush the opposition in Kufa. The consensus in Damascus was to send Ibn Ziyad, a man known to be as ruthless and bloodthirsty as his father, at the head of a contingent of Umayyad supporters with full authority to handle the situation as he saw fit. Thus, both Husayn and Ibn Ziyad were to converge on Kufa from different directions. Ibn Ziyad arrived early enough to terrorize the Kufans by executing some of their leaders. He captured Muslim before the latter had a chance to warn his trusting cousin against coming to

Kufa and made it clear that if Husayn's supporters rose up against Yazid, a blood bath for all the sons of Hashim would result.

The news of Ibn Ziyad's campaign of terror reached Husayn as he was approaching Kufa. Husayn and his household camped near Karbala, where he reportedly dismissed his warriors, instructing them not to resist Yazid's rule. Knowing that Husayn was dangerous while living, Ibn Ziyad sent a message to him asking him to renounce his claim and announce publicly his support for Yazid. Husayn rejected this ultimatum and requested an interview with Yazid himself in Damascus. Ibn Ziyad refused this request and sent a message to the Umayyad commander encamped near Karbala declaring that Husayn should die unless he accepted the original ultimatum. The Umayyad commander gave the message to Husayn, whose dignity forced him to reject the humiliating proposal. Perhaps being the grandson of the Prophet made him believe that no Muslim, regardless of tribal affiliation or clan loyalty, would dare harm him or any of his household.

As the Umayyad troops approached Karbala, Husayn reportedly began to pray and admonish his followers to fortify themselves with courage and faith, believing that God would undoubtedly uphold his cause. However, his hopes were dashed as Umayyad soldiers rained arrows on his camp, killing his relatives one by one. One of Husayn's sons was killed beside him. As Husayn was carrying him inside, another son fell dead. He placed his sons' bodies side by side and then stood to remind his assailants of his relation to the Prophet. At that moment he was wounded by an arrow and stumbled over the bodies of his relatives. Finally, a warrior named Shammar aimed a fatal arrow at the swaying form of Husayn, and he fell atop the bodies of members of his household. It is estimated that at least seventy-two of the sons of Hashim were murdered in defense of Husayn, whose head was cut off and sent to Ibn Ziyad. The brutality of the tragedy of Karbala was so repulsive that many Muslim historians, in referring to it, frankly express great embarrassment at the treachery of the Muslim warriors who dared to kill the grandson of the Prophet.

Husayn's remains are believed to have been buried in Karbala where his gravesite has become a sacred shrine for the Shi'ite sect (followers of Ali). On the anniversary of Husayn's murder, Shi'ite Muslims everywhere assemble to mourn the brutal assassination of their martyred leader. Even today, as these Shi'ite pilgrims visit Husayn's shrine, they re-enact the passion play of his murder, weep bitterly, and beat their breasts in an effort to atone for his betrayal.

Sack of Madina

Yazid's troubles did not end with the death of his arch-rival Husayn; Ibn Zubayr in Madina aroused the Arabs of Hijaz against Yazid's brutality. In 682 they announced their secession from the Arab Empire, dismissed the Umayyad governor in Madina, and besieged the houses of members of the Umayyad clan. As news of the Madinan rebellion reached Yazid in Damascus, he ordered about twelve thousand men under Ibn Uqba to discipline the insurgents of Hijaz and free the Umayyad hostages. In 683 Ibn Uqba sent an ultimatum to the people of Madina asking them to pledge their allegiance to Yazid. When at the end of the third day the Madinans refused to accept the ultimatum, Ibn Uqba ordered his soldiers to attack the city. Although disorganized and ill-equipped, the people of Madina fought bravely but futilely against Ibn Uqba's organized army. The Umayyad troops stormed the city for three days, looting and murdering hundreds of Hashim supporters.

First Bombardment of Makka

Hearing of the attack against Madina, Ibn Zubayr took refuge in Makka and refused to surrender. Apparently he believed that no matter how ruthless the Umayyads could be, they would never dare to desecrate the most sacred place in Islam. However, Yazid, who had ordered the conquest of Madina in 682, did not hesitate to order a march against Makka itself to fight the dissident Ibn Zubayr. In 683 Yazid's commander, Ibn Uqba, led the Umayyad army toward Makka, but suddenly became sick and died. According to Yazid's orders, another warrior named Numayr succeeded Ibn Uqba and resumed the march against Makka. He besieged the city for two months during which his soldiers bombarded its walls with mangonels that hurled fireballs made of burning burlap fibers dipped in what the Arabs called *nafd* (possibly raw petroleum). In this bombardment many houses were destroyed, and the Ka'ba itself was burned and its shrine demolished.

During the siege, news arrived from Damascus of the sudden and mysterious death of Caliph Yazid, who was then only thirty-eight years old. Since Yazid's son and expected successor, Mu'awiya II, was only a boy of thirteen, Numayr became apprehensive of more trouble for the Umayyads in Damascus. He therefore halted the siege of Makka and invited Ibn Zubayr to accompany him to Syria, where he promised to help acclaim him caliph. Ibn Zubayr, however, was suspicious of Numayr's gestures and flatly refused, perferring to accept the allegiance of Muslim delegations in Makka itself. Disillusioned with the Umayyads in Damascus and disappointed by Ibn Zubayr in Makka, Numayr reportedly called the siege off and returned to his home in Syria.

MU'AWIYA II, 683

The impact of Yazid's death on the Arab Empire is difficult to evaluate because of the occurrence of many simultaneous but geographically scattered events. Near anarchy prevailed as local leaders acted according to their own wishes and inclinations.

In Damascus, Mu'awiya II was acclaimed caliph. However, many reports mention that the youth refused this acclamation and asked the Muslims to choose their commander as they pleased. This apparent abdication caused a sharp split within the Umayyad ranks; one group, called the Yamanites, wished to retain the caliphate within their own clan; and others, called the Qaysites, hoped to end Arab rivalries and unite their ranks under the leadership of Ibn Zubayr in Makka. The Yamanites, who tried to retain the Umayyad line, in turn split among themselves while trying to nominate a candidate to succeed Mu'awiya II. Some of them preferred Khalid, the younger son of Yazid, and others preferred Marwan, who had been governor of Madina during Uthman's caliphate. To add to the confusion, as the Umayyads in Syria were deliberating among themselves on their course of action, Mu'awiya II died suddenly only forty days after the death of his father. The Qaysite faction of the Umayyads set out to acclaim Ibn Zubayr, while the Yamanites totally failed to agree on a candidate to succeed Mu'awiya II.

MARWAN I, 683-685

Marwan, the eldest of the Umayyad leaders, had almost decided to surrender to Ibn Zubayr, when Ibn Ziyad, the Umayyad governor of Kufa, convinced him to champion the Umayyad cause. To retrieve their position, the Yamanites held a conference at Jabiya, south of Damascus, in which they agreed to support Marwan as caliph to be followed by Khalid, son of Yazid. Marwan assumed the caliphate in Damascus against heavy odds and began immediately to consolidate his position. His first task was to face the Qaysite group of the Umayyads, who had already found a leader in the person of Dahhak and were on their way to acclaim Ibn Zubayr as caliph.

The Situation in Iraq and Egypt

After Yazid's death, Ibn Ziyad, who had previously terrorized Iraq for the sake of the Umayyad cause, made a local bid for the caliphate. Whether in fear or real support, the people of Kufa acclaimed him caliph while the Kharijites and Shi'ites of Basra strongly resisted his claim. As he attempted to strengthen his position in Basra, a secret movement in Kufa successfully staged a surprise coup against Ibn Ziyad and forced him to flee. He then appeared in Damascus and convinced Marwan to assume the leadership of the Umayyad cause. Both Basra and Kufa selected local governors, who immediately decided to give their allegiance to Ibn Zubayr in Makka.

While Marwan was desperately trying to unite his supporters, Egypt slipped away from Umayyad control and welcomed Ibn Zubayr's emissary as governor. Ibn Zubayr was by this time acclaimed caliph in almost every major province of the Arab Empire except Syria. Even

there the Qaysite Umayyads under Dahhak were on the verge of announcing their support to him. However, the tide of events was to turn
sharply against Ibn Zubayr, mainly because of his insistence on staying
in Makka rather than going out to rally his supporters behind him.
Marwan and his son Abd al-Malik led their Yamanite supporters from
victory to victory until they cornered Ibn Zubayr in his own stronghold
and seized the caliphate once more for their own household.

Battle of Marj Rahit, 684

In order to end civil war, the Qaysite group under Dahhak decided
to support Ibn Zubayr's cause in Makka. A delegation was chosen to
travel to Hijaz and acclaim Ibn Zubayr caliph of all Muslims. On the
other hand, Marwan had already been appointed caliph by the Yamanite group and began to consolidate his position. He first decided to
discipline the dissident Qaysites and dispatched his troops to Marj
Rahit, where he surprised his enemies. A fierce battle followed between
the Yamanites and the Qaysites in which Marwan's troops defeated the
Qaysites. Despite Marwan's clear victory, a new feud began within the
ranks of the Umayyad supporters. The Yamanites were descendants of
the Kalb tribe of South Arabia and the Qaysites belonged to the Mudar
tribe of the North. Accordingly, the Qaysite blood spilled at Marj
Rahit made the Arabs of the North hold a grudge against the Arabs of
the South in almost every part of the Arab Empire. This feud continued
within Umayyad ranks and played a major role in bringing about the
eventual fall of the Umayyad regime.

Death of Marwan I

After his victory at Marj Rahit, Marwan marched against Egypt
to restore it to Umayyad control. Fierce battles followed between his
troops and those of Ibn Zubayr's governor, but Marwan's troops were
victorious. Upon his return to Damascus, Marwan mobilized two
armies, one directed toward Hijaz and the other toward Iraq, for the
purpose of restoring Umayyad control over these two regions. However,
the strain of fighting against heavy odds impaired Marwan's health; he
died in 685 leaving the troubled Umayyad regime in the hands of his
son, Abd al-Malik.[2]

---

[2] After Marj Rahit, Marwan succeeded in persuading Khalid, son of Yazid,
to renounce his claim to the caliphate in favor of Abd al-Malik.

CHAPTER 26

ABD AL-MALIK, 685-705

PROBLEMS FACING ABD AL-MALIK

Abd al-Malik and the Byzantines

When Abd al-Malik became caliph in 685, only Egypt, under
the governorship of his brother Abd al-Aziz, was relatively peaceful and loyal to the Umayyad regime. In the rest of
the Arab Empire Abd al-Malik had to fight for his dynasty
against enormous obstacles.

In Syria, the Qaysite opposition within the Umayyad clan
was revived under the leadership of Dhufar who took advantage
of Abd al-Malik's absence on a military trip to stage a rebellion in Damascus itself. The two armies sent earlier by Marwan to put down the Hashimite resistance were defeated as
Ibn Zubayr formally announced himself caliph over Hijaz,
Iraq, and Persia.

Moreover, as Abd al-Malik was preparing to crush the
Iraqi revolt, news came from Antioch that a Byzantine army
was attacking Syria's northern borders. Disturbed by discouraging reports from all sides, Abd al-Malik handled the
situation with extreme care and prudence. He knew well that
the conflicting forces inside Iraq, especially the Shi'ites and
the Kharijites—already a source of trouble to the Umayyad
dynasty—would rise also against Ibn Zubayr. He therefore
turned his attention from Iraq to the Byzantine armies in
Asia Minor. His tactics were successful, and in the next few
years he struck hard against the Byzantines and ensured the
security of his northern frontiers. In the meantime, Ibn

Zubayr's forces in Iraq, which had been weakened by the Shi'ite rebellion in Basra and Kufa, were exhausted and unable to resist a fresh attack. In 691 the situation in Iraq was ripe for Abd al-Malik to restore Umayyad supremacy over the entire Arab Empire.

Battle of Warda, 685

Following the death of Yazid in 683, a *coup d'état* had been staged against Ibn Ziyad in Kufa, forcing him to leave Iraq for Syria. This coup ended the terror with which Ibn Ziyad had suppressed the Shi'ite elements in Iraq. Once more, members of the Hashim clan were able to meet openly and demand revenge for the blood of their martyr, Husayn—mercilessly slain at Karbala. A special group of Shi'ite supporters assembled under the name of "Penitents" and began a campaign against the Umayyads to avenge the death of Husayn and atone for the Alids' crime of betraying him at Karbala. Ibn Zubayr's forces tried in vain to join them and form a united front against the Umayyads, but the Penitents rejected such cooperation on the grounds of a basic difference of opinion regarding their ultimate goals. Their only purpose, the Penitents insisted, was to avenge Husayn's blood free of ambition for territorial gains or political advantages. Accordingly, about 3,000 Penitent warriors gathered under the leadership of Surad, who urged them to follow in the footsteps of Husayn and be ready for martyrdom. Most of them left their wives, children, and property expecting never to return. Muslim annals record several incidents in which wives of Shi'ite warriors with babies in their arms wept as their husbands departed forever.

It may be recalled that the two armies sent by Marwan against the forces of Ibn Zubayr in Hijaz and Iraq had been defeated. The Penitents, therefore, followed the trail of the Umayyad army as it retreated from Iraq until they reached the borders of Syria at a place called Ayn al-Warda. There the Umayyad army was reinforced by additional forces under Ibn Ziyad, the same commander who had ordered the murder of Husayn. A fierce battle followed in which the Umayyads poured their arrows into the ranks of the Penitents, who actually exposed themselves to death. Within a few days, most of the Penitents had been killed and the remnant began a retreat toward Iraq. Some of the retreating Penitents, shamed at fleeing, reportedly returned to the battlefield and requested martyrdom in order to enter paradise without delay. The Umayyad forces willingly obliged, and, according to reports, killed them all on the spot. This battle of Warda exemplifies the strange sense of honor and dignity among the Arabs. Apparently these Shi'ite supporters had been so frequently scorned for abandoning their leader Husayn that they could bear it no longer. To wipe away their humiliation and redeem their honor, they preferred death to bequeathing their shame to their descendants—a noble, if somewhat catastrophic sense of dignity.

MUKHTAR'S REBELLION IN IRAQ

Mukhtar in Kufa

The Penitents had two original purposes: (1) avenging Husayn's blood, and (2) atoning for their own failure to protect him. They succeeded only in expiating their guilt and this only by willfully exposing themselves to death. However, the murderers of Husayn, especially Ibn Ziyad, who had ordered the murder, were still alive. According to Arab blood custom, Husayn's blood still required the murder of his assassins. Therefore, after the battle of Warda in 685, a popular movement began to crystallize among the supporters of the house of Ali in Iraq for the sole purpose of avenging the blood of Husayn. This new Shi'ite movement was led by a gallant warrior named Mukhtar, who himself had carried a grudge against Ibn Ziyad during the latter's rule in Kufa.

At the head of his excessively enthusiastic and willing Shi'ite supporters, Mukhtar staged a quick *coup d'état* against Ibn Zubayr's representative in Kufa. The latter moved to Basra and prepared his forces for an expected offensive by Mukhtar, which never took place. Instead of attacking southern Iraq, Mukhtar sent his forces toward Mosul to stop the advancing armies of Ibn Ziyad himself, the Shi'ites' main target.

Mukhtar's army suffered an initial defeat; but as his foothold in Kufa was strengthened, he sent a reliable warrior named Ashtar at the head of another army to fight Ibn Ziyad. Ashtar's forces took Ibn Ziyad's army by surprise and defeated it amid loud cries of "O, defenders of the faith, vengeance for Husayn." Three hundred of the Shi'ite warriors vowed to kill Ibn Ziyad, and reportedly crossed the Umayyad lines. Exposing themselves to enemy arrows, they fought their way to Ibn Ziyad's headquarters, killed him in cold blood, and carried his severed head to Mukhtar in Kufa, where a few years earlier Ibn Ziyad himself had received the severed head of Husayn.

With this great victory over their archenemy, the Shi'ite supporters joyfully celebrated the revenge of Husayn as Mukhtar's forces occupied the whole territory of northern Iraq. The Shi'ite warriors then returned to Kufa having fulfilled their vows. Although Mukhtar indicated a strong desire to become caliph, his followers and Shi'ite supporters did not encourage him to press his claims—due perhaps to the fact that he was not a descendant of Ali.

Fall of Mukhtar

Once the Shi'ite warriors had satisfied themselves with the murder of Ibn Ziyad, their enthusiasm for further fighting waned. While Mukh-

tar's soldiers were occupied in northern Iraq, Ibn Zubayr of Hijaz
appointed his brother Mus'ab as commander-in-chief of his forces in
Basra with instructions to quell Mukhtar's rebellion. Mus'ab obtained
the support of Muhallab, governor of Persia, who, after defeating the
Kharijites near Ahwaz, was free to side with either group. Muhallab
rallied to Ibn Zubayr's cause, as Mus'ab's forces marched from Basra
to Kufa in April, 687. Although the Shi'ite warriors under Mukhtar's
leadership fought only half-heartedly, they inflicted heavy losses upon
Mus'ab's forces before they were themselves finally defeated. Mukhtar
took refuge inside Kufa's main castle, which was then heavily besieged
by enemy forces. Mukhtar decided to go out in the open and face his
fate. He was killed as soon as he emerged from the castle and his
followers dispersed.

CONQUEST OF IRAQ

After Mukhtar's Death

With Mukhtar out of the way, the struggle for the caliphate was
confined to Abd al-Malik of Damascus and Ibn Zubayr of Makka who
divided the Arab Empire almost equally. Abd al-Malik ruled Egypt
and Syria, and Ibn Zubayr controlled Hijaz, Iraq, and Persia. Since
each rejected the other's claim to the caliphate, it was inevitable that
the sword should determine their destiny as well as the destiny of the
entire Islamic domain.

Realizing that defeat by Ibn Zubayr's forces would mean the end of
Umayyad rule in Damascus, Abd al-Malik decided against rushing into
disastrous premature war. He instructed his advisors to study the
military situation from all directions, especially since his northern
frontiers lay exposed to a possible attack from Byzantium. To ensure
against such an attack, Abd al-Malik entered negotiations with the
Byzantine emperor and reportedly agreed to pay the emperor twelve
thousand dinars a year to refrain from attacking northern Syria.

Mus'ab's Defeat and Death

Having placated the Byzantines, Abd al-Malik turned his attention
to the east. He realized that the Arabs of Iraq had become dissatisfied
with Ibn Zubayr's rule because the latter insisted on remaining in
Makka and considered Iraq a province to be ruled by a governor.
Accordingly, in the summer of 691 Abd al-Malik deemed the time ripe
for a military campaign against Iraq. His calculations proved correct,
for when the Umayyad army faced Mus'ab's forces in Iraq, the latter
were utterly discouraged and lacked the zeal to fight. In vain did Mus'ab
call upon his warriors to defend their land. Finally, when all odds were

against Mus'ab, the Umayyad commander offered him the choice of surrender and allegiance to Abd al-Malik or death. Preferring death to surrender, he dashed into the Umayyad lines followed by his son. An Umayyad horseman reportedly drove his lance through Mus'ab and then severed his head, which was sent to Abd al-Malik. With Mus'ab's defeat and death, all Iraq and Persia lay open to Umayyad reoccupation. Abd al-Malik arrived in Kufa and accepted the allegiance of many Iraqi leaders and chiefs of tribes while Mus'ab's head reportedly lay beneath his feet. Since the beginning of the Umayyad rule, four famous heads were carried to almost the same spot as a result of bitter factional rivalries among the Arabs. Husayn's head was brought to Ibn Ziyad, Ibn Ziyad's head was brought to Mukhtar, Mukhtar's head to Mus'ab, and now Mus'ab's head to Abd al-Malik. It is said that upon hearing this, Abd al-Malik ordered the demolition of the building that had witnessed these tragic and horrid events.

THE SECOND BOMBARDMENT OF MAKKA

Hajjaj Sent to Makka

Mus'ab's defeat and death in Iraq left his brother, Ibn Zubayr, in Makka in a hopeless situation. Although he controlled Hijaz and almost all of the Arabian Peninsula, his supply line from the rich provinces of Iraq and Persia had been cut off. Common sense dictated that Ibn Zubayr should have surrendered to Abd al-Malik; instead, he took refuge at the Ka'ba desperately hoping that the Umayyads would not dare to attack the holy shrine as they had done during the struggle with Yazid. Abd al-Malik, who had suffered because of Ibn Zubayr's per-sistence in claiming the caliphate, was in no mood to spare his deter-mined rival, even at the expense of the Ka'ba. He appointed for the task of obtaining Ibn Zubayr's surrender a ruthless warrior named Hajjaj and sent him at the head of a substantial force to Hijaz in 692.

Surrender and Death of Ibn Zubayr

Hajjaj besieged Makka for over eight months. His forces, controlling the mountains around the holy city, bombarded it with rocks hurled by mangonels, severely damaging its walls and buildings, especially the Ka'ba. Ibn Zubayr held tenaciously to his claim and refused to surren-der. Hajjaj, however, used trickery and announced a general amnesty to all those who would abandon resistance and join his ranks. Tired of fighting with extremely limited supplies and anxious to end the disas-trous bombardment of their revered city, Ibn Zubayr's forces began to defect in great numbers to Hajjaj's side. When almost all his fol-lowers, including two of his sons, deserted him, Ibn Zubayr turned for advice to his aged mother. She is reported to have urged him in the dignified tones of age to be willing to die for the cause in which he so firmly believed. Ibn Zubayr thereupon walked alone through the city gates into Umayyad lines where two missiles struck and killed him.

With the death of Ibn Zubayr, the Umayyad dynasty became firmly established in Damascus, and the household of Islam once more was united under one regime. The year 692 is therefore known in Islamic annals as the second year of unity; the first was 661, when Mu'awiya succeeded in uniting the Arab Empire.

ABD AL-MALIK AS CALIPH

Hajjaj, Governor of Iraq

No sooner had Hajjaj captured and pacified Makka and Hijaz under Umayyad rule than trouble broke out again in Iraq and Persia, where Kharijites fomented rebellion in Ahwaz and Khuzistan. Recalling the experience of his predecessor Yazid, Abd al-Malik concluded that the Iraqi Arabs would not yield except by terror and intimidation. So he dispatched Hajjaj as governor and commander-in-chief of the Umayyad forces.

When Hajjaj reached Kufa, he reportedly stood in the pulpit of the central mosque and delivered his famous, fiery speech in which he said, "O people of Kufa, I see among you heads ripe for the harvest. The time of harvest has arrived and I am the harvester. . . . Blood will soon flow below the turbans and above the beards." He made a similar speech in Basra. The result, according to Arab historians, was complete acquiescence by the people of Iraq to Hajjaj's reign of terror.

Hajjaj then enlisted in southern Persia the help of Muhallab, an experienced fighter against the Kharijites, to put down the latter's rebellion. Hajjaj's campaign against the Kharijites, even with the help of Muhallab, was not easy. However, after more than a year of fighting, he defeated them in a decisive battle after which they ceased to be of any vital importance.

Hajjaj was promoted to the governorship of both Iraq and Persia and was asked to pacify the far eastern frontiers of the Arab Empire. He dispatched Muhallab to Khurasan and Ash'ath to Kabul. However, Ash'ath, having been reprimanded by Hajjaj for his failure to achieve his earlier mission against the Kharijites, led a rebellion against the Umayyads and marched back with his forces to Kufa and Basra. The Iraqis supported him and Hajjaj sent urgent appeals to Abd al-Malik for reinforcements, which he received in time to face Ash'ath in a battle at Dayr al-Jamajim in 702 on the outskirts of Kufa. Many were killed on both sides as the balance of power swayed back and forth between the two armies. Finally Ash'ath's forces were defeated, and he fled to Kabul, where he was killed.

Abd al-Malik's Reforms

After Hajjaj's victory over Ash'ath, Umayyad control was firmly established over all territories of the Arab Empire. Abd al-Malik's subsequent efforts were devoted to expansion and organization. In North Africa he ordered Hassan to march against Carthage and proceed westward. In Persia, he directed Muhallab, and later on Muhallab's son, to expand the Islamic frontiers beyond the Oxus River. At home he used some Qaysite Arabs, an opposition group within the Umayyads, in raids on the Byzantine borders in Asia Minor. To protect his regime against Qaysite opposition, he sent the rest of them to Hijaz and appointed his brother governor there. In Iraq, Hajjaj built the city of Wasit to be the headquarters of the Umayyads from which both Kufa and Basra could be controlled.

A man of highly refined literary taste, Abd al-Malik encouraged Arabic literature as well as the use of Arabic script. He is credited with ordering Arabic to be used as the official language of state documents in Egypt, Syria, Iraq, and Persia in place of the local languages of these countries. He also ordered Arabic to be used on coins instead of earlier non-Arabic inscriptions. Muslim annals mention that he also directed that dots and points be added to the Qur'anic text in order to make it more easily read.

Abd al-Malik died in 705 while his commanders in Persia and North Africa were expanding the frontiers of the Arab Empire both east and west, leaving his son Walid a stable, well-organized, and growing regime. While Mu'awiya is credited with founding the Umayyad dynasty in 661, Abd al-Malik may be considered the man who placed the regime on a firm foundation.

CHAPTER 27

WALID I, 705-715

ON THE ROAD TO EXPANSION

Walid's Expansion Plans

A year before his death, Abd al-Malik asked his governors, as well as the Arab chiefs in the empire, to swear allegiance to his son Walid as his successor. Therefore, when Abd al-Malik died in 705, Walid became caliph almost without opposition; his father's prestige had been so great and far-reaching that the prospects of rebellion were dim. Nevertheless, Walid's responsibilities were complicated by the continual existence of strong elements of opposition, forcing him to use great care and prudence. His father had advised him always to consult with the governors of the provinces, especially Hajjaj, and to follow their counsel. The consensus among Walid's governors and army commanders was to occupy the Arab warriors with further conquests, thereby keeping them away from sedition and intrigue. Accordingly, Walid charged three commanders with expanding the borders of the Arab Empire. Qutayba was to lead the Arab forces in Persia east of the Oxus with his destination Samarqand and China; Ibn Qasim was given charge of the forces in southern Persia and his goal was the River Sind in India; and Musa ibn Nusayr was appointed as commander of the troops in North Africa with his destination the Atlantic Ocean.

These three commanders were independent of each other. As they penetrated new territories they also became self-supporting and independent of the center of the empire, Damascus. Walid did not exercise full control over these armies; however, he received periodic reports of their progress while his attention was focused on improving the internal conditions and guarding the Islamic frontiers against the Byzantines in Asia Minor.

Summer Raids Against Byzantium

Walid dispatched his brother Maslama at the head of an Umayyad army to invade the Byzantine possessions north of Syria. In a number of summer raids Maslama was able to penetrate Asia Minor and reach the vicinity of Constantinople. However, the fortifications of the city were very strong, and when his supplies were exhausted, he returned home.

Walid's Domestic Reforms

Walid I is reported to have widened the central mosque in Damascus and added more embellishments and decorations to it than any other caliph. He dug canals carrying enough water to allow many houses in the city to maintain water fountains or marble cisterns. Walid was also known for his welfare measures, especially for lepers and the blind. Moreover, he is reported to have started a system of charity to support the poor and the beggars of Damascus. Such benevolent acts undoubtedly increased Walid's popularity and promoted peace and security at home. The internal stability of the empire also greatly contributed to the successful and uninterrupted military expansions abroad, making Walid's rule the high point of power and prosperity for the Umayyad regime.

CONQUEST OF TRANSOXIANA

Beyond the Oxus River

During Abd al-Malik's time, Muhallab and his son Yazid succeeded in crossing the Oxus River and attacking a number of Persian and Turkish principalities along the trade routes from China to Persia. Marv became the capital city of the Arab governor of Khurasan, and when Qutayba was appointed by Walid — at the suggestion of Hajjaj — to cross the Oxus River, he used it as his military headquarters and a rallying point from which to launch further campaigns.

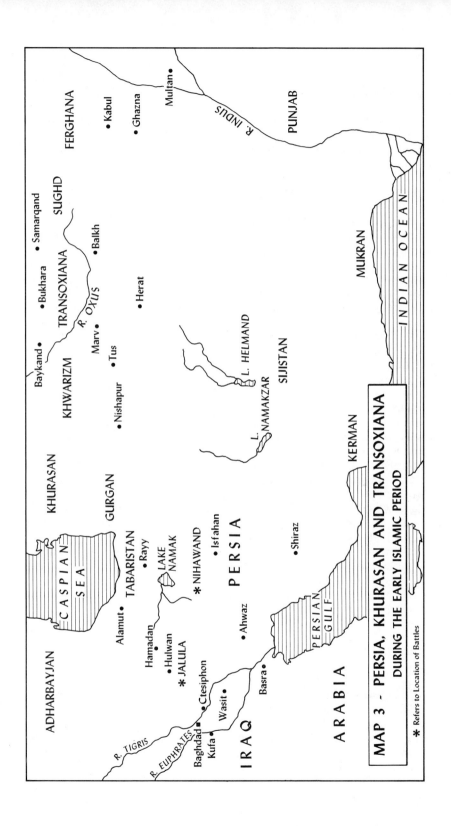

MAP 3 - PERSIA, KHURASAN AND TRANSOXIANA
DURING THE EARLY ISLAMIC PERIOD

* Refers to Location of Battles

Fall of Bukhara and Samarqand

Qutayba did not waste time. Immediately after his appointment to his post in late 705 he marched toward the Oxus, accompanied by native warriors. In 706 he reportedly crossed the river and captured the city of Baykand, after inflicting heavy defeats upon its chieftains. He appointed a governor at Baykand and continued his march eastward. Before reaching Bukhara, news reached him of a rebellion at Baykand, and he returned to subdue the city, declaring its possessions and supplies as booty for the Arabs. Qutayba's soldiers helped themselves to the wealth of Baykand and returned to spend the winter of 707 in Marv.

In the spring of 707, Qutayba marched again toward Bukhara, which finally surrendered after heavy fighting. He guaranteed its population peace and protection, forbidding his soldiers to loot or destroy. In Bukhara the Arab commander had a chance to reorganize his army; he requested the chieftains of Bukhara to supply him with local soldiers to join Arab warriors in battles. Thus far Arab warriors had monopolized the privilege of fighting and obtaining war booty; however, knowing that the supply line behind him was too long for practical purposes, Qutayba allowed non-Arabs to enroll among his regular troops. Thus equipped with local supplies and ample manpower, he advanced toward Samarqand.

To prepare his troops for the attack on Samarqand, Qutayba first pacified the whole region of Khwarizm and brought it under Arab control. In 712 he captured Kish and proceeded toward his target city – Samarqand. Heavy fighting ended in the surrender of the city and several trading posts around it to the Arabs. Qutayba advanced even further, toward the region of Ferghana; however, the warlike Turkish tribes which he had conquered at both Bukhara and Samarqand revolted against the Arabs, and Qutayba had to return from Ferghana. Muslim annals mention that in order to establish Arab rule over the tribes of Transoxiana, Qutayba used harsh measures to convert the inhabitants of both Bukhara and Samarqand to Islam. For example, when he collected idols at Samarqand for destruction, he was cautioned against it and told that destroying the idols might lead to rebellion; nevertheless, he marched forward and set fire to the heap.

On the Borders of China

In 715, having stabilized his position beyond the Oxus River, Qutayba felt secure enough to lead a campaign against the outlying provinces of China. Instead of merely controlling Chinese trade routes to the Middle East, he thought of adding part of the Chinese territory to the Arab Empire. He marched eastward till he approached the borders of China where he received news of the death of the caliph in Damascus. However, he continued his march till he reached the border; from there he sent a delegation to the Chinese Emperor headed by an eloquent Arab called Hubayra. Muslim annals supply the following report on the discussions that presumably took place between the Chinese Emperor and Hubayra.

After three days of negotiations, the Chinese Emperor said to Hubayra, "Go back to your ruler and tell him to return because I know his greed and the meagerness of his troops. Otherwise I shall send (an army) to destroy both you and him." Hubayra then said, "How could his forces be meager while their front is at your territory and their back is in the olive groves? And how could he still be greedy when he has conquered so much territory as to be able to invade your land? As for your threat to destroy us, we believe that fates are determined, and nothing is more honorable for us than to die (by the sword); we neither hate it nor fear it." Upon hearing these statements, the Chinese Emperor is reported to have asked, "What will satisfy your ruler?" Hubayra answered, "He swore not to go back unless he treads your soil, obtains hostages from your kings, and receives your tribute." The Emperor then said, "We shall absolve him of his oath; we shall send to him some dust of our soil to tread, we shall send to him some young men as hostages, and a tribute that would please him." The report goes on to say that the Chinese Emperor sent with the Arab delegation some dust in golden pots, four of the royal children, and a gift of silk and gold to Qutayba. The latter is said to have trodden the Chinese dust, received the homage of the royal children, and accepted the gift as tribute. After releasing the four royal children to return to China, Qutayba and his forces returned to Marv; and thus, according to Arab annals, China avoided Arab occupation.[1]

After Qutayba's retreat from China, relations between the Chinese Emperor and the Arab caliphs were generally cordial. It is reported that during the reign of the second Abbasid caliph, the Chinese Emperor faced a rebellion in his own country and requested military aid from the caliph. A contingent of Arab soldiers is believed to have been dispatched by the caliph; after completing its task it reportedly remained to become the nucleus of an Arab Muslim community in China.

On the Borders of India

The River Sind on the northwestern borders of India was presumably known to the Arabs from pre-Islamic times when merchants traveled to the region carrying herbs, spices, and other commodities. Muslim annals report that Uthman once asked the governor of Iraq to explore the military situation in India and that the governor described the land as susceptible to invasion. However, no serious attempt at conquest was made until Walid appointed Ibn Qasim in 705 to invade India. During Mu'awiya's caliphate, Muhallab is reported to have raided the borders of India and gone as far as Multan; but the Arab forces retreated to Iraq without making any claims of conquest.

[1]Al-Tabari, *Tarikh*, Volume 8, pp. 100, 101.

Ibn Qasim crossed into India in 711, having captured several towns between the Kerman region and the River Sind. According to Arab historians, the Muslim troops defeated the Indian forces led by a commander named Dahir. Ibn Qasim then advanced beyond the Sind and captured most of the territory now comprising West Pakistan. He then moved toward Multan, a religious center of the Indian Brahman caste, which had a temple containing a statue of their god whose eyes were made of precious stones and whose head was covered with gold. The Arabs are reported to have stormed the temple and looted its gold and precious stones.

The Indians resisted conversion to Islam. Until the time of Caliph Umar II, (717-720) there were very few conversions; however, when the caliph promised the Indians equality with the Arabs if they became Muslims a great number of them, including the son of their defeated commander Dahir, were reportedly converted to Islam. Nevertheless, the Indians revolted several times against Arab rule until al-Mansur, the second Abbasid caliph, was forced to recapture the whole territory previously conquered by Ibn Qasim.

CONQUEST OF NORTH AFRICA

Background of Ifriqiya

As early as the ninth century B.C., the Phoenicians, or more specifically the Sidonians, founded Carthage in North Africa and used it as a commercial colony. Having been driven out by the Assyrians after 722 B.C., many Phoenicians settled in Carthage and the surrounding area, giving rise to a strong regime. After lengthy and brutal battles between the Romans and Carthaginians, under the great leader Hannibal, the Carthaginians were defeated and their territory became a Roman colony in 146 B.C. The Romans and later the Byzantines ruled Carthage as a colony known as Africa. When the Arabs captured Carthage from the Byzantines, they called the area between Egypt and Carthage "Ifriqiya," which is the Arabic name for Africa. Their conquests west of Carthage were called al-Maghrib, meaning "the western land," a name still used to refer to present-day Morocco.

In his efforts to avoid unnecessary expansion, Umar—the second orthodox caliph—ordered Ibn al-As, his commander in Egypt, to halt military operations at Barqa near the frontiers of Egypt. However, the Arabs raided North Africa several times and returned to their base at Barqa with abundant booty. In 647 one of these raids reportedly reached as far as the frontiers of modern Tunisia.

Founding of Qayrawan

In 670, during Mu'awiya's caliphate, Uqba was appointed commander of the Arab forces in North Africa. He followed the coastal line west of Barqa, passed Tripoli, and turned north with the curve of the Mediterranean till he came within fifty miles of Carthage. Uqba's main enemies were the Byzantine regular forces in the coastal strip and the Berber tribesmen of the mountains. He therefore followed a route between the two groups and built an Arab city called Qayrawan about thirty-five miles inland to serve as an Arab military headquarters and supply depot. Many Arabs settled in Qayrawan, which soon became one of several purely Arab settlements in the Arab Empire.

Uqba's Conquests in Ifriqiya

In 682, after Mu'awiya's death, Uqba again set out to conquer the West. He marched a few miles south of the Mediterranean coast to avoid encountering either the Byzantines or the Berbers. He speedily penetrated Ifriqiya till he reached Tangier near the Atlantic. In 683 he reportedly looked at the ocean and asked his troops to witness before God that only the water prevented him from marching farther west. Having reached as far as he could in al-Maghrib, he ordered his forces back toward Qayrawan. However, Berber raiders from the Atlas Mountains ambushed Uqba's column and, according to Arab historians, killed Uqba and most of the three hundred horsemen escorting him. The surviving troops, discouraged by the loss of their commander, swiftly retreated to Barqa.

Capture of Carthage

In 695, having settled most of his problems with Iraq and the East, Abd al-Malik turned his attention to Africa and the West. He appointed a warrior called Hassan to command the Arab troops and once more capture Ifriqiya. Hassan advanced westward from Barqa and, instead of avoiding the Byzantines, he decided to meet them on their own ground. After heavy fighting in the coastal strip, Hassan broke through the defenses of Carthage and captured the city. To ensure that the enemy would never return, he completely demolished the city of Carthage, founded more than a millennium and a half before. With their capital in Africa razed to the ground, the rest of the Byzantine troops evacuated Ifriqiya, forcing their emperor to abandon his last foothold on the African continent.

Arabs and Berbers

No sooner had Hassan established Arab control over Ifriqiya, than Berber mountain tribes suddenly descended on the coastal territories surprising the Arabs. The unprepared Arabs were defeated at the battle of Tebessa in 698, losing many warriors. Hassan reassembled the remnant of his forces and retreated to Barqa, which he had left three

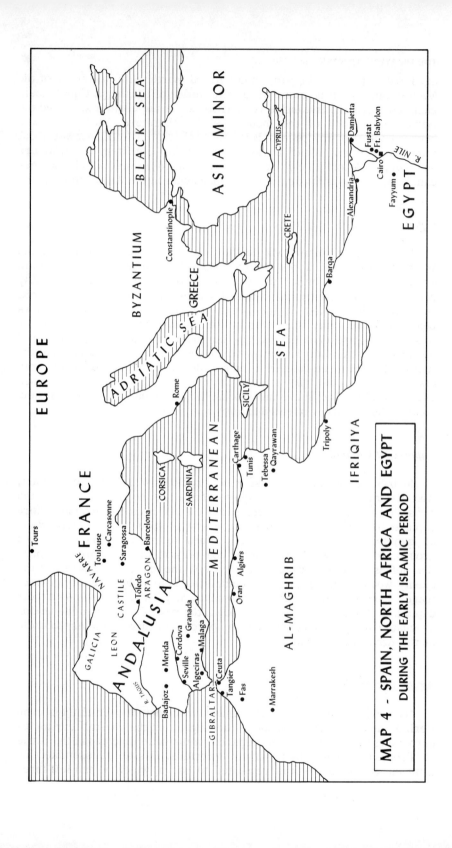

MAP 4 - SPAIN, NORTH AFRICA AND EGYPT
DURING THE EARLY ISLAMIC PERIOD

years before. Notwithstanding this defeat, the Arabs received reinforcements from Abd al-Malik in 702 and once more felt strong enough
to reconquer Ifriqiya. The Berber raiders followed a scorched earth
policy destroying property and cattle to discourage reconquest. As a
result, the sedentary population of the coastal plains turned against the
mountain Berbers, and as the Arab forces marched again toward
Ifriqiya, the sedentary inhabitants fought with them against the Berbers.
Hassan recaptured Qayrawan and reached the vicinity of Carthage.
Near its site he laid the foundations of the city of Tunis, which later
became the capital of what is now known as Tunisia.

CONQUEST OF SPAIN

Berbers in the Muslim Forces

When Walid became caliph in 705, he dismissed Hassan as commander in North Africa, reportedly because of his tough policies with
the Berbers, and appointed in his place Musa ibn Nusayr. Musa's
first aim was to win the Berbers' good will in order to end their raids.
His policy was successful, for the Berbers not only accepted Islam,
but also became active warriors on the Arab side. Among them was
Tariq ibn Ziyad, a great warrior who later became the Muslim commander destined to cross the Strait of Gibraltar (which incidently is
named after him[2]) and conquer Spain.

Having won the Berbers to his side, Musa established Arab rule
over the rest of North Africa in a relatively short time. When he
reached Tangier, he appointed Tariq as governor of al-Maghrib and
entrusted to him the task of invading Spain.

The Situation in Spain

The Arabs call Spain "Andalusia," a term presumably derived
from the word "Vandals," after certain barbarian European tribes that
came to North Africa from Spain and established a strong empire in
Carthage about 439. In Spain the Vandals were followed by the Visigoths,
who about 530 founded a kingdom which ruled most of the peninsula.
The conquering Goths became a ruling elite replacing the old Roman
aristocracy, while the rest of the inhabitants of Spain languished in
slavery.

About 587 the Goths were converted to Christianity, giving rise
to a new branch of aristocracy, the clergy. Under their influence the
Jews of Spain suffered greatly. As the Arabs reached North Africa, the
Spanish masses included serfs, slaves, and oppressed Jews living in
misery and deprivation.

[2] Gibraltar is Arabic *jabal Tariq* meaning "the mountain of Tariq."

Between Goths and Romans

Many Romans who were driven out of Spain by the Visigoths had settled in North Africa, which for a short while, became a part of the Byzantine Empire. When the Arabs conquered North Africa, the area closest to Spain, known as Ceuta, remained independent under a prince named Count Julian presumably of Roman origin. Julian owned estates in Spain and was married to the daughter of Witiza, the Gothic King of Spain. However, when the latter died, a new king named Roderic seized power. Witiza's sons pretended to support the new king, but in secret they plotted with their brother-in-law Julian to stage an attack against Roderic from Ceuta, in which they would turn the army against the king.

Some annals mention that King Roderic had once mistreated Julian's daughter, which greatly angered her father and uncles. In any case, in order to launch an attack against Spain from North Africa, Julian needed the help of the Arabs. He is therefore reported to have asked Musa ibn Nusayr for a small regiment of Muslim warriors to raid the Spanish coast.

Tariq's Conquest of Spain

Musa agreed first to send an exploratory mission to report to him about conditions in Andalusia. The mission's report favored conquest and, accordingly, Tariq invaded Andalusia in 711. The Arab contingent numbered only 12,000 troops, while Roderic's forces were estimated at over 25,000. However it is also reported that most of the Gothic troops were under the command of Witiza's two sons, who had been secretly in agreement with Julian and the Arabs. Accordingly, as the two armies met near Cadiz, Roderic was suddenly abandoned by his commanders, and the Muslims secured a brilliant victory over the Goths.

According to the agreement with Musa ibn Nusayr, the Muslims, having completed their task, should have returned to Africa leaving Spain to Julian and his brothers-in-law. However, without waiting for orders from Musa, Tariq made use of the fearful effects of his sudden victory and advanced northward, capturing Spanish cities one after the other with the remainder of his small contingent. Before the Goths could react, Tariq had reached Toledo in central Spain, bringing Cordova and most of the southern areas of the peninsula under Islamic control.

Musa's Campaign

Tariq's swift campaign in Andalusia completely foiled Julian's plan to recapture Spain; instead, most of the peninsula came under Muslim control. Musa ibn Nusayr is reported to have been greatly annoyed, not because Tariq had captured most of southern Spain, but because he had done so without Musa's permission. Musa therefore in 712 led another Muslim army to complete the conquest of Spain and locate his victorious runaway commander. His mission, however, was less fortunate than Tariq's; by the time Musa entered the unconquered Spanish cities, the inhabitants had recovered from their shock and were ready to defend themselves. Nevertheless, Musa captured Sidonia and Seville after heavy fighting, but when he reached Merida, he was effectively repulsed by its strong fortifications. He therefore besieged the city for several months till its supplies were completely exhausted. Faced with starvation and disease, the inhabitants of Merida negotiated an honorable surrender.

In 713 Musa set out for Toledo to meet Tariq, who had been engaged in subjugating the northern areas of Spain. It is reported that when the two commanders met, Musa ordered Tariq to be flogged in punishment for failure to take orders from him. However, in appreciation of Tariq's deeds, Musa allowed him to retain his command and complete the conquest of Spain.

By 714 most of Andalusia except for the mountainous district of Galicia, was held by the Arabs. Many of the Spanish cities capitulated without a struggle and received considerate treatment from the Muslims. Cities that resisted and were won by the sword were treated as spoils of war. In any case, since most Spaniards were either serfs or slaves to Gothic nobles, a number of them professed Islam and were automatically freed. In spite of the fact that Spain became a part of the Arab Empire by conquest, the bulk of its population was apparently happier under the Arabs than it had been under the Goths. Muslim rulers in Spain eliminated the Spanish aristocracy, freed slaves, and stopped persecution of the Jewish minority. However, the Muslim rule in Spain was not always benevolent; at the top of the social order was the Arab aristocracy, which considered all non-Arabs inferior subjects in their vast empire.

Musa's Recall to Damascus

In late 714, Musa ibn Nusayr explored the situation in Europe and requested Walid's permission to invade Central Europe and reach Damascus by way of Greece. However, the caliph, fearful of the growing prestige of Musa, denied his request and ordered him home instead. A disciplined warrior, Musa obeyed Walid's command when he could well have turned the whole empire against him. The great conqueror of North Africa and Spain returned in great splendor and pomp. Walid received him at his palace, congratulated him for his splendid achievement, and then relieved him of his command.

Walid died in 715 and was succeeded by his brother Sulayman. Sulayman had contacted Musa while Musa was on his way back to Damascus and asked him to stay at Tiberius in Palestine. Musa disregarded Sulayman's request because the latter had not yet been acclaimed

caliph. When Sulayman became caliph in 715, he flogged the great ex-
commander, stripped him of all his wealth, and sent him to Arabia to
live a Bedouin life. As if these measures were not enough, Sulayman
reportedly ordered assassins in North Africa to bring to him the head
of Musa's son. In an unbelievable act of hatred and jealousy, Sulayman
sent the severed head to the aged father. Thus ended the career of one
of the greatest Arab commanders.

CHAPTER 28

DECLINE OF THE UMAYYAD REGIME

Following is a list of the Umayyad caliphs and their dates:

1.	Mu'awiya I	661-680
2.	Yazid I	680-683
3.	Mu'awiya II	683
4.	Marwan I	683-685
5.	Abd al-Malik	685-705
6.	Walid I	705-715
7.	Sulayman	715-717
8.	Umar II	717-720
9.	Yazid II	720-724
10.	Hisham	724-743
11.	Walid II	743-744
12.	Yazid III	744
13.	Ibrahim	744
14.	Marwan II	744-750

Their relationship to each other is illustrated by the following chart:

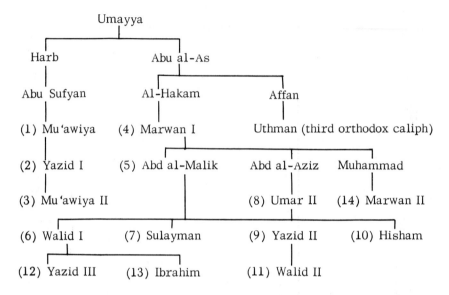

Until the time of Walid I, succession to the caliphate was hereditary from father to son, except in the case of Marwan I, who followed Mu'awiya II. During the first six caliphates of the Umayyad regime, there was a relative continuity of government as each caliph attempted to build upon previous foundations. However, when Walid I died in 715, his brother Sulayman hastened to snatch the caliphate from Walid's son before the latter could consolidate his claim. From that time on, the death of an Umayyad caliph usually meant bloodshed with several of the close relatives of the deceased caliph claiming the caliphate. When one of them would prevail over the others, the new administration would proclaim a *coup d'état* against the preceding administration and eliminate most of its supporters. Accordingly, after 715 the Umayyad regime suffered greatly from frequent interruptions in government coupled with bitter feuds and internecine wars between its two main factions – the Qaysites and the Yamanites – leading ultimately to its final collapse.

SULAYMAN, 715-717

Sulayman's Acclamation

Abd al-Malik had already designated Sulayman to follow Walid I as caliph. However, as Walid I was trying to gain support for his son against his brother Sulayman, the latter mustered enough followers to press his claim. As soon as Walid's death was known, Sulayman announced his claim to the caliphate and hurried to receive the acclamation of his loyal supporters. Sulayman assumed office in 715 against the desires of many of Walid's followers. The new caliph could hardly hide his bitter hatred and revengeful feelings toward those who had earlier supported his brother's attempts to disqualify him. The result was a reign of terror against Sulayman's opponents, in which he tried to punish and remove from office almost all governors and army commanders of the preceding administration. Sulayman not only dismissed his brother's officials throughout the empire, but also tortured them, stripped them of all their wealth, and sent them into desert exile.

Among the great commanders who suffered at his hands were Qutayba, the conqueror of China; Ibn Qasim, the conqueror of India; and Musa ibn Nusayr, the conqueror of North Africa and Spain. In Iraq, Sulayman appointed Ibn Muhallab, a bitter enemy of Hajjaj, as governor. Ibn Muhallab tortured and killed several members of Hajjaj's household; Hajjaj himself may be considered fortunate to have died a few months before Walid's death. Moreover, since most of the deposed commanders belonged to the Qaysite faction of the regime, the old feud between the Qaysites and the Yamanites was rekindled and gathered momentum until the final collapse of the empire.

Siege of Constantinople, 717

Sulayman's rule was not totally consumed in internal strife and bitter revenge against Walid's supporters. Arab warriors continued their periodic attacks on the Byzantines in Asia Minor. The Arabs were led by Maslama, son of Abd al-Malik, who had been assigned this task during Walid's administration. Sulayman sent reinforcements to Maslama and ordered him to advance against Constantinople.

It is reported that by the year 716, a usurper named Theodosius seized the throne of Byzantium from Emperor Anastasius II. Earlier a Byzantine warrior named Leo had been appointed by Anastasius II as commander of the eastern front against the Arabs. Leo spoke fluent Arabic and was well acquainted with Arab manners and military tactics. However, when Theodosius assumed the rule in Byzantium, Leo rebelled against him and at least outwardly cooperated with the Arab troops against Constantinople. It is assumed that Leo's tactics were planned to face Theodosius with a serious military threat at home in order to force him off the throne, thus clearing the way for Leo's own accession to the emperorship. Leo then thought to lure the Arabs into Thrace on Greek soil and deal them a fatal blow.

When the Arab forces under Maslama reached the vicinity of Constantinople, the whole city was churning in complete fear and disorder resulting from the final overthrow of Emperor Theodosius. At this decisive moment Leo is reported to have defected from Arab ranks and reached Constantinople in time to be acclaimed Emperor Leo III, Savior of the Empire.

By this time, Arab ships were guarding the entrances of Constantinople from its three waterfront sides as massive land forces laid siege to its western borders. Having failed to negotiate peace with the Arabs, Leo III equipped his ships with catapults which threw fire-projectiles at the enemy. This new invention, called "Greek fire," as used in naval operations took the Arabs by complete surprise; their ships on the Bosphorus were either burned or disabled. Instead of laying siege to Constantinople, the Arabs, whose land forces had been transferred to the western side of the city through the Dardanelles, themselves became trapped and besieged by the Byzantines on the east and the barbarians on the west. Moreover, the winter of 717 happened to be exceptionally cold, and the Arabs suffered greatly. Nevertheless, Sulayman insisted on maintaining the siege by all means until reinforcements were sent. However, the ailing caliph died before any substantial forces could be dispatched. His peace-loving successor, Umar II, called the siege off as his troops retreated to Syria with considerable losses in both manpower and supplies.

UMAR II, 717-721

His Piety

Umar II is known in Islamic history as the pious caliph. It is reported that once his wife found him weeping. When she inquired about the reason, he said, "I have been put in charge of Muslims and non-Muslims alike, I remember now the poor who starve, the sick who are deprived, the needy, the persecuted, the imprisoned, the miserable, and the unattended elders. I am afraid God will hold me responsible for them all; and therefore I cried."

On his mother's side, Umar II was a great-grandson of the second caliph, Umar I. He sought to bring about some reconciliation between the two feuding Arab clans, the Umayyads and the Hashimites. To this end he outlawed the customary curse pronounced upon Ali and his descendants in the mosques of Damascus, a procedure which had been instituted during Mu'awiya's time. In its place he asked the Muslims to say, "Forgive our sins, O Lord, and forgive also the sins of those who have preceded us in faith; and help us not to bear a grudge against those who believed; O Lord, thou art compassionate and merciful."

Umar II was thoroughly convinced that Islamic mores, as influenced by the political behavior of his time, had deviated greatly from the original pattern of the Prophet and his two successors. The caliphs themselves had openly taken to wine, women, and luxury. Contrary to Muhammad's instructions, non-Arab converts to Islam were required to pay taxes, a matter which greatly retarded the progress of conversions. Furthermore, personal liberties were quite restricted since mere suspicion of crime could send a person not only to prison but also to death.

Known for his piety and intense dislike of luxury, Umar II ordered sweeping changes in almost every branch of government. In his personal life Umar completely shunned the style of living of his immediate predecessors; instead he wore a patched shirt, ate simple food, and avoided any display or pomp. He reportedly asked his wife to turn all her jewelry and precious gifts, estimated at thousands of dinars, into the main treasury. She obeyed and refused to take them back after his death even when offered them by his successor.

His Reforms

Regarding state administration, Umar II ordered that no person, regardless of background or religion, be arrested without clear evidence of crime. He lifted all restrictions against the Shi'ites and Kharijites and returned to them all their confiscated possessions. He also returned, to the Jews and Christians respectively, several synagogues and churches taken over by the preceding regimes. In Arabia, he ordered the return of the territory of Fadak, which had been usurped by Marwan I, to the house of Hashim since it had been previously the personal property of the Prophet himself.

Perhaps the most significant legislation attributed to this pious caliph was his order to exempt non-Arab Muslims from paying taxes. It may be remembered that Muhammad himself had freed non-Arabs from paying taxes if they became converted to Islam. However, since so many accepted Islam and became tax-exempt, the treasury of the Arab Empire suffered great losses. In an effort to replenish their treasury, the early Umayyad caliphs had taxed non-Arab Muslims – a measure which not only differentiated between Arab Muslims and non-Arab Muslims, but also aroused the hostility of the latter. Without giving much thought to the consequences of his actions, Umar II exempted non-Arab Muslims from taxes. As the income of the state sharply decreased, conversions to Islam are reported to have greatly increased, especially among the Turks of Transoxiana. Sudden confusion followed within the Arab communities whose regular state annuities were sharply reduced. As the Arab warriors were preparing for a coup against the caliph, he suddenly died at the age of thirty-nine. He had ruled for only two and a half years. His death brought an abrupt end to a relatively pious and benevolent rule.

YAZID II, 720-724

Yamanites Against Qaysites

Yazid II was the third son of Abd al-Malik to become caliph. Umar II had tried to instill in him the virtues of justice and piety, but Yazid II turned out to be the complete opposite of his predecessor. One of his first acts was, of course, to tax non-Arab Muslims. This action greatly angered the converts who had accepted Islam during the rule of Umar II, and sowed seeds of sedition, especially in Persia where non-Arab Muslims were in the majority.

Yazid II was closely related to the household of Hajjaj by marriage, and therefore favored the Qaysites against the Yamanites. This attitude renewed the factionalism among Umayyad supporters, which Umar II had tried to restrain. To sharpen antagonisms, Yazid II encouraged the Qaysites of Iraq to take revenge on the Yamanites for the blood of Hajjaj and his household, reportedly causing fierce factional strife not only in Iraq, but throughout the Arab Empire.

Revolution of Ibn Muhallab

Ibn Muhallab was the Yamanite governor appointed by Caliph Sulayman (715-717) to exterminate the supporters of Hajjaj. When Ibn Muhallab learned of Yazid's accession to the caliphate he escaped from his prison and fomented a rebellion in Basra. Yazid II sent an army headed by his brother Maslama to quench this revolt. A battle between the two factions was fought near Karbala in which the rebels were defeated and Ibn Muhallab himself, together with his supporters, killed. Although this battle was a victory for the loyalist Umayyad army, its results were greatly detrimental to the Umayyad cause. Throughout the whole empire, factional disputes intensified, contributing to the final collapse of the Umayyad regime.

Other than these reckless measures, nothing of any importance was recorded about Yazid II's reign, except perhaps his love affairs. It is reported that he was strongly attached to two beautiful slave girls. When the first of them died, he became grief-stricken and died soon after, ending a life wasted mainly on wine and the immature conduct of state.

HISHAM, 724-743

Hisham's Problems

Hisham was the fourth son of Abd al-Malik to be designated caliph. He brought a certain amount of dignity to the office of caliph after it had been carelessly abused by his brother Yazid II. Hisham became caliph at a critical period in the Umayyad regime, when rebellions flared in almost all parts of the empire. Had it not been for Hisham's perseverance and firm control of the state, perhaps the Umayyad dynasty would have been liquidated during his own reign by the Turkish tribesmen of Transoxiana in the east and the Berbers of North Africa in the west. It is no wonder, therefore, that Muslim annals associate

Hisham's name with those of Mu'awiya and Abd al-Malik as the three heroes of the Umayyad dynasty.

Hisham's rule was marked by the following main events:

1. The Muslims' defeat in France
2. Rebellion in Khurasan and Transoxiana
3. Rebellion in Egypt
4. Rebellion in North Africa
5. Rebellion in Iraq
6. Birth of the Abbasid underground movement

The Muslims' defeat in France marked the end of Arab expansions; the four rebellions were put down by Hisham's loyal forces, but the Abbasid underground movement led ultimately to the collapse of the Umayyad regime.

The Muslim Defeat in France

It may be recalled that in 714 the great conqueror of North Africa and Spain, Musa ibn Nusayr, was suddenly recalled to Damascus by Caliph Walid I. This left the Muslim troops in Spain without a strong commander. Nevertheless, in 718 they crossed the Pyrenees and captured Carcassonne, and in 725 took Nîmes. In 732 the Arabs, under the new commander Abd al-Rahman, penetrated deep into Aquitaine as far as the vicinity of Bordeaux. Eudes, Duke of Aquitaine, requested help against the Arabs from Charles Martel, then Mayor of the Palace of the Frankish kingdom. Charles Martel met the Arab forces at a point between Tours and Poitiers, where, in a hard-fought battle, the Arabs were defeated. The victorious Charles Martel added Aquitaine to his kingdom, thus establishing a strong barrier in France against further Arab invasions. The battle of Tours and Poitiers in 732 (exactly one hundred years after the death of the Prophet) marked the limits of Islamic expansion in Western Europe.

Rebellion in Khurasan and Transoxiana

During the rule of Umar II, much effort was exerted to win new converts to Islam. However, many converts later recanted and took refuge in the mountains of Transoxiana. Since death was theoretically the penalty for apostasy, severe measures were taken against recanting believers. This led to open rebellion in Khurasan and Transoxiana by 728. The rebels not only resisted Arab sovereignty and rule, but they also requested Turkish tribesmen from adjacent mountains to come to their aid. For several years Arab armies desperately fought numerous Turkish tribes, of which a certain group known as the Khazars penetrated deeply into Muslim territories as far as Mosul in Iraq. They were a source of continuous affliction to the Arabs until they were finally defeated by the caliph's own brother, Maslama, who ejected them after a surprise attack.

On the eastern frontier, a certain Turkish leader known as the Khaqan fought Arab armies near Samarqand for several years before he was finally defeated in 737. His defeat caused a considerable rift within the ranks of his own tribesmen, resulting in factional warfare rather than raids against Muslim territories. When Hisham received the news of the Khaqan's defeat, he reportedly offered a special prayer of thanks to Allah for granting victory to the Arabs.

Rebellion in Egypt

Since the beginning of Islamic rule in Egypt, the Copts had quietly paid their taxes and patiently endured their role as second-class citizens. However, toward the end of the administration of Umar II, their patience was tried by numerous oppressive measures. For example, a new law was passed requiring relatives of a deceased taxpayer to pay his overdue taxes. When the Copts protested, their churches were damaged and their sacred icons desecrated. Furthermore, during Hisham's regime, taxes were suddenly increased on the pretext that Egypt had been captured by the sword and thereafter the Copts and their property could be considered as booty. Finally, when Hisham transferred a number of the Qaysite tribes to the Hawf of Egypt, driving many Coptic families from their homes, the Copts rose in rebellion. The Coptic rebellion spread throughout the Nile Valley into both Upper and Lower Egypt, threatening Arab control of the land. When the Copts succeeded in pushing the Arab army as far north as Damietta on the Mediterranean in 739, Hisham sent reinforcements under the leadership of Handhala, who crushed the revolt, with the loss of several thousand Coptic lives.

Rebellion in North Africa

It may be recalled that when Hajjaj was appointed governor in Kufa in 695, one of his main tasks was to quell the Kharijite revolt in Iraq. When he pursued them into Persia, many Kharijites fled to North Africa and began to spread their teachings among the Berbers. Antagonized by the sudden recall of their beloved leader Musa in 714, the Berbers were evidently willing to listen to any anti-Umayyad slogans. However, the main principle which won most of the Berbers to the Kharijite side was the latter's belief in complete equality between Arabs and non-Arabs under the banner of Islam — a doctrine which the Umayyads had always refused to admit. Accordingly, in 740 the Berbers, under the leadership of the Kharijite sect, declared an open revolt in North Africa. They captured Tangier in 740 after the bloody battle of the Nobles, in which all Arab defensive units were completely destroyed. From there, the Berbers marched toward Qayrawan, imposing their authority over most of North Africa.

Realizing the seriousness of the situation, Hisham ordered more Arab troops to join the reinforcements he had already sent to Egypt under Handhala, who was charged with crushing the Berber revolt. Handhala rushed to defend Qayrawan, and instead of waiting to face a united Berber force, defeated their scattered units one by one until the last surrendered on the outskirts of Qayrawan in 743.

Rebellion in Iraq

In 738 Hisham replaced the governor of Iraq, whom the Kufans liked, with a relative of Hajjaj. This aroused doubts among the Iraqis, especially the Shi'ites, who were always looking for a pretext to withdraw their allegiance from the Umayyad caliphate. Therefore, in 740 the Shi'ites of Kufa sent messages to Zayd (a grandson of Husayn, the martyr of Karbala) who had been residing in Madina, inviting him to come to Kufa and assume the caliphate. Perhaps Zayd thought the time was opportune, since during that year the Umayyad caliph was preoccupied with the revolution in North Africa. At any rate, he accepted the invitation and started on his way to Kufa according to a plan which called for his arrival at the same moment that his supporters would stage a coup against the Umayyad governor. However the plot was discovered by the governor, who invited the chief Shi'ite supporters to the great mosque where he purposely detained them past the appointed time of Zayd's arrival. When the latter arrived, only a few supporters were on hand to greet him. As Zayd rode before them through the streets of Kufa, the Umayyad governor arrested the whole group, and Zayd was mercilessly slain. His body was crucified and his head severed and sent to Hisham in Damascus. Thus ended in complete failure the Shi'ites' second attempt to install their own caliph; instead they had another martyr to lament.

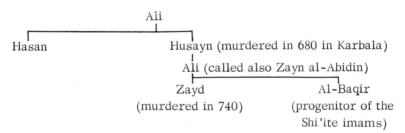

Descendants of Ali through Husayn

Birth of the Abbasid Underground Movement

Revolutions may be crushed and revolutionaries put to death, but popular dissatisfaction can never be extinguished without basic reforms.

Hisham might have succeeded in putting down four revolutions, but all his forces could not change prevailing anti-Umayyad sentiment, especially among the non-Arab Muslims of the empire. While Umayyad troops were busy fighting in Khurasan and North Africa, a certain descendant of the Prophet's uncle Abbas, a Hashimite named Muhammad, organized a secret society whose main purpose was to enlist supporters for the Abbasid cause throughout the Arab Empire. Working for the transfer of the caliphate to the Hashimite clan of Quraysh, underground cells spread throughout Iraq and Persia. Converts to the new movement were drafted secretly and plans were carefully made for a coup. The movement was successful; only seven years after the death of Hisham, the Umayyads were destroyed and the Abbasids firmly established as rulers of the Arab Empire.

CHAPTER 29

FALL OF THE UMAYYAD DYNASTY

THE LAST UMAYYAD CALIPHS

Walid II, 743-744

Toward the end of his administration, Hisham tried to exclude Walid II from the caliphate, to which he (Walid) had been designated by his father, Yazid II. At first he requested Walid to withdraw his claim in favor of Maslama, Hisham's own son. When Walid refused to do so, the caliph reportedly cut off his stipend and persecuted him, allowing common people to insult him openly. However, Hisham's son died suddenly before his father making way for Walid's accession to the caliphate in 743, when Hisham himself died. Naturally, Walid II was indignant against the household of Hisham and its supporters. He reportedly confiscated all their properties, imprisoned and flogged many of Hisham's sons, and dismissed from office several of his Yamanite supporters.

These actions brought adverse repercussions. The Yamanite faction of the Umayyad clan revolted against Walid II and chose his cousin Yazid III as their candidate. While Walid II was away from Damascus, the Yamanites marched on the capital, captured it, and announced their coup and Yazid III's assumption of the caliphate. Assured of their position in Damascus, they besieged Walid's desert residence. Walid begged in vain to be spared. When his pleas were rejected, he began reading the Qur'an reportedly saying, "Another day like Uthman's."[1] Nevertheless, according to Arab

---

[1]He was referring to the assassination of Uthman. See p. 156.

historians, his adversaries marched inside, severed his head, and
carried it away to Damascus.

Yazid III, 744

No sooner had Yazid III become caliph than the Qaysite faction
of the Umayyad clan revolted against him. However, with the help of
the Yamanite faction, he started a campaign of attrition against all
Qaysite leaders and potential troublemakers. So many atrocities were
committed that many of Yazid's enemies sought safety by disguising
themselves. One of them, Walid II's governor of Iraq, reportedly disguised himself as a woman and hid for several days. Yazid III's rule
was short-lived; he died in the sixth month of his reign and was followed by his brother Ibrahim.

Ibrahim, 744

As a caliph Ibrahim was timid and unwilling to extend his claims
outside Damascus. The Qaysites of northern Syria rallied behind
an Umayyad warrior named Marwan, who led them against Ibrahim.
Ibrahim's forces met Marwan's well-trained army near Baalbek, where
a desperate battle took place in which Ibrahim and his supporters
were defeated. Muslim annals report that before Marwan reached
Damascus and while the Yamanites were still in control, the latter
took revenge by killing the two sons of Walid II and a number of his
supporters.

As Marwan reached Damascus, Ibrahim and his followers fled the
city, which was soon restored to law and order. To save his life,
Ibrahim abdicated after reigning for only two months and ten days.

Marwan II, 744-750

Marwan II was a military man by profession. He fought with his
cousin, Maslama, commander of the Arab armies, along the northern
frontiers and Asia Minor. In 732 Maslama assigned Marwan the
responsibility of defending the Islamic frontiers against the Turkish
tribesmen of Adharbayjan. There he learned military tactics and became
an experienced warrior. Upon hearing of the assassination of Walid II
in 744, he left the frontier and set out for Damascus to seek revenge for
the murdered caliph. However, during Marwan's march on Damascus
after defeating Ibrahim, the Yamanites killed Walid II's two sons and
several others of his household leaving none of his supporters to claim
the caliphate. Accordingly, when the city was captured there was no
surviving heir to Walid II; the Qaysites had no alternative but to nominate Marwan as their caliph. Marwan II accepted their nomination and
became the last of the Umayyad caliphs.

END OF THE UMAYYAD DYNASTY

Umayyad Civil War

It is important to note that Marwan II assumed the Umayyad caliphate not by majority acclamation such as Mu'awiya I and Marwan I, nor by designation by a preceding caliph such as the rest of the Umayyad caliphs. A military man, he used the army to defeat the disorganized forces of the ruling caliph, Ibrahim. When Ibrahim abdicated, he did not designate Marwan II to replace him. This meant that Marwan II became caliph by nomination of only one faction of the Umayyad clan, namely the Qaysites, leaving the Yamanite faction throughout the empire under no obligation to accept him as caliph.

To add to the strife, Marwan II avenged the murder of Walid II's two sons by opening Yazid III's tomb and crucifying his corpse and by murdering a number of the Yamanite leaders who had supported Yazid III against Walid II. Marwan's action triggered the Yamanite faction to declare open revolt in almost every corner of the empire against the Damascus regime. Civil war broke out. Yamanites fought Qaysites not only in Syria and Iraq, but also as far as Khurasan in the east and Spain in the west. To suppress the rebels, Marwan II had to start from home. He dispatched two armies –one to northern Syria and another to Palestine –to put down rebellions there. The two armies succeeded in their missions and the Syrian region of the empire was stable for some time.

Kharijite Rebellion in Iraq

While the Umayyad armies were engaged at home, Yamanites and Qaysites fought in Iraq. There the Kharijites, having been suppressed for a long time, took advantage of the chaotic situation. Under the leadership of a warrior named Dahhak, they first fought the two warring factions of Umayya. But the Yamanite leader concluded a pact with the Kharijites by which the Kharijites and the Yamanite Umayyads would become allied against Marwan II. This rather unholy alliance succeeded for a time, and the Kharijite army soon occupied Kufa and Wasit in southern Iraq. As the Kharijites marched northward, Marwan II swiftly moved eastward to suppress the rebellion in Iraq. In 747 his armies met the Kharijite forces under Dahhak near Nasibin in northern Iraq. Marwan's forces fought gallantly against the Kharijites, defeated them, and moved on to recapture Kufa. In 748, after crushing the rebellion in Iraq, Marwan II dispatched his troops to suppress another rebellion in Hijaz and then returned to his residence in Harran in Syria.

Rebellion in Khurasan

As Marwan II was busy crushing rebellions in Syria, Iraq, and Hijaz, he could not direct his attention to problems elsewhere. It has been mentioned above that a Hashimite claimant to the caliphate from the line of Abbas named Muhammad had organized a secret society which spread itself in Khurasan under the slogan of *ahl al-Bayt,* which means "the Prophet's household." The Persian Muslims of Khurasan were anxious to join the Hashimite society because it promised sweeping religious reforms and social equality between Arabs and Muslim non-Arabs. The organization was so secret that its own members did not know most of their leaders nor the vast majority of their fellow members.

A year before his death in 743, Muhammad met a freed Persian slave named Abu Muslim and introduced him to his son, Ibrahim the Imam, who succeeded his father as head of the secret Abbasid organization. Later Ibrahim appointed Abu Muslim to lead the organization in Khurasan and form an underground army. Ibrahim the Imam, incidentally, was captured and killed by Marwan II, but his brother Abu al-Abbas had already been designated to succeed him.

When Marwan II faced civil war, Ibrahim the Imam decided that the time was ripe for the Abbasid movement to come out in the open. He ordered Abu Muslim to call upon members of his organization throughout Khurasan to begin the fight for the Hashimite cause. Since the Umayyad governor of Khurasan was deeply involved in the Yamanite-Qaysite dispute, Abu Muslim's forces scored an easy victory over their Umayyad enemies. Gaining control over Khurasan, they marched against Iraq, defeated the Umayyad forces near Nihawand, and captured Kufa. Marwan II gathered the remnant of his troops and marched toward Iraq, where he met the Abbasid forces on the banks of the Upper River Zab, a tributary of the Tigris. There in January, 750, at the battle of the Zab, Marwan's troops were badly beaten. Marwan II himself fled to Egypt leaving Syria and the whole Arab Empire virtually in the hands of the Abbasids. In August, 750, Marwan was captured in the Fayyum region in Egypt and immediately killed. With his death the Umayyad dynasty ended after ruling the Arab Empire for almost a century.

REASONS FOR THE UMAYYAD COLLAPSE

It is evident that the first of the fatal blows that struck the Umayyad dynasty was not foreign in origin. It was caused by internal rifts and bitter feuds within the Umayyad regime. Many reasons can be cited to explain the fall of the Umayyad dynasty; however, the following four generalizations seem to summarize the main weaknesses:

1. Discontinuity of government
2. Tribal factionalism
3. Blood revenge
4. Differentiation between Arab and non-Arab Muslims

Discontinuity of Government

Mu'awiya introduced to the Islamic world a dynastic system in which each caliph designated his successor in order to ensure peaceful transition of government and alleviate the strife and contention that usually accompanied the death of a caliph and the selection of his successor. However, Mu'awiya's system left designation completely at the discretion of each caliph without providing uniform regulations concerning succession. As it turned out, some caliphs designated more than one (usually two brothers) to follow each other. Undoubtedly, whenever the first one of these designates became caliph, he would try to disqualify the other one in favor of his own son. The second caliph-designate would then attempt to muster the support of as many high officials as possible to confirm and strengthen his own claim. If he succeeded and became caliph, he would discontinue his predecessor's work and follow an almost diametrically opposite course. This behavior naturally impeded continuity of government, brought about several splits in the political structure of the state, and drastically weakened the whole regime.

Perhaps the best illustration of this point is the case of Abd al-Malik and his two sons, Walid I and Sulayman. The damage resulting from Sulayman's attitude toward Walid's policies cannot be over-emphasized. The empire not only lost its great army commanders, but also its greatest opportunity to expand into Europe and several other fronts in the East. Furthermore, the internal structure of the empire suffered a great blow when Sulayman encouraged his own supporters to avenge themselves against the families of the high-ranking officials of his predecessor.

Tribal Factionalism

It may be recalled that only seven years after the capture of Makka in 630, the Arab armies defeated the armies of both the Byzantine and Persian Empires and founded their own empire. This meant that desert Arabs with their tribal customs suddenly found themselves the ruling class in sedentary communities such as Syria, Iraq, Persia, and Egypt. Waves of Arab Bedouins migrated to these countries; however, according to Umar's injunctions, they established their own Arab cities and retained their own way of life. When non-Arabs became Muslims they were required to associate themselves with Arab tribes at the level of *mawali,* meaning "clients" or "subordinates." This meant that, generally speaking, Arabs did not have to mingle with non-Arabs; on the contrary, non-Arab Muslims were the ones who had to join Arabs and emulate their way of life.

Of course the Arabs borrowed many material features of the cultures they had conquered, but it is important to note that they continued to live in their new settlements as tribes. Since the Qur'an did not explicitly outlaw the tribal way of life, the social unit of the Arabs within their empire continued to be the tribe with its main subdivisions, the clans, and the sub-clans. Later on, as tribal boundaries expanded, Islamic society became divided into several factions, each representing some earlier tribe or clan. These factions within the Arab Empire required from their members the same loyalty that a tribe or a clan had earlier required from desert Bedouins. Accordingly, as factional loyalties began to supercede state loyalties, splits and schisms beleaguered the Arab Empire. The first split divided the Islamic world into two major factions—the Umayyads versus the Hashimites. Within the Umayyad group two sub-factions existed—the Qaysites and the Yamanites. Unfortunately for the Umayyad dynasty, some imprudent caliphs had played these two factions against each other with the catastrophic result of many factional fights throughout the empire. These factional wars reached serious proportions during Marwan II's rule, allowing a movement such as the Abbasid one in Khurasan to bring about the collapse of the Umayyad dynasty.

Blood Revenge

One of the legacies of tribalism that was allowed to continue within the Arab political structure was blood revenge. In the desert this custom apparently helped prevent murder and bloodshed; but in a large empire it only perpetuated enmity and bitter feelings. It was the murder of Uthman that caused the first Arab civil war between Ali and Mu'awiya. The murder of Ali and his son, Husayn, split the Islamic world into several religio-political factions. During the Umayyad dynasty itself, the murder of Walid II is an example of the fateful results of blood revenge. As soon as Marwan II heard of Walid's murder, he left his command headquarters in northern Syria and in revenge defeated Caliph Ibrahim and murdered a number of Umayyad Yamanites. The latter avenged their blood by murdering Walid's two sons and other Qaysite leaders. Again in revenge, Marwan II murdered many Yamanite leaders in Damascus and hanged the exhumed body of Yazid III on a cross. This led to an open revolt by the Yamanites throughout the empire, allowing the Abbasid movement in Khurasan to bring about the downfall of the divided Umayyad regime.

Differentiation Between Arab and Non-Arab Muslims

The Umayyad regime is generally characterized by its policies of Arab supremacy. Arabs throughout the empire constituted the ruling elite. Non-Arab Muslims were *mawali,* "clients." In other words, the Umayyad society was divided into the following four groups in the order of their prestige: (1) Arab Muslims, (2) non-Arab Muslims *(mawali),* (3) scriptuaries[2] *(dhimmis),* and (4) slaves. Since the Qur'an condemned segregation among Muslims due to race or national origin, non-Arab Muslims within the Umayyad regime were justified in their grudge against their rulers. Moreover, when more funds were needed for the treasury, non-Arab Muslims were asked to pay taxes in spite of Islamic traditions which had made them tax-exempt. These actions on the part of Umayyad caliphs immensely angered the non-Arab Muslims. It may be recalled that the Kharijites easily incited the Berbers of North Africa to revolt against Hisham in 740. Moreover, it was due mainly to the dissatisfaction of the non-Arab Muslims of Khurasan that the secret Abbasid organization spread and gained momentum. When the time was ripe, Abu Muslim launched his fatal attack against the Umayyad regime.

[2] These included Christians, Jews, and any other group that believed in a revealed book.

IMPORTANT TERMS

Abd al-Malik: Fifth Umayyad caliph (685-705). During his reign Iraq revolted under Mukhtar, and Hijaz seceded under Ibn Zubayr. When Ibn Zubayr's forces defeated Mukhtar, Abd al-Malik defeated Ibn Zubayr and saved the Umayyad regime from collapse.

Charles Martel: Mayor of the Palace in the Frankish kingdom who defeated the Arabs at the battle of Tours and Poitiers in 732.

Dahhak the Kharijite: A warrior who staged a rebellion against Marwan II in Iraq. Although he was defeated at Nasibin in 747, he engaged the Umayyad troops during the early stages of the Abbasid revolt.

Dahhak the Qaysite: A leader of the Qaysite faction of the Umayyads. He opposed Marwan I in favor of Ibn Zubayr, but Marwan I defeated him at Marj Rahit in 684.

Hajjaj: A warrior under Abd al-Malik. He besieged and bombarded Makka in 692. Later on he was appointed governor of Iraq and succeeded in inhibiting further rebellions there.

Handhala: An Arab warrior under Hisham who put down the Coptic rebellion of Egypt in 739. He then moved to Qayrawan and defeated the Berbers in 742, ending the North African rebellion.

Hisham: The tenth Umayyad caliph (724-743). In his reign rebellions broke out almost everywhere in the Arab Empire. However, due to his firm attitude and good judgment, he succeeded in suppressing them and reaffirming the authority of the Umayyad regime.

Husayn: A grandson of the Prophet Muhammad who claimed the caliphate after Mu'awiya's death with the support of the Alids in Kufa. However, Ibn Ziyad, Yazid's governor in Iraq, put down the Alid rebellion, and Husayn was killed near Karbala in 680.

Ibn Qasim: An army commander known for his conquests in India during the reign of Walid I.

Ibn Ziyad: The governor of Iraq under Yazid I. He ordered the murder of Husayn near Karbala in 680.

Ibn Zubayr: A pretender to the caliphate in Makka during the reign of Abd al-Malik. The Umayyad army defeated his forces in Iraq and besieged him in Makka till he surrendered and was killed in 692.

Ibrahim: The thirteenth Umayyad caliph. As soon as he was acclaimed caliph in 744, Marwan II defeated him north of Damascus forcing him to renounce his rights to the caliphate.

Ibrahim the Imam: Son of Muhammad, head of the Abbasid secret organization. He was designated by his father as successor, but Marwan II took him prisoner at Harran, where he was killed in 749 and succeeded by his brother Abu al-Abbas.

Karbala: Site of the martyrdom of Husayn in 680.

Khaqan: Chief of the Turkish tribesmen who attacked Transoxiana during Hisham's rule. He was defeated in 737, and his warriors disbanded.

Marj Rahit, battle of: The battle in 684 in which Marwan I defeated the Qaysite faction under Dakhak.

Muhammad, son of Ali: Organizer and leader of the secret Abbasid movement. He died in 743 and was followed by his son Ibrahim the Imam.

Mukhtar: Self-appointed avenger of the murder of Husayn. He staged a coup in Iraq against the Umayyads in 685, but was defeated by Mus'ab in 687.

Marwan I: Fourth Umayyad caliph. During his reign the Umayyads sharply split into two factions, the Qaysites and the Yamanites. By defeating his opponents, the Qaysites under Dahhak at Marj Rahit in 684, he consolidated his rule over the Arab Empire.

Marwan II: Fourteenth and last of the Umayyad caliphs. He was acclaimed caliph in 744 when he defeated the forces of his predecessor, Ibrahim. However, the Abbasid revolution overtook him as he was battling the Kharijites in Iraq, and he was finally defeated at the battle of the Zab in 750.

Musa ibn Nusayr: The great conqueror of North Africa. Together with Tariq he completed the capture of Spain between 711 and 714. In the zenith of his power, Caliph Walid I recalled him to Damascus.

Mus'ab: Brother of Ibn Zubayr, a claimant of the caliphate in Makka. He commanded his brother's troops toward Iraq and defeated Mukhtar in 687, but was defeated himself by the Umayyad forces in 691.

Poitiers: See Tours.

Qaysites and Yamanites: Two factions within the Umayyad dynasty. The feud between them continued throughout the Umayyad regime, contributing to its weakness and final collapse.

Qutayba: The great conqueror of Transoxiana. He reached the borders of China during Walid's caliphate; however, he was recalled and detained by Walid's successor Sulayman.

Sulayman: Seventh Umayyad caliph, (715-717). Due to a feud between him and his predecessor, Walid I, he detained and persecuted all of his predecessor's warriors and governors. These actions rekindled the Qaysite-Yamanite feud, which ended with the fall of the empire.

Tariq: A Berber commander in the Arab army of North Africa. In 711, according to orders from his own commander, Musa, he crossed Gibraltar and captured southern Spain for the Arabs.

Tours and Poitiers, battle of: The decisive battle between the Arabs and Charles Martel of France in 732, in which the Arabs were defeated. This battle marks the farthest extent of Arab expansion in Western Europe.

Umar II: Eighth Umayyad caliph, (717-720). His piety and sense of justice won him the hearts of his people. He legislated many social and financial reforms for which the Arab Empire was not yet ready.

Uqba: A great Arab warrior who conquered North Africa in 670 and founded the Arab city of Qayrawan.

Walid I: Sixth Umayyad caliph (705-715). During his reign the Arab Empire expanded until it reached the borders of China in the east and northern Spain in the west. His period was one of prosperity and internal reforms.

Walid II: Eleventh Umayyad caliph (743-744). He was killed in a manner similar to that of the assassination of Uthman in 656. This caused a sharpening of the feud within the Umayyad dynasty and was mainly responsible for its collapse.

Warda, battle of: The Shi'ite followers of Husayn were greatly ashamed of themselves for having abandoned him during the massacre of Karbala in 680. They formed a group of about 3,000 warriors called the Penitents and marched against the Umayyads in Syria. They were completely routed at the battle of Warda in 685, and many were killed.

Yazid I: Second Umayyad caliph (680-683). During his rule, Husayn was murdered at Karbala, and Makka was besieged and bombarded for the first time.

Yazid II: Ninth Umayyad caliph (720-724). He followed Hisham and reversed most of his internal reforms. Otherwise, he was devoted to pleasure, women, and wine.

Yazid III: Twelfth Umayyad caliph (744). He reigned for only six months after which the Umayyad dynasty began its sharp downfall.

Yamanites: See Qaysites.

SUPPLEMENTARY READINGS

ALI, AMEER, *A Short History of the Saracens* (London, 1957).

BROCKELMANN, CARL, *History of the Islamic Peoples* (New York, 1947).

DENNET, D.C., *Conversion and Poll Tax in Early Islam* (Cambridge, 1950).

GIBBON, EDWARD, *The Decline and Fall of the Roman Empire,* An Abridgement by D.M. Low (London, 1960).

GLUBB, SIR JOHN BAGOT, *The Empire of the Arabs* (London 1963).

GRUNEBAUM,G.E. VON,   *Medieval Islam* (Chicago, 1946).

HITTI, PHILIP K., *History of the Arabs* (New York, 1960).

——, *History of Syria* (London, 1957).

LAMMENS, H., *Études sur le siècle des Omayyades* (Beirut, 1930).

LANE-POOLE, STANLEY, *The Moors in Spain* (New York, 1911).

LEWIS, A.R. *Naval Power and Trade in the Mediterranean, A.D. 500-1100* (Princeton, 1951).

MUIR, WILLIAM, *The Caliphate* (Edinburgh, 1924).

TRITTON, A.S., *The Caliphs and their non-Muslim Subjects* (Oxford, 1938).

VASILEV, A.A., *History of the Byzantine Empire* (Madison, Wisconsin, 1964).

WATT, W.M., *A History of Islamic Spain* (Edinburgh, 1965).

WELLHAUSEN, T., *The Arab Kingdom and its Fall* (Calcutta, 1927).

PART viii

THE EARLY ABBASID PERIOD, 750-861

Following are excerpts from the inaugural speech of the first Abbasid caliph, Abu al-Abbas al-Saffah, delivered in the mosque of Kufa early in the year 750:

> Praise be to God, who has chosen Islam for Himself as a religion . . . and supported it by us, establishing us as its upholders, its protectors, and its strength . . . He has honored us by allowing us to be direct descendants and relatives of the Prophet of God and by making us a part of his clan, a branch of his tree, and a tributary of his stream. . . .
>
> He (God), great is His bounty, has made clear to them (the Muslims) our favor, binding upon them our right (for the caliphate) and their loyalty to us. He has allowed us to receive booty and spoils of war as a sign of our high office and an indication of His kind favor upon us. God is most gracious and bountiful. . . .
>
> When God claimed Muhammad to Himself, his companions became leaders after him. . . . They ruled with justice and divided things fairly, giving each one his rightful share while they themselves obtained nothing. Soon, however, the sons of Harb (Umayyads) and Marwan plunged themselves in the middle and devoured everything. When they ruled unjustly and mistreated the people, God appointed for them a time, but

they angered Him. Accordingly, He took revenge against them through us, returning to us our usurped right, and using us to save our *umma*, (the Islamic community). . . .

We, the Prophet's household, receive guidance from God. O, people of Kufa, you are the center of our devotion and focal point of our love, you yourselves whose (loyalty) never changed. You have kept up your (zeal), in spite of the tribulations brought upon you by the tyrants, until you reached our era, when God graced you with our rule. With us you will be the most prosperous of all people. [1]

The striking contrast between the words and actions of the first Abbasid caliph becomes evident as the story of the rise of the Abbasid regime unfolds in the following chapters.

[1] Al-Tabari, *Tarikh,* Volume 9, pp. 125, 126.

CHAPTER 30

ABBASIDS VERSUS UMAYYADS

BEGINNING OF THE ABBASID MOVEMENT

Muhammad the Abbasid

It may be recalled that during the early battles between Makka and Madina following the Prophet's emigration in 622, one of his uncles named Abbas residing in Makka secretly supported the Prophet against his Makkan enemies. However, for some unknown reason Abbas hesitated to announce his conversion to Islam till Muhammad's final victory over Makka in 630. It does not appear likely that Abbas himself, nor any of his sons, ever aspired to the caliphate since their allegiance to Ali and his son Husayn was strong. Nevertheless, during the Umayyad period, Walid I is reported to have greatly humiliated a grandson of Abbas named Ali by flogging him publicly for marrying his (Walid's) divorced wife. Apparently this action aroused in Ali's son, Muhammad, such bitter resentment that he made up his mind to avenge his family's prestige by plotting in earnest to overthrow the Umayyad regime.

Secret Organization

Muhammad, the great-grandson of Abbas, was an efficient administrator and organizer. Knowing that the Umayyad regime was too strong to be overthrown by an ill-conceived or hasty plot, he planned to win support for his movement first by giving

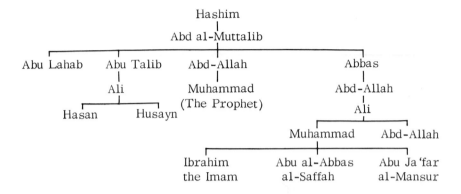

The Abbasid Branch of the Hashimites.

it a slogan and sending out missionaries to recruit followers. The slogan was purposely left vague, calling on people to support *ahl al-bayt,* "the Prophet's household," without making clear whether it was supporting Ali or Abbas. This of course, attracted many Shi'ite adherents. Besides advocating the return of the caliphate to its rightful possessors, the Prophet's household, Muhammad's platform included other reforms, such as the restoration of justice and equality among all Muslims regardless of their ethnic backgrounds. This platform appealed strongly to the Persian Muslims, who resented being treated as second-class Muslims by the Umayyads. To ensure its success, Muhammad organized his movement in utmost secrecy. Even the identity of the top leaders was withheld from the majority of their supporters. The exact goals of the movement apart from its slogan and promised reforms were unclear. At any rate, so long as Umayyad caliphs continued to commit atrocities, the Abbasid movement continued to gain momentum throughout the Arab Empire. Muhammad, the founder of the movement, reportedly formed a high council of twelve supervisors, each in charge of recruiting adherents in designated areas. The recruiters were selected from traveling merchants who went from town to town enlisting supporters. During the pilgrimage season, Muhammad met with members of his high council to receive their reports and issue his orders.

Abu Muslim Joins the Movement

Arab historians have related different stories about the early life of the warrior named Abu Muslim and how he joined the Abbasid movement. However the following account is the best available.

In 742 Bukayr, one of the movement's organizers in Kufa, saw a young Persian named Abu Muslim waiting upon some prisoners in one of the city jails. The youth was seen weeping as he heard unhappy prisoners talk about Umayyad malevolence and brutality. Bukayr brought Abu Muslim to the attention of Muhammad himself, who im-

mediately freed him and introduced him to his son, Ibrahim the Imam.
Abu Muslim was then sent to Khurasan to campaign for the Abbasid
cause in his own home country.

Shortly afterward, Muhammad, founder of the Abbasid secret
movement, died, after having designated his son Ibrahim the Imam as
his successor. Recognizing Abu Muslim's success in recruiting converts to the Abbasid movement, Ibrahim the Imam in 746 appointed him
commander-in-chief of the organization in Khurasan. His efficiency
and shrewdness won over many inhabitants around the city of Marv,
as well as the Yamanite faction of the Umayyad regime.

Open Revolt

As mentioned before, by 745 revolts by the Yamanite faction of the
Umayyad regime had already broken out against Marwan II in many
parts of Syria, Palestine, Iraq, and Persia. As the embattled caliph
was trying to put down these revolts, the Kharijites declared war
against him in Kufa and sent their army northward to occupy Mosul.
Marwan II marshaled all his forces against the Kharijites at the battle
of Nasibin in 747. However, during these operations the Yamanites
in Khurasan were fighting the Qaysite governor Nasr, who was able
to check their progress but could not defeat them. Yamanites in
Khurasan joined Abu Muslim's ranks, adding more weight to his
movement. At this stage, Ibrahim the Imam presumably issued his
orders to Abu Muslim to openly revolt.

Nasr was extremely alarmed at the alliance of Abu Muslim with
the Yamanites and sent urgent pleas to Marwan II for reinforcements.
One of his pleas reportedly included some eloquent verses:

> I see a glimmer within the ashes, that soon will
>   burst to flame.
> If the wisemen of the land could not quench it,
>   many corpses will it claim.
> Are the Umayyads awake or fast alseep?
> In my wonder I did exclaim.

Marwan II was so busy battling the Kharijites that Nasr's continued
pleas to him went in vain. With the help of the Yamanites, Abu Muslim
captured Marv in 748 and used it as a base for his campaigns.

BEGINNING OF THE ABBASID REGIME

Outbreak of War

Without divulging the name of the person for whom he was fighting,
Abu Muslim called upon his Khurasanian recruits to come into the open
and enlist in the movement's army. They did, and in a short time he had

a standing army of several thousand warriors bearing black banners, which later became the emblem of the Abbasid regime. Abu Muslim immediately appointed a warrior named Qahtaba to lead the black-bannered army against Iraq and Syria. Wasting no time, Qahtaba started from Marv in 748 and moved west toward Kufa, capturing on his way Nishapur, Rayy, and Isfahan, where the Umayyad governor Nasr was defeated and killed. With practically all of Persia in Abbasid hands, the army of the revolution triumphantly proceeded toward Iraq, the stronghold of the Shi'ites.

Murder of Ibrahim the Imam

As soon as Abu Muslim declared open war against the Umayyads in Marv, Marwan II ordered his officials to find the identity of the Hashimite leader of the revolt. Mail was inspected and a letter was intercepted which had been sent by Ibrahim the Imam from his residence in Transjordan to Abu Muslim himself. Once the identity of Ibrahim was known, Marwan II easily had him captured and sent to Harran, where he was detained as a hostage. However, when the Abbasid army moved west, Marwan II had Ibrahim the Imam murdered in order to discourage his supporters from pursuing the war. Nevertheless, Marwan's efforts were in vain, for Ibrahim, recognizing the urgency of leaving Syria as soon as possible, had already designated his brother Abu al-Abbas to succeed him. Abu al-Abbas secretly moved to Kufa with his household, arriving there in time to meet the victorious Abbasid armies.

Capture of Kufa

In 749 Qahtaba's troops captured Nihawand and pushed toward Kufa. Failing to receive any reinforcements from Marwan II, Ibn Hubayra, the Umayyad governor of Iraq, gathered his loyal Umayyad soldiers and moved to check the fast-advancing Abbasid army. Ibn Hubayra re-dug an old trench around the small town of Jalula and camped inside waiting for Qahtaba. However, Qahtaba marched directly toward Kufa, crossed the River Tigris, and camped on the banks of the Euphrates only a few miles away from Kufa. To prevent the Abbasids from crossing the Euphrates to Kufa, Ibn Hubayra rushed his troops from Jalula to Qahtaba's encampment. In a hard-fought battle the Umayyads were defeated; however, they caused so much disorder and alarm among the Abbasid troops, that in the midst of the confusion Qahtaba himself was drowned. His son Hasan immediately assumed command of the troops, restored their morale, and swiftly proceeded toward Kufa. Ibn Hubayra abandoned the defense of Kufa, where the Shi'ite population would have certainly supported the Hashimite cause of the Abbasids, and retreated to Wasit, where he took refuge within its fortified walls. The Abbasid army, advancing under Hasan, captured Kufa without opposition. There the caliph-designate, Abu al-Abbas, met his Persian army for the first time.

Abu Al-Abbas Declared Caliph

No sooner had the army of Khursan occupied Kufa than the Shi'ites announced their desire to select a caliph from the descendants of Ali. At that time the commander-in-chief of the conquering army publicly proclaimed Abu al-Abbas the designated caliph. Finding it too late to resist, the Shi'ite supporters had to recognize the new caliph and pledge him their allegiance. Abu al-Abbas triumphantly rode through the streets of Kufa to the great mosque, where he was officially proclaimed caliph and commander of the faithful. The new caliph immediately stood behind the pulpit and gave his inaugural speech, in which he denounced the brutalities of the Umayyads and announced a new era, to be characterized by piety and justice under the banner of the Prophet's own household and guided by the principles of the Islamic religion. As he sat down, his brother Abu Ja'far received the allegiance of the supporters of the new regime.

END OF THE UMAYYAD REGIME

The Battle of the Zab, 750

Although reports from Kufa were discouraging indeed, Marwan II considered the Abbasid takeover in Iraq only a rebellion to be crushed before its roots could take hold and spread throughout the empire. He therefore marshaled all his forces and proceeded east, hoping to deal his enemies a decisive blow while their movement was young.

One of Abu al-Abbas's first acts as caliph was to appoint his uncle Abd-Allah commander-in-chief of the Abbasid forces with orders to fight the Umayyads in Syria and consolidate his regime throughout the empire. Thus as Marwan II and his forces were moving east, Abd-Allah and his troops were marching north. The armies of the two opposing regimes met head-on in January, 750, near Mosul on the banks of the Upper Zab River, a tributary of the Tigris. A number of Marwan's soldiers reportedly failed to obey his orders to cross the river and fight on the other side. Nevertheless, in a hard-fought battle the Umayyad forces were badly defeated and Marwan II himself fled the battlefield.

After this decisive battle of the Zab, most of the Syrian cities surrendered to the Abbasid forces with little or no resistance. The Umayyads of Damascus, however, put up a last minute fight to save their city, forcing the Abbasid commander Abd-Allah to order its siege. After a few days of resistance, the Umayyads of Damascus surrendered and the victorious Abbasid army triumphantly occupied their city, murdering a number of Umayyad leaders and digging up the graves of several of their dead caliphs.

With Damascus under their control, the Abbasids had no trouble capturing the rest of the Syrian cities along the Mediterranean. In fact, as soon as the Umayyad capital surrendered to the besieging Abbasid army, it became clear that the Umayyad regime had reached its ignominious end. Governors of the provinces, who had not yet proclaimed their allegiance to the Abbasid regime, hastened to announce their loyalty and subordination to the new caliph in Kufa. Thus after ninety years of Umayyad rule, the Arab Empire had a new Hashimite caliph, a direct descendant of the Prophet's own clan; ironically enough, the main force behind this new Hashimite caliphate was not Arab but Persian.

Extermination of the Umayyad Clan

Soon after the battle of the Zab, Abu al-Abbas appointed his uncle Abd-Allah as governor of Syria, ordering him to exterminate all members of the Umayyad clan. Abd-Allah's first target was the fugitive Umayyad caliph, Marwan II, who had fled through Harran and Damascus to Palestine. The victorious Abbasid army pursued him from city to city. He finally sought refuge in Egypt, but Abd-Allah sent an Abbasid contingent to find out his hiding place. In August, 750, the Abbasid detachment surprised him in the Fayyum region of Egypt and killed him on the spot, carrying his head to Abd-Allah in Damascus. With the death of Marwan II, the last vestige of Umayyad authority disappeared, and the Abbasid regime in Kufa was firmly established.

The greatest act of revenge against the Umayyads took place in Damascus, where Abd-Allah reportedly celebrated the capture of the city by ordering the murder of all Umayyad leaders and their supporters. Hundreds of men, women, and children of the Umayyad clan were mercilessly killed while the Abbasids enjoyed a festive banquet. A few Umayyads fled to Palestine, but Abd-Allah reportedly followed them and deceitfully announced a general amnesty if they would pledge allegiance to the new caliph. When about seventy desperate Umayyads accepted the Abbasid terms, and agreed to meet at a designated place to proclaim their loyalty to the new regime, Abd-Allah treacherously ordered their massacre. Islamic annals report that while the helpless Umayyads were being killed, Abd-Allah brought food and ate together with his high officials undisturbed by the pitiful moans of the dying victims.

With the exception of one young man named Abd al-Rahman, who fled to Spain, all members of the Umayyad clan are reported to have been massacred by the Abbasids. It is no wonder, therefore, that when Arab historians referred to Abu al-Abbas, who had originally ordered these massacres, they called him al-Saffah, "blood shedder"—an indication that the Arabs themselves considered his brutality extreme.

CONSOLIDATION OF THE ABBASID REGIME

With the exception of Spain, which later became the seat of a new Umayyad dynasty, the chief provinces of the Arab Empire pledged their allegiance to the Abbasid caliphate. A few instances of rebellion broke out in northern Syria, but all were easily crushed as peace and stability began to prevail over the Islamic domain. While all these battles between the Abbasids and the Umayyads were taking place, Abu Muslim, the great Persian warrior who organized the armies of the Abbasid movement, remained behind as governor of Khurasan. Besides keeping the Persians under control, he was also responsible for supplying the main Abbasid forces with reinforcements and material, especially during the first decisive battles.

On the Syrian front, Abd-Allah continued to guard the interests of the regime by keeping a watchful eye on counter-revolutionary movements. A few scattered riots occurred, but he was able to suppress them easily. In Iraq itself there was no commander strong enough to capture Wasit and recover it from the Umayyad governor Ibn Hubayra. The latter fortified the city and held out against Abbasid

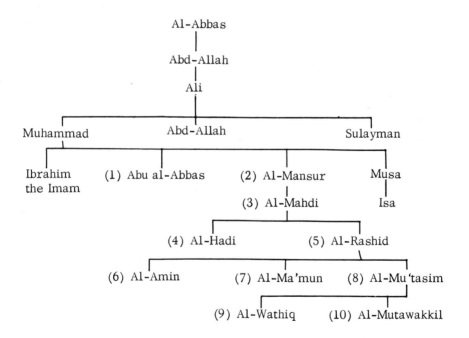

Genealogy of the First Ten Abbasid Caliphs [2]

2 Consult the list of the names and dates of the Abbasid caliphs on pp. 381,382.

attacks until almost all military activity came to an end. All else failing, the new caliph dispatched his brother Abu Ja'far to negotiate terms with Ibn Hubayra. The two agreed on surrender of the city on condition that Ibn Hubayra be given a safe conduct. Abu Ja'far guaranteed the safe conduct on behalf of his brother; however, when the city surrendered, the new caliph treacherously ordered the murder of Ibn Hubayra and his followers.

At this point, one might recall the promises which Abu al-Abbas himself made during his inaugural speech in Kufa, in which he pledged a reign of piety and justice according to the laws of religion. As soon as he attained power, his promises proved to be only means to an end. Compared to the brutal Umayyad caliphs, the first Abbasid caliph showed himself to be not only brutal, but also treacherous.

CHAPTER 31

THE FIRST TWO ABBASID CALIPHS

ABU AL-ABBAS AL-SAFFAH, 750-754

Dealing With Counterrevolutions

Having eliminated his Umayyad opponents, the new Abbasid caliph—known by his well-deserved title, al-Saffah, "blood-shedder"—carried the Abbasid banner throughout the Arab Empire, with the exception of Spain. However, when he embarked on reorganizing the provinces, he met several problems, chief of which was the refusal of certain areas to obey his newly appointed governors. Al-Saffah therefore decided to punish these counterrevolutionaries with severity, in order to make them object lessons for others who might think of defying his orders.

The first experiment of this kind took place in Mosul in northern Iraq, where a majority of the population succeeded in driving out their new governor. Al-Saffah promised security to Mosul's dissatisfied inhabitants and requested them to gather in the courtyard of the central mosque to voice their complaints. As the record goes, about ten thousand citizens of Mosul accepted the caliph's promise of security; but instead of sending his officials to listen to their grievances, al-Saffah sent his army, which suddenly surrounded the crowd and killed them all. The city was then laid open to looting and raping by army troops for several days till a brave woman reached the army commander and pleaded with him to save the honor of the Prophet's descendants. The commander reportedly ordered his soldiers to stop their looting, but not before counterrevolutionaries everywhere had noted the caliph's determination to crush any revolt.

Al-Saffah and His First Wazir

Apparently the ruthless actions of Caliph al-Saffah did not agree with the policies of his *wazir* (administrative assistant) Abu Salma, who had previously supported the house of Ali before serving the Abbasids. Abu Salma left the residence of the caliph and lived at Anbar, where several influential supporters began to rally around him. Fearing the outcome of such a clique only a few miles away, al-Saffah consulted with Abu Muslim, who reportedly advised him against publicly murdering Abu Salma. Accordingly, the caliph ordered one of his court officials to walk in the city's main streets and proclaim the caliph's praises for his *wazir*, Abu Salma, in order to convince the citizens that there was no ill-feeling at all between himself and his *wazir*. Meanwhile, an assassin had been secretly hired to murder Abu Salma that same night. Although official announcements accused the Kharijites of this murder, almost everyone recognized the plot and quietly understood who the real assassin was.

Death of Al-Saffah

With Abu Salma removed, al-Saffah confirmed his brother Abu Ja'far as governor of Iraq, Armenia, and Adharbayjan; his uncle Abd-Allah remained governor of Syria, and Abu Muslim governor of Khurasan. He built a palace at Anbar, and employed a certain Khalid ibn Barmak as his treasurer. Plots and intrigues started between Abu Ja'far and Abu Muslim, as the two departed for Makka on a pilgrimage tour. Abu Ja'far requested his brother to eliminate Abu Muslim, but the caliph hesitated to do so for fear of the Khurasanian reaction.

While these plots were going on in Kufa, the Byzantines attacked the Muslim borders in Asia Minor, forcing Abd-Allah to move his forces northward to defend the frontiers. However, the caliph came down unexpectedly with smallpox and was seriously ill. His son was too young to become caliph, and, by-passing his uncle Abd-Allah, who was busy fighting the Byzantines, al-Saffah designated his brother Abu Ja'far as his successor. Since Abu Ja'far was on a pilgrimage tour, the caliph appointed his nephew Isa to receive acclamation for Abu Ja'far during the latter's absence.

After ruling only four years, al-Saffah died in June, 754, at the age of thirty-five. Although he is known in history as *al-saffah*, "blood shedder," his domestic life was one of temperance and hospitality. He had only one wife and refused to bring concubines or dancing girls to his palace. He was reportedly most generous and cheerful at home.

However, as a revolutionary, he was always fearful of counter-revolutionaries, and therefore he applied the most ruthless and treacherous means at his disposal to protect his newly established regime.

ABU JA'FAR AL-MANSUR, 754-775

Al-Mansur Proclaimed Caliph

Hearing the news of his brother's premature death, Abu Ja'far hastened back to Kufa and then to Anbar, where he was proclaimed caliph under the title al-Mansur, meaning "the victorious." Al-Mansur may be considered the real founder of the Abbasid dynasty for two reasons. First, all Abbasid caliphs who ruled the Arab Empire for centuries after him were his descendants. Second, during the twenty years in which al-Mansur was caliph, he was so successful in crushing all counterrevolutions and destroying all potential rivals that the Abbasid regime became indeed firmly established. He consolidated his regime so well that the regnal years of the five caliphs immediately after him were the most successful and prosperous years in the history of the Arab Empire. They were so productive in literature, art, philosophy, jurisprudence, and all other branches of science and scholarship that historians have rightly referred to them as the classical period of the Arab Empire.

Al-Mansur's regime itself was fraught with dangers and difficulties so that his reign was one of continuous struggle and bloodshed. However, due to his cleverness, ruthlessness, and wily devices, he surmounted one crisis after another until he finally managed not only to survive, but also to become the undisputed ruler of the empire.

Al-Mansur Versus Abd-Allah

The first to oppose al-Mansur was his own uncle Abd-Allah, the military commander and hero of the great battle of the Zab. He was fighting the Byzantines in Asia Minor when he learned of the death of al-Saffah and the accession of al-Mansur. Aware that his nephew did not have a standing army, he proclaimed himself caliph and ordered his troops to march eastward in order to stage a coup against the newly proclaimed caliph.

Al-Mansur proved more wily than his uncle. He turned to Abu Muslim of Khurasan, whose murder he had plotted shortly before his brother's death, and, showering praises upon him, the young caliph won both his allegiance and armed support. Abd-Allah and his army moved east, while Abu Muslim and his troops were moving westward; the two commanders met near Nasibin in northern Iraq. Islamic annals report that besides his regular Arab troops, Abd-Allah's forces included about 17,000 soldiers from Khurasan, whose loyalty to him was doubtful. To avoid possible treason on their part, he ordered them all killed in cold blood—a characteristic act of treachery. This enormous butchery undoubtedly enraged Abu Muslim and his troops, who fought gallantly against their enemies, inflicting a ruinous defeat. Abd-Allah himself ignominiously fled to his brother in Basra, where he lived in hiding most of the time.

According to some records, a few months later when al-Mansur decided to get rid of his rebellious uncle, he built him a house whose foundations included blocks of salt. Giving him a safe conduct, the caliph ordered his uncle to move to the new house where he could live "safely." When the rainy season came, the whole house reportedly collapsed upon the old man, killing him and all his household. Thus the man who had treacherously slaughtered thousands in Palestine, Syria, and Iraq, died a victim of the same perfidy he had himself so frequently perpetrated.

Al-Mansur versus Abu Muslim

Abu Muslim's triumph over Abd-Allah represented a tremendous victory of non-Arab forces over Arabs. Although it resulted in establishing the rule of the Abbasid caliph, al-Mansur, the main beneficiary was the victorious commander himself, who became chief of the only military force in the whole empire. The wily caliph knew very well that if Abu Muslim and his troops were allowed to return to Khurasan they could ally themselves to any counterrevolutionary movement and bring about his downfall. Since al-Mansur lacked a military force with which to challenge the troops from Khurasan, the battle between the caliph and Abu Muslim had to be one of wits and craftiness.

First, al-Mansur sent to the victorious warrior a message praising his brilliant victory over the revolution's enemies and expressing his full confidence and support. At the end of the message the caliph indicated his appreciation of his commander's loyalty by appointing him governor of both Egypt and Syria. Abu Muslim, who was on his way back home with his troops, realized from al-Mansur's message that the caliph wanted to separate him from his forces. Accordingly, he answered the caliph's message by thanking him for his trust and confidence and politely suggesting that the Abbasid cause would be served better by his being in Khurasan rather than Syria. Despite the polite correspondence between the caliph and his army commander, each one sensed with foreboding the true intent of the other. Without waiting for the caliph's answer to his message, Abu Muslim continued his eastward march homeward. As soon as al-Mansur received Abu Muslim's reply, he understood that his commander was firm on rejecting the new appointment. Without wasting time, the caliph sent another message approving Abu Muslim's suggestion and allowing him to proceed to Khurasan if he would pass first by the capital and receive his due honors for his victory over the rebels.

Al-Mansur's scheme was, of course, to try by all possible means to separate Abu Muslim from his troops. To encourage Abu Muslim to come to the capital, al-Mansur dispatched a number of trusted emissaries with the special assignment of convincing Abu Muslim of the caliph's sincerity and good intentions. Apparently, the emissaries fulfilled their task faithfully, for, contrary to the advice of his own chief officers, Abu Muslim decided to accept the caliph's invitation to see him at Mada'in, ancient Ctesiphon.

A big camp was pitched on the bank of the Tigris River near Mada'in to witness the caliph's gala reception for Abu Muslim. The royal compartment was equipped with curtains behind which al-Mansur ordered five armed men to hide and come out only at the sound of the clapping of his hands. With great show and pomp, Abu Muslim entered the caliph's presence, kissed his hands, and began deliberations. Having succeeded in separating the commander from his troops, the wily caliph came right to the point. He reminded Abu Muslim of his refusal to go to Syria when he was asked to do so, and of many other past instances in which the powerful commander had slighted the caliph's orders. Aware of his precarious position, Abu Muslim, stripped of his weapons and separated from his troops, pleaded guilty and requested the caliph's pardon. Al-Mansur clapped his hands, and immediately the five soldiers came out from behind the curtains. He ordered them to kill the helpless warrior and wrap him in a carpet. The soldiers were then ordered to roll the carpet with the corpse to the side of the room. Shortly afterward, al-Mansur showed the body to high officials of the state and ordered it dropped into the Tigris River near the camp. When certain senior officers of the Persian army inquired about Abu Muslim's absence in the caliph's camp, al-Mansur talked them out of pursuing the matter any further by showering upon them generous gifts and promises of promotion. Accordingly, when an uprising took place among the Khurasanian troops, it was easily put down by al-Mansur's Persian supporters. This ended the career of Abu Muslim, without whose help and continuous support the Abbasids would never have gained power, and without whom al-Mansur himself would have never been able to keep his post.

Al-Mansur and the Alids

Despite their devotion to the cause of Ali, the Prophet's cousin, in their several attempts at gaining authority and staging revolutions, the Alids had always been characterized by timidity and hesitation. Almost invariably, whenever they supported one of the descendants of Ali for the caliphate, they ended up with a martyr. The first of these ineffective movements was Husayn's rising in 680 against Yazid I, son of Mu'awiya, which was climaxed by the massacre of Karbala. The second was Zayd's rising against Caliph Hisham, which ended with the Kufan fiasco in 740. From that time on, Ali's descendants in Hijaz led a quiet life devoted to religion and scholarship. However, when the Abbasid secret organization was launched during Hisham's rule under the slogan of "the Prophet's household," the Shi'ites thought that if the movement succeeded, one of the descendants of Ali should be called upon to assume the caliphate. Accordingly, a call was sent out by the descendants of Ali to several representatives of the Hashimite groups, inviting them to a conference in Madina in order to designate a nominee for the Hashimite caliphate. Unaware that the secret organization already had its own leaders, the Hashimite conference convened shortly before the collapse of the Umayyad dynasty in Madina and began deliberations. Al-Mansur himself, known then as Abu Ja'far, attended the conference in behalf of the Abbasids. He and the rest of the Hashimites, approved a proposal designating Muhammad—called the Pure Soul—a great grandson of Hasan, son of Ali, as their nominee, should the newly launched movement succeed. However, the Alids were greatly disappointed when the Khurasanian troops under Qahtaba's son supported Abu al-Abbas after capturing Kufa in 749. Since there was little they could do, they accepted the *fait accompli* and waited for another chance to press the nomination of Muhammad the Pure Soul. Following the death of Abu al-Abbas and the accession of his brother in 754, the Alids thought they had a chance of gaining the support of many Arabs in both Iraq and Hijaz against al-Mansur, especially since the latter was the son of a Berber woman. They continued to meet in Madina plotting a coup to wrest the caliphate from al-Mansur.

Apparently the Abbasid caliph did not forget the Hashimite conference in Madina in which Muhammad the Pure Soul was nominated for the caliphate. He reportedly surrounded the Alids with an effective network of secret intelligence. As soon as he could organize an army to replace Abu Muslim's forces, he sent a contingent to Madina to bring Muhammad the Pure Soul and his brother Ibrahim to Kufa. The two brothers escaped, but their father Abd-Allah and many of their relatives were taken prisoners. Al-Mansur ordered Abd-Allah, Muhammad's aged father, to be flogged several times to extract from him the hiding place of his son, but all his efforts went in vain. Meanwhile, Muhammad the Pure Soul remained in Madina while his brother Ibrahim fled to Basra and rallied support for his brother's cause.

Many of the citizens of Madina supported Muhammad, including an important Muslim jurist named Malik ibn Anas, who absolved his fellow citizens from their oath of allegiance to the Abbasids. Encouraged by this support, Muhammad publicly announced himself caliph in Madina in 762. Al-Mansur responded by sending Muhammad a letter in which he promised to pardon him and his followers if they would abandon their counterrevolution. Muhammad the Pure Soul answered the Abbasid caliph with an eloquent letter in which he emphasized his superior claim to the caliphate, being a direct descendant of the Prophet himself through his daughter Fatima, as compared to al-Mansur, a descendant of the Prophet's uncle and son of a slave woman. He also declared that al-Mansur's promises of security and safe conduct were worthless, citing as examples of broken promises the safe conducts given to Ibn Hubayra, to the caliph's own uncle Abd-Allah, and to

Abu Muslim. He closed his letter by promising al-Mansur amnesty and security if he were to relinquish the caliphate and support the Alid cause. Al-Mansur immediately answered explaining that according to Arab customs inheritance did not follow through a daughter but through a son, and since Muhammad had no sons his nearest male kin was his uncle al-Abbas, whose descendants should be the rightful owners of the caliphate. [1]

Finally, when Muhammad refused to give up his claim, al-Mansur dispatched his newly organized army under the leadership of his nephew Isa to Hijaz. The Abbasid army bombarded the holy city, which soon surrendered. Muhammad the Pure Soul and the members of his household were mercilessly murdered, and many of his supporters were imprisoned and flogged, including the great jurist Malik.

Soon after, apparently with the encouragement of another great Muslim jurist in Iraq, Abu Hanifa, Muhammad's brother Ibrahim rallied some supporters from Basra and Ahwaz and marched against Kufa. Weakened by fighting in Hijaz, the Abbasid army, under Isa, was near defeat; but suddenly, as the victorious Ibrahim was galloping forward, a stray arrow struck him fatally. His supporters abandoned the battle and another Alid movement ended in tragic failure.

Thus by slyness, perfidy, and luck, al-Mansur eliminated his three formidable rivals — his uncle Abd-Allah, his army commander Abu Muslim, and his fellow Hashimite, Muhammad the Pure Soul.

Building of Baghdad

Kufa, the capital of the Abbasid regime, was hard to defend since it lay exposed to attacks from two directions — Basra and Wasit. It may be recalled that the Umayyad governor Ibn Hubayra was forced to abandon its defense against the Abbasids in 749 and take refuge in the better fortified city of Wasit. For this and many other reasons, al-Mansur in 762 decided to build a new capital whose location would be acceptable to him as well as his army officers.

He chose a site near the old Persian capital Ctesiphon (Arabic Mada'in) on the western bank of the Tigris River, where a small Persian village called Baghdad [2] once existed. Al-Mansur is reported to have asked his best engineers to plan the new city, enlisting for its construction hundreds of artisans. The caliph himself laid the foundation stone in a great ceremony, reportedly saying to the builders, "The earth is God's and He gives it to whomsoever He wills." As he gave

---

[1] See Appendices 3 and 4, pp. 375-378.

[2] The original meaning of Baghdad is still uncertain. According to some interpretations, *Bagh* means "garden" and *dad* is a shortened form of the proper name *Dadhawayh*. The two words together would mean "the garden of Dadhawayh." Other interpretations attach the meaning "lord" to *Bagh* and "giveth" to *dad* making the whole word mean "the lord giveth."

the order to begin building, he called the city *Madinat al-Salam* which means "the city of peace." However, its ancient name Baghdad still prevails.

The city was designed to be circular in shape, one and a half miles in diameter, with double thick walls around it. Its circumference had four equidistant gates named Kufa, Syria, Khurasan, and Basra. In its midst stood the caliph's palace and the city's main mosque. Around this glorious nucleus, government buildings were built, to be surrounded near the circumference by residential quarters and market places. Four main roads traversed the city from its gates, and from these main arteries narrower streets branched to every quarter of the city.

No sooner had the builders begun their work on the walls than the Alid rebellion flared up and the work was interrupted for almost a year, till Ibrahim's attack against Kufa in 763 ended in failure. Work was then resumed and al-Mansur moved to his new capital by the end of the year.

Al-Mansur's Death

The last part of al-Mansur's rule was mostly peaceful and devoted mainly to internal reforms. He encouraged agriculture and trade, patronized artists and poets, and greatly improved the living conditions of his people. Apparently al-Mansur's ruthless suppression of rebels and potential rivals paid dividends at last. When rebels no longer dared to disturb the peace of the empire, and when the caliph became the supreme commander of his domain, peace, tranquility and prosperity dominated the empire.

Toward the end of his rule, al-Mansur, having disqualified his nephew Isa from the caliphate, designated his son al-Mahdi to succeed him. He reportedly brought his heir into his presence and gave him ample advice on discharging the responsibilities of the state. He concluded his admonitions by urging his son to give his unabated attention to the prosperity of the state, reminding him of his own treasury which contained, he declared, enough wealth for ten years to come.

In 775 while on a pilgrimage to Makka, al-Mansur died in the outskirts of the holy city. His followers reportedly dug one hundred graves and laid him to rest in one of them, lest some of his enemies should exhume his body and disfigure his corpse.

SECESSION OF SPAIN UNDER
ABD AL-RAHMAN THE UMAYYAD

The lone fugitive of the Umayyad dynasty was a grandson of Caliph Hisham called Abd al-Rahman, who had escaped the tragic massacre of his clan. He traveled in disguise for five full years till he, together with his brave servant Badr, reached Ceuta opposite Gibraltar. From Ceuta he sent Badr to Spain to study the situation there and report to him as soon as possible. In a few months the servant returned with an encouraging report in which he assured his master of the willingness of the Yamanites to support him.

Abd al-Rahman entered Spain in September, 755, and camped near Malaga, where Yamanite supporters rallied around him. The Qaysite governor, known as Yusuf al-Fihri, sent a delegation to Abd al-Rahman to negotiate peaceful terms of co-existence; however, negotiations failed to produce any results. Al-Fihri began preparing his troops to attack Abd al-Rahman the following spring, but the latter stole a march on his opponent by attacking first. In March, 756, Abd al-Rahman captured Seville. As al-Fihri's forces tried to recapture the city, they were badly defeated and retreated toward Cordova. Abd al-Rahman's forces pursued their enemies to Musara, where al-Fihri's troops were defeated again. On May 14, 756, the victorious Abd al-Rahman entered Cordova triumphantly. The Qaysite governor al-Fihri surrendered his authority and requested amnesty for his supporters. When he betrayed the amnesty a short time later, and together with his supporters attacked Seville, another battle was fought in which al-Fihiri was finally defeated and killed and his supporters scattered.

Al-Mansur Versus Abd al-Rahman

No sooner had Abd al-Rahman begun to consolidate his victories over his Qaysite enemies than al-Mansur dispatched an Abbasid contingent under Mughith to the Umayyad forces in Spain. The Abbasid army was badly defeated and several of its leaders were killed — including Mughith himself, whose body was dismembered, pickled in salt, and sent to al-Mansur, together with his letter of appointment. Upon receiving this horrible package, al-Mansur reportedly thanked Allah that such a formidable enemy as Abd al-Rahman was so far away from the center of the Abbasid Empire. The best al-Mansur could do was to seek the friendship of Pepin, king of the Franks, in order to keep Abd al-Rahman always fearful of a Frankish attack against him.

Nevertheless, Abd al-Rahman consolidated his rule over Spain and prevented the mention of the Abbasid caliph in public prayers. Although he accepted the title *amir* "prince," he never proclaimed himself caliph. He ruled successfully for thirty-two years, contemporaneously with four Abbasid caliphs, including Harun al-Rashid.

It is reported that once al-Mansur asked a group of his friends, "Who is the stork of Quraysh?" When they gave various names which he rejected, he added, "It is Abd al-Rahman of Spain." Asked the reason for this, he said, "Abd al-Rahman crossed seas and traversed deserts; he reached a foreign country all alone; . . . there, he established a kingdom by the strength of his own personality." Such a statement by an archenemy is perhaps the greatest testimony of Abd al-Rahman's courage and audacity. Abd al-Rahman founded in the prosperous land of Spain an Umayyad regime ruled by his descendants for almost three centuries.

CHAPTER 32

THE ABBASID GOLDEN AGE

AL-MAHDI, 775-785

His Designation

Al-Mahdi could not have been officially designated for the caliphate without the abdication of his cousin Isa, originally designated by Abu al-Abbas himself. Al-Mansur in vain tried all possible means of coercing Isa to renounce his rights to the caliphate. The credit for persuading Isa to abdicate is attributed to Khalid ibn Barmak, the Persian treasurer of the first two Abbasid caliphs. He reportedly offered Isa fabulous amounts of money, until he was finally able to convince him to withdraw his claim in favor of al-Mahdi. Undoubtedly, Ibn Barmak's maneuver to secure the caliphate for al-Mahdi endeared him to the new caliph, who appointed both him and his son Yahya as assistants to his own son al-Rashid in his war campaigns against Byzantium.

Internal Reforms

Raised as a prince protected from the atmosphere of plots and revolutions, al-Mahdi was relatively trustful. He released many Umayyad and Alid supporters from prisons, returning to them their wealth and property. Contrary to the predictions of those who had disagreed with him about such measures, only a few insignificant uprisings were instigated by those enemies, and these were quickly and easily suppressed.

235

Al-Mahdi is known to have fortified a number of cities, especially the city of Rusafa, (near Baghdad), where he was brought up as a prince. Suburban Baghdad grew rapidly due to numerous territorial grants donated to Abbasid supporters, many of whom were non-Arab freedmen. Baghdad soon became a center of trade and culture for the whole empire; merchants and professionals alike were attracted by its booming prosperity.

Among al-Mahdi's reforms was the construction of rest stations with water supplies along the route from Baghdad to Makka. He is also known to have organized fast mail service within the empire, extending its routes as far as Yaman in the South and Qayrawan in North Africa.

It is worth mentioning that al-Mahdi ordered state allowances to be granted to those families whose providers were imprisoned and to those who had been disabled, in order to spare them from the shame of begging. The reign of al-Mahdi was the beginning of a period of wealth and prosperity in which fear and terror subsided while peacefulness and quiet prevailed within the empire.

State Reforms

Al-Mahdi divided the government of his caliphate into three *diwans*, "departments"—finance, justice, and defense—with a chief for each *diwan.* Overseeing these departments was a chief minister or *wazir*, responsible directly to the caliph. This arrangement relieved the ruling caliph from many responsibilities which henceforth fell within the jurisdiction of the *wazir*. It is important to note here that most of the department chiefs and *wazirs* during the Abbasid dynasty were non-Arabs. Apparently, having fought against both the Umayyads and the Alids, Abbasid caliphs felt a strong inhibition against placing Arabs in high-ranking offices.

Having improved mail services within the empire, al-Mahdi appointed court representatives to accompany mail pouches and report to him regularly about the behavior of his governors in the provinces. Consequently, the governors had to abstain from mistreating their citizens, accepting bribes, or accumulating unearned wealth. Furthermore, he gave more authority to the state judges and lawmakers in order that they might exercise their duties without fear or inhibition. It is reported that once a common citizen requested an audience with al-Mahdi while one of the judges was in the caliph's presence. As soon as the request was granted, the visitor made a complaint to the judge against the caliph regarding a piece of property. The caliph allegedly ordered the judge to use his prerogative, as if he (the caliph) were an ordinary citizen. After hearing the case, the judge ruled against the caliph, who approved the verdict and returned the property to his visitor.

War with Byzantium

Border skirmishes with the Byzantines were annual events during the Umayyad regime. Although Arab attacks against Constantinople failed at least twice, the Umayyads continued to assert themselves by periodically raiding the frontiers. During the Abbasid-Umayyad struggle for power, these raids in Asia Minor ceased almost completely; the result was an attempt on the part of the Byzantines to push their borders in Asia Minor deep into Islamic territory. To regain military prestige, al-Mahdi prepared an Arab force under the leadership of his son al-Rashid to invade Asia Minor. With the help of his assistants, Khalid ibn Barmak and his son Yahya, al-Rashid defeated the Byzantine forces in 781. When the Abbasids repeated military operations in 782, reaching the vicinity of Constantinople itself, Empress Irene of Byzantium, ruling in the name of her son, requested peace negotiations. Al-Rashid agreed to halt his attacks for an annual tribute of 70,000 dinars, which the Byzantines promised to pay.

Al-Mahdi and Zindiqism

As a result of Umayyad endeavors to keep the Arabs a social elite superior to other groups in the empire, many local movements arose in Khurasan and Transoxiana reviving old Persian ideologies, chief of which was Manichaeism—a mixture of Zoroastrianism, Christianity, and paganism. The Manichaean doctrines, first proclaimed by a Persian prophet called Mani (ca. A.D. 216-277), emphasized dualistic concepts such as light and darkness, good and evil, body and soul, etc. The Arabs called the revival of Manichaeism among Muslims in Persia and Iraq, Zindiqism, a term which originally meant "heterodoxy." Zindiqism appealed to certain Muslims because some of its rituals were found in Islam, such as ablutions and prayers several times daily. In any case, besides their belief in more than one god, Zindiqs were described (perhaps unfairly) to al-Mahdi as believing in marriages among close blood relatives, the use of urine for cleansing purposes, and the kidnapping of children of orthodox Muslim believers to be brought up as Zindiqs.

Although no zealot for Islamic theology, upon hearing about Zindiq doctrines, al-Mahdi was reportedly outraged and ordered the establishment of a department of government whose main task was to uproot Zindiqism from the empire. Zindiq adherents were asked first to recant; if they refused, they were immediately put to death. Thousands of them, including several individuals in high-ranking offices, were hunted down and mercilessly murdered. Islamic annals emphasize al-Mahdi's hatred of Zindiqism by asserting that once he ordered a chief official of the court to kill his own son who was accused of Zindiqism. The old man allegedly stumbled and fell to the ground in a state of shock. However, when a cousin of al-Mahdi pleaded with him to relieve the father from this painful ordeal, the caliph ordered someone else to sever the youth's head. In spite of all the efforts to exterminate Zindiqism, it survived underground for many years till the end of the Abbasid dynasty.

Al-Mahdi's Death

One of the legacies of the Umayyad period which the Abbasids apparently inherited was the custom of designating more than one (usually two brothers) for the caliphate. Accordingly, al-Mahdi designated his two sons, Musa al-Hadi and Harun al-Rashid, to succeed him in that order.

Things went well at first, but, perhaps due to the influence of al-Rashid's mother upon al-Mahdi, he tried to reverse the order of succession and designate the younger al-Rashid to rule before the older al-Hadi. However, on a hunting trip in 785, al-Mahdi's horse reportedly galloped into a building. He died almost instantaneously of a broken back and was immediately succeeded by al-Hadi, his eldest son, whose appointment he wanted to delay. Thus, in spite of al-Mahdi's great works and outstanding reforms, he left behind the seed of a grudge between his two sons.

AL-HADI, 785-786

Al-Hadi and al-Rashid

As expected, al-Hadi tried hard to disqualify his brother al-Rashid in favor of his son Ja'far, citing as precedent al-Mansur's successful attempt to exclude his nephew Isa and designate his son al-Mahdi as caliph. However, al-Rashid's behavior toward his brother al-Hadi was very cautious and polite. He was the first to acclaim him caliph and swear allegiance to him, sparing no effort to declare his complete devotion and loyalty to his brother. Nonetheless, since al-Hadi had been greatly annoyed by his father's biased attitude toward his brother, he spitefully persecuted al-Rashid and his associates to the extent that he imprisoned the latter's chief advisor, Yahya ibn Barmak, for taking al-Rashid's side. Furthermore, when his mother, Khayzuran, tried to mediate between her two sons, al-Hadi refused to listen to her and prevented her from interfering in the affairs of the state as she had during his father's reign. Following the advice of Yahya, his friend and assistant, al-Rashid left the capital, living almost as a fugitive till his brother died.

A New Alid Rebellion

It may be recalled that al-Hadi's father had declared a general amnesty under which many Umayyad supporters, Alids, and Kharijites were freed. However, al-Hadi himself, moved by a thirst for revenge, reversed his father's policies and embarked on a fresh campaign to

persecute those groups. Their leaders were again jailed, their properties confiscated, and their followers ridiculed.

In Hijaz, the Abbasid governor capriciously paraded in the streets
of Makka some members of the house of Ali accused of drinking and
disorderly conduct. This episode greatly angered the whole Alid clan
in the holy city, where a revolution broke out under the leadership of
Husayn, a cousin of Muhammad the Pure Soul. Al-Hadi sent an Abbasid
force to Hijaz, and it suppressed the revolution and killed Husayn
in 785.

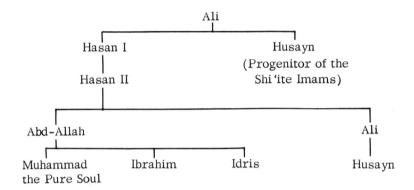

Ali's Descendants Through Hasan

Idris's Flight to North Africa

A cousin of Husayn named Idris (brother of Muhammad the Pure
Soul), who participated with him in the abortive Alid revolution of 785,
escaped from Hijaz to Egypt and then North Africa. He was reportedly
assisted by the chief of the mail service in Egypt, who not only aided him
in his flight, but also kept the whole affair hidden from the caliph's
intelligence reporters till Idris finally reached Tangier. With the support of the Berbers in the Atlas Mountains, Idris established an Alid
dynasty in 788 in the far west of North Africa in the region known as al-
Maghrib (modern Morocco). With the establishment of the Idrisid dynasty
in North Africa, the Islamic domain became divided into three main
regions, each ruled by a descendant from Quraysh: (1) the Umayyads in
Spain, (2) the Alids in al-Maghrib, and (3) the Abbasids in the remaining
areas of the Middle East.

Al-Hadi's Death

After only one year of rule, al-Hadi was stricken with a serious
illness. Realizing the nearness of his end, he reportedly invited his
mother, Khayzuran, whom he had previously rebuked, and began to
apologize for his earlier misdeeds in an effort to convince her that

he had acted only to keep her reputation above blame. In any case, as he was clasping his mother's hand, assuring her of his great love and respect, he died on September 15, 786. Some Arab historians have accused his mother Khayzuran of secretly contriving his death by sending him poisoned food; but others have emphatically absolved her of this charge, attributing the caliph's death to natural causes. Be this as it may, al-Hadi's death ushered in the renowned and widely celebrated era of Harun al-Rashid, under whose rule the Arab Empire reached new heights of wealth and prosperity.

HARUN AL-RASHID, 786-809

Al-Rashid's Immediate Reforms

Al-Rashid was proclaimed caliph on the evening of al-Hadi's death. During the same night, his son al-Ma'mun (another noted caliph) was born. A few followers of al-Hadi's son attempted to rally support for their candidate, but their efforts collapsed as al-Rashid's followers won for their candidate almost unanimous acclamation.

Al-Rashid's policies followed those of his father al-Mahdi. He released from jail many of the Umayyad and Alid leaders whom his brother al-Hadi had imprisoned, declaring a general amnesty to all the political groups of Quraysh. He promoted security and encouraged trade, thus restoring prosperity and gaiety to Islamic cities, especially Baghdad, which became famous for its fabulous Arabian nights.

Moreover, taxes were regulated so that, besides the poll tax binding upon non-Muslims, all citizens were required to pay property and land taxes according to the return of their holdings. Not only was the treasury replenished, but citizens of the empire became prosperous as agriculture expanded and trade mushroomed. Furthermore, to regulate justice, al-Rashid appointed a noted jurist, Abu Yusuf, a student of the great master of jurisprudence Abu Hanifa, to be the supreme judge in the empire. Besides writing his basic work on the land tax, Abu Yusuf helped in organizing lower courts and establishing certain laws, regulations, and precedents as guidelines to be followed by lesser judges.

Perhaps the first thing that al-Rashid did upon assuming office was to release his teacher and counselor Yahya ibn Barmak from prison. Yahya and his sons, especially Ja'far and al-Fadl, reached very high ranks in the administration of the state, rendered faithful service to al-Rashid, and of all officials became the closest to the caliph's private life. Due to their influence and wise counsel, the state reached that glorious peak which characterized al-Rashid's rule.

Al-Rashid restored to his mother Khayzuran (confined by al-Hadi) the freedom and authority which she had possessed during his father's rule; she was allowed to live in her own palace and to conduct her personal affairs. Apparently she exercised some influence upon her son, since all indications are that she was chiefly responsible for the great attachment that existed between al-Rashid and the Barmak family.

The Abbasid Regime and North Africa

It may be recalled that immediately after the Alid revolution in 785, a brother of Muhammad the Pure Soul named Idris fled to western North Africa, where he established his independence from Baghdad in 788 with the help of the local Berbers. Al-Rashid faced the task of suppressing the Idrisid movement in North Africa at a very critical time of his reign, when riots and uprisings in Persia, Khurasan, and Adharbayjan were occupying his forces. By the time he had suppressed these riots and could send an army to North Africa, skirmishes along the unstable Byzantine borders were resumed, forcing the caliph to concentrate his forces in Asia Minor. Meanwhile, the Idrisids not only strengthened their hold on al-Maghrib, but also threatened to expand into the rest of North Africa. To thwart their efforts, al-Rashid appointed al-Aghlab as governor of the volatile North African area of the empire with almost absolute authority to check the aggressive ambitions of the Idrisids. Although al-Aghlab established firm control over central North Africa, now known as Algeria and Tunisia, he did not seriously attempt to recapture the Idrisid territory. The Idrisids continued their dynasty in al-Maghrib, and the Aghlabids, gradually losing contact with their own headquarters in Baghdad, around 800 became another independent dynasty in central North Africa.

War with Byzantium

Mention has already been made of an Arab-Byzantine war during al-Mahdi's reign, in which al-Rashid, then commander of the Abbasid army, defeated the Byzantine forces near Constantinople, forcing Empress Irene (ruling in the name of her son) to seek for peace. Since the Byzantines agreed to pay a yearly tribute to the Arabs, al-Rashid agreed to halt his military activities and thus peace was restored. However, in 785 Irene's son became of age and ruled under the name of Constantine VI. Shortly after he began his independent rule, he denounced his mother's agreement with al-Rashid, allowing skirmishes to resume along the Arab-Byzantine borders.

In 797 Irene removed her son from the throne, had him blinded, and ruled in his place as Empress Augusta for five years. During these years she observed her original agreement with al-Rashid, and peace was again restored to the uncertain frontiers. In 802, however, a Byzantine aristocrat staged a coup against Augusta in Constantinople and took the throne as Nicephorus I. The new emperor reversed his predecessor's agreement with the Arabs and reportedly sent to al-Rashid the following message:

From Nicephorus, king of the Romans, to Harun, king of the Arabs. The queen who preceded me . . . carried to you from her wealth that which you should have doubled and carried to her. However, this was due to women's weakness and foolishness. Therefore, when you read my message, return the wealth which you have received and save yourself the consequences. Otherwise, the sword will determine matters between us and you.

According to Islamic reports al-Rashid answered saying:

In the name of the Lord, the merciful, the compassionate. From Harun, the Commander of the Faithful, to Nicephorus, the dog of the Romans. I read your message, O son of a pagan mother. My reply to you will be seen rather than heard.[1]

In 804 hostilities began on a large scale between the Arabs and the Byzantines. Al-Rashid marshaled most of his forces, reportedly totaling 135,000 troops, into Asia Minor, where he took personal command and attacked the Byzantine borders, penetrating their territories till he reached Heraclea on the Black Sea. With Arab troops only one hundred and fifty miles from Constantinople, Nicephorus became alarmed and sought peace. Once more, al-Rashid dictated his terms and forced the Byzantine emperor to agree to pay tribute.

Feeling safe after the departure of the Arab troops, the fickle Nicephorus reneged on his agreement, thinking that al-Rashid's forces would not dare renew hostilities while snow covered the mountain passes. However, the Arabs returned to battle more determined than ever to crush the Byzantine forces. Nicephorus was again defeated and Byzantine possessions in Asia Minor between the Mediterranean and Black Seas were open to looting and plunder. Al-Rashid once more dictated his terms, this time making ample provisions against default. As a corollary to al-Rashid's wars against Byzantium, Arab forces recaptured Cyprus in 802; it had been lost shortly after 649 when the Arabs first captured it. Why al-Rashid decided against conquering Constantinople and bringing an end to the Byzantine Empire is hard to answer. From a military point of view, his troops had demonstrated undeniable superiority by winning several decisive battles against the Byzantines. From a diplomatic point of view, Nicephorus's defaults and procrastinations were provocative enough to allow any monarch with a slight military advantage to pursue his victories till the enemy was crushed. Perhaps al-Rashid thought from past experiences that his armies could not overcome the strong fortifications of Constantinople, or perhaps he did not want to expand his empire beyond what he could firmly control. The task which al-Rashid failed to do was left to the Ottoman Turks more than six centuries later.

[1]Al-Tabari, *Tarikh*, Volume 10, pp. 92, 93.

The Debacle of the Barmakids

The Barmakids had been a priestly family in Balkh whose members served in a native monastery of Buddhist origin known as the "New Spring." Later, when the Arabs captured Persia, many of them were converted to Islam, including Khalid ibn Barmak, who supported the Abbasid movement and was employed by both Abu al-Abbas and al-Mansur as administrative assistant and state treasurer. The Barmakid family was known for its intense loyalty to the Abbasid caliphs, who reciprocated their loyalty with absolute trust and confidence. Khalid ibn Barmak was effective in convincing Isa, a nominee for the caliphate by Abu al-Abbas, to renounce his rights in favor of al-Mahdi, son of al-Mansur, thereby keeping the caliphate in the latter's household. In response, al-Mahdi appointed Yahya, son of Khalid, as a tutor-advisor to his son al-Rashid. Relations between al-Mahdi and Yahya were so cordial that, according to several reports, their wives used to nurse each other's babies. Accordingly, al-Rashid and Yahya's children grew up as close friends. Their friendship was undoubtedly cemented when Yahya undertook the tutoring of the young prince.

It may be recalled that Yahya continued to oppose al-Hadi's efforts to disqualify al-Rashid and nominate his own son until Yahya was finally relieved of his post and put in jail. Therefore, when al-Rashid became caliph, he immediatley released Yahya, appointed him as *wazir*, i.e., chief minister, and honored him publicly by calling him "Father." Moreover, he appointed Yahya's sons, especially al-Fadl and Ja'far, to high-ranking offices. Al-Fadl was his own father's assistant, holding the office of deputy *wazir*, and Ja'far was appointed governor of Egypt and Syria. Yahya's family served al-Rashid faithfully, bringing law and order to public affairs. Some historians have attributed the outstanding record of the Abbasid regime under al-Rashid to their firmness, efficiency, and organizing ability.

At any rate, al-Rashid was more attached to Ja'far ibn Barmak, son of Yahya, than to Ja'far's brother al-Fadl, perhaps because the former was more congenial and adaptable than the latter. When their father was too old to continue as *wazir*, al-Rashid appointed Ja'far rather than al-Fadl to replace him. Nevertheless, due to the discipline within the Barmak family, this apparent slight to al-Fadl did not cause any problems or ill-feelings between the two brothers. Ja'far's personality seems to have greatly overshadowed that of al-Rashid in several matters, including private family affairs. Islamic annals report that Ja'far was so confident in conducting al-Rashid's private life that he once negotiated the marriage of the caliph's own daughter without consulting her father.

The Barmak family served al-Rashid's court for seventeen years before the tide turned sharply against them. It is generally believed that Ja'far's personal friendship with al-Rashid had given him such great authority that he could control even the harem section of the palace. Apparently, a palace intrigue against Ja'far, which involved him in a scandal in the harem, had been carefully planned and suddenly brought to the caliph's attention. Outraged against his devoted minister for bringing disgrace upon his honor and family reputation, al-Rashid reportedly acted both speedily and impulsively. While Ja'far was unsuspectingly entertaining some friends at home, the caliph's order went out to bring him to the palace, where he was immediately put to death. His aging father and all members of the Barmak family were jailed and their wealth and properties were confiscated. The fall of the Barmakids in 802 stands out in Islamic history as a vivid illustration of the two extremes of hospitality and hostility that generally characterized life in the vast Arab Empire.

End of Al-Rashid's Rule

The last years of al-Rashid's rule were spent in a northern border town called Raqqa, where he established command headquarters against the Byzantines. Although legend portrays al-Rashid as an oriental monarch used to the luxurious court life of Baghdad, much of his life was spent in wars and conflicts, especially with the Byzantines.

On the diplomatic scene, al-Rashid extended his friendship to Emperor Charlemagne of the Franks, sending him fabulous gifts and exchanging diplomatic representatives with him. Apparently al-Rashid thought that by strengthening his relations with the Franks he could thwart any expansionist attempts made against him by the Umayyads of Spain. At the same time, Charlemagne welcomed al-Rashid's friendship, perhaps as a check against the Byzantines in case they sought to interfere with his kingdom in Europe.

On the domestic scene, besides his agricultural and trade reforms,[2] al-Rashid encouraged many literary and learned guilds, allowing poets, jurists, and theologians to compete with each other without fear of molestation. During his rule the Arab Empire reached its cultural peak.

On various occasions before his death, al-Rashid had nominated his three sons al-Amin, al-Ma'mun, and al-Mu'tamin respectively to succeed him as caliphs. However, toward the end of his rule he permitted the second son, al-Ma'mun to disqualify his younger brother, al-Mu'tamin, if he so desired. Finally in March, 809, while al-Rashid was in Tus, away from his capital, he became seriously ill and died,[3] leaving behind an empire at the peak of its glory and two main rival heirs, each preparing for a hard battle to decide their own destinies as well as the destiny of their prosperous empire.

[2] It is reported that al-Rashid proposed to dig a canal between the Mediterranean and the Red Seas, but Yahya ibn Barmak advised against it.

[3] See Appendix 5, p. 378.

CHAPTER 33

FRATRICIDAL CONFLICTS

AL-AMIN, 809-813

Al-Rashid's Will

Before his death, al-Rashid left a will in which he designated his three sons, al-Amin, al-Ma'mun, and al-Mu'tamin — already appointed governors of Persia, Iraq, and the Northern Frontiers respectively — to succeed him in that order. As if he had sensed that his sons would engage in fratricidal wars, he ordered his will to be hung on the sacred walls of the Ka'ba so that none of his sons would dare to alter it.

Al-Rashid's precautions, however, could not change the pattern of fratricidal wars that evolved whenever two brothers were designated to the caliphate. The rivalry between al-Amin and al-Ma'mun, represented not only two brothers competing for the high office, but two different nationalities within the Arab Empire competing for supremacy. It so happened that al-Amin's mother was an Arab from the family of Abbas, and al-Ma'mun's mother was a Persian concubine. Moreover, al-Amin had been tutored by an Arab teacher and represented the Arab political heritage, while al-Ma'mun had been tutored by the noted Persian statesman Ja'far ibn Barmak and thus became a symbol of Persian cultural pride. Since al-Ma'mun was governor of Khurasan — a post that made him almost independent from Baghdad — he inevitably aroused the suspicion of his brother al-Amin, especially when the latter assumed the caliphate in 809.

245

Al-Amin as Caliph

A noted Arab historian described al-Amin as follows:

> He was a handsome young man, fair and tall, with out-
> standing physical strength combined with extreme courage. He
> was reported to have killed a lion with his bare hands. He was
> eloquent in speech and a lover of literature. However, he was
> known for his mismanagement and waste of money. Moreover,
> he was clumsy, with a weak personality and never was fit to be
> a prince.[1]

As soon as he ascended to the caliphate, al-Amin tore down the
document of succession which his father had hung on the walls of the
Ka'ba. He then dismissed his brother al-Mu'tamin from his post as
governor of the Northern Frontiers. Having easily prevailed over
al-Mu'tamin, he turned to al-Ma'mun in Khurasan. First, he ordered him
to remit some of the state revenues to Baghdad, then informed al-
Ma'mun of his desire to replace certain high officials in Khurasan
itself, and at last he ordered him to relinquish his rights of succession
to the caliphate. These requests forced al-Ma'mun to choose either
to surrender with humiliation or to resist and fight. As much as he
hated to fight with his brother, he was virtually compelled to reject his
demands and prepare for battle. The fratricidal war between al-Amin
and al-Ma'mun lasted several months, ending with the defeat and death
of al-Amin in September, 813.

AL-AMIN VERSUS AL-MA'MUN

Preparation for Battle

During the early part of al-Amin's rule, all indications pointed to
an impending conflict between the two brothers as each was strongly
backed by one of the two competing blocks of the Arab Empire —the
Arabs and the Persians. Al-Amin appointed as his chief minister an
Arab named al-Rabi', and entrusted his troops to a warrior named Ali
ibn Isa, who had previously been governor of Persia. On the other hand,
al-Ma'mun's chief minister was al-Fadl ibn Sahl, whose continuous
support and encouragement greatly influenced the young prince in his
determination to stand against his brother. The commander of al-
Ma'mun's troops was a capable warrior named Tahir, who trained and
organized a strong Persian army.
As al-Amin's provocations increased, al-Ma'mun closed his borders
with Iraq in order to prevent any subversives or agitators from enter-

[1] Al-Suyuti, *History of the Caliphs* (Cairo, 1931), p. 197.

ing Persia. At the same time, due to the insistence of al-Rabi', his chief minister, al-Amin agreed to announce formally the designation of his son Musa to replace his brother al-Ma'mun as successor to the caliphate. Having made this formal announcement, he sent a call to his brother to return to Baghdad and officially renounce his claims. There was absolutely no choice left to al-Ma'mun but to reject his brother's orders and announce his insistence upon maintaining his rights as heir to the caliphate. Troops were ordered to move as civil war once more beleaguered the Arab Empire.

Battle of Hamadan, 811

Failing to secure the obedience of his brother al-Ma'mun, al-Amin left the whole matter of war to his minister, al-Rabi', and remained in his palace reportedly sipping wine and watching dancing girls with several friends. Meanwhile, his armies advanced under the leadership of Ali ibn Isa into the interior of Persia till they reached Rayy in 811. In their first combat with al-Ma'mun's Persian troops under the leadership of Tahir, Ali ibn Isa was killed and his army retreated toward Hamadan, where they were pursued by the Persian troops. A hard-fought battle followed in which al-Amin's forces were badly defeated and forced to take refuge within the walls of Hamadan. Tahir ordered the siege of the city until the desperate Arab warriors surrendered and opened the gates for the triumphal entry of the Persian troops.

After the fall of Hamadan, Tahir advanced at the head of his victorious troops toward the southern region of Iraq, where he captured Ahwaz, Basra, and Wasit. Early in 812 he reached the vicinity of the strongly fortified city of Baghdad in preparation for the next round of the civil war.

In contrast to the victorious and well-disciplined troops of al-Ma'mun, the Arab army of al-Amin was composed mainly of mercenaries. Besides fighting half-heartedly, they were always asking for higher stipends, which al-Amin always granted despite their continuous defeats. To add to the Arab confusion, a local revolt broke out in Syria, which demanded the division of Arab troops. Al-Amin's forces put down the Syrian revolt, but utterly failed to stand against al-Ma'mun's well-disciplined and hard-fighting Persian troops.

Al-Ma'mun Proclaimed Caliph

No sooner had al-Ma'mun's chief minister received the news of his army's initial victories at Rayy and Hamadan in 811 than he advised the young prince to proclaim himself caliph in Marv. Having been assured of the support of many provinces, al-Ma'mun accepted the acclamation of his followers and delivered his inaugural speech at the mosque of Marv, in which he promised to devote his energies to the service of Islam. Soon after his acclamation, a Hashimite delegation from Hijaz arrived in Marv to offer its allegiance to the new caliph. In April, 812, the leaders of Kufa and Mosul announced the deposition of al-Amin and proclaimed their support of his victorious brother. Furthermore, a number of Arab army commanders, who were unhappy with al-Amin's frivolous behavior, defected to join the ranks of the newly proclaimed caliph. As al-Ma'mun's caliphate gathered momentum and won supporters throughout the empire, al-Amin continued to lead a life of self-delusion inside Baghdad, putting his trust in the double wall which his great-grandfather al-Mansur had built around it.

Bombardment of Baghdad and Death of al-Amin, 813

The fortified city of Baghdad was not an easy prize for al-Ma'mun's forces. In September, 812, Tahir ordered his troops to bombard the city with rocks and arrows for several days; however, all attempts to capture the city during that year ended in failure. Encouraged by al-Amin's promises to give them all the wealth of his treasury, the defenders of Baghdad put up a very strong resistance against the attackers and refused to surrender. Tahir had no alternative but to order the city under siege.

However, when the siege had lasted for a whole year without results, Tahir ordered his troops to attack without mercy and to burn the city if necessary in order to force its capitulation. In September, 813, hostilities resumed as al-Ma'mun's army bombarded the city heavily with mangonels and missiles, completely demolishing a number of its huge structures. House to house fighting followed until the besieging forces reached the caliph's own palace, where al-Amin was still holding out. Before al-Ma'mun's troops could enter the palace, al-Amin managed to escape by boat across the Tigris. However, his boat was intercepted, and he was captured and killed. His severed head was immediately sent to al-Ma'mun and his body dragged along the streets of Baghdad.

AL-MA'MUN'S CALIPHATE, 813-833

Revolts and Riots in Iraq

As soon as al-Amin was killed, Tahir sent to al-Ma'mun in Marv the robe, sword, and insignia of the caliphate —official symbols of his high office However, as had happened before between caliphs and their army commanders, al-Ma'mun became fearful of his victorious commander, relieved him of his post, and exiled him to Raqqa in northern Syria. In his place he appointed al-Hasan, brother of his chief minister, al-Fadl ibn Sahl, and assigned to him the task of governing Iraq.

Heeding the advice of his chief minister, al-Ma'mun decided against returning to Baghdad, the city of his fathers, preferring rather to reside in faraway Marv, which he adopted as his Persian capital. Their territory having been reduced to the level of a province ruled by a governor, the people of Iraq became greatly displeased with al-Ma'mun for abandoning his Arab ancestry in favor of his Persian maternal relatives. In their anger, they revolted against the new governor, al-Hasan, forcing him to leave Baghdad for Wasit, where he tried in vain to restore order.

Meanwhile, the citizens of Baghdad, having heard of al-Ma'mun's intentions to designate a Shi'ite descendant named Ali al-Rida as his successor, hastened to acclaim one of the sons of al-Mahdi, Ibrahim, as their caliph.[2] To add to the confusion, al-Hasan's forces in Wasit mutinied and elected as their commander Mansur, the other son of al-Mahdi[3], who refused to accept the post without al-Ma'mun's endorsement. Al-Ma'mun, however, retained al-Hasan as commander, but appointed Mansur as his personal representative to administer affairs till further notice. Thus, during al-Ma'mun's absence in Marv, there was a rival caliph in Baghdad and two governors in Wasit, one suspended and the other temporary. This hopeless situation continued till al-Ma'mun finally decided to leave Marv and return to his strife-torn capital in Iraq.

Al-Ma'mun and the Shi'ites

While matters were going from bad to worse in Iraq, demonstrations against al-Ma'mun broke out in Hijaz for almost the same reasons, namely, al-Ma'mun's apparent renunciation of Arab interests and championship of the Persian cause. Taking advantage of the deteriorating situation in Iraq and Hijaz, the Shi'ites in Kufa, Basra, Madina, Makka, and also Yaman rioted and plundered the houses of many Abbasids. Apparently, al-Ma'mun's chief minister, al-Fadl ibn Sahl, had concealed from the caliph vital information about the disorder in Iraq, and at the same time exaggerated to him the seriousness of the Shi'ite riots. And so, in an effort to placate the seemingly powerful Shi'ites, al-Ma'mun invited their imam (religious leader) to Marv for negotiations. Islamic records reveal that when Ali al-Rida, the Shi'ite imam, met with al-Ma'mun, he impressed him so much that the caliph publicly proclaimed him as the most admirable and praiseworthy individual of all the Hashimites. In an unprecedented gesture of kindness to Ali al-Rida, the man just pronounced the most deserving of all, al-Ma'mun designated him as his successor, thereby approving the transfer of the caliphate from the house of Abbas to that of Ali. In a transport of delight, the Shi'ites hailed al-Ma'mun's decision as the most welcome and

[2] Ibrahim, son of al-Mahdi, was al Ma'mun's uncle.

[3] Mansur was also al-Ma'mun's uncle.

gratifying news in all their history. After many struggles and martyr-
doms, it appeared for awhile that they were about to gain the caliphate
without violence.

Al-Ma'mun's Journey to Baghdad

As mentioned above, angered by al-Ma'mun's behavior, the citizens
of Baghdad acclaimed Ibrahim, son of al-Mahdi, as a rival caliph, while
they practically severed all relations with the Persian regime. Meanwhile, a revolt against al-Ma'mun broke out in the northern part of
Iraq for almost the same reasons. Al-Hasan (al-Ma'mun's commander
in Wasit) sent a small contingent under a brave warrior named Harthama
to put down the new revolt. Recognizing the chief causes of the troubles
in the empire, Harthama decided to risk his life[4] and travel to Marv
to inform the caliph of the truth. Al-Ma'mun was reportedly incensed
at al-Fadl ibn Sahl, his chief minister, for his disloyalty in concealing
vital matters. Receiving confirmation of Harthama's reports from other
sources, al-Ma'mun decided to move his court to Baghdad, requesting
both his chief minister, al-Fadl ibn Sahl, and his heir to the caliphate,
Ali al-Rida, to accompany him.

During the royal trip from Marv to Baghdad, both al-Fadl and Ali
al-Rida met untimely deaths through mysterious circumstances. In the
first incident, which took place shortly after the party had left Marv,
four armed men murdered al-Fadl as he was bathing in his camp. In
the second incident, which took place at Tus while al-Ma'mun was
visiting his father's tomb, al-Rida died suddenly—reportedly after
eating poisoned grapes. With the death of their iman, the Shi'ites' hopes
of gaining the caliphate were dashed. Arab historians have speculated
that al-Ma'mun, having decided to start a new era in Baghdad, arranged
the murders of the two men who could have posed considerable problems
for him in Baghdad. Al-Ma'mun's party reached Baghdad in September,
819, after five years' residence in Marv, during which the empire came
to the verge of collapse.

Al-Ma'mun in Baghdad

When news reached the citizens of Baghdad that al-Ma'mun was
coming without al-Fadl ibn Sahl or Ali al-Rida, the two figures that
caused their main concern, they immediately abandoned their own hand-
picked rival caliph, Ibrahim, son of al-Mahdi. The first act of the triumphant caliph was to forgive his enemies and declare a general amnesty
for all political prisoners. Among those restored to favor was al-
Ma'mun's great commander, Tahir, hero of the war of 809-813 against
al-Amin. Desiring to avoid another clash with the caliph, Tahir requested

---

[4]As a matter of fact, Harthama was treacherously killed by al-Fadl ibn
Sahl for his brave action.

to be sent to Khurasan where he had wanted to live before his exile. Al-Ma'mun not only granted him permission to live in his own home country, but in a gracious mood also appointed him governor of Khurasan. Later, Tahir gained for his family the hereditary governorship of the whole region and established a semi-independent regime ruled by a Tahirid dynasty similar to the Aghlabids in Qayrawan and the Idrisids in al-Maghrib.

Almost every citizen in Baghdad celebrated with joy the return of the caliph to his original capital and the restoration of peace and security to the land. One man, however, was especially unhappy and greatly terrified by al-Ma'mun's return to Baghdad—his uncle Ibrahim, the designated caliph abandoned by the fickle citizens of Baghdad. In his fear, he disguised himself as a woman and fled the country; after several years he was suddenly uncovered by one of al-Ma'mun's officials, arrested, and brought to the caliph's palace in his women's clothes. After inviting certain guests to laugh at the runaway caliph, al-Ma'mun released his uncle unharmed. The gesture of magnanimity on the part of al-Ma'mun toward his rival uncle was repeated in the cases of several other potential enemies whom he had released.

Since the death of al-Rashid, Iraq for almost ten years had witnessed considerable confusion and turmoil—the whole reign of al-Amin plus the years of al-Ma'mun's absence in Khurasan. These were ten years of frustration and tragedy for the city of Baghdad; riots and outbreaks of trouble dimmed Baghdad's gay Arabian nights, causing a sharp decline in prosperity. However, after the caliph's return to the capital of his fathers, peace and security were gradually restored. Its torn streets were reconstructed while roads were opened and new buildings erected. Trade soon revived, bringing wealth and prosperity not only to its own people, but to the whole Arab Empire as Baghdad once more became the undisputed metropolis of the entire Middle East.

In January, 826, in one of the most extravagant weddings of the East, al-Ma'mun was married to the beautiful daughter of al-Hasan ibn Sahl, his loyal commander in Wasit. Fabulous sums of money were spent on lavish decorations and generous gifts were thrown to the crowds in the streets. It has been reported that no less than fifty million dirhams[5] were spent by the bride's father on jewelry for his daughter and gifts for the guests. The caliph's mother, Zubayda, is reported to have showered upon the bridegroom a heap of one thousand pearls, which were all collected and given to the bride.

Al-Ma'mun and the Mu'tazilites

The Mu'tazilites[6] were a group of intellectuals who tried to subject religious doctrines and beliefs to rational examination. They did not hesitate, therefore, to embrace new ideas or argue about matters

[5] One dirham is estimated to be one quarter of a dollar.

[6] The Mu'tazilites are also discussed on pp. 344, 345.

previously taken for granted. Among their most controversial beliefs were (1) the doctrine of "the intermediate state of Muslim believers," and (2) the doctrine of "the createdness of the Qur'an." The first one implied that Muslim believers who committed grave sins could neither be considered believers as orthodox Muslims maintained, nor could they be considered infidels as the Kharijites asserted. The Mu'tazilites believed that impious Muslims belonged in an intermediate state which they called "the state between the two states," in which a believer would be considered as a transgressor of his religious duties without necessarily becoming an infidel.

The doctrine about the createdness of the Qur'an implied that, contrary to orthodox Muslim belief, the Qur'an could not be associated with the essence of God but rather with his works. The controversy in this issue revolved around the answer to one question: Should the word of God be considered a part of his essence or his works? Muslim theologians have always maintained that the word of God belonged to his essence and not his works. Therefore, the Qur'an, being the word of God, could not have been created. It may be noted here that some Christian theologians have applied this argument about the noncreatedness of the Qur'an to Jesus Christ—already described in Islam as "a word from God." Their main objective was to show by using orthodox Islamic arguments that Christ was divine.

Caliph al-Ma'mun was well known for his intellectual interests and love of theological debates. He not only encouraged the translation of Greek works into Arabic, but also allowed scholars of various schools to debate their positions before him. After years of debates, he publicly announced his adherence to the Mu'tazilite doctrines. His enthusiasm for their unorthodox beliefs led him to use force in demanding many of his officials, especially jurists, to do the same. The issue which particularly caused unhappy repercussions was the Mu'tazilite belief in the createdness of the Qur'an, a doctrine which many of the chief orthodox jurists and theologians refused to accept. The result was an actual war against them declared by al-Ma'mun, in which many renowned leaders of the Muslim community were tortured and imprisoned. Toward the end of al-Ma'mun's rule matters became worse as he ordered an inquisition against those who refused to embrace the doctrine of the createdness of the Qur'an. Under this inquisition some jurists were killed and many were imprisoned, chief among them was the great jurist Ibn Hanbal, founder of a school of jurisprudence known by his own name. He tenaciously held to his belief in the "uncreated and eternal" aspect of the Qur'an, refusing to obey the caliph's decrees.[7] According to al-Ma'mun's orders, Ibn Hanbal and a few others were sent in chains to Tarsus to wait for the caliph's return. However, the caliph died on his way to Tarsus; thus Ibn Hanbal's life was spared by chance.

[7] See Appendix 6 pp. 379,380.

Al-Ma'mun's Military Campaigns

Al-Ma'mun's rule was not very tranquil because of the internal turmoil that followed the civil war against al-Amin. On the home front, al-Ma'mun had to deal with three important revolts: (1) Nasr's rebellion in northern Iraq, (2) the Copts' rebellion in Egypt, and (3) the Khurramite rebellion in Adharbayjan. Externally he had to wage no less than three campaigns against Byzantium, whose new emperor, Theophilus, renewed hostilities by extending help to the Khurramites of Adharbayjan.

In 820 an Arab warrior called Nasr rebelled against al-Ma'mun, backed mostly by Arab malcontents who disliked the caliph's pro-Persian attitude. Nasr's rebellion spread over the whole Jazira region in the northern part of Iraq and Syria covering a sizable area of the Arab Empire. Al-Ma'mun appointed Abd-Allah, son of Tahir, as governor of Syria with orders to put down Nasr's rebellion. From his headquarters in Raqqa, Abd-Allah fought Nasr's forces for five years before the latter was finally defeated and brought to Baghdad in submission.

In Egypt some rebels from Spain managed to reach Alexandria and, with help from the Copts, seized the city and declared an independent state. In 825, after he had successfully suppressed Nasr's rebellion in Iraq and Syria, Abd-Allah turned to Egypt. He easily put down the rebellion in Alexandria. The rebels fled, capturing Crete on their return to Spain. However, in 830, just three years before al-Ma'mun's death, the Copts rebelled against their governor. Al-Ma'mun sent one of his most ruthless commanders named al-Afshin, who put down the Coptic rebellion after several thousand Copts had been killed. Al-Afshin replaced them by settling in Egypt two new tribes from Arabia, who greatly increased the Arab population. It is generally believed that as a result of these events the Coptic population strikingly decreased in number, becoming a minority group in the land of their ancestors.

In Khurasan a religious movement called Khurramiyya, based on beliefs drawn from Islam and Zoroastrianism, gained political momentum in 815 under the leadership of an excellent guerrilla fighter named Babek. The Khurramites professed to be followers of Abu Muslim. As soon as al-Ma'mun left Marv and returned to Baghdad in 819, Babek called upon his followers to avenge the murder of Abu Muslim and to rise in revolt against the Abbasid regime. Their rebellion, which started in Adharbayjan, caught al-Ma'mun's forces by surprise. Operating from the mountains with skillful guerrilla maneuvers, the Khurramites continued their rebellion throughout the rest of al-Ma'mun's reign till they were finally defeated by his brother al-Mu'tasim in 837.

In 830 Babek the Khurramite made an agreement with Emperor Theophilus of Byzantium, by which he received Byzantine assistance for his rebellion against al-Ma'mun in Armenia and Adharbayjan. To counteract this pact, al-Ma'mun renewed hostilities against Byzantium. During the last three years of his reign, he personally led three campaigns into Asia Minor, penetrating deep inside Byzantine territory. He succeeded in putting pressure on the Byzantine emperor and preventing him from giving substantial aid to the Khurramites. Although al-Ma'mun did not live to see the results of his campaigns, his successor, al-Mu'tasim, was able to deal a decisive blow to Babek and his rebellious movement in Adharbayjan.

Death of al-Ma'mun

On his way back to Tarsus from his last campaign in Asia Minor, al-Ma'mun was reportedly enjoying the company of some of his friends as they sat with their feet dipped in the cool water of a running stream. Soon afterward, he became very ill with a high fever and was unconscious most of the time. During the few moments in which he regained consciousness he designated his brother al-Mu'tasim as his successor, giving him important counsel and advice regarding the state affairs. He died in August, 833, at the age of forty-eight, after ruling the Arab Empire for twenty years. In spite of the upheaval through which the empire passed during his reign, al-Ma'mun is considered among its greatest caliphs. His name is closely associated with literature and scholarship since he not only encouraged scientists and scholars but also supported the translation of famous Greek and Persian writings into Arabic. Great works such as those of Plato and Aristotle were introduced to the Western world mainly through their Arabic translations.

CHAPTER 34

THE BEGINNING OF DECLINE

AL-MU'TASIM, 833-842

His Personality

To avoid open conflict between Persians and Arabs, al-Ma'mun bypassed his own son, who was strongly supported by Arab troops, and designated his brother, al-Mu'tasim. During the last moments of his life, al-Ma'mun reportedly gave his brother the following advice:

> O, Abu Ishaq (al-Mu'tasim's original name), come near me and take heed of what you see. Follow your brother's path regarding the Qur'an and deal with the caliphate—if God grants it to you—according to His will, fearing only His punishment and torment. Do not be deceived by God's endurance, and act as if death were trailing you. Do not neglect the welfare of the people, the people, the people, the common people, because they are the source of authority. . . ."[1]

Upon his appointment, al-Mu'tasim hastened to Baghdad, where he was faced with a serious movement initiated by Arab army officers who wanted to nominate his nephew al-Abbas as caliph. However, after some negotiations, al-Abbas himself agreed to respect his father's designation and renounce

[1]Al-Tabari, *Tarikh*, Volume 10, p. 294.

his own claims to the caliphate. The army movement collapsed, and al-Mu'tasim was duly proclaimed caliph in August, 833.

Al-Mu'tasim is described as a courageous and robust man capable of lifting a weight of one thousand pounds and carrying it several steps. Despite his youthfulness when he became caliph, in a very short time he took firm control of the affairs of state. He acted decisively against his enemies by renewing his brother's war against those who resisted the Mu'tazilite views regarding the createdness of the Qur'an. He flogged some of them and imprisoned others after severe torture. Among those who suffered greatly was Ibn Hanbal, the great jurist, who had already been persecuted by al-Ma'mun in 833.

Al-Mu'tasim and the Gypsies

In 835 some non-Arab nomadic immigrants whom the Arabs called *zatt* reached Basra from the east. Totaling between seventeen and twenty-seven thousand persons, the *zatt* people harassed the trade routes of southern Iraq and became a menace to Arab merchants in the area. To counter their depredations, al-Mu'tasim dispatched a strong contingent of his army, which completely routed them and sent them all in ships to Baghdad. The caliph sent them to Asia Minor, allowing them to cross to Byzantine territory. They reportedly migrated to Thrace and the rest of Europe, where they continued to live as gypsies.

War with the Khurramites

Among the troubles which al-Mu'tasim inherited from al-Ma'mun's reign was Babek's Khurramite rebellion in Adharbayjan. Their training as mountain-fighters enabled the Khurramites to hold out against the Abbasid troops in Khurasan for almost twenty-two years.

Finally, al-Mu'tasim determined to put an end to this rebellion. He dispatched a new army under the leadership of the ruthless commander al-Afshin, who had crushed the Coptic rebellion in Egypt during al-Ma'mun's reign. With skill and organization, al-Afshin combed the mountains of Adharbayjan, where the Khurramites had been hiding, and dealt mercilessly with their warriors wherever he found them. Finally in 837 he reached the hiding place of their leader, Babek, whom he captured and carried in chains to al-Mu'tasim's new residence in Samarra. After being paraded in the streets, Babek was brought before the caliph, who ordered his soldiers to cut him slowly to pieces. After his head was severed, his body was hanged on a wooden post in one of the streets of Samarra. Arab historians have estimated the number of casualties during the twenty-two years of the Khurramite rebellion at two hundred thousand persons killed, besides the wounded and those taken slaves. Al-Afshin's prestige was greatly increased as he became, much to his personal misfortune, the most valuable warrior in the empire.

War With Byzantium

In 837 Emperor Theophilus of Byzantium, seeing that most of the Islamic forces were engaged in Adharbayjan against the Khurramite rebellion, suddenly renewed hostilities against al-Mu'tasim and occupied vast areas of Arab-controlled territories in Asia Minor. During the summer of 837, Byzantine troops reached Zebetra, al-Mu'tasim's own birthplace, and destroyed it, paying no attention to a personal message from al-Mu'tasim pleading with Theophilus to spare his town. As soon as al-Afshin captured Babek and ended the Khurramite rebellion, al-Mu'tasim ordered him to proceed to Asia Minor. Meanwhile, the determined caliph sent messages to all parts of the Arab Empire, asking his governors to urge the people to forget personal feuds and regional rivalries in order to recruit a united army against their common enemy, Byzantium. When Byzantium was mentioned, feuding factions of the Arab Empire united and formed one front against their non-Muslim enemy. Arab historians have estimated the Islamic army recruited to fight in Asia Minor at no less than two hundred thousand warriors.

Al-Mu'tasim divided his troops into two armies, one under al-Afshin that moved overland toward Hadeth, and the other led by himself that moved along the coastal line. Thinking that al-Afshin's soldiers would be weary after crossing the Taurus Mountains, Theophilus decided to meet the overland army first. The Byzantine forces surprised al-Afshin north of the mountain pass at Hadeth, and managed to spread disorder and confusion among his troops. However, the experienced Abbasid commander soon reorganized his troops in a counterattack and inflicted upon the Byzantine forces a decisive defeat, causing Emperor Theophilus himself to flee in June, 838. Meanwhile al-Mu'tasim's forces, upon receiving news that the Byzantines were fighting al-Afshin in the north, hurried to his help. As the two Muslim armies met, they pursued their victories till they reached Amorium, the native city of the Byzantine emperor. In revenge for the deliberate sack of his birthplace, Zebetra, al-Mu'tasim captured Amorium, laid it waste, and massacred most of its inhabitants. Having regained his lost prestige in Asia Minor, al-Mu'tasim and his army triumphantly returned to Iraq to face a new Persian plot against his regime, secretly encouraged by none other than his victorious commander al-Afshin.

Al-Afshin's Revolt

When al-Ma'mun left Marv for Baghdad, the Persians became unhappy about the loss of their status in the empire. No sooner were the Khurramites defeated and their leader Babek eliminated than a related regional movement under a native leader called Mazyar emerged in Tabaristan, south of the Caspian Sea. Al-Afshin sympathized with Mazyar's movement and secretly supported it against Ibn Tahir, whose family had become hereditary governors of Khurasan from the

days of al-Ma'mun. It is generally believed that al-Afshin, realizing
the danger of his possible elimination as commander-in-chief of the
army due to his continued victories in Egypt, Adharbayjan, and Asia
Minor, purposely encouraged Mazyar, in order to establish an independent Persian state free from Arab domination. However, Ibn Tahir's
forces succeeded in defeating Mazyar's troops and were able to seize
al-Afshin's secret letters to him. Al-Mu'tasim immediately jailed his
victorious commander al-Afshin. When he died, reportedly of poisoning,
his body was hung in a public square and then burned in ridicule.

Introduction of Turkish Mercenaries

Al-Mu'tasim assumed the caliphate at a critical time in the history
of the Arab Empire when regionalism was beginning to undermine its
unity and solidarity. It may be recalled that the civil war between al-
Amin and al-Ma'mun actually had been a regional conflict between the
former's Arab supporters and the latter's Persian backers. From that
time on, regional rivalry between Arabs and Persians was clearly
demonstrated by riots and revolts in either Iraq or Persia depending
on the orientation of each ruling caliph. From al-Ma'mun's experience,
al-Mu'tasim soon realized that siding with either faction surely meant
a revolt by the other side. He therefore decided to follow a nonaligned
course, treating the two main groups of the empire with absolute
equality. Al-Mu'tasim's decision was undoubtedly fair and just, but he
soon discovered that neither the Arabs nor the Persians could be trusted
to defend the caliphate against any revolt or *coup d'état*. Himself the
son of a Turkish concubine and well-acquainted with the warlike
behavior of the Turkish tribesmen, al-Mu'tasim thought of introducing
to Baghdad a contingent of Turkish mercenaries, whose loyalty to the
caliph could be fairly well assured, and who would rally to him in time
of emergency or regional revolt. He therefore sent orders to his
officials in Samarqand, Ferghana, and other outposts in Transoxiana
to recruit for him Turkish bondsmen, whom he brought to Baghdad and
trained for military service. These Turks, known in Arabic as Mamluks, were owned by the caliph; however, they were promised freedom
upon performing some gallant deed in the defense of their master.
Thousands of these unpolished Turkish mountaineers poured into
Baghdad, nominally accepted Islam, and began their military training
as mercenaries. Al-Mu'tasim extended to them his full trust and confidence, and they became not only his personal bodyguard but also the
backbone of his standing army. Later on, many of them were granted
freedom and promoted to high-ranking offices in the state administration in Baghdad itself and throughout the empire.

Building of Samarra

Al-Mu'tasim was very proud of his newly acquired Turkish mercenaries, especially when they marched about his palace in their
colorful uniforms. As they gained favor with the caliph, they gradually

assumed greater authority than the Arab soldiers, whom they began to overshadow. Their arrogant attitude toward the Arabs in Baghdad resulted in many skirmishes between the caliph's daring bodyguards and his proud subjects. Al-Mu'tasim had no other choice but to move his Turkish mercenaries to a new residence north of Baghdad called Samarra, which he founded and adopted as his second capital in 836. Samarra grew rapidly and was mostly inhabited by Turkish warriors, who enjoyed the full confidence of the caliph and became his closest associates. This was the beginning of a new era in Islamic history, in which regionalism led not only to the deterioration of the two feuding parties – Arabs and Persians – but also to the introduction of a new unpredictable element within the empire, namely, the Turkish mercenaries. This new Turkish element, brought in originally to protect the empire from rivalry and competition, continued to gain power and prestige until Arabs, Persians, and all others were brought under its control. At the time of al-Mu'tasim's death in 842, he hardly realized that by using Turkish mercenaries to protect himself and his descendants he had actually procured the vanguard of a force that was destined not only to usurp power from his successors, but to subject them to all kinds of anguish and torture.

AL-WATHIQ, 842-847

His Intolerance

Al-Wathiq assumed the caliphate in 842 by designation of his father al-Mu'tasim. He lived in Samarra among his father's Turkish mercenaries, whom he not only retained but also promoted in the state administration. Al-Wathiq's rule did not suffer from the rise of rival claimants as much as from outbreaks and revolts that embattled almost the whole empire. Like his father and uncle before him, he was a firm believer in Mu'tazilite doctrines, especially that of the createdness of the Qur'an. He therefore carried on, perhaps with more severity, the persecution of several orthodox theologians who refused to admit that the Qur'an was created.

His relentless intolerance in this respect led his enemies in Baghdad to plot against his life. However, two members of the conspiracy drank excessively on the night of the planned execution, and the whole plot was revealed to the caliph. He ordered its leader Ibn Nasr to his presence in the palace and reportedly argued with him at length concerning theological matters, but Ibn Nasr tenaciously held to his orthodox views. The caliph looked at his palace officials and asked their opinions regarding the kind of punishment the man deserved. As soon as one of them suggested his death as an infidel, al-Wathiq ordered one of his officials to cut off Ibn Nasr's head, which was then paraded in the streets of Baghdad with the following caption attached to one of its ears:

This is the head of the misguided infidel and polytheist Ibn
Nasr. God has ordered his death by the Commander of the
Faithful, al-Wathiq, after evidence had been heard against him
regarding the createdness of the Qur'an. . . .

Praise be to God, who hastened to take him to hellfire for
severe punishment.

Rebellion in Hijaz

In 845 several dissatisfied Bedouins of Arabia rebelled against al-
Wathiq's authority in Hijaz. They defeated his governor in Madina and
looted a number of market places and trading posts in the area. To
suppress this revolt, al-Wathiq dispatched to Hijaz some of his mercenaries under a Turkish warrior named Bugha. Before the Turks
restored law and order in Hijaz, they ravaged several places and fought
many scattered insurgent Bedouins, killing some and taking others as
prisoners. The most striking feature about the suppression of this
revolt in Hijaz was the fact that for the first time Turkish troops, still
considered pagan in essence, were sent to Arabia where they fought
Arabs in and around the two holy cities of Madina and Makka.

Al-Wathiq and the Turks

Al-Wathiq was among those caliphs who preferred to stay at home
rather than travel or lead military campaigns. Most of the time he
remained at his residence in Samarra surrounded by his Turkish officers
upon whom he became greatly dependent. He granted large fiefs outside
Samarra to some of them, promoted others to high administrative posts,
and appointed others as governors of provinces in Syria and Iraq. No
doubt the Turks, who were rapidly increasing in number, felt themselves
capable of controlling vital departments in the state administration.
Arabs and Persians alike had to appease and even bribe them if they
ever wanted their requests to reach the caliph's attention. Accordingly,
corruption increased as bribery became the only way to reach any
high-ranking office in the state.

After a rule of less than six years, al-Wathiq died in 847 of an
incurable disease. During his illness he was asked to nominate his
successor, but he refused saying, "I do not want to bear your burdens
alive and also dead." The matter of appointing his successor had to be
decided by none other than the chief commanders of the Turkish
mercenaries – a clear indication of the fast-declining authority of the
Arabs in their own empire.

AL-MUTAWAKKIL, 847-861

Al-Mutawakkil's Appointment

In conjunction with top palace officials, Turkish commanders thought first of appointing al-Wathiq's own son to succeed him, but finding him too young and completely disinterested in the post, they sought another candidate. Finally, they chose the deceased caliph's brother al-Mutawakkil, whom they thought would be an easy master to deal with. However, as soon as he was proclaimed caliph in 847, al-Mutawakkil proved himself a man of wit and power. Hardly two months had passed before he dismissed and executed his chief minister, Ibn Zayyat, who had earlier ridiculed him during al-Wathiq's rule. Later on, he lured the Turkish commander of his bodyguard to go to Baghdad, the stronghold of anti-Turkish sentiments, where he plotted to imprison him and put him to death. In fact, almost all of al-Mutawakkil's rule was a battle between Arab and Turkish authority. For some time it appeared that the Arabs, led by the caliph himself, had the upper hand; however, due to tactical mistakes on his part, al-Mutawakkil fell victim to Turkish intrigues which led to his assassination and the transfer of authority from the Arab caliphs to the Turkish mercenaries.

Return to Orthodoxy

Al-Mutawakkil completely reversed the Mu'tazilite policies of his predecessors in an effort to bring the Arab Empire back to the path of traditional orthodoxy. He dismissed Mu'tazilite officials from the state administration and released from prison all orthodox jurists and local judges whom al-Wathiq and al-Mu'tasim had previously imprisoned and persecuted. Moreover, al-Mutawakkil called upon all Muslims to observe faithfully the oracles of religion according to the Sunnite (traditional) system of worship. This call meant almost open war against other religious sects including the Shi'ites, who believed in the sacred merits of Ali and his sons through Husayn. In an effort to break the Shi'ite influence in the empire, al-Mutawakkil sent troops to tear down Husayn's tomb in Karbala, a sacred shrine visited by almost all Shi'ites of the Islamic domain. As a further humiliation to the Shi'ites, he ordered the tomb site plowed over and sown with corn. Furthermore he publicly insulted the memory of Ali, the Prophet's cousin, subjecting his name to contempt.

As al-Mutawakkil pursued his fanatic return to traditional orthodoxy, he turned his anger against the Jews and Christians, demolishing many churches and synagogues. He ordered Christians to wear identifying marks in public and forbade them to ride horses; if they rode mules or donkeys, they were ordered to use only wooden knobs upon their saddles. He prevented them also from displaying the cross in their religious activities and from putting tombstones or raised markers over the tombs of their dead.

As al-Mutawakkil was busy restricting the freedom of all religious groups other than the orthodox Muslims, the empire began to feel the pinch of bankruptcy. He is therefore reported to have encouraged bribery in the process of appointing officials to high-ranking offices, appointing only those who offered large sums of money. Furthermore, his indiscreet behavior gave the Turkish commanders an opportunity to plot against him.

Al-Mutawakkil's Assassination

At different times in his reign, al-Mutawakkil designated his three sons, al-Muntasir, al-Mu'tazz, and al-Mu'ayyid, respectively to succeed him. However, during a romantic exchange of verse with one of his wives named Qabiha, mother of al-Mu'tazz, he decided to promote her son over al-Muntasir. When al-Muntasir refused to renounce his claims, his father reportedly abused him, insulted him publicly, and excluded him from official business. When al-Muntasir could no longer take his father's humiliation, he joined hands with Wasif and Bugha,[2] two Turkish conspirators. In 861 he allowed these two plotters to enter his father's palace with a number of their soldiers, and before the caliph could call for help, he was brutally murdered, together with one of his assistants. With the tragic death of al-Mutawakkil at the hands of Turkish officers, the Arab Empire may be said to have reached the sad stage of Ichabod, since glory indeed departed from the Abbasid household. As long as the Turkish mercenaries held power, most of the succeeding caliphs were appointed and dismissed at the whim of their Turkish protectors, who frequently confined them within the palace walls, torturing them in order to force them to submit to their demands. An Arab poet described the Abbasid caliph after al-Muta-wakkil's death as follows:

> A caliph in a cage between Wasif and Bugha.[3]
> He repeats whatever they tell him exactly as the parrot does.

As the Turkish mercenaries assumed control over the caliphate, they utilized their authority mostly to promote their own desires and financial ambitions. They accepted fantastic bribes from equally corrupt high-ranking officials, in order to obtain from the reigning caliph whatever they desired. Accordingly, some governors were able to establish hereditary status for their dynasties, and began to rule almost independently of Baghdad. This state of affairs inevitably led to the

[2] He was the son of Bugha who put down the rebellion in Hijaz, see p. 260.

[3] Wasif and Bugha were the two Turkish officers who killed al-Mutawakkil and assumed control of the caliphate after him.

establishment of a number of independent regional dynasties in various areas of the Islamic domain; however, as curious as it might appear, all these regional dynasties derived their legitimate rights to rule from the Abbasid caliph in Baghdad, who was most of the time only a symbol of power without much authority or control.

REASONS FOR THE DECLINE OF THE ABBASID REGIME

It may be recalled that when leaders of the Abbasid movement began their campaign to win adherents against the Umayyad regime during Hisham's rule, they emphasized two weak features in the Umayyad regime: (1) intertribal feuds, and (2) the policy of Arab superiority. Accordingly, when the Abbasids took power, they particularly avoided these two Umayyad weaknesses and always tried to maintain solidarity within their own household and universality among the various regions of their empire. The Abbasid caliphs failed, however, to recognize the other weaknesses of the Umayyad regime, namely: (1) discontinuity of government, and (2) blood revenge, both of which crept into their own regime. These two weaknesses, inherited from the Umayyads, plus a third weakness peculiar to the Abbasid period, namely the rise of regionalism, may be considered the main causes of the decline of the Abbasid caliphate.

Discontinuity of Government

The same pattern of succession to the caliphate adopted by the Umayyads, with all its tragedies and misfortunes, was also practiced by the Abbasids. It may be recalled that al-Mahdi had designated both his sons to succeed him with the inevitable result that al-Hadi tried to exclude al-Rashid; were it not for al-Hadi's premature death, the empire would have been engulfed in fratricidal feuds as early as al-Rashid's time. The most severe disturbance caused by lack of smooth continuity of government during the Abbasid period was the well-known civil war between al-Amin and al-Ma'mun (809-813). As a direct result of this war and similar feuds, regionalism was strengthened, leading to the introduction of Turkish mercenaries, who finally usurped control from the caliph about 861.

Blood Revenge

The savagery of blood revenge during the Abbasid regime is well illustrated by their ruthless massacres of the Umayyads, resulting in the establishing of a rival Umayyad state in Spain, and in the ever-increasing suspicion which the Arabs throughout the Arab Empire harbored against the Abbasid caliphs. In other words, the Abbasids fell victims of their own tyranny to the extent that they could never afterward trust their own Arab warriors. On the other hand, when they incurred the distrust of the Persian leaders during the latter part of al-Ma'mun's rule, riots and revolts beleaguered their empire, forcing al-Mu'tasim to introduce Turkish mercenaries. However, instead of protecting their masters, the Turkish warriors advanced themselves by wielding a firm control over the caliphs. Curiously enough, both Arabs and Persians had apparently become so offended by Abbasid atrocities that no real effort was exerted to save the caliphs who suffered under the control of their Turkish masters.

Rise of Regionalism

The Abbasid dynasty came to power as a direct result of Persian support. However, as certain Persian commanders gained prestige due to their superior military ability, they were eliminated by the Abbasid caliphs, who eyed them with doubt and suspicion. A clear example of this behavior is the case of Abu Muslim, whose gallant efforts allowed the Abbasid dynasty to come into being in the first place, and who was finally murdered by order of al-Mansur, its second caliph. This case and other incidents in which Persian leaders were put to death by the Abbasids led to the rise of Persian regionalism as exemplified by the Khurramite movement as well as that of Mazyar and al-Afshin during al-Mu'tasim's reign. When regional rivalry between Arabs and Persians increased beyond repair, al-Mu'tasim was almost forced to rely on a new element, namely, the Turkish mercenaries, who finally brought about the decline of the Abbasid dynasty and the rise of several autonomous regional regimes.

IMPORTANT TERMS

Abd-Allah: Uncle of Caliph Abu al-Abbas. He led the Abbasid forces against Marwan II at the battle of the Zab in 750. Later, he was eliminated by Caliph al-Mansur.

Abd al-Rahman: An Umayyad fugitive who fled his people's massacre in Syria and managed to reach Spain, where he established an Umayyad dynasty in 756.

Abu al-Abbas: First Abbasid caliph (750-754). During his short reign, he ordered the massacre of all Umayyad descendants, winning for himself the title al-Saffah, meaning "shedder of blood."

Abu Muslim: Organizer of the Abbasid movement in Khurasan. He raised a Persian army which defeated the Umayyads in 750. Later he was put to death by Caliph al-Mansur.

Abu Salma: Chief minister of the first Abbasid caliph, Abu al-Abbas. The caliph eliminated him shortly after taking office.

Al-Afshin: A ruthless warrior under al-Ma'mun and al-Mu'tasim. He put down the Coptic rebellion in 830 and the Khurramite rebellion in 837. After his victory over the Byzantines in the same year, he participated in the abortive Mazyar rebellion and was sent to jail where he died.

Al-Amin: Sixth Abbasid caliph (809-813). He lost the war against his brother al-Ma'mun and was killed in 813.

Al-Fadl ibn Barmak: One of the sons of Yahya, chief minister of al-Rashid. He was jailed with members of his family during the Barmakid debacle.

Al-Fadl ibn Sahl: Chief minister of al-Ma'mun who encouraged the caliph to stay in Marv. He was assassinated while he accompanied al-Ma'mun on the return to Baghdad.

Al-Fihri: The Umayyad governor of Spain during the Abbasid takeover. Abd al-Rahman defeated him in 756 and established a new Umayyad dynasty.

Al-Hadi: Fourth Abbasid caliph (785-786).

Ali al-Rida: An Alid leader whom al-Ma'mun once designated as his successor. He died during al-Ma'mun's trip to Baghdad in 819.

Al-Mahdi: Third Abbasid caliph (775-785).

Al-Ma'mun: Seventh Abbasid caliph (813-833). He was proclaimed caliph after defeating his brother al-Amin. During his reign, the Abbasid regime reached new heights of prosperity and scholarship.

Al-Mansur: Second Abbasid caliph (754-775). Upon his accession to the caliphate he eliminated his uncle Abd-Allah, the commander of his army Abu Muslim, and the Alid claimant Muhammad the Pure Soul. He is credited with building the city of Baghdad in 762.

Al-Mu'tasim: Eighth Abbasid caliph (833-842). He won many battles against the Byzantines. His most significant action, however, was his introduction of Turkish mercenaries who later stripped the caliphs of their authority.

Al-Mutawakkil: Tenth Abbasid caliph (847-861). He was a fanatic traditional caliph who persecuted several non-orthodox religious movements. The Turkish mercenaries plotted his assassination in 861, ushering in the period of Turkish supremacy.

Al-Rashid: Fifth Abbasid caliph (786-809). During his reign the Abbasid regime reached new heights of wealth and prosperity.

Al-Saffah: See Abu al-Abbas.

Al-Wathiq: Ninth Abbasid caliph (842-847).

Augusta, Empress: A Byzantine empress who reached the throne in 797 by dismissing and blinding her son for whom she acted as guardian. She made peace with al-Rashid, but her successor Nicephorus disregarded it and embarked upon several military campaigns against the Abbasids.

Babek: Leader of the Khurramite rebellion in Adharbayjan, which was finally put down in 837.

Bugha: A Turkish mercenary who plotted the murder of al-Mutawakkil in 861.

Ibrahim the Iman: Son of Muhammad, the first organizer of the Abbasid movement. He was designated by his father to lead the Abbasid cause, but was murdered by Marwan II in 749 shortly before the battle of the Zab. His brother Abu al-Abbas (al-Saffah) succeeded him and became the first Abbasid caliph in 750.

Idris: Brother of Muhammad the Pure Soul. He participated in the abortive Alid revolution in 785 against al-Hadi. However, he managed to escape to North Africa, where he started the Idrisid dynasty in 788.

Ja'far ibn Barmak: Son of Yahya, al-Rashid's first chief minister. Ja'far was greatly liked by al-Rashid, who chose him to replace his father. A few years later, because of a palace intrigue, the caliph's anger was kindled against the Barmakids. He killed Ja'far, confiscated the property of his family, and jailed all his relatives.

Khalid ibn Barmak: The first of the Barmak family to be employed by the Abbasids. He served as treasurer of the first two caliphs.

Khurramites: See Babek.

Mazyar: A Persian rebel who staged a rebellion against al-Mu'tasim with the support of al-Afshin. The rebellion was suppressed and al-Afshin was put in jail where he died.

Muhammad, son of Ali: A Hashimite descendant from the line of Abbas. He was the first organizer of the Abbasid movement.

Muhammad the Pure Soul: An Alid claimant to the caliphate against al-Mansur. He staged an abortive anti-Abbasid revolution in 762, in which Madina was bombarded and he was killed.

Mu'tazilites: A group of Muslim theologians who believed in certain heterodox doctrines chief of which was the createdness of the Qur'an. Al-Ma'mun and his two successors supported them, promoting several of their scholars to high-ranking offices.

Nicephorus: The Byzantine emperor who succeeded Empress Irene in 802. He renewed war with al-Rashid and was defeated.

Qahtaba: Commander of the Persian troops that marched westward in 749 against the Umayyad regime. He was drowned before his troops reached Kufa.

Samarra: A city north of Baghdad built by al-Mu'tasim to be the residence of his Turkish mercenaries.

Tahir: Commander of al-Ma'mun's forces against al-Amin. After he won the war in 813, he was confined for awhile. However, a few years later al-Ma'mun appointed him governor of Khurasan, where he established the regional Tahirid dynasty.

Yahya ibn Barmak: Son of Khalid, treasurer of the first two Abbasid caliphs. Yahya was the tutor of al-Rashid and was later promoted to become his chief minister. When the Barmakids fell in disgrace, Yahya was imprisoned with members of his family.

Zab, battle of: A battle fought in 750 between the Abbasid forces under Abd-Allah and the Umayyads under Marwan II. It marks the end of the Umayyad regime and the beginning of the Abbasid dynasty.

SUPPLEMENTARY READINGS

ABBOTT, N., *Two Queens of Baghdad* (Chicago, 1937).

ALI, AMEER, *A Short History of the Saracens* (London, 1951).

BEN SHEMESH, A., *Taxation in Islam* (Leiden, 1958).

BUCKLER, F., *Harun' l-Rashid and Charles the Great* (Cambridge, Mass., 1931).

BOWEN, H., *The Life and Times of Ali ibn 'Isa, "The Good Vizier"* (Cambridge, 1928).

BROCKELMANN, CARL, *History of the Islamic Peoples* (New York, 1947).

GIBB, H.A.R., *The Arab Conquests in Central Asia* (London, 1923).

GIBBON, EDWARD, *The Decline and Fall of the Roman Empire*, An abridgement by D.M. Low (London, 1960).

GLUBB, SIR JOHN BAGOT, *The Empire of the Arabs* (London, 1963).

GRUNEBAUM, G.E. VON, *Medieval Islam* (Chicago, 1946).

HITTI, PHILIP K., *History of the Arabs* (New York, 1960).

LANE-POOLE, STANLEY, *The Muhammadan Dynasties* (Paris, 1925).

LE STRANGE, GUY, *Baghdad During the Abbasid Caliphate* (London, 1924).

LEVY, REUBEN, *A Baghdad Chronicle* (Cambridge, 1929).

MUIR, WILLIAM, *The Caliphate* (Edinburgh, 1924).

PIRENNE, H., *A History of Europe: From the Invasions to the XVI Century* (New York, 1956).

"The Expansion of the Saracens," *Cambridge Medieval History*, Volume 2.

PART **IX**

REGIONAL DYNASTIES DURING THE LATE ABBASID PERIOD, 861-1258

Before the rise of Islam, individual Arabs owed allegiance in principle to leaders of their respective tribes. Through this allegiance they became entitled to the protection and support of the tribes, as well as the honor and prestige of the leaders. When the Islamic state was established in Madina shortly after 622, Muhammad introduced to the Arabs a religio-political concept known as the *umma,* "Islamic community," that promoted Arab unity. However, within the structure of the *umma,* Muhammad allowed the Arab tribes, under certain conditions, to function both administratively and socially as independent units. In so doing he actually caused the Arabs to divide their loyalty between the *umma* and the tribe, thereby allowing the dichotomy of "dual allegiance" to become a part of their social outlook.

As long as the Arabs lived as tribes during the early period of the Arab Empire, they continued to owe allegiance both to their tribal leaders, who symbolized social prestige, and to the reigning caliph, who symbolized the *umma.* During the Abbasid period, however, social integration between Arabs and non-Arabs took place, causing many Arab tribes to become submerged in the new Islamic society. Nevertheless, tribal loyalties did not altogether disappear from the Islamic state; they were transformed into what may be called "factional loyalties." The principle of dual allegiance, therefore, continued to function as Muslims owed allegiance both to the

269

Islamic *umma* as a whole, and to their respective factions within the *umma*.

After the death of al-Mutawakkil in 861, when the Abbasid caliphs became weak, factional loyalties superseded state loyalties, allowing many regional dynasties to rule almost independently of the central government. The following chapters attempt to outline the history of these regional dynasties in Iraq itself, in Western Asia, in Spain, in North Africa, and in Egypt.[1]

---

[1] The history of these regional dynasties has been purposely treated separately in order to present a unified account of each one of them instead of referring to them sporadically here and there in one main account about the late Abbasid period. Accordingly, a few statements in regard to direct relations among these dynasties have been unavoidably repeated.

CHAPTER 35

FORCES CONTROLLING
THE ABBASID CALIPHATE

After the murder of al-Mutawakkil in 861, the Abbasid caliphate began to decline. Authority slipped away from the caliphs till they possessed nothing of the former prestige of the office except its title. Even the title became a source of trouble to several caliphs who were jailed, persecuted and tortured by the various forces which controlled them. Between 861 and the sack of Baghdad by the Mongols in 1258, four different forces succeeded each other in controlling the Abbasid caliphate and usurping the powers of many individual caliphs in both Baghdad and Samarra.

1. The Turkish mercenaries, 861-946
2. The Buwayhids of Persia, 946-1055
3. The Seljuq Turks, 1055-1180
4. The Khwarizm shahs, 1180-1258.

THE TURKISH MERCENARIES, 861-946

Caliphs Controlled by the Turks

The twelve caliphs that followed al-Mutawakkil[1] were more or less controlled by various commanders of the Turkish mercenaries between 861 and 946. These commanders were frequently divided among themselves and suspicious of each

[1] See p. 382.

other's intentions. While they exercised authority, each commander followed his own wishes. In the midst of all this confusion, six of the caliphs were murdered; one of them, al-Muqtadir, was slaughtered like a lamb. The other six were dismissed, blinded, or left to die in prison.

During this period of Turkish supremacy, many provincial governors, whether by force of arms or bribes, gained autonomy over their areas and began to rule semi-independently. The empire, therefore, was gradually dismembered until by the reign of al-Muqtadir (d. 932) nothing was left to the caliphs save Baghdad and its neighboring cities. At this low ebb, al-Muqtadir's successor, in an effort to spare himself the dangers of his office, appointed one of his officials as *amir al-umara,* "chief prince," to whom he delegated full authority to deal with the problems of the empire. As it turned out, the new chief prince during the reigns of al-Muttaqi (940-944) and al-Mustakfi (944-946) became involved in many tragic quarrels and disputes with both the arrogant Turkish commanders and the ambitious governors of the provinces. Finally, while the chief princes were busy with local problems, a regional dynasty in Persia under the leadership of the Buwayhids captured Baghdad and usurped the powers of the three quarreling forces—the Turkish mercenaries, the chief princes, and the caliphs themselves.

The Negro Rebellion

It may be of some interest to note here that a serious rebellion flared among the *Zanj,* "Negro slaves," in Iraq during the first twelve years of Caliph al-Mu'tamid's reign, 870-892. It started when a Persian leader called upon Negro slaves (brought from East Africa and owned by numerous masters in Persia and Iraq) to announce their freedom and start a rebellion. Several thousand Negroes responded to his call and rallied behind him in 870, operating mostly in southern Iraq and the Ahwaz district in Persia. By this time the caliphate had become so weak that the Negroes seized Basra and threatened both Wasit and Baghdad. Al-Mu'tamid appointed his brother al-Muwaffaq to suppress the Negro revolt. Short of money and equipment, al-Muwaffaq requested Ahmad ibn Tulun, then a semi-independent governor of Egypt, to send him financial help. Even with this help, the war against the Negroes dragged on for several years, during which al-Muwaffaq was also busy with other problems both at home and in Persia. Finally, al-Muwaffaq was able to trap the rebels' leader, defeat him, and have him murdered in 883. Without their leader and emancipator, the Negroes surrendered to al-Muwaffaq and asked for his pardon. The rebellion subsided as many slaves were returned to the homes of their masters. The fact that the suppression of this rebellion by a few thousand slaves occupied the authorities in Baghdad for about twelve years is a clear indication of the low ebb the caliphate reached during the years of Turkish supremacy.

THE BUWAYHIDS, 946-1055

Origin of the Buwayhids

During the years of anarchy in Iraq under the Turkish mercenaries, several forces were struggling for power in Persia in an effort to achieve regional autonomy. Among the ambitious warriors fighting to gain some measure of independence were three sons of the house of Buwayh (traditionally linked to the old Sassanians of Persia), who expanded their rule from Kerman to Isfahan and Ahwaz. It is reported that in 940 Caliph al-Muttaqi had asked one of the sons of Buwayh to enter Baghdad with his forces; however, the Turks defeated the caliph before the Buwayhids reached the vicinity of the city.

The Buwayhids and the Abbasid Caliphs

Throughout the reigns of al-Muttaqi and his successor al-Mustakfi quarrels and disputes continued in Iraq between the forces of the chief prince and those of the Turkish commander, leading to the weakening of both groups. A Buwayhid named Ali consolidated his rule over southern Persia and sent his brother Ahmad, reportedly at the invitation of Caliph al-Mustakfi, with an army to capture Baghdad. In 945 Ahmad ibn Buwayh took complete control of Baghdad, bringing an end to the lawless rule of the Turkish mercenaries and adding Iraq to his brother's domain in southern Persia. Caliph al-Mustakfi granted Ali, the chief Buwayhid ruler in Persia, the title *rukn al-dawla*, "supporter of the state," and granted Ahmad, his brother and viceroy in Iraq, the title *mu'izz al-dawla*, "strengthener of the state."

In a desperate effort to regain his lost authority, al-Mustakfi asked the Buwayhids to rule under him as administrators of the Arab Empire. However, recognizing the low estate of the fragmented empire, the Buwayhids refused the caliph's offer and, instead, dismissed him from office and in 946 appointed as his successor their first puppet caliph, al-Muti'. From that time till their final overthrow by the Seljuqs in 1055, the Buwayhids ruled as a dynasty over southern Iraq and Persia. They took over all caliphal authority and allowed the caliphs a small subsidy on which to live. The Buwayhid dynasty ruled Baghdad for over a century during which four Abbasid caliphs succeeded each other as titular heads of the state.[2]

The Buwayhid Regime

During the Buwayhid regime relative peace and security were restored to Iraq. Trade began to flourish, and scholarship, especially

[2] See p. **382.**

literature, jurisprudence, and philosophy, made great strides. The first Buwayhid rulers were so powerful that they ordered Muslim worshipers to mention their names during Friday congregational prayers. They also ordered coins to be issued bearing their own names instead of those of the Abbasid caliphs.

While the first Buwayhid ruler, Ahmad – known as Mu'izz al-Dawla[3] – reigned in Iraq, his brother Ali, known as Imad al-Dawla, ruled in Persia, and his second brother, al-Hasan, known as Rukn al-Dawla, ruled in Hamadan. Each ruler appeared to have his own independent administration. Relations among the Buwayhid brothers were cordial, as each cooperated with the other two to strengthen his own regime.

Their sons, however, did not maintain the harmony and cooperation that prevailed during their fathers' rule; they allowed contentions and disputes, caused mainly by the easy life and irresponsible actions of Izz al-Dawla of Iraq, to arise among them. This led Izz al-Dawla's cousin Adud al-Dawla of Persia to eliminate him and take over his administration, bringing about some political cooperation between Persia and Iraq. During the reign of Adad al-Dawla, the Buwayhid regime reached its peak of power and authority, especially when he succeeded in controlling regions as far away as Rayy.

The Buwayhid dynasty in Persia came to an end when Mahmud the Ghaznavid defeated the Buwayhid forces in 1029, thus extending his regime to the Punjab in the east and Persia in the west. His death in 1030 prevented his armies from reaching Iraq and capturing Baghdad itself. According to some reports, in 1055, a Seljuq Turk named Tughril Beg, on a pilgrimage tour with his warriors in Hijaz, asked for permission to visit Baghdad. Granted this permission by Caliph al-Qa'im, Tughril Beg and his troops camped in the Abbasid capital until local demonstrations broke out against his forces. Tughril Beg then ordered his troops to take control of the city and capture all Buwayhid officials, bringing an end to the Buwayhid regime in Iraq.

[3] Following is a list of the Buwayhid rulers:

1.	Mu'izz al-Dawla (Ahmad)	946-967
2.	Izz al-Dawla	967-977
3.	Adad al-Dawla	977-982
4.	Sharaf al-Dawla	982-989
5.	Baha' al-Dawla	989-1012
6.	Sultan al-Dawla	1012-1024
7.	Imad al-Dawla	1024-1048
8.	Fayruz al-Rahim	1048-1055

THE SELJUQ TURKS, 1055-1180

Origin of the Seljuqs

The history of the Seljuqs can be traced as far back as 970, when a certain group of Turkish tribesmen known as Ghuzz descended from the eastern mountains of Khurasan, led by an ambitious family known as the Seljuqs. These Seljuq Turks soon established themselves in Bukhara and expanded their rule over adjacent areas. In 1040 Tughril Beg (referred to above) led them to Marv and Nishapur, from where he advanced to the footholds of the Buwayhid dynasty in southern Persia and Iraq till he captured Baghdad in 1055.

Establishment of the Seljuq Regime

In 1058, while Tughril Beg was fighting in Mosul and Nasibin, a leader of the original Turkish mercenaries, Basasiri, captured Baghdad and drove the Abbasid caliph away. Basasiri then announced his allegiance to the Fatimid caliph[4] of Cairo ordering the citizens of Baghdad, center of the Abbasid caliphate, to mention the rival caliph in their prayers. However, this situation did not last long, for Tughril Beg returned to Baghdad with the Abbasid Caliph al-Qa'im and drove Basasiri to Wasit, where he was killed in 1060.

Tughril Beg was followed in 1063 by his nephew Alp Arslan, during whose reign the Seljuq regime reached the peak of its power and authority. He expanded his rule to include most of Syria by capturing Damascus from the Fatimids in 1072. The Seljuq rulers were called sultans; however, the Abbasid caliphs granted them the title ''kings of the West and East.'' Their chief ministers were known as''atabegs'', whose authority and prestige increased so much during the latter period of the Seljuq regime that many of them overshadowed the sultans themselves. At any rate, the Abbasid caliphs in Baghdad during the Seljuq rule fared slightly better than their predecessors under the Buwayhids; however, they continued to act only as figureheads, in spite of the fact that authority legally emanated from them.

The Abbasid Caliphs During the Seljuq Supremacy

The Seljuq regime was marked by the following important developments: (1) rise of the cult of Assassins, (2) attempts on the part of certain caliphs to regain independence, and (3) coming of the Crusaders.

[4]See p. 312.

The Assassin Cult

A certain Shi'ite extremist named Sabbah rebelled against the authority of both the Seljuq sultanate and the Abbasid caliphate around 1090. He organized a secret society whose members were later known as Assassins (derived from *hashish,* a drug extracted from hemp), whose main task was to surprise and assassinate those persons deemed enemies of their alleged true faith. This fanatical movement started in Alamut near Adharbayjan and caused the Seljuq regime countless problems due to the Assassins' extreme secrecy and daring actions. The sultan's troops attempted in vain to subdue them as they continued to victimize high-ranking officials and theologians. Several noted orthodox scholars were murdered by the daring Assassins, who continued to seek shelter in the mountains and travel in disguise to slay their victims.

Struggle of the Caliphs for Independence

While the Seljuq sultans were consolidating their regime in the east, Baghdad was left almost completely in the hands of the Abbasid caliphate. By 1122 Caliph al-Mustarshid (1118-1135) could muster an Arab army of about 30,000 troops and defy the Seljuq sultan in Persia. The latter entrusted his forces to a warrior named Zanki, who marched against Baghdad from Basra, forcing the caliph to come to terms. However, due to his courage and determination in battle, Zanki was sent to Syria to fight the Crusaders. While Zanki was away from Iraq, al-Mustarshid again rebelled against Seljuq rule, but he was soon captured and put to death in 1135.

Al-Mustarshid was succeeded by his son al-Rashid (1135-1136) who followed his father's example and announced Baghdad's independence from Seljuq supremacy. The Seljuq sultan hastened to Iraq, where he besieged the Abbasid strongholds in Baghdad, forcing the city to surrender and the caliph to abdicate. After these two attempts, the Abbasid caliphate reverted once more to Seljuq control till the Seljuq sultans were finally overthrown by the Khwarizm shahs.

Coming of the Crusaders

In 1097, when the first Crusaders under Godfrey reached Antioch, Syria was ruled by a Seljuq governor whose contacts with the central government were almost cut off. By that time, the great Sultan Alp Arslan had died, and his successor was deeply involved in internal troubles, especially those caused by the rise of the Assassins. At the same time, Fatimid caliphs in Egypt were in a period of decline, which prevented them from taking any serious action against the Crusaders. The Christian forces were thus able to capture Antioch after a siege of nine months and to move to Jerusalem, where Godfrey was proclaimed king in 1099.

The European kingdom in Jerusalem was almost unopposed by the Arabs, many of whom fled Palestine for Baghdad, where they rallied some opposition to the Crusaders among their fellow Arabs. However, Seljuq sultans took no decisive action against the Crusaders for many years, during which their authority in Persia was threatened, and their foothold in Iraq was about to slip away. It may be recalled that in 1122 Caliph al-Mustarshid actually declared war against the Seljuqs in an effort to achieve independence, but was finally defeated by a Seljuq warrior named Zanki, who was then appointed governor of both Iraq and Syria and charged with fighting the Crusaders. Zanki did not decisively defeat his Christian enemies; however, he did succeed in checking their expansion into the interior of Syria and northern Iraq and in restoring Aleppo to Islamic rule. Zanki established a new regional dynasty in Mosul called the Atabeg dynasty, which may be considered an offshoot of the Seljuq regime of Baghdad. In 1146 while he was slowly but successfully battling the European forces in Syria and Palestine, he was assassinated, affording the Crusaders an opportunity to resume the expansion of their kingdom.

The Second Crusade was launched in 1147. The Christians, under Louis VII of France and Conrad III of Germany, besieged Damascus for several months. However, a son of Zanki named Nur al-Din replaced his father in Mosul and took charge of the Seljuq troops, forcing the European kings to lift their siege and return home. Meanwhile, Nur al-Din consolidated his regime (inherited from his father, Zanki) over northern Iraq and Syria. In 1166 he dispatched a campaign under Shirkuh against the tottering Fatimid regime in Egypt. However, due to the Franks' intervention in Egypt, Shirkuh allied himself with the Fatimid commander against their common enemy. The combined Muslim forces defeated the Crusaders in 1169, after which the Fatimid caliph appointed Shirkuh as his chief minister, a post which the latter held for only two months before he died. His nephew Salah al-Din (Saladin) replaced him as prime minister and viceroy of the Atabeg Sultan Nur al-Din of Mosul. However, upon the death of the Fatimid caliph in 1171, Salah al-Din restored Egypt to the Abbasid caliphate, bringing an end to the Fatimid dynasty.

THE KHWARIZM SHAHS

Caliph al-Nasir and the Khwarizm Shahs

While these events were taking place in Syria and Egypt, a new Abbasid caliph called al-Nasir was acclaimed in Baghdad in 1180. By that time, the Seljuq atabegs[5] of Mosul were consolidating their

[5] This was the name of a Seljuq subdynasty started in Mosul by Zanki, see p. 287.

rule in northern Iraq and Syria and the original Seljuq sultans were occupied with the Assassins and other rebellious groups in Persia. Al-Nasir proclaimed his complete independence from the authority of the Seljuq Turks and ruled without opposition over southern Iraq.

Meanwhile, in the region of Khwarizm in Persia, a local regime ruled by the Khwarizm shahs had emerged, posing a great threat to the authority of the Seljuq sultans. Realizing that the Seljuqs might defeat him in Baghdad, al-Nasir instigated the Khwarizm shahs against the Seljuq regime in Persia. The Persian forces from Khwarizm in 1181 marched against the Seljuqs, defeated them decisively, and killed their sultan, thereby ending their rule in Persia.

Coming of the Mongols

For a while relations between Caliph al-Nasir and the reigning Khwarizm shah were amiable, but soon intrigues and counter-intrigues caused the two rulers to turn bitterly against each other. In a deliberate move to annoy the Abbasid caliph, the Khwarizm shah appointed a certain Alid as rival caliph in Khwarizm, causing al-Nasir to hunt for quick assistance in order to maintain his own independence. In the meantime, Jenghiz Khan, who had laid the foundations of the Mongol Empire in Central Asia around 1206, threatened the very existence of the Khwarizm shah. As the latter was planning to march against Baghdad in 1220, the Mongol hordes not only conquered Khwarizm, but also captured Bukhara and Samarqand on the eastern borders of Transoxiana. This abrupt end of the Khwarizm supremacy at the hands of the pagan Mongols undoubtedly brought some relief to the Abbasid caliphate in Baghdad.

Sack of Baghdad, 1258

Things went well with the remainder of al-Nasir's rule and those of his two successors, but this was only the glimmer that preceded ashes. When al-Musta'sim, the last of the Abbasid caliphs in Baghdad, assumed office in 1242, the end was not far away. Hulagu, a descendant of Jenghiz Khan, was granted the Middle East as his portion of the already dismembered Mongol Empire.

In 1256 Hulagu marched westward to carve for himself a new empire. He sent a message to Caliph al-Musta'sim to surrender and tear down the walls of Baghdad. However, the caliph refused to do so. In January, 1258, Hulagu, at the head of his Mongol warriors, reached Baghdad and sacked the city, razing the caliph's palace to the ground. He captured al-Musta'sim together with many of his kinsmen and executed them all, thereby bringing an end not only to the Abbasid caliphate in Baghdad, but also to the Arab Empire that had ruled over vast areas of the Middle East for over six hundred years.

CHAPTER 36

REGIONAL DYNASTIES IN WESTERN ASIA

THE TAHIRID DYNASTY, 820-872

As mentioned before, in 820 al-Ma'mun's victorious commander Tahir, who fought against al-Amin's forces in Baghdad, was restored to the caliph's favor and permitted to return to his home in Khurasan. He was then appointed governor of Persia and the East, where he began a semi-independent regime ruled by his sons and known as the Tahirid dynasty.

The Tahirids ruled Khurasan from their capital at Nishapur and were on good terms with the Abbasid caliphs in Baghdad, who continued to recognize the Tahirids' full authority over their region. As long as the Tahirids ruled in Persia and Khurasan they were able not only to bring the whole region under firm control but also to prevent serious revolts against their own authority or that of the caliphate in Baghdad. However, when the Turkish mercenaries reduced the caliphs' authority over the empire, conditions in Persia and the East began to change; many local rulers emerged to compete for power, leading to the establishment of several regional dynasties.

THE SAFFARID DYNASTY, 872-910

The founder of the Saffarid dynasty was a warrior named Ya'qub al-Saffar, who had been sent by the caliph to suppress the Kharijites in Transoxiana. He succeeded in rallying an army and capturing Sijistan from the Tahirids in 867. Soon Ya'qub al-Saffar expanded his rule over adjacent areas till he captured Nishapur in 872, bringing an end to the Tahirid dynasty that had ruled there for over fifty years. Ya'qub moved northward, subjugating most of the regions of Khurasan, Gurgan, and Tabaristan.

Ya'qub's expansions greatly disturbed the Abbasid caliph al-Mu'tamid (870-892), who hastened to send letters to the local rulers of the area revealing his complete disavowal of Ya'qub's actions. In the meantime, Ya'qub marched toward Baghdad itself till he reached Ahwaz. There he sent a message to the caliph asking him to concede to him officially the territories previously controlled by the Tahirids in addition to the eastern frontiers of Transoxiana. Fearful of losing his own capital, al-Mu'tamid granted Ya'qub's demands, elevating him officially to supreme rulership over all Persia and Transoxiana.

Moreover, the caliph reportedly sent messengers with gifts of good will to Ya'qub in an obvious effort to win his friendship and persuade him not to strike against Baghdad. However, Ya'qub al-Saffar died suddenly in 879 after challenging the caliph to pursue their struggle until one of them destroyed the other. Ya'qub's death probably prevented the collapse of the Abbasid caliphate as early as the reign of al-Mu'tamid himself, around the year 880.

Amr al-Saffar, 879-901

Ya'qub was succeeded by his brother Amr al-Saffar, who obtained the caliph's authorization to rule over his brother's domain. However, in 887 Caliph al-Mu'tamid withdrew his appointment of Amr as supreme ruler of Persia and Transoxiana and sent an army to restore his control over the whole region. In 892, during the war between al-Mu'tamid's forces and those of Amr al-Saffar, the caliph died and was followed by al-Mu'tadid, who brought an end to fighting by recognizing Amr's position based on inheritance from his brother Ya'qub.

However, Amr's troubles were not yet over; a rival named Isma'il al-Samani emerged from a frontier region on the eastern borders of Transoxiana. Isma'il sent a message to Amr asking Amr to be content with his large domain in Persia and Khurasan and leave for Isma'il the border region in Transoxiana. Amr refused and led an army to subjugate Isma'il al-Samani. Trapped by Isma'il's forces, Amr himself was taken prisoner in 901 and his army dispersed westward.

End of the Saffarid Dynasty

Two years after Amr's capture, a son of Isma'il named Ahmad al-Samani moved westward, conquering Sijistan. Continuing his expansion north and south, he captured Khurasan and Kerman. In 910 he sent several Saffarid claimants and army commanders as prisoners to Baghdad, bringing to a rather abrupt end the once-strong Saffarid dynasty.

THE SAMANID DYNASTY, 910-999

Founding of the Samanid Dynasty

The Samanids belonged to a prominent Persian family whose founder, Saman, reportedly accepted Islam during the Umayyad dynasty. Both the Umayyad and Abbasid caliphs appointed several descendants of Saman to high-ranking offices in Khurasan and Transoxiana. When the Tahirids gained supremacy over the whole area, they appointed Nasr al-Samani as governor of Transoxiana. Nasr's son Isma'il al-Samani succeeded his father at a time when the Saffarids coveted supremacy over the whole region east of Iraq, including Transoxiana. Isma'il wrote to Amr al-Saffar requesting him to cease attempts to add the eastern frontier region to his domain. Amr refused and in 901 war began between the Saffarids and the Samanids, resulting in Isma'il's victory. From that time the house of al-Saffar declined, mainly because of internal conflicts, while the house of Saman made substantial progress toward capturing Sijistan and Khurasan. In 903 Ahmad al-Samani, son of Isma'il, took command of his father's troops. In 910 he brought about the final collapse of the Saffarids, whose leaders were sent to Baghdad as captives. In that year Caliph al-Muktafi confirmed Ahmad al-Samani as ruler of Khurasan and Transoxiana, thereby recognizing the supreme authority of the new Samanid dynasty. Relations between the Samanids and the Abbasid caliphs of Baghdad were fairly amiable as the former tried always to establish the caliphate's authority over several adverse heterodox movements in their regime, especially that of the Qarmatians.[1]

Seven Samanid rulers governed Khurasan and Transoxiana as follows:

1.	Ahmad	910-913
2.	Nasr	913-942
3.	Nuh I	942-954
4.	Abd al-Malik	954-961
5.	Mansur I	961-976
6.	Nuh II	976-997
7.	Mansur II	997-999

The Samanid Rulers

Although Isma'il al-Samani (Ahmad's father) was the founder of the Samanid dynasty, Ahmad fought the Saffarids till he captured their

[1] See p. 342.

leaders and ended their rule in 910. While he was still fighting the last Saffarid descendants in 907, his father died, and he became leader of the Samanid dynasty. In 910, the caliph officially recognized him as ruler of Khurasan and Transoxiana, making him the first sovereign of the Samanid dynasty. His reign was short, for he was assassinated in 913 and succeeded by his son Nasr, a young man about eighteen years old.

No sooner had Nasr become the Samanid leader than his uncle rallied forces against him on the grounds of Nasr's youthfulness. However, Nasr's supporters defeated their enemies, forcing them to flee to Ferghana in 922. From that time on the Samanid dynasty never recovered from internal conflicts and quarrels. Its authority gradually waned as the Buwayhids of Persia in the west and the Ghaznavids on the borders of India in the east flanked it on both sides. By the reign of Mansur I, the central government required seven years to put down a rebellion by a local governor in Sijistan—a clear indication of the tragic weakness of the Samanid regime by that time.

Moreover, when Nuh II in 976 became the Samanid ruler at the tender age of thirteen, his mother, acting as his guardian, seized control. This led to the rebellion of several army commanders and the inevitable interference of the Buwayhids of Persia and the Ghaznavids of the east. Ambitious to expand westward, the Ghaznavids gradually intervened in the internal affairs of the Samanids till they brought about the Samanid downfall in 999.

Despite its weaknesses, the Samanid regime was a period of Persian cultural revival. As a result of Islamic expansion into Persia and Khurasan, the Persians not only adopted Islam as a religion, but they also became upholders of Islamic theology and champions of Arabic literature. The Samanids, however, are believed to have encouraged the reassertion of Persian culture. Persian scholars were strongly urged to write in their native language instead of Arabic, giving rise to such great works as the epic *Shahname* of al-Firdawsi. During the Samanid period distinguished literary works, such as the historical annals of al-Tabari from Arabic and the two stories of *Kalila wa Dimna* and *Sindbad* from an Indian book of fables, were translated into Persian.

Fall of the Samanid Dynasty

Soon after Mansur II became ruler of the Samanid regime the ambitious Mahmud the Ghaznavid asked him to concede Khurasan. When Mansur's chief minister refused, Mahmud led his armies against the Samanids, capturing Nishapur and Bukhara. He proceeded westward, conquering Khurasan and taking Mansur and his household captive. They were later put to death, and the Ghaznavid regime became firmly established in the whole region east of Isfahan.

With the collapse of the Samanid dynasty in 999, it may be said that authority in Khurasan and Transoxiana shifted for the first time from the grip of native Persians to the hands of alien Turks, halting thereby the Arab-Persian feuds that had started with the rise of the Abbasid regime.

THE GHAZNAVID DYNASTY, 999-1186

Beginning of the Ghaznavid Regime

The Ghaznavids were a dynasty of Turkish warriors who settled in the city of Ghazna, south of Kabul, in what is now Afghanistan. Their military ability attracted the Samanid rulers as early as 954 when Abd al-Malik appointed a Ghaznavid Turk named Alptigin as governor of Khurasan. Alptigin returned to Ghazna after Abd al-Malik's death and organized his followers into a fighting force, but he died in 977 and was followed by his son-in-law Subuktigin. Continuing Alptigin's work, Subuktigin led his Turkish troops south into India in 980, forcing Jaybal, king of the Punjab, to surrender to him vast areas of Indian border territory. Having carved out a state, Subuktigin began a Ghaznavid regime south of Kabul with himself as sultan. His prestige continued to increase as he was acclaimed throughout the Islamic domain as conqueror of the Indian infidels. In 997 Subuktigin died and was followed first by his oldest son Isma'il, who showed little interest in carrying out the responsibilities of his father's regime. Isma'il's younger brother Mahmud, a courageous warrior, forced him to abdicate. As soon as Mahmud became sultan, he turned his attention toward expanding his father's domain. As mentioned above, he marched against the Samanid regime in 998 when its ruler Mansur II refused to yield Khurasan to him. In the following year Mahmud defeated the Samanids, ending their regime abruptly and establishing Ghaznavid rule over most of the Islamic domain east of Isfahan.

Expansion of the Ghaznavid Regime

Mahmud's victory over the Samanids gained him the official support of the Abbasid caliph, who not only recognized him as sultan of the East, but also granted him the title *yamin al-dawla*, "right hand of the state." Encouraged by this support, Mahmud consolidated his regime by suppressing several pockets of resistance to his rule in the two regions of Sijistan and Tabaristan. In the northeast region of Transoxiana, he fought several Turkish tribes, chief of which were the Ghuzz tribes, from whom the Seljuq Turks are reported to have descended.

Having achieved these victories both within and beyond the Islamic domain, Mahmud turned once more to India, capturing Multan in 1004 and defeating King Anandpal, who had just replaced his father Jaybal as king of the Punjab. Mahmud penetrated deeply into India, capturing most of the Punjab region with its rich capital, Lahore, which became the seat of a Ghaznavid dynasty that ruled in India for more than one hundred and fifty years.

Turning north, Mahmud subjugated the Ilek Khan Turks, who tried to control the Balkh area in the northeast corner of Khurasan. He also defeated the local leaders of the two regions of Khwarizm and Gurgan north of Khurasan. In the west, he drove the Buwayhids out of Rayy and Hamadan, expanding the Ghaznavid empire to include the whole area between Hamadan in the west and Lahore in the east.

In 1026 Mahmud led an expedition into India beyond the Ganges River, occupying Gujarat and destroying the chief Indian temple dedicated to an idol called Somnath. The destruction of this pagan idol won for Mahmud tremendous prestige throughout Islam, besides paving the way for the conversion of many disillusioned Indians to Islam. Mahmud died in 1030, leaving behind a vast empire established mainly by the force of his own personal prestige as an administrator and military commander.

Fall of the Ghaznavid Regime

After Mahmud's death, fifteen successive sultans ruled the Ghaznavid regime, which lasted till 1186. However, his successors lacked Mahmud's administrative and military ability. The regime suffered greatly from internal quarrels and disputes, which enabled several Turkish tribes north of Marv to force the Ghaznavid sultans to withdraw gradually to the south. The Seljuq Turks soon emerged as a great power under Tughril Beg, who carved a sizable state at the expense of the Ghaznavids in Khurasan. Tughril Beg later captured Bukhara and Samarqand in the east and the region of Tabaristan in the west, eventually reaching Baghdad and ending Buwayhid rule in Iraq in 1055.

As the Seljuq Turks were consolidating their regime in the north and west, the Ghaznavids were gradually driven out of Transoxiana until they were confined mostly to their Indian possessions in the Punjab. They continued to rule in Lahore until the Ghorids (originally from the region of Ghor near Ghazna) marched against them from the north and defeated them in 1186.

THE HAMDANIDS OF MOSUL AND ALEPPO, 931-1003

The Hamdanids in Mosul

The Hamdanid dynasty sprang from an Arab tribe which had settled in northern Iraq during the early period of Islamic expansion. Around 870 several members of the Hamdanid family attained recognition when, in cooperation with certain Kharijites, they rebelled against

Caliph al-Mu'tadid (892-902) in Baghdad. Later on, however, the Hamdanids were reconciled to the Abbasid caliphs and efficiently helped them in suppressing several rebellious movements in northern Iraq. As a result, Caliph al-Muqtadir (910-932) appointed three sons of the Hamdan family to high-ranking positions in Mosul and its adjacent cities, adding to the family's prestige throughout northern Iraq.

In 931 al-Muqtadir promoted a certain Hamdanid named al-Hasan as governor of the district of Mosul. Using his family's prestige to advance his own ambitions, he expanded his rule to include several other districts around Mosul. As al-Hasan's influence and power increased, Caliph al-Muttaqi (940-944) officially recognized him as ruler of the whole region of northern Syria and Iraq, bestowing upon him the honorary title *nasir al-dawla*, "the supporter of the state." Al-Hasan gained so much favor with al-Muttaqi that the latter elevated him to the rank of *amir al-umara*, "chief prince," of the Abbasid regime, moving his residence to Baghdad. However, being an Arab, al-Hasan did not have much success among the many Turkish leaders around the caliph; therefore he returned to Mosul, where he began to consolidate his own regime in 942.

The Hamdanids Against the Turks and Buwayhids

While in Mosul, al-Hasan faced several attacks against his regime led by Turkish mercenaries in an effort to prevent an alliance between the Hamdanids and the Abbasid caliphate. Had it not been for the timid attitude of the Abbasid caliph, who offered the Hamdanids no help at all, al-Hasan probably would have been able to defeat the Turks and restore Arab supremacy over the empire. Instead, the Turks blinded the hesitant Caliph al-Muttaqi, removed him from office, and appointed al-Mustakfi (944-946) as his successor.

In the meantime, the Buwayhids appeared on the eastern borders of Persia and in 946 reached Baghdad and defeated the Turkish mercenaries. It may be recalled that after the Buwayhids established their authority in Baghdad, they continued to control the ruling Abbasid caliphs in spite of the Abbasids' efforts to restore some authority to their office. When relations between the Persian Buwayhids and the Abbasid caliphs deteriorated sharply, the Buwayhids were apprehensive of the Hamdanid Arab threat in Mosul. In 947 war broke out between these two powers situated in the southern and northern regions of Iraq, resulting in a truce by which the defeated Hamdanids agreed to pay tribute money to the Buwayhids. In 956, as the Buwayhids were engaged in suppressing a revolt in Ahwaz, al-Hasan attacked Baghdad but was soon driven back by the Buwayhids, who defeated him and forced him to pay more tribute.

The Hamdanids in Aleppo

Al-Hasan had a brother named Ali upon whom Caliph al-Muttaqi had earlier bestowed the honorary title *sayf al-dawla*, "sword of the state." Ali proved his military ability during the sporadic fighting between his brother's forces and the Turkish mercenaries. In 944 he led some Hamdanid forces against Syria and captured Aleppo and the surrounding district. There he established a branch of the Hamdanid dynasty, which often came to the aid of its sister dynasty in Mosul, especially during the wars with the Buwayhids.

In the meantime, the Ikhshidids of Egypt [2] threatened the new Hamdanid regime in Aleppo as both camps competed for possession of Damascus. At last the Ikhshidids made peace with the Hamdanids, conceding Damascus when the latter agreed to pay indemnities. From that time on the Hamdanid ruler in Aleppo often interfered in behalf of his brother in Mosul, to bring about peace and reconciliation between Mosul and the Buwayhid regime in Baghdad. However, tranquility in Aleppo was short-lived because of several attacks Ali launched against Byzantium. In spite of Ali's failure to deal the Byzantines a decisive blow, his prestige increased considerably among other Muslim rulers who were forced on religious grounds to give him respect for fighting against the "polytheist" Christians.

Fall of the Hamdanid Dynasty

The golden age of the Hamdanid regime both in Mosul and Aleppo ended with the death of its two founders, al-Hasan, known as *nasir al-dawla*, and Ali, known as *sayf al-dawla*. Like several other regional dynasties, their later rulers were both weak and divided. Disputes arose between al-Hasan's and Ali's successors leading to the rapid deterioration and collapse of the whole regime. In 979 the Buwayhids captured Mosul and held it for about ten years until the last Hamdanid ruler mustered enough power in 989 to restore it to his shaky regime. However, only five years later the Buwayhids drove the Hamdanid ruler out of the Mosul area completely and replaced him with one of their followers, ending the Hamdanid regime of Mosul in 994.

In Aleppo internal troubles among Ali's descendants permitted the emerging Fatimids of Egypt [3] to gain control over several cities in Syria. However, in 1003 Lu'lu, the chief counselor of the last Hamdanid ruler, sided with the Fatimids against his own master, whom he betrayed and murdered, bringing to an end the tottering Hamdanid regime in Aleppo. After a short rule as a vassal of the Fatimids, Lu'lu himself died, allowing the whole area of Syria and Palestine to revert to Fatimid control.

[2] See pp. 308-310.

[3] See pp. 310-313.

THE ATABEGS OF MOSUL, 1127-1182

Rise of the Atabegs

The later sultans of the Seljuq regime (1055-1180) were known for their weakness and incompetence. Therefore, they relied heavily on their chief ministers or "atabegs." A famous atabeg during the reign of the Abbasid Caliph al-Mustarshid (1118-1135) was called Zanki. When the caliph attempted to regain his independence in 1122, Zanki upheld the Seljuq sultan against al-Mustarshid, who was later on removed and put to death.

In 1127 the Seljuq sultan appointed his atabeg, Zanki, as ruler of the district of Mosul in northern Iraq. Here Zanki participated in the wars against the Crusaders, and was acclaimed by the Muslims of Syria and Iraq as one of their great heroes. When the Seljuqs of Baghdad were finally defeated by the Khwarizm shahs of Persia, Zanki became virtually independent in Mosul, where he established an Atabeg dynasty whose authority reached beyond northern Iraq to include Syria.

The Atabegs under Nur al-Din

Zanki was treacherously killed in 1146 by one of his own people while fighting against the Crusaders. He was followed as Atabeg of Mosul and Aleppo by his son Nur al-Din. Nur al-Din was a brave and unflinching ruler. He won many battles against the Crusaders, forcing Louis VII of France and Conrad III of Germany to lift the siege of Damascus in 1148 and return to Europe. While Nur al-Din was fighting the Crusaders on the Syrian front, he sent an army under his commander Shirkuh to bring the Fatimids of Egypt under his control. Shirkuh defeated the Franks near Alexandria and ruled Egypt as viceroy of Nur al-Din. After his death in 1169, Shirkuh was succeeded by his nephew Salah al-Din (Saladin), a daring and ambitious soldier who terminated the Fatimid dynasty in Egypt, refusing to allow a successor to reign after the death of its last caliph, al-Adid.

End of the Atabeg Rule

Salah al-Din ruled Egypt in the name of Nur al-Din, Atabeg of Mosul, whose domains extended from Iraq to Egypt with the exception of the Christian state in Palestine. However, when Nur al-Din died, his descendants divided the Atabeg regime between Aleppo and Mosul. Several disputes arose which led Salah al-Din to announce his independence from the Atabeg dynasty. Having distinguished himself both militarily and administratively, Salah al-Din was able to win the support of sev-

eral groups of Muslims in Egypt, Syria, and Iraq, who requested him
to lead their armies against the Crusaders. In 1182, after a number of
battles between Salah al-Din and Nur al-Din's descendants, the last
Atabeg ruler of Mosul forfeited his rights in favor of Salah al-Din, who
then became sole ruler over a realm extending from Egypt to Iraq.
After the final collapse of the Atabeg dynasty in Mosul, Salah al-Din
united Egypt, Syria, and northern Iraq under the rule of a new dynasty
known as the Ayyubid dynasty, which ruled in the Middle East from
1171 to 1260.

CHAPTER 37

THE UMAYYAD DYNASTY IN SPAIN, 756-1031

BEGINNING OF THE UMAYYADS IN SPAIN

Abd al-Rahman's Fateful Trip

It may be recalled that when the Abbasids took control of the Arab Empire, they embarked upon a vicious campaign to exterminate the Umayyad household. While the Abbasids were joyously celebrating their hard-won victory over Marwan II, hundreds of Umayyad princes and leaders were treacherously massacred throughout Syria and Palestine. Nevertheless, one Umayyad prince named Abd al-Rahman managed to evade Abbasid soldiers and escape all the way to Spain. Islamic annals include a report attributed to Abd al-Rahman himself, in which he described his historic escape from Syria as follows:

> When we were promised security and then deceived at the river of Abu Fadras, I received news of the orders to spill our blood. With the feelings of an outcast, I returned to my home in desperation trying to find a way to save myself and my household. Extremely fearful, I walked out till I reached a village on the Euphrates known for its trees and shrubs. While there, my son Sulayman, who was then only four years old, was playing with me. He left me for a short while then returned crying with fear, hanging onto me as I was pushing him away. Finally I went outside

to find out what was the matter and discovered that the whole village was in turmoil as the black banners (of the Abbasids) were unfurled everywhere. My younger brother said to me, "Escape! Escape! These are the black banners!" I took some money with me and escaped with my brother after telling the rest of my family about my intentions, requesting them to send my bondman Badr after me. Accordingly, when the horsemen reached the village, they could not find me. I met one of my acquaintances and asked him to buy for me some beasts of burden and other necessities; but he informed the governor Abd-Allah against me. When he (the governor) came after me, we fled on foot as his horsemen followed. We crossed through some orchards toward the Euphrates, preceding the horsemen to the river, where we swam. The horsemen promised us safe conduct if we returned, but I did not go back. My brother, how-ever, could not persevere in swimming, and, believing in their safety promises, he returned. Albeit, they murdered him while I was watching—he was thirteen years old. I bore my grief for him and continued on my way till I disappeared from sight. I hid till they stopped searching for me; then I came out of hiding and started on my trip to North Africa. [1]

Although Abbasid soldiers throughout the empire were ordered to arrest Abd al-Rahman if they found him, he managed to win a few friends who helped him escape to Egypt and then to North Africa. In 755 he crossed into Spain and managed to win considerable support for himself, especially among the followers of the Yamanite faction of the Umayyad regime. After some skirmishes with the Qaysite faction, Abd al-Rahman was proclaimed ruler of Spain in 756 with the title *amir,* "prince."

Abd al-Rahman's Reign, 756-788

Abd al-Rahman adopted Cordova as his capital, where he built a palace and a mosque. His regime was far from tranquil; during his thirty-two year reign he faced many problems and had to suppress several revolts before he achieved stability near the end of his rule. Besides wars against the Qaysite leader al-Fihri and later the Abbasid commander Mughith, [2] Abd al-Rahman met perhaps the most dangerous challenge to his new regime at the hands of Charlemagne, who, in collusion with the Arab governors of Barcelona and Saragossa, attacked the northern borders of the new Islamic state.

In 774 al-Arabi, governor of Barcelona, and al-Ansari, governor of Saragossa, allied themselves against Abd al-Rahman. Unable to

[1] Ibn al-Athir, *al-Kamil* (Bulaq, 1860) Volume 5, p. 198.

[2] See p. 233.

accomplish very much by themselves, they reportedly asked Charlemagne for aid, promising him certain advantages in northern Spain. This unholy alliance contemplated that as Charlemagne crossed the Pyrenees to Spain, al-Arabi and al-Ansari would announce their revolt and bring about the downfall of the new Umayyad regime. In 778 Charlemagne crossed the Pyrenees into Navarre and marched toward Saragossa. In the meantime, al-Arabi and al-Ansari disagreed about the timing of their rebellion, while news of the impending revolt leaked to Abd al-Rahman. Abd al-Rahman dispatched his forces to Barcelona and prevented its governor al-Ansari from carrying out his part of the original plan. Hearing of the capture of Barcelona by Umayyad forces, the people of Saragossa rose in revolt against their own governor, al-Arabi. Thus when Charlemagne reached the vicinity of the city, instead of finding its people on his side, he found its gates closed and its inhabitants ready to resist.

After a short skirmish, Charlemagne captured Saragossa's governor, Al-Arabi, and returned with him toward the Pyrenees. However, Abd al-Rahman's forces, joined by those from Barcelona and Saragossa, followed Charlemagne into the valley of Roncevaux, where the Basques had already been fighting the retreating Frankish army. The Franks fought against heavy odds; nevertheless, their soldiers exhibited great courage, giving rise to the well-known epic [3] about a gallant hero named Roland. After incurring heavy casualties, Charlemagne withdrew, while the Arabs and Basques continued fighting against each other. In 780 the Arab forces returned to Cordova after subjugating the Basques and stabilizing the otherwise shaky and unsteady frontier. Abd al-Rahman died in 788, leaving a strong, stable, and well-established regime. He reigned contemporaneously with four Abbasid caliphs: al-Mansur, al-Mahdi, al-Hadi, and al-Rashid. Of his eleven sons, he chose Hisham, a younger son, to succeed him as ruler of his prosperous and hard-won regime. Hisham I (788-796) continued to stabilize the Umayyad regime in Spain. He frequently consulted theologians in regard to state administration; in fact, many Islamic jurists and scholars attained high-ranking positions during his reign. Before his death, he designated his son al-Hakam I to succeed him as *amir* (prince) of the Umayyad regime.

DEVELOPMENT OF THE UMAYYAD RULE IN SPAIN

Problems Facing the Umayyads in Spain

Perhaps the best way to help the reader understand some of the problems facing the Umayyad rulers in Spain is to enumerate the various groups composing its heterogeneous population. Besides the Arabs, who

[3] The name of the epic is *Chanson de Roland.*

themselves were divided into various factions, there were: (1) the Berbers, (2) the Muslim Spaniards, (3) the Arabicized Christians (Arabic-speaking Spaniards), and (4) the Spanish Christians. Each of these groups tried, of course, to advance its own interests against those of the others in an atmosphere of plots, intrigues, local revolutions, and counterrevolutions. In fact, the major portion of Umayyad rule in Spain was devoted mainly to suppressing revolts and dealing with riots and factional rivalries.

Moreover, the Christian kingdoms ruling in the north and west of Spain continued to apply considerable pressure against the borders of the Islamic state. Thus besides coping with numerous internal problems, the Umayyad rulers always had to be on guard against sudden attacks on their territory. In spite of all these problems, several Umayyad rulers managed to maintain control and to devote much of their energies to the promotion of prosperity, literature, and scholarship. The Umayyad regime was among the most prosperous and culturally advanced eras in the history of medieval Spain. Mention is given here only to the Umayyad rulers whose reigns were characterized by significant events.[4]

Al-Hakam I, 796-822

Al-Hakam I was a young man when he became ruler in Spain; however, he was a ruthless autocrat who cared little about the consequences of his rigid policies. His rule was marked by continuous struggle against almost every contending group within the state, including two of his own uncles. Therefore al-Hakam introduced from the east about five thousand mercenaries to suppress internal revolts and to act as his personal bodyguards.

Perhaps the most serious threat that faced al-Hakam I was several revolts inside his own capital Cordova, which reached their critical stage in 814. Contrary to the policies of his predecessor, al-Hakam I excluded all theologians from interfering in the state's affairs. The alienated theologians began to preach against him in the numerous mosques of the city in an effort to arouse the population against his rule. This led to several revolts in Cordova beginning in 805, all of which were ruthlessly suppressed by al-Hakam's loyal forces. These revolts culminated in 814 with the greatest rebellion ever staged in the capital city during the Umayyad regime. Indignant at al-Hakam's humiliation of their theologians, the inhabitants of Cordova reportedly left their houses and gathered around the royal palace shouting derogatory slogans against their ruler. Al-Hakam quickly ordered his bodyguards to rush to the citizens' empty homes and set fire to them. This maneuver forced the rebels to return hurriedly to put down the holocaust, forgetting for a while the goals of their rebellion. Al-Hakam's forces rushed after the disarrayed populace and massacred thousands of them.

----

[4]A complete list of the Umayyad amirs and caliphs in Spain is given in Appendix 9, pp. 382, 383.

Al-Hakam ordered three hundred leaders of the revolt to be hanged on posts throughout the town; the rest of those who took part in the rebellion were driven out of Spain and reportedly migrated as far as the island of Crete.

The rest of al-Hakam's reign was spent in consolidating the Umayyad regime in Spain against both internal and external threats. Before his death in 822 he left a stable and prosperous regime to his son Abd al-Rahman II, who spent most of his time promoting art and scholarship. Abd al-Rahman II erected magnificent buildings, constructed fabulous mosques decorated in all styles of Islamic art, and encouraged trade with Europe, Africa, and the Middle East. During his reign, Cordova became one of the richest capitals of the Islamic world; only Baghdad could compete with it.

Abd al-Rahman III, 912-961

Between the reigns of Abd al-Rahman II and Abd al-Rahman III, Spain was ruled by three amirs whose reigns were not as stable as those of the early founders of the regime. As the authority of the central government weakened, several local chieftains, especially in the frontier areas of the state, ruled almost independently. When Abd al-Rahman III began his rule in 912, he set out to restore to his control several of those autonomous districts, in addition to suppressing a number of riots and revolts in the interior of his realm. Having stabilized his administration, Abd al-Rahman III followed the example of the new Fatimid caliphate in North Africa and proclaimed himself caliph in 929. This was the beginning of a schism which divided Muslim loyalties among three independent caliphates: the Fatimids in North Africa, the Umayyads in Spain, and the Abbasids in Iraq.

In 922 the Christian king of Leon reportedly attacked the borders of Abd al-Rahman III's territory, forcing the Umayyads to send troops against the scattered Christian kingdoms in northern Spain. Islamic forces fought against Leon, and also Navarre and Castile, defeating their respective kings, who were forced to accept the caliph's peace terms.

Abd al-Rahman III is known also for building a new residence for the Umayyad caliphate in a suburb of Cordova called al-Zahra'. Islamic annals use extremely elaborate terms in describing the beauty and elegance of the new residence. Unfortunately, however, al-Zahra' became the target of so many riots and attacks during the shaky reigns of succeeding caliphs that none of its splendid structures survived the downfall of the Umayyad regime.

Despite the good works attributed to Abd al-Rahman III, he was chiefly responsible for strengthening the non-Arab elements against the Arab population of his state. He reportedly dismissed from high-ranking offices a number of loyal Arab officials, replacing them with Berbers and non-Arabs. Moreover, Abd al-Rahman III introduced to his court a corps of slaves from Europe known as *saqaliba,* or "Slavs."

He trained them in the art of warfare and used them as his own bodyguards in a way similar to the function of the Turkish mercenaries of
Baghdad. Undoubtedly these actions caused animosity and dissatisfaction
among his own kinsmen, the Arabs, whose resentment increased with
the passing years, leading to the great revolution that ended the
Umayyad regime.

Al-Hakam II, 961-976

Al-Hakam II succeeded his father Abd al-Rahman III as caliph in
Cordova. Immediately, the Christian kingdoms in northern Spain revoked their previous agreements with Abd al-Rahman III and attacked
certain outposts on the Islamic borders. Consequently, in 963 al-Hakam
II led a campaign, first against the king of Castile, and then against the
king of Navarre, forcing both to acquiesce to his peace terms.

In the meantime, the Fatimids were beginning to meet some success
in North Africa as they promoted Shi'ite over Sunnite doctrines. Al-
Hakam II in 972 dispatched an army to North Africa to suppress the
Shi'ite threat. However, the Umayyad army succeeded only in conquering a few coastal districts in the region of al-Maghrib (Morocco),
leaving the interior of North Africa open to the Fatimids.

Al-Hakam II distinguished himself above all other Umayyad caliphs
by his love for learning. He encouraged scholars of all fields to come to
Cordova, where he established a spacious and well-stocked library.
By his time, Baghdad's fame as a center of learning was beginning to
decline; this encouraged many philosophers, historians, poets, and other
scholars to flock to the Umayyad capital in Spain, making it the undisputed metropolis of Islamic learning in the later tenth century. Besides
the attraction of the rich library which al-Hakam II erected, scholars
were also drawn to Cordova by the great sums of money distributed by
the caliph to encourage writing and research. It is reported that he
spent one thousand gold dinars to secure a collection of Arabic poems
known as *al-Aghani* by Abu al-Faraj al-Isfahani, whom the Umayyad
caliph finally persuaded to send his work to Cordova rather than
Baghdad.

DECLINE OF THE UMAYYAD RULE IN SPAIN

Rising Power of the Hajibs, "Bodyguards"

Al-Hakam II died in 976, leaving as his successor a ten-year-old
son named Hisham II. Hisham's guardian was his mother, who entrusted
the young caliph's future to a certain bodyguard (Arabic, *hajib*) called
al-Mansur. Being in charge of the caliph's personal security, al-
Mansur embarked on a campaign in which he liquidated his own enemies
and potential rivals under the pretext that they were a threat to the

young caliph. One of the groups which he tried to eliminate was the *saqaliba,* "Slav mercenaries," introduced by Abd al-Rahman III as palace guards and courtiers. Having removed all potential opponents, al-Mansur began to control the young caliph himself, confining him to his palace and stripping him of most of his authority.

Al-Mansur's rule in behalf of the Umayyad Caliph Hisham II was rather prosperous. He continued to encourage scholarship and literature, especially poetry and Islamic history. He built a new residence, competing with that of the caliph and called it *al-Madina al-Zahira,* furnishing it in splendor. When al-Mansur died in 1003, his son continued his father's rule as the caliph's *hajib* for seven years until Muhammad II, a relative of Caliph Hisham II, staged a revolt in Cordova, forcing the caliph in 1009 to abdicate in Muhammad's favor.

Period of Disorder

From that time on the Umayyad caliphate in Spain became the scene of bloody disputes among members of the Umayyad household and among several local chieftains aspiring for leadership. Following Muhammad II's *coup d'état* in 1009, an Umayyad named Sulayman staged another coup in the same year and seized the caliphate from Muhammad II. The three Umayyad claimants to the caliphate then fought among themselves, each trying to win certain elements of Spain's heterogeneous population. At last Sulayman won the battle after soliciting the help of both the Christians and the Berbers. His reign, however, ended shortly thereafter, for in 1016 an ambitious warrior named Ali ibn Hammud from the Idrisid dynasty of North Africa staged a coup in Cordova, seizing the caliphate and executing Sulayman.

END OF THE UMAYYAD RULE IN SPAIN

Rise of the Hammud Dynasty

While Ali ibn Hammud was consolidating his rule in Spain in an effort to establish his own dynasty, he was suddenly murdered in 1018 by one of the Slav mercenaries. Upon his death the Umayyads proclaimed Abd al-Rahman IV as their caliph while al-Qasim, Ali's son, assumed his father's Hammud rule. Because of the bitter rivalry between al-Qasim and his nephew, Yahya, the rulership rotated between the two till 1023, when al-Qasim was finally defeated and jailed.

The Umayyads now tried to find within their own household a caliph strong enough to restore the Umayyad caliphate to its previous strength. Their choices of Abd al-Rahman V in 1023 and Muhammad III in 1024 failed to produce any useful results since the new caliphs were no match for Yahya of the Hammud dynasty. When Muhammad III died in

1025, the inhabitants of Cordova invited Yahya to assume rule once more in the name of the Hammud dynasty. Yahya's rule lasted only two years, after which the Umayyads made a last effort to install a caliph of their own. Choosing Hisham III as their caliph, they staged a coup against Yahya in 1027, forcing him to flee the capital city northward where he was soon trapped and killed.

The Umayyad Caliphate Abolished

The four years of Caliph Hisham III's reign were marked by bloody riots and several plots fomented by the various groups within the Spanish population. In 1031 several demonstrations in the streets of Cordova were organized against the government of Hisham III. Unable to suppress these riots, the caliph requested his ministers to study the situation. Hisham's ministers met and decided to request the caliph to abdicate and leave the rule to the leaders of Cordova. Unable to resist or disobey, Hisham III abdicated and went into retirement. Thereupon, the ministers announced publicly the end of the caliphate and the beginning of the people's rule.

A council composed of Cordova's leading citizens was organized to govern. However, as soon as the council's chairman requested the governors of the various districts to pledge allegiance to the new republican government, he was sharply rebuffed; the result was the rise of several regional petty dynasties at times numbering about twenty-five separate principalities. From 1031 to 1054 the Hammud regime survived in Malaga and Cordova, as the chief state among numerous other petty states. They were followed in leadership by the Abbad dynasty that ruled in Seville for over twenty-five more years. Harassed by the Christian kings of the north, the last Abbad ruler requested the help of the Murabit regime in North Africa in 1086 and also in 1090. As the Murabits defeated the Christian kingdoms of Spain, they also abolished the Abbad Arab regime, adding Spain to their fast-growing empire in Africa. From that time till the end of the Christian reconquest in 1492, Spain's history was closely tied to that of North Africa.

CHAPTER 38

REGIONAL DYNASTIES IN NORTH AFRICA

THE IDRISIDS, 788-922

Backgrounds of the Idrisid Dynasty

Early in the Abbasid regime, when al-Hadi became caliph (785), he reversed his father's policies in regard to the toleration of non-Abbasid elements in the empire. He jailed and eliminated many Umayyad and Alid leaders for the slightest suspicion of disloyalty. In Hijaz, for instance, a group of Alids were publicly paraded in the streets of the holy cities by Abbasid officers, allegedly for excessive drinking. This humiliation aroused deep feelings of resentment among the whole Alid community in Makka and Madina, resulting in a revolt led by an Alid named Husayn and supported by his cousin Idris, brother of Muhammad the Pure Soul. Al-Hadi sent an Abbasid army to Hijaz to suppress the Alid revolt; during the skirmishes which ensued Husayn was killed, but his cousin Idris managed to escape.

Assisted by certain officials in charge of the mail service between Hijaz and North Africa, Idris traveled safely to al-Maghrib where he appealed to the Berbers for support. In 788 a Berber tribe recognized him as their *imam*, "religious leader," the first step toward also recognizing him as their political leader. However, during al-Rashid's reign, a special messenger, reportedly a physician, was sent from Baghdad to al-Maghrib to assassinate the Alid leader. The messenger succeeded in poisoning Idris, who died in 793 leaving behind no heir to lead the youthful movement. His followers waited until his pregnant concubine bore a son whom they called Idris II and immediately proclaimed the child as their imam.

As Idris II grew up, he established under his rule an independent Alid regime. To consolidate his rule over the northwest corner of Africa he built as his capital a city called Fas.

Following are the Idrisid princes who ruled in al-Maghrib between 788 and 922:

1.	Idris I	788-793
2.	Idris II	793-828
3.	Muhammad	828-836
4.	Ali I	836-849
5.	Yahya I	
6.	Yahya II	
7.	Ali II	849-904
8.	Yahya III	
9.	Yahya IV	904-922

Rise and Fall of the Idrisid Regime

Idris II died in 828, leaving behind a stable regime whose core consisted mainly of Muslim Berbers. The next three princes, Muhammad, Ali I, and Yahya I, were strong rulers who further strengthened the Idrisid regime. During the reign of Yahya I, Fas reached its pinnacle of prosperity becoming a trade center for routes between Africa and Europe.

Yahya I was followed by his nephew Yahya II, whose reign was less successful. The Berbers revolted against him forcing him to go into hiding. Following Yahya II's death, the regime lapsed into anarchy as different segments of the population supported various descendants of Idris. The chaotic situation which ensued was further complicated by the open opposition of the Kharijites to the Alid rule, leading to civil war within the Idrisid regime. Trade diminished, prosperity declined, and poverty spread everywhere. Furthermore, in 881 a great earthquake shook most of the state, tearing down buildings and burying several communities under its debris while terror and disease spread from village to village. These were indeed the lean years of the Idrisid dynasty during which political events were so confused that historians could not reconstruct the regnal years of the Idrisid rulers between Yahya I and Yahya IV.

In 904 Yahya IV was proclaimed prince and imam of the gradually recovering regime. During his reign relative stability and security were restored to the North African state as trade resumed and wealth flowed again to Fas. However, this prosperity was brief; soon the Fatimids, another Alid movement in central North Africa, gained strength under the leadership of Ubayd Allah al-Mahdi. In 919, only fifteen years after his accession to the imamate of the Idrisid regime,

Yahya IV faced war against his neighbors the Fatimids. Recognizing his weak position, Yahya IV preferred to negotiate peace terms with the Fatimids, who agreed to let him continue as ruler of Fas on the condition that he pay tribute and pledge allegiance to the Fatimid caliph. In 922, however, the Fatimids suddenly decided to dismiss Yahya IV and add al-Maghrib to their expanding regime, ending the Idrisid dynasty, which had ruled in North Africa for one hundred and forty years.

Al-Afiya's Household

The Fatimids chose a certain relative of the Idris family called al-Afiya to be governor of al-Maghrib. Yet as soon as Abd al-Rahman III of Spain landed forces on the shores of North Africa, al-Afiya seceded from the Fatimid regime and joined the Umayyad cause. Fighting followed immediately between the Umayyads and the Fatimids, resulting in Umayyad supremacy over the coastal area with al-Afiya as their governor, while the Fatimids retained the remainder of the Idrisid regime. This division of territory soon was changed; the Fatimids moved their residence to Egypt, abandoning western North Africa to the rule of al-Afiya's household, which continued to govern almost independently for over one hundred and fifty years till the Murabits came to power around 1050.

THE AGHLABIDS, 800-909

Rise of the Aghlabids

In 800, while Idris II of al-Maghrib was still a child supported by the Berbers, al-Rashid was advised to appoint a capable administrator named Ibrahim al-Aghlab as governor of North Africa and give him a free hand in dealing with any Berber rebellions that might break out. Al-Aghlab reportedly accepted al-Rashid's appointment only after the caliph promised him hereditary rights over North Africa. Thus fortified with a fief, Ibrahim al-Aghlab set out for Qayrawan, where he established the headquarters of a new Aghlabid dynasty destined to rule in the region of Tunis for over a century.

Following is a list of Aghlabid rulers:

1.	Ibrahim I	800-811
2.	Abd-Allah I	811-816
3.	Ziyadat Allah I	816-837
4.	Abu Iqal	837-840
5.	Muhammad I	840-856
6.	Ahmad	856-863
7.	Ziyadat Allah II	863-864

8.	Muhammad II	864-874
9.	Ibrahim II	874-902
10.	Abd-Allah II	902-903
11.	Ziyadat Allah III	903-909

High Points of the Aghlabid Regime

Although the primary goal of Ibrahim's appointment in North Africa was to suppress the Idrisid rebellion in al-Maghrib, neither Ibrahim I himself nor any of his descendants ever attempted to displace the Idrisids from their western stronghold. No sooner had Ibrahim I reached Qayrawan than the inhabitants of Tripoli rose in revolt against their governor. In 804 Ibrahim set out to suppress the Libyan revolt, but soon the restless Berbers staged several revolts in different regions of North Africa, forcing Ibrahim I to concentrate most of his efforts against them. At last, and only a short time before his death, Ibrahim I succeeded in bringing Tripoli and most of the Berber population under control. In 811, at the peak of his power and prestige, he died having ruled for only eleven years.

His son Abd-Allah I (811-816) was neither as firm nor just as his father. He used stern measures to collect taxes, giving little heed to the advice of his jurists and theologians. He was mysteriously murdered after ruling for only five years.

Ziyadat Allah I (816-837) followed his brother Abd-Allah I as ruler of North Africa. He was more inclined to take his counselors' advice than was his predecessor, and his rule was characterized by relative stability. In 825 a serious revolt broke out led by a certain Mansur, who managed to recruit some followers and threaten Qayrawan. However, the following year Ziyadat Allah defeated Mansur who died shortly after in jail. In 827 Ziyadat Allah launched a campaign against Sicily, where he defeated the Byzantine forces first in 828 in Syracuse and then in 830 in Palermo. Despite their victories in these cities, the Aghlabids could not maintain their supply line with Qayrawan and were gradually forced to abandon their hold over them.

After the death of Ziyadat Allah I in 837, five Aghlabid rulers followed each other in relatively rapid succession. Internal quarrels and local revolts were common until Ibrahim II assumed rule in 874. He was firm and generous, spending most of his time hearing his peoples' complaints and alleviating their ills. He generously showered gifts and extended liberal financial assistance to his subjects. Accordingly, the common people were always ready to rally around him and support him during times of emergency.

During Ibrahim II's rule, a son of Ibn Tulun of Egypt named al-Abbas attempted to displace his father and carve for himself an empire in North Africa. Al-Abbas reportedly sent a message to Ibrahim II in 880 informing Ibrahim that he had been appointed governor of North Africa and asking Ibrahim II to vacate his post immediately. Upon hearing this message, Ibrahim II raised an army to fight al-Abbas ibn

Tulun, who had already advanced toward Qayrawan. In the battle that followed al-Abbas was defeated and forced to retreat to Barqa. This Aghlabid victory greatly strengthened the prestige of Ibrahim II among his own people, and he continued to rule in Qayrawan till 902.

End of the Aghlabid Dynasty

Ibrahim II was followed by his son Abd-Allah II, who was treacherously assassinated by his own servants after ruling for only nine months. Abd-Allah II was followed by Ziyadat Allah III, the last Aghlabid ruler to reign in Qayrawan. During his rule, the Fatimids began their religious movement, which spread widely among the inhabitants of North Africa. By 904 Abu abd-Allah, the organizer of the Fatimid movement in Africa, had gathered a large number of supporters —enough to capture several cities within the Aghlabid domain. From this nucleus, he advanced against Qayrawan in 909, forcing Ziyadat Allah III to flee the city.

Soon after the capture of Qayrawan, the imam of the Fatimid movement, Ubayd Allah al-Mahdi, arrived in the capital and was proclaimed the first Shi'ite caliph, thereby sealing the final collapse of the Aghlabid dynasty.

THE MURABITS, 1062-1145

Backgrounds of the Murabit Regime

It may be recalled that ever since Uqba first conquered North Africa in 682, the Berbers had been a source of trouble to Arab rulers. Although the Berbers of North Africa accepted Islam, they were devoted to their earlier customs and were never quite happy with the conduct and behavior of the Arabs. Revolts followed in quick succession until 705 when Caliph Walid I was forced to pacify the whole area. Under the wise leadership of Musa ibn Nusayr, North Africa was restored to Arab rule within a relatively short time as Berbers were chosen to fight side by side with Arabs, especially during the conquest of Spain in 711. With the recall of Musa, their beloved commander, the Berbers reverted to rebellion, making it very hard for Arab governors to keep them under control.

It was not very difficult for Idris, who fled Hijaz in 785, to find supporters among the Berbers of the western corner of North Africa and to establish in al-Maghrib an independent regime which lasted over one hundred and fifty years. When al-Rashid in 800 appointed Ibrahim al-Aghlab as governor of North Africa with a free hand to deal with the Idrisids, the Berbers of Tripoli revolted against the caliph and his successors, preventing the Aghlabids from destroying the Idrisid regime.

The Berbers as early as 904 also supported the Fatimid reform movement preached to them by Abu Abd-Allah. However, the Berbers were greatly disillusioned by the Fatimid reformation, especially when the latter moved to Egypt in 969. At the turn of the eleventh century, the Berbers were not satisfied with the religious mores of the Arab Muslims and were willing to support any local reform movement.

Berber missionary groups were organized and sent to spread Islamic teachings among the Negroes of Africa. By 1048 a strong religious revival rose among the Muslim Berbers of the Atlas Mountains under the spiritual leadership of a theologian named Ibn Yasin, who established missionary outposts known in Arabic as *ribats,* from which the term "Murabits," the name under which the movement spread, was derived.[1] Ibn Yasin delegated the political responsibilities of his religious movement to a warrior named Yusuf ibn Tashfin, who organized a sizable number of the Murabits into a fighting corps. When Ibn Yasin died in 1059, Tashfin assumed both the religious and political responsibilities of the fast-growing movement on both sides of the Sahara Desert in western Africa.

In 1062 Tashfin founded the city of Marrakesh and made it the capital of his newly established regime. From there he gradually expanded into Fas, Tangier, and Algiers, leaving the Fatimid rule in North Africa limited to Tunis and Tripoli.

The Murabits in Spain

By 1085 Tashfin became the undisputed ruler over a large territory extending from the shores of the Mediterranean in the north to Senegal in the south. After the collapse of the Umayyads in 1031, Spain was divided among several petty Arab dynasties, each ruling a local region or district. Chief of these dynasties were the Hammuds in Cordova and the Abbads in Seville. In the meantime, King Alfonso VI united the kingdoms of Castile and Leon and applied considerable pressure against the Arab rulers of the south in conjunction with a certain warrior named Rodrigo Diaz de Bivar, known in Spanish literature as El Cid. Al-Mu'tamid, the last ruler of the Abbad dynasty in Seville, sent an urgent appeal to Tashfin of Africa for immediate help. Tashfin crossed into Spain in 1086 at the head of a Berber army, and, after occupying Algeciras, proceeded northward to Badajoz. There he sent a message to Alfonso VI demanding surrender. Alfonso refused to yield and a battle followed in which the Christian troops were defeated by the Murabit forces.

According to his agreement with al-Mu'tamid, Tashfin left behind about three thousand Berber troops and returned to Africa. However, bitter quarrels arose among several Arab rulers in Spain, allowing the Christian forces to resume their pressure against the scattered petty states. In 1090 Tashfin crossed once more to Spain and this time

[1] The Murabits are also known as Almoravides.

was able to obtain a *fatwa,* "legal opinion," from the jurists of several cities, denouncing the rule of existing regional dynasties and supporting a united Muslim rule under Murabit control. Thereupon he dismissed all local Arab rulers, including al-Mu'tamid of Seville himself, adding all of Islamic Spain to his regime in Africa.

Fall of the Murabit Regime

Yusuf ibn Tashfin died in 1106 leaving his son Ali to rule over a vast empire extending from Saragossa in Spain in the north to Senegal in Africa in the south.   Ali frequently consulted with several Murabit jurists who strongly advised him against tolerating any religious groups other than their own. In fact, the authority of Murabit jurists under Ali's rule increased so much that the great work of the noted Muslim philosopher al-Ghazali *Revival of the Sciences of Religion* was branded by them as heretical, and its pages were publicly burned in the streets of Cordova. In other words, under Murabit rule Islamic jurisprudence rested heavily on the personal opinion of local jurists rather than on the traditional path outlined by the various orthodox schools of law. This characteristic of Murabit rule undoubtedly angered many orthodox Muslims both in Spain and in Africa, causing dissension and discontent to spread throughout the region. As opposition mounted against the Murabits in Spain, the king of Aragon in 1118 marched against their northern frontiers, capturing Saragossa and advancing as far south as the outskirts of Granada. In the meantime a certain Berber theologian named Muhammad ibn Tumart, a student of the Ash'arite doctrines[2], began a religious reformation in the Atlas Mountains resulting in the rise of the Muwahhid movement. Tumart's movement attracted many Berber followers, who captured Marrakesh from the Murabits in 1140. Soon the Muwahhids drove the Murabits out of all their North African possessions, leaving only Spain under the rule of Ali, son of Tashfin.

Ali died in 1143 and was followed by his son Tashfin II. Stripped of his African possessions by the Muwahhids, Tashfin II was desperately fighting the Christian forces pressing on his northern frontiers when he suddenly decided to regain his lost African possessions. In 1145 he sailed at the head of a small fleet to the African coast where he was defeated and killed by Muwahhid forces. After his death the Murabit regime ended abruptly while the Muwahhid movement rapidly expanded over both North Africa and Spain.

[2] See p. 356.

THE MUWAHHIDS, 1145-1223

Beginning of the Muwahhid Movement

The unreasonable expansion of the authority of Murabit jurists in their state's administration caused many Muslim theologians to seek popular support against what they termed deviation from orthodoxy. Among those who managed to win substantial support among the Berbers was the noted theologian Muhammad ibn Tumart, mentioned above. In 1107 he went to Baghdad, where he was tutored by distinguished Ash'arite scholars, among whom was al-Ghazali. Upon his return to al-Maghrib, Tumart called for immediate reforms in Islamic beliefs and practices among his own people, laying more emphasis on the doctrine of the oneness of God, known as *tawhid*, from which the term ''Muwahhids'' was derived. [3]

Under the religious leadership of Tumart, the Muwahhid movement gained many supporters, chief of whom was a noted warrior called Abd al-Mu'min, who assumed the political leadership of the movement. Abd al-Mu'min organized the Muwahhid followers into a strong army, which captured main Murabit strongholds. In 1140 Abd al-Mu'min succeeded in capturing Marrakesh, the Murabit capital in al-Maghrib, thereby establishing the new Muwahhid regime on the remains of the fast-declining Murabit empire.

Consolidation of the Muwahhid Regime

Following is a list of the Muwahhid rulers:

1.	Abd al-Mu'min	1130-1163
2.	Muhammad	1163
3.	Yusuf I	1163-1184
4.	Ya'qub	1184-1199
5.	Al-Nasir	1199-1214
6.	Yusuf II	1214-1223

After the defeat of Tashfin II in al-Maghrib, the Murabit regime in Spain reverted to local regionalism as each leader of a province or district became its independent ruler. In North Africa, Abd al-Mu'min expanded his rule eastward from al-Maghrib until he reached Barqa. In the meantime, the Christian kingdoms in northern Spain took advantage of the weakening Arab rule and captured a few Muslim cities; Alfonso VII of Castile is reported to have reached the outskirts of Cordova itself. Abd al-Mu'min died in 1163 and was followed

---

[3]The Muwahhids are also known as Almohades.

by his son Muhammad, who was soon deposed because of incompetence by the high officials of the state. He was followed by his brother Yusuf I, who embarked on a campaign to recapture several lost cities in Spain. Yusuf I died in 1184 without accomplishing his goal. He was succeeded by his son Ya'qub during whose reign the Muwahhid regime reached its zenith of power and prosperity.

At first Ya'qub made a truce with Alfonso VIII of Castile, which the latter revoked by launching the largest Christian offensive ever attempted against the Muslims in Spain. Ya'qub rushed his troops to meet the Christian threat and the two armies met near Badajoz in 1195. In a hard-fought battle Alfonso VIII and his troops were defeated. Ya'qub's brilliant victory at the battle of Badajoz won for him great prestige in his own regime and throughout the rest of the Muslim world. His contemporary Salah al-Din (Saladin) of Egypt reportedly exchanged gifts and embassies with Ya'qub's Muwahhid court. A distinguished commander and administrator, Ya'qub was also a great promoter of literature and philosophy. It may be of some interest to note here that the great jurist and philosopher Ibn Rushd (Averroes) held the post of chief judge of Cordova during his reign.

Collapse of the Muwahhid Regime

Ya'qub was followed by his son al-Nasir, who took to a life of pleasure and luxury. During his rule, the Christian forces resumed their attacks west of Seville and Cordova, while Pope Innocent III encouraged the kings of northern Spain to unite in a Crusade against the Muwahhids. In 1212 a huge Christian army led by Alfonso VIII of Castile met the Muwahhid forces at the battle of Las Navas de Tolosa. The Muslim army was almost annihilated and al-Nasir escaped to Africa, where he died two years later. Local Muslim dynasties soon emerged and continued to rule till 1492, when Ferdinand and Isabella recaptured the last Muslim stronghold of Granada. In 1610, King Philip III deported about half a million Muslims from Spain into Africa, leaving the Muslim rule in the Iberian Peninsula only a memory.

In North Africa, al-Nasir was followed in 1214 by his teen-age son Yusuf II. During his reign authority was transferred to several Muwahhid elders and princes who quarreled among themselves, causing the decline and fragmentation of their regime. When Yusuf II died in 1223, the Muwahhid regime ended and authority reverted to regional dynasties under local rulers.

CHAPTER 39

REGIONAL DYNASTIES IN EGYPT

THE TULUNIDS, 868-905

Ibn Tulun 868-883

The founder of the Tulunid dynasty in Egypt was Ahmad ibn Tulun, a Turk whose father had been recruited from Trans-oxiana during the reign of al-Mu'tasim (833-842). From that time on, the Abbasid caliphs depended heavily upon recruited Turkish mercenaries, some of whom were selected as body-guards and others promoted to be governors of certain provinces. Except for rare exceptions, Egypt was governed by Turkish rulers from 833 till the Fatimids assumed rule in 969. The early Turkish governors used to appoint deputy governors to represent them in their respective provinces, while they themselves resided in Baghdad to be on guard against any developing plots or intrigues.

In 854 a Turk named Bayakbek was appointed governor of Egypt. He chose as his deputy governor Ahmad ibn Tulun and limited his authority to the capital and its outskirts. In 868 when Bayakbek died and Ibn Tulun's father-in-law, Yarjukh, became governor, the latter established Ibn Tulun as deputy governor over all Egypt. In 873, however, Yarjukh died and Ibn Tulun was officially appointed by Caliph al-Mu'tamid (870-892) as governor of Egypt.

In the first few years of Ibn Tulun's administration relations between him and al-Mu'tamid were so amiable that the caliph granted him in addition to Egypt the governorship of the frontier region in Asia Minor. When the Negro revolt broke out in southern Iraq,[1] Ibn Tulun reportedly donated about a million dinars to the caliph's brother al-Muwaffaq, who was in charge of suppressing that revolt. However, al-Muwaffaq showed no gratitude for Ibn Tulun's aid and began to foment misunderstandings between the caliph and his governor. In the meantime, Ibn Tulun thought of adding Syria to his own regime. In 878 he led an Egyptian army against Palestine and Syria, and, before the year was over he was undisputed master of the whole area between the Euphrates and the Nile.

Consolidation of the Tulunid Regime

Following is a list of the rulers of the Tulunid dynasty in Egypt:

1. Ibn Tulun   868-883
2. Khumarawayh   883-895
3. Abu al-Asakir   895-896
4. Harun   896-905

No sooner had Ibn Tulun established his autonomous regime in Egypt than he faced two major problems, either of which could have destroyed his administration. The first was the rebellion of his own son al-Abbas, and the second was the adverse propaganda directed against him by al-Muwaffaq, the caliph's brother.

Taking advantage of his father's absence in Syria in 878, al-Abbas rallied some soldiers from Egypt, declaring his own independent rule. Desirous of carving for himself an empire south of the Mediterranean, al-Abbas marched against Ibrahim II (874-902) of the Aghlabid regime in North Africa. After being defeated near Barqa by the Aghlabids, al-Abbas returned to Egypt only to find his father, back from Syria, defeating the remnant of his forces. When al-Abbas's rebellion was completely suppressed, Ibn Tulun returned to Syria in 882 to consolidate his rule there.

The propaganda from Baghdad against Ibn Tulun encouraged many district governors in Syria to rebel against him and side with al-Muwaffaq. This forced Ibn Tulun to embark on a vigorous campaign to recapture the seceding districts. While fighting in 883 in Anatolia at Tarsus, he died and was followed by his son Khumarawayh.

As Khumarawayh assumed rule over the Tulunid regime, his father's armies outside the Nile Valley were suffering rapid defeats. He therefore recruited new troops from Egypt and in 886 marched against Syria, and fought the caliph's forces on the borders of Syria and Iraq. Since neither side could claim a clear victory, the two sides negotiated a peace agreement by which the caliph granted Khumarawayh hereditary rights to rule over the region between the Euphrates in Iraq and the Nile in Egypt in return for a certain amount of tribute money which the Tulunid ruler agreed to pay. To confirm this peace, Khumarawayh consented to give his beautiful daughter Qatr al-Nada in marriage to Caliph al-Mu'tamid.

[1]See p. 272.

For this occasion, Khumarawayh is reported to have built several magnificent palaces along the mail route from Fustat to Baghdad to allow his daughter to lodge every night in comfort and luxury. The celebrations held in Baghdad for the wedding and the gifts with which the bride was showered are described by Arab historians as phenomenal and unprecedented.

During the last years of Khumarawayh's reign relative peace and prosperity prevailed in Egypt and the rest of the Tulunid regime. It is reported that Khumarawayh's budget for entertaining guests at his palace reached over a quarter of a million dinars a year — strong testimony not only to the ruler's great bounty and hospitality but also to the regime's high level of prosperity.

Decline and Fall of the Tulunid Regime

Khumarawayh died in Damascus in 895 and was followed by his son Abu al-Asakir, whose indiscreet behavior turned many local leaders against him and caused several army officers to defect to Baghdad. A number of district governors in Syria rebelled against the central government in Egypt. To reverse the growing chaos, several leaders and army officers agreed to dismiss Abu al-Asakir and proclaim his younger brother Harun as ruler in his place.

The appointment of Harun in 896 failed to solve all the problems facing the Tulunid regime; the army officers who had defected to Baghdad succeeded in planting seeds of hatred and animosity between the Abbasid caliph and the Tulunid regime. In the meantime, the Qarmatians, an extreme Alid sect known for their violent acts of sabotage, began open hostilities in Syria, causing havoc and confusion to spread throughout the region. In 904 Caliph al-Muktafi (902-910) sent his commander Sulayman at the head of an Abbasid force to restore both Syria and Egypt to his direct control. Harun and his supporters rushed northward to check the march of the advancing Abbasid army, and the two sides met in battle near Tarsus. Harun's army was badly defeated and he was killed as Sulayman continued his march toward Fustat.

Harun's uncle Shayban succeeded his nephew in 905 while the Tulunid regime was rapidly collapsing. In spite of Shayban's desperate efforts to save his administration, Sulayman's troops captured Fustat and forced the last Tulunid ruler to surrender unconditionally, bringing an abrupt end to the Tulunid regime.

THE IKHSHIDIDS, 935-969

Muhammad al-Ikhshid, 935-946

The Ikhshidids originally belonged to a Turkish family which moved to Baghdad from Ferghana during the reign of al-Mu'tasim (833-842). They steadily gained prominence and prestige under al-Mu'tasim and his immediate successors until one of them, Muhammad al-Ikhshid, was appointed deputy governor of Egypt in 910 shortly after the collapse of the Tulunid regime. His military ability was clearly demonstrated when in 919 he defeated a Fatimid army sent by Ubayd Allah from North Africa. This victory encouraged the caliph to make Muhammad al-Ikhshid deputy governor not only of Egypt, but also of Palestine.

In 934 the Fatimids attempted once more to capture Egypt, but again Muhammad al-Ikhshid scored a brilliant victory against them, and greatly enhanced his own prominence and prestige. In 935 the caliph elevated him officially to the rank of full governor of Egypt and Palestine, bestowing upon him the title "Ikhshid," which was originally adopted by the kings of his home in Ferghana as a sign of special honor and prestige.

However, in 940 as a result of sharp differences between himself and the chief prince, *amir al-umara,* of the court of Baghdad, al-Ikhshid announced his complete autonomy and withdrew his allegiance to the Abbasid caliphate. Shortly after this, the troublesome chief prince died and al-Ikhshid was persuaded to announce once more his allegiance to Baghdad after the caliph granted him sovereignty over Makka and Madina in Hijaz. When al-Ikhshid died in 946, he had already established a new dynasty which ruled Egypt, Syria, and Hijaz. Before his death, since both of his sons were young, al-Ikhshid designated a member of his family called Kafur to act as guardian of his children and to rule in their names until they were of age. However, Kafur soon usurped authority from the two young sons, who reportedly died under mysterious circumstances, allowing their guardian to assume sole rulership over the firmly established Ikhshidid regime.

Kafur, 946-967

Besides removing the young heirs of his predecessor, Kafur eliminated many of his enemies who opposed his rule and considered it illegitimate. His military activities included an attack against the Hamdanids of Aleppo in Syria, who captured Damascus and were on their way to capture Palestine. However, Kafur inflicted upon them a humiliating defeat, forcing them to accept his peace terms by which Damascus was restored to Ikhshidid rule.

Kafur's reign was marked by several tragic events, caused in part by extremist Qarmatians, and also by certain natural catastrophies including earthquake, fire, and famine. In 965, toward the end of his reign, as opposition mounted against him, Kafur obtained from the Abbasid caliph a decree officially confirming him as ruler of the Ikhshidid regime. This enabled him to stamp out all pockets of resistance against his rule in Egypt and then turn his attention to the Fatimid forces advancing against his western frontiers. However, he died in 967 without having had the opportunity to defeat the Fatimids.

End of the Ikhshidid Regime

Since Kafur had eliminated almost all potential leaders because of their stand against his illegitimate rule, there was no strong personality to assume control after his death. Accordingly, the court officials appointed a grandson of Muhammad al-Ikhshid named Abu al-Fawaris, a youngster less than eleven years of age. This appointment caused many quarrels among local leaders and army commanders. A shrewd Fatimid caliph in North Africa named al-Mu'izz took advantage of the deteriorating situation among the Ikhshidids and dispatched his commander Jawhar to invade Egypt. In 969 Jawhar easily captured Egypt, adding it to the Fatimid rule as the Ikhshidid regime came to an end.

THE FATIMIDS, 969-1171

Rise of the Fatimid Movement

After the death of Ali ibn Abu Talib, the fourth orthodox caliph, who was murdered by the Kharijites in 661, his Shi'ite followers tried unsuccessfully several times to install a caliph of their own. Their desperate efforts to achieve their goals by means of open revolt always ended in frustration and usually the murder of their aspiring imam (religious leader). When their revolt in Hijaz during al-Hadi's reign ended in 785 with the murder of its leader Husayn, whose cousin Idris escaped to North Africa, the Shi'ites and all their Alid supporters resumed their normal underground activities. They spread throughout the Arab Empire calling secretly for the right of Alid descendants to lead the Islamic community both spiritually and temporally. Being a scattered group without any particular unified command, the Shi'ites split among themselves into several sects, each calling for the rights of its own imam to assume the caliphate.

One of the Shi'ite sects that appears to have been better organized was that of the Isma'ilites, followers of the line of Isma'il, brother of Musa al-Kadhim, the seventh imam.[2] They started their organization in Syria and promoted the Alid cause in various parts of the Arab Empire by supporting regional leaders whose duty it was to call in secret for the right of their imam to rule over the Arab Empire.

The Isma'ilite sect soon split into several branches, chief of which was the Fatimid group. About 900 the Fatimids nominated as their imam a certain Alid called Ubayd Allah (al-Mahdi) and asked their representatives throughout the Islamic domain to call for him as imam and candidate for the caliphate. One Fatimid representative named Abu Abd-Allah of North Africa succeeded in winning to the new Shi'ite cause many Berbers. He organized his followers into an army and fought several battles with the Aghlabids until he finally captured Qayrawan in 909 from the last Aghlabid amir, Ziyadat Allah III.

For the first time, the Fatimids had a movement, a state, and an

[2]More about the Isma'ilites is discussed on pp. 341, 342.

organized army. Abu Abd-Allah sent a message to his imam, Ubayd Allah, to come to Qayrawan and proclaim himself caliph of the Shi'ites. Ubayd Allah set out to travel from Syria to North Africa but was detained several times on the way. Finally he managed to reach Qayrawan, where Abu Abd-Allah received him with great honor, proclaiming him caliph of the new Fatimid regime.

The Fatimids in North Africa[3]

Ubayd Allah was officially proclaimed caliph in the mosque of Qayrawan with the title "al-Mahdi Commander of the Faithful." He expanded his authority over territories in both al-Maghrib in the west and Libya in the east. His forces attacked Egypt at least three times, but were driven out both by Abbasid and Ikhshidid forces. The third attack was met by Muhammad al-Ikhshid of Egypt in 934, who rebuffed the Fatimids in a brilliant victory after which he was officially elevated to the rank of full governor of Egypt and Palestine. Back in 915 Ubayd Allah founded the city of Mahdiyya on the southern outskirts of Qayrawan and adopted it as his official residence. He died in 934 after ruling for twenty-five years during which he laid a strong foundation for the first Shi'ite regime.

Ubayd Allah's two successors were occupied mainly in consolidating the new regime against internal disturbances. There was little foreign activity since Egypt was greatly strengthened by the vigorous rule of al-Ikhshid, while al-Maghrib was further fortified by Umayyad forces sent to check Fatimid expansion toward the west.

The fourth caliph, al-Mu'izz, was both vigorous and ambitious; upon his assumption of the Fatimid rule in 952, he completed the conquest of al-Maghrib and made extensive preparations to conquer Egypt. He entrusted the command of his army to a Muslim warrior from Sicily named Jawhar, who began moving eastward against Egypt in 969. He captured Barqa and Alexandria, which surrendered almost without a struggle. He then marched toward Fustat, capital of the fast-declining Ikhshidid regime. In Fustat the Abbasid forces offered to surrender to Jawhar's forces on one condition, namely, that the Egyptians be left free to choose between accepting the Shi'ite doctrines or maintaining their orthodox beliefs. Jawhar accepted this condition and victoriously entered Fustat, proclaiming Egypt part of the Fatimid regime. He then marched north to Palestine and Syria, succeeding in winning the allegiance of several local leaders in both regions.

Jawhar then founded the city of Cairo, known in Arabic as al-Qahira, which he adopted as capital of the Fatimid regime, and where he erected a spacious mosque called al-Azhar to serve as a university for Islamic studies—which it does to this day. Jawhar sent a detachment to occupy

[3]See the list of the Fatimid caliphs in Appendix 10, p. 383.

Hijaz, thus adding the two holy cities to the Fatimid regime. In 973, when the east appeared under control, Jawhar invited Caliph al-Mu'izz to move his residence to Cairo, where he had built for the caliph a palace decorated with the best of Islamic art. On June 11, 973, al-Mu'izz transferred his capital from Qayrawan to Cairo, from where the Fatimid dynasty ruled over a Shi'ite empire for another hundred years.

Al-Mu'izz ruled only two years in his new capital of Cairo. He attempted to strengthen the fast-growing Shi'ite regime extending from Syria in the north to Yaman in the south, and from al-Maghrib in the west to Hijaz in the east. Upon the completion of conquests necessary for the consolidation of his regime, al-Mu'izz relieved his famous commander Jawhar from both the military and political roles that he had assumed in Egypt prior to the caliph's arrival in Cairo. However, Jawhar was restored to his military office soon after the death of al-Mu'izz when some of the Qarmatians posed a real threat to the security of the Fatimid regime.

In 975 al-Mu'izz died and was succeeded by his son al-Aziz (975-996) during whose rule the Qarmatians were finally defeated and their menace ended. Otherwise, the reign of al-Aziz was among the most stable and prosperous periods of the Fatimid regime. Al-Aziz is known to have encouraged Islamic missionary endeavors, allowing trained theologians to travel far and wide to spread Shi'ite doctrines. He also encouraged poets, historians, and physicians to pursue their studies and record their findings, attracting a number of eminent scholars in these fields to add luster to the Fatimid regime in Egypt.

Al-Aziz died in 996 and was followed by his son al-Hakim (996-1020), one of the most controversial caliphs of the Fatimid regime. His violence against all non-Shi'ites, both Muslim and non-Muslim, was accompanied at times by unprecedented fanaticism for the advancement of his own Shi'ite views. These tendencies led him finally to claim divine prerogatives in an attempt to force several rules and regulations upon his bewildered subjects. Al-Hakim meddled not only in their religious beliefs but also in their private affairs and other matters such as diet and clothes. For instance, he is reported to have prohibited the planting of grapes in order to prevent the manufacture of wine, and to have penalized shoemakers for making ladies' shoes in order to prevent women from going out in the streets. Furthermore, he reportedly required the Jews to wear a bell and the Christians a five pound cross as distinguishing marks of their religions.

Al-Hakim is credited with establishing an academy for arts and sciences, which he called *dar al-hikma*, "the house of wisdom," and which gathered outstanding scholars in the fields of theology, astrology, grammar, and history, attaching to it a spacious library called *dar al-ilm*, "house of knowledge," which contained hundreds of books written in Egypt and other centers of learning throughout the Islamic world. Al-Hakim died in 1020, possibly by assassination at the hands of certain members of his own court. Many of his subjects undoubtedly were relieved, yet with his death ended the greatness and vigor of the Fatimid regime. His successors began to indulge in the comforts and luxuries of their courts, and gave little or no attention to state affairs.[4]

End of the Fatimid Regime

By 1071 the Seljuq Turks had wrested all Syria and Palestine from the Fatimid regime, while the Murabits simultaneously were expanding their regime in North Africa at the expense of the Fatimids till they almost reached Barqa. Moreover, in 1099 the Crusaders of Europe established a Christian kingdom in Jerusalem, posing a serious threat to the very existence of the Fatimid regime. Nevertheless, the Seljuqs of Syria kept the Crusaders occupied for several years until the reign of the last Fatimid Caliph al-Adid (1160-1171) when, in the face of a Crusade threat, the caliph appointed a warrior of the Seljuq regime by the name of Shirkuh to be his chief minister.

In 1169 Shirkuh inflicted on the Crusaders a decisive defeat which greatly boosted his position in Egypt. However, he died shortly afterward and was succeeded by his nephew Salah al-Din (Saladin). As an orthodox Muslim, Salah al-Din ruled Egypt in the name of the Seljuq Atabeg of Syria, completely bypassing the Fatimid Caliph al-Adid. Accordingly, when the latter died in 1171, Salah al-Din refused to allow another Shi'ite caliph to be installed, bringing an end to the Fatimid regime, which had ruled over a sizable portion of the Islamic world for more than two centuries.

THE AYYUBIDS, 1171-1260

Origin of the Ayyubid Dynasty

The Ayyubids belonged to a presumably Kurdish family in northern Iraq, whose fame was established when two brothers, one named Ayyub and the other Shirkuh, entered the service of the Atabegs in Syria and Iraq respectively. During the siege of Damascus by the Crusaders in 1146, Ayyub was promoted to the rank of governor of Damascus by Nur al-Din, who replaced his father Zanki as Atabeg of Syria.

In 1160 Nur al-Din dispatched Shirkuh at the head of a Syrian army to Egypt, which was ruled by the last Fatimid caliph al-Adid (1160-1171). Because of a feud between the Fatimid caliph and his chief minister Shamar, the caliph requested Shirkuh to take command of the Egyptian army and to suppress Shamar's rebellion. Shamar then re-

---

[4]After the death of al-Hakim in 1020, some of his followers claimed that he was still living and began a movement to promote the doctrine of deifying him. However, they were driven out of Egypt; those who succeeded in reaching Lebanon were called Druzes after Darazi, one of their noted missionaries.

quested and received help from the Crusaders, forcing Shirkuh to war against the Christian forces which launched an attack against Egypt. Shirkuh decisively defeated the invading European armies, forcing them to evacuate Egypt in 1169. Thereupon, Caliph al-Adid appointed Shirkuh as his own chief minister, requesting him to restore order to his embattled realm. As mentioned above, Shirkuh died two months later and was replaced by his nephew Salah al-Din, son of Ayyub, who served as chief minister of Caliph al-Adid till the latter died in 1171. As a vassal of Atabeg Nur al-Din of Syria, Salah al-Din refused to allow another Fatamid caliph to succeed al-Adid, assuming for himself full authority over the extinct Fatimid regime and ushering in his own Ayyubid dynasty, destined to rule in Egypt and Syria until 1260.

Salah al-Din, 1171-1193

When Salah al-Din assumed rule in Egypt in 1171, he was acting as viceroy for his superior Nur al-Din, Atabeg of Syria, who was a follower of orthodox Islam under the spiritual leadership of the Abbasid caliphate. As soon as the last Fatimid caliph died, Salah al-Din embarked on a campaign to restore Egypt to orthodoxy after it had been under Shi'ite rule for almost two centuries. For the first time since 969, the Egyptians, by order of Salah al-Din, began to mention the Abbasid caliph during their Friday prayers. Shi'ism gradually declined until, shortly afterward, most of the inhabitants of Egypt returned to the doctrines of orthodox Islam.

Salah al-Din then began to create a strong Egyptian army to resist the increasing threat to his rule posed by the alien Crusader kingdom in neighboring Palestine. However, his growing military power soon aroused suspicion in the mind of Atabeg Nur al-Din, in whose behalf Salah al-Din was ruling. In 1172 Nur al-Din reportedly gathered his forces in order to trim his vassal's authority in Egypt, but he died before he could accomplish his goal. Salah al-Din was now encouraged to continue his plans to establish a strong Egyptian army to stand not only against the Christians in Palestine, but also against possible attack from the Atabegs of Syria.

At any rate, the death of Nur al-Din in 1172 greatly weakened the Atabeg regime since his son and successor Isma'il was only eleven years old. Recognizing that the Christian kingdom in Palestine could not be defeated without cooperation between Egypt and Syria, Salah al-Din decided to seize Syria from the Atabegs and add it to his regime in Egypt. In 1173 after several battles against the forces of Isma'il's guardians, Salah al-Din wrested almost all of Syria from the Atabegs, leaving only Aleppo to the young Atabeg and his family. In 1181 Isma'il died and was followed as sultan of Aleppo by Zanki II. In the meantime, Salah al-Din won the support of several Muslim leaders in both Syria and northern Iraq (the two main strongholds of the Atabegs) who requested him to end the Atabeg regime, which had completely failed to defeat the Crusaders in Palestine. Accordingly, in 1182 Salah al-Din captured both Aleppo and Mosul, establishing his rule over a united territory composed of Egypt, Syria, northern Iraq, and some parts of Hijaz and Yaman.

Salah al-Din and the Crusaders

Having stabilized his expanding regime, which he administered with wisdom and tact, Salah al-Din decided to crush the Christian kingdom of Jerusalem. Early in 1187 his forces met the Christian troops near Tiberias in a fateful battle during which the Crusaders were badly defeated. In the same year, Salah al-Din pursued his victory by marching against Jerusalem itself, which he finally restored to Muslim rule.

After the fall of Jerusalem in 1187, Salah al-Din continued his campaign to recapture the remaining Christian cities of Palestine while the kings of Europe were preparing another Crusade. A huge Christian army under the leadership of Richard the Lionhearted of England captured Acre in 1192 after a siege of several months. Since casualties were very heavy on both sides, Salah al-Din entered into serious negotiations with Richard in order to end the bitter conflict between Muslims and Christians. Salah al-Din agreed to permit unarmed Christian pilgrims to visit Jerusalem freely if Christian troops withdrew completely from Palestine. Anxious to return to England as soon as possible, Richard accepted Salah al-Din's promise and signed a peace agreement with him in September, 1192, restoring most of Palestine once more to Islamic rule.

Salah al-Din's great dignity before Richard the Lionhearted and other commanders of the Christian armies won him fame in several European countries, where he became known by the name Saladin as one of the great rulers in Islam. However, Salah al-Din himself did not live long enough to enjoy the fruits of his own victories; he died in Damascus in 1193, only five months after signing the peace agreement with Richard.

Besides his military accomplishments against the Atabegs and the Crusaders, Salah al-Din was known also for his administrative reforms and love of learning. He established in Cairo an academy for Islamic theology and jurisprudence in honor of the noted Islamic scholar al-Shafi'i, founder of one of the four schools of Islamic law. In Jerusalem he restored the great mosque known as al-Jami' al-Aqsa, which had been desecrated by the Crusaders during their occupation of Palestine. Furthermore, he is credited with building the great citadel of Cairo on the hills of al-Muqattam.

Conflicts within the Ayyubid Dynasty

Following is a list of the Ayyubid rulers in Egypt who (with the exception of Salah al-Din) reigned under the title of *al-malik,* meaning "king," from 1171-1260:

1.	Salah al-Din	1171-1193
2.	Al-Aziz	1193-1196
3.	Al-Adil	1196-1218
4.	Al-Kamil	1218-1238
5.	Al-Adil II	1238
6.	Al-Salih	1238-1249
7.	Turanshah	1249-1250
8.	Shajarag al-Durr	1250-1257
9.	Qutuz (Turkish Mamluk)	1257-1260

After the death of Salah al-Din in 1193, the Ayyubid regime was split among his three sons: al-Afdal in southern Syria, al-Aziz in Egypt, and al-Dhahir in northern Syria. However, Salah al-Din's sons soon quarreled among themselves regarding matters of territorial claims, allowing their uncle, al-Malik al-Adil to succeed in uniting the Ayyubid regime under his sole rule in 1196.

Nevertheless, this unity did not last beyond his lifetime since after al-Adil's death in 1218, the Ayyubid regime was once more divided — this time among his own sons. With the Ayyubid's regime in a state of confusion, a new Crusade under the auspices of King Andrew of Hungary was launched to attack and capture Damietta (in Egypt) a few months after the death of al-Adil. As soon as al-Kamil, a son of al-Adil, consolidated his rule in Egypt, he recovered Damietta in 1221 after defeating the European contingent that had occupied it two years before.

The Crusaders' failure to retain Damietta caused Pope Innocent III to call for another Crusade to recapture Jerusalem. This call was renewed by Pope Gregory IX in 1227 when Frederick II of Germany agreed to lead a campaign to liberate Jerusalem from Islamic rule. While Frederick II was launching his campaign against Palestine from Italy, al-Kamil of Egypt was deeply involved in bitter quarrels and disputes with his brothers in Syria over the unification of their regime. Therefore, when Frederick II arrived in Palestine in 1228, al-Kamil's troops, already engaged in recapturing Syria, were not available to fight the new invaders. Al-Kamil and Frederick II entered into immediate negotiations in order to find a quick solution to the situation. Frederick II insisted on possession of Jerusalem and a few other cities in Palestine, giving al-Kamil the choice between war and concession. Obtaining a solemn promise from the Crusaders not to attack Syria, al-Kamil finally conceded Jerusalem to Frederick II together with the Mediterranean coast from Jaffa in the south to Sidon in the north.

Al-Kamil died in 1238 and was succeeded by his son al-Adil II. However, two months later another son, al-Salih, ousted al-Adil II. Al-Salih's main objectives were to unite the Ayyubid regime and drive out the latest Crusaders from Jerusalem. To accomplish his purpose he inducted into his army a number of Turkish warriors who had fled in large numbers to Egypt and Syria before the ravaging campaigns of the Mongols under Jenghiz Khan. With this substantial help he was able to restore Jerusalem to Islamic rule in 1244 and add Damascus to his regime in 1245.

While al-Salih was struggling in Syria to unify the Ayyubid regime, King Louis IX of France surprised him by capturing Damietta in 1248. Al-Salih was forced to return to Egypt in 1249, but he died en route and was replaced by his son Turanshah. Faced with a new Crusade in Damietta, Turanshah used Turkish mercenaries known as Mamluks to serve in the Egyptian army. With their help he defeated the invading European forces in 1250, liberating Damietta and taking King Louis IX as captive. After this victory, Turanshah himself fell an easy victim to the cruel intrigues of the Mamluks, whose commander Aybek, desiring to attain supreme rule in Egypt, plotted his assassination

End of the Ayyubid Dynasty

After the murder of Turanshah at the hands of the Mamluks, his mother, Shajarat al-Durr, convinced the Mamluk commander Aybek to retain her as ruler of Egypt while he assumed the post of army commander. Shortly afterward, she reportedly married him, but the marriage was not very successful. In 1257 she plotted her husband's murder in an attempt to win popular support. Her schemes apparently backfired, for she herself was murdered soon after, leaving the Ayyubid regime in the hands of several ambitious Turkish Mamluks.

After Aybek's death, authority shifted to a Mamluk commander named Qutuz acting as guardian for Aybek's son. Faced with the Mongol threat, Qutuz assigned the task of checking their advance into Syria to a capable warrior named Baybars. At the battle of Ayn Jalut in 1260, Baybars defeated the Mongols so badly that they withdrew to Central Asia never to return. This victory boosted Baybars' prestige in Syria enough to motivate him to decide to end the Ayyubid regime and rule in his own name. He marched against Egypt, defeated and murdered its sultan, Qutuz, and took the throne. His rule marks the end of the Ayyubid dynasty and the official beginning of the Mamluk rule.

Baybars brought into Egypt a scion of the Abbasid caliphate who had survived the destruction of the Mongols, and proclaimed him caliph in Cairo but denied him any political authority. In this way the Abbasid caliphate, which had collapsed in Baghdad in 1258, was resumed in Egypt and maintained under Mamluk control till the Ottoman sultan, Selim, claimed it for himself in 1517.

IMPORTANT TERMS

Abbadids: A dynasty that ruled in Spain after the fall of the Umayyad regime. In 1090 the last Abbadid ruler requested Murabit help from North Africa, resulting in the Murabit takeover of Spain.

Abd al-Rahman   I: Founder of the Umayyad dynasty in Spain in 756. He escaped the Abbasid massacre of his clan in Damascus in 750, reaching Spain five years later. Supported by the Yamanite faction of the Umayyads, he defeated the Qaysite opposition and established his own regime.

Aghlabids: A semi-independent dynasty ruling in Qayrawan in central North Africa, (800-909). Its founder was Ibrahim al-Aghlab, a capable organizer sent by Caliph al-Rashid to check the Idrisids in al-Maghrib.

Al-Azhar: A magnificent mosque built by the Fatimids in Cairo soon after their capture of Egypt in 969. Al-Azhar was then used as a theological school to train Shi'ite students for missionary work. Later on it became a Muslim university that still functions today.

Atabegs: Counselors to the Seljuq sultans. They ruled in Iraq between 1055 and 1180. One of them called Zanki became independent in Mosul, where he established the Atabeg dynasty that ruled in northern Iraq and Syria between 1127 and 1182.

Ayn Jalut, battle of: A famous battle fought in 1260 between a newly organized Syrian army under the leadership of the Mamluk Baybars and the invading Mongols from Asia. Baybars's brilliant victory drove the Mongols out of the region of the Middle East, allowing him to establish a new Mamluk regime in Egypt.

Ayyubids: An independent dynasty in Egypt established by Salah al-Din (Saladin) in 1171. The Ayyubids are credited with terminating the rule of the Crusaders in Jerusalem. However, the Ayyubids were overthrown by Baybars in 1260 after the latter's victory over the Mongols in the battle of Ayn Jalut in 1260.

Baybars: See Ayn Jalut and Ayyubids.

Buwayhids: A dynasty which started an autonomous rule in southern Persia around 940. When the Abbasid Caliph al-Muttaqi (940-944) invited them to protect him against the Turkish mercenaries, they took full control of the caliphate in Baghdad and continued to rule in Iraq and Persia till 1055.

Fatimids: A Shi'ite movement which succeeded in establishing political rule in central North Africa around 909 when their forces captured Qayrawan. They established an independent Shi'ite caliphate ruling in North Africa till 973, and then in Egypt till 1182, when they were overthrown by the Ayyubids.

Ghaznavids: A dynasty of Turkish warriors who settled first in Ghazna. In 999 they defeated the Samanids and established their own dynasty, which reached from Hamadan in Persia to Lahore in India.

Hamdanids: An Arab dynasty that ruled in Mosul and Aleppo.

Hulagu: A descendant of Jenghiz Khan. In 1258 he led the Mongol warriors against Baghdad.

Idrisids: An Arab Alid dynasty established in 788 in al-Maghrib by Idris, brother of Muhammad the Pure Soul. It continued to rule there till 922 when the Fatimids assumed complete control over North Africa.

Ikhshidids: A Turkish dynasty that ruled in Egypt between 935 and 969.

Jawhar: A Muslim warrior from Sicily who led the Fatimid forces that captured Egypt in 969. He is credited with founding Cairo and building the al-Azhar mosque.

Jenghiz Khan: A Mongol commander who captured Bukhara and Samarqand from the Khwarizm shahs in 1220.

Khwarizm Shahs: A local Persian dynasty that ruled in Khwarizm and exercised authority over the Abbasid caliphate between 1180 and 1258.

Mamluks: Turkish warriors first introduced into the Arab Empire as slave mercenaries by al-Mu'tasim (833-842). They were actually bought from several regions in the mountains of Transoxiana and freed after demonstrating military ability. Many of them occupied high-ranking offices under the Abbasid regime, including those of governors of provinces.

Mercenaries: See Mamluks.

Murabits: A Berber dynasty that ruled in North Africa and Spain between 1062 and 1145.

Muwahhids: A Berber dynasty that ruled in North Africa and Spain between 1145 and 1223.

Saffarids: A Persian dynasty that ruled in Persia and Transoxiana between 872 and 910.

Saladin: See Salah al-Din.

Salah al-Din: Founder of the Ayyubid dynasty. In 1187 he recaptured Jerusalem from the Crusaders and in 1192 he negotiated a treaty with Richard the Lionhearted by which most of Palestine was restored to Islamic rule.

Samanids: A Persian dynasty which ruled in Khurasan and Transoxiana between 910 and 999.

Seljuqs: Turkish warriors who first established themselves in Bukhara. In 1040 their leader Tughril Beg expanded his rule to include Marv and Nishapur; in 1055 he defeated the Buwayhids in Iraq. From 1055 until 1180 the Seljuqs controlled the Abbasid caliphate in Baghdad.

Tahirids: A Persian dynasty that ruled in Khurasan between 820 and 872. They were on good terms with the Abbasid caliphate in Baghdad.

Tashfin: Military commander of the Murabit movement. He established the Murabit dynasty and founded the city of Marrakesh in 1062.

Tughril Beg: See Seljuqs.

Tulunids: A Turkish dynasty founded by Ahmad ibn Tulun. It ruled in Egypt and some regions of Syria between 868 and 905.

Tumart: Religious leader of the Muwahhid movement that in 1145 succeeded the Murabits.

Ubayd Allah: First caliph of the Fatimids. His army commander Abu Abd-Allah captured Qayrawan and invited him to move there in 909 where he laid the foundations of the Shi'ite Fatimid dynasty.

Zanki: See Atabegs.

SUPPLEMENTARY READINGS

ARBERRY, A.J., ed., *The Legacy of Persia* (Cambridge, 1953).
ATIYA, AZIZ S., *Crusade, Commerce and Culture* (London, 1962).
BOSWORTH, C.E., *The Ghaznavids: their Empire in Afghanistan and Eastern Iran* (Edinburgh, 1963).
DANIEL, N., *Islam and the West* (Edinburgh, 1960).
HITTI, PHILIP K., *Usamah ibn Munqidh, Memoires* (New York, 1929).
HODGSON, M.G.S., *The Order of Assassins* (The Hague, 1955).
LANE-POOLE, STANLEY, *The Moors in Spain* (London, 1887).
——, *The Muhammadan Dynasties* (Paris, 1925).
——, *Saladin and the Fall of the Kingdom of Jerusalem* (New York, 1898).
LE STRANGE, GUY, *Baghdad during the Abbasid Caliphate* (Oxford, 1924).
LEVY, REUBEN, *A Baghdad Chronicle* (Cambridge, 1929).
LEWIS, BERNARD, *The Origins of Isma'ilism* (Cambridge, 1940).
MEZ, A., *The Renaissance of Islam* (London, 1937).
MUIR, W., *The Caliphate* (Edinburgh, 1924).
O'LEARY, DE LACY E., *A Short History of the Fatimid Khalifate* (London, 1923).
RICE, T.T., *The Seljuqs in Asia Minor* (London, 1960).
RUNCIMAN, STEVEN, *A History of the Crusades* (Cambridge, 1951).
SPULER, B., *Les Mongols dans l'Histoire* (Paris, 1961).
WATT, W.M., and CACHIA, P., *Islamic Spain* (Edinburgh, 1965).

PART X

THE ARABIC-ISLAMIC SOCIETY

In his *Muqaddima,* Ibn Khaldun refers to Arab factional loyalties as follows:

> Let it be known that although clans and sub-clans within tribes may constitute individual communities bound together by one general relationship, they engender several factional loyalties belonging to special relationships that may be stronger than that general relationship. These special relationships may be represented, for example, by members of one family, or one household, or by descendants of one father as opposed to near or distant cousins. While such sub-groups (engendering sub-loyalties) are bound together by special relationships, they nonetheless continue to share with other sub-groups in the general relationship. In such circumstances, loyalty is due to the special as well as the general relationship; however, it (loyalty) would be stronger among members of the special relationship because of the closeness of kin. Leadership of course would be restricted only to one group rather than (rotating among) all groups. Since leadership (in a multifactional society) is achieved by prevailing, the factional loyalty demonstrated by the group (producing leadership) must be stronger than the factional loyalties demonstrated by other groups in

order to overcome them and secure leadership for its own group. If this is attained, leadership becomes restricted to that particular group which has prevailed, since if leadership were to be taken away from them and assigned to another nonprevailing group, the latter would not be able to preserve it. Accordingly, leadership continues in that particular group, moving from one of its branches to another, and always moving toward the strongest branch in harmony with the law of prevalence.

Societies and factional loyalties are like chemical compounds. If the ingredients in a chemical compound are equally strong, there will be no reaction; one must prevail over the others in order to produce a new substance. This is the mystery of prevalence among groups exhibiting factional loyalties by which the leadership continues to reside only in one particular group.[1]

In the following chapters, Islamic civilization is discussed in terms of state administration, sects, scholarship, and the legacy of tribalism. In the discussion about tribalism, the reader is advised to trace Ibn Khaldun's concept of asabiyya, translated here as "factional loyalty," to its pre-Islamic tribal origins.

---

[1] Tarikh al-Allamah Ibn Khaldoun, Volume I, Dar al-Kitab al-Lubnani (Beirut, 1956) pp. 233-234.

CHAPTER 40

STATE ADMINISTRATION

THE CALIPHATE

Responsibilities of the Caliph

The term "caliph" comes from Arabic *khalifa* meaning literally "successor." Abu Bakr, the first caliph, was officially called "successor of the messenger of God," while Umar, the second caliph, became known as "the successor of the successor of the messenger of God." When it became evident that such a title could not continue very long to include the entire chain of succession, Umar accepted the simple title *khalifa*, caliph, without any further embellishments. The caliph was also known by two other titles: (1) *imam*, "religious leader," and (2) *amir al-mu'minin*, "commander of the faithful."

These three titles by which a Muslim caliph was commonly known, namely, *khalifa*, *imam*, and *amir*, reflect perhaps better than any other criteria the main functions of the highest and most revered of all Islamic institutions, the caliphate. Muhammad was not only the leader of Islam as a state, but also the leader of Islam as a religion and Islam as a military movement. Inasmuch as the caliph was invested with all the prerogatives of Muhammad except that of prophecy, i.e., receiving divine revelations, his duties were political, religious, and military.

As a political leader, the caliph appointed (or deposed) all governors of provinces and other high-ranking officials. In this respect, all officials were responsible to him, but the

caliph was responsible only to God, from whom all authority was derived.
As a religious leader, he was in charge of defending Islam against
internal heresy and external infiltration by either pagans or polytheists; furthermore, he was expected to lead Muslim worshipers
during public prayers. As a military leader, he was responsible for
protecting the frontiers of *dar al-Islam*, "the household of Islam."
He maintained a standing army along the borders and declared the
jihad, "holy war," whenever he deemed that such an action was
necessary for the security of the Islamic state.

Selection of the Caliphs

The first caliph, Abu Bakr, was chosen by the leaders of Muhammad's supporters, known as the *muhajirun*, to become *khalifa*
or "successor of the messenger of God." According to Arab custom,
once he was chosen, leaders of the Arab tribes pledged him their
allegiance, giving him full authority to lead the Islamic state. The
selection of Abu Bakr may be called, therefore, "selection by acclamation." Umar, however, was designated by his predecessor, Abu Bakr,
whose personal as well as official prestige allowed his designation to
become valid with little opposition. Umar's appointment may be called
therefore "selection by designation." Before his own death, Umar
named seven leaders to a council to select his successor. The seven
members of the council met, but their votes were split between Uthman
and Ali. Their chairman cast his vote for Uthman, who became the third
caliph and was followed by Ali as the fourth caliph. Accordingly, the
appointment of Uthman and Ali may be called "selection by consultation."

Although three methods were employed to select the first four
caliphs, one feature was common to all four appointments, namely,
the requirement of a declaration of allegiance by local Arab chiefs
following the selection of each caliph. In other words, whether the
selection took place by acclamation, designation, or consultation, the
allegiance of the Islamic community was necessary to confirm the
caliph in his high office.

In 661 Mu'awiya announced his candidacy for the caliphate by
virtue of being heir of the murdered Caliph Uthman. However, Mu'awiya's
claim was confirmed only after leaders of the Arab community, desiring to end the civil war between Damascus and Kufa, pledged their
allegiance to him. Mu'awiya wanted to retain the caliphate within his
own clan, and therefore he designated his son Yazid to succeed him and
asked the leaders of the Islamic community to pledge allegiance to the
caliph-designate during his own lifetime. In other words, Mu'awiya
added two major modifications to the system of designation by which
Umar had been selected: (1) he limited designation to his own family,
thus making the caliphate dynastic, and (2) he forced the Muslim community to pledge their allegiance (necessary to confirm any designation) before the new caliph was ready to assume office. Most of

Mu'awiya's successors also designated their own sons or close relatives and sought the allegiance of their supporters in advance. This modified system of succession made the caliphate virtually a semi-dynastic monarchy in which the caliph was the supreme ruler and designated his successors during his own lifetime. Since there were no regulations by which a certain son was automatically chosen as heir to the caliphate, each individual caliph was at liberty to choose whomsoever he wished to succeed him. Many caliphs designated two of their sons to succeed each other; others felt free to disqualify one son and designate another, causing rifts and civil wars to disrupt the continuity of government in the Arab Empire.

Weakening of the Caliphate

The Umayyad caliphate established by Mu'awiya in 661 was followed by the Abbasid caliphate established by Abu al-Abbas al-Saffah in 750, who followed the same system of dynastic succession introduced by his predecessors. Accordingly, the Abbasid caliphate was also afflicted with quarrels and disputes among designated sons and/or relatives of deceased caliphs. Between 750 and 861, the Abbasid caliphs ruled as absolute monarchs exercising full political, religious, and military authority over the Arab Empire. However, between 861 and 1258 the Turkish mercenaries, followed by the Buwayhids, Seljuqs, and Khwarizm shahs, exercised almost complete control over the Abbasid caliphs. The contrast between the prestige of the Abbasid caliphs before and after 861 is sharp indeed. Around that time the caliphs made a transition from a position of absolute power and authority to one of complete weakness and lack of authority. The main reason for this was the lack of adequate and stable provisions for the succession to the caliphate.

ADMINISTRATION OF THE PROVINCES

Arabia under Muhammad

When Muhammad entered Madina in 622, he announced the establishment of the *umma*, "Islamic community," to which all Arab tribes pledged allegiance. However, Islam as a state did not attempt to destroy the loyalty of individual Muslims to their own tribes; on the contrary, on various occasions it recognized the local authority of each tribe by holding it responsible for the safety and protection of its individual members. Moreover, when Muhammad set out to organize his own administration, he appointed *amils*, "official administrators," to represent him not only in each town but also before each tribe. The Prophet's representatives were ordered to perform two duties: (1) to lead Muslims in public prayers, and to receive the religious tax *(zakat)*, required

from all Muslims and collected from individual tribes acting as
separate administrative units within the Islamic state.

The Empire under Umar

Abu Bakr followed more or less the same method used by Muhammad
to administer Arabia. It was the refusal of certain tribes (acting as
units) to pay the religious tax that led to apostasy and civil war during
Abu Bakr's reign. However, soon after Khalid's victory over the false
prophets, especially at Yamama, the Arab tribes joined the army of the
victorious warrior and agreed to advance northward to Hira and Iraq
in 634. Under the leadership of Umar, the Arab forces were able in less
than ten years to conquer all the countries of the Middle East Proper
outside of Arabia and to establish an empire in which the nomadic Arabs
suddenly emerged as the ruling elite. This situation created many administrative problems for Umar, who apparently recognized the differences
in behavior patterns between the Arabs and the inhabitants of the conquered territories. He therefore ordered the Arabs to establish for themselves separate settlements and to retain their own way of life without
becoming involved in the activities of the non-Arab inhabitants with
whom they came in contact. Undoubtedly, those Arabs who moved to
countries such as Egypt, Syria, Palestine, Iraq, and Persia lived in
their own Arab settlements in some sort of tribal organization since
the *ata'at,* "state allowances," were distributed to them by the various
governors of the provinces not as individuals but as tribes.

Divisions of the Arab Empire

The Arab Empire was generally divided into five major divisions,
each administered by an Arab *wali,* "governor," appointed by the
caliph. These divisions were as follows:

1. The Arabian Peninsula (i.e., Hijaz, Yaman, and Najd).

2. Egypt.

3. Southern Iraq and Persia, including Khurasan and most of
   Transoxiana.

4. Northern Iraq and Syria including Armenia, Adharbayjan, and
   the frontier territories in Asia Minor.

5. North Africa and Spain.

Each of these divisions was further divided into local provinces
or districts, each ruled by an *amil,* appointed either by the caliph himself or by the local governor of the division. During the Umayyad
caliphate all the *amils* within the major divisions were chosen from the
Arab population, giving the Umayyad regime a distinct Arab character.

However, during the Abbasid caliphate these *amils* were sometimes chosen from among the local non-Arab Muslim inhabitants.

The main duties of the *wali*, "governor," sometimes also called *amir*, "commander," have been summarized in Islamic annals as follows:

1. Recruiting warriors for the standing army that was supposed to be always ready for combat.

2. Appointing district judges to investigate and rule in local disputes according to Islamic law.

3. Collecting the different taxes, paying local allowances, and sending the balance to the main treasury.

4. Defending religion against innovations.

5. Leading public prayers.

6. Protecting the frontiers against attacks—a duty which allowed governors of frontier territories to penetrate deep into adjacent lands and acquire booty.

During the Umayyad regime, some governors began the practice of appointing deputies to rule in their names, while they resided in Damascus at the caliph's court. This habit continued throughout the Abbasid regime and was common during the period in which the Turkish mercenaries held control of the caliphate. Islamic annals record several events in which deputy governors usurped the rule, usually by plots and intrigues, from their masters and started their own regimes—a practice that led ultimately to the fragmentation and collapse of the Arab Empire.

OTHER OFFICES AND PUBLIC SERVICES

Byzantine and Persian Influence

Although Islam as a religion prohibits orthodox Muslims from accepting religious innovations, it does not bar them from borrowing non-religious patterns of culture from other nations as long as these patterns do not clash with the main principles of their religion. This peculiar feature of Islam allows Muslims to be both conservative and liberal; it allows them to be conservative as far as religious dogma is concerned, but very liberal in other matters not explicitly proscribed in the Qur'an or Traditions. Accordingly, after Islamic expansions in the Middle East, the Arabs are known to have been indifferent to the religious practices of both Persia and Byzantium while at the same time they copied several material administrative features of the local cultures, ranging from royalty to dancing and entertainment. In fact the Umayyads in Damascus and the Abbasids in Baghdad borrowed from Byzantine and

Persian court life much of its panoply and such administrative offices as the *wazir,* "minister"; *hajib,* "bodyguard"; and *katib,* "secretary"; in addition to public establishments, such as the police and mail services.

Office of the Wazir

The title *wazir,* "minister," was used in Islamic annals to refer to the administrative assistant of the caliph. During the orthodox caliphate the position of *wazir* was not filled officially in spite of the fact that the first four caliphs sought help from their companions regarding several matters of state administration. However, during the Umayyad regime, as the Arab caliphs became acquainted with the Byzantine system of public administration, they appointed a number of officials directly responsible to them, each in charge of a certain branch of government. Yet there is no clear evidence that the Umayyad caliphs ever granted the title *wazir* to any of their political advisors.

On the other hand, the Abbasid caliphs, who were greatly influenced by the Persian culture are reported to have used the title *wazir* to refer to the highest official in charge of administering state affairs in behalf of the caliph. The *wazir* was virtually the right hand of the caliph, and was in charge of the state budget. He maintained the army, employed state officials, and, upon his recommendations the governors of the provinces were appointed or deposed. It is reported that when al-Rashid promoted Yahya ibn Barmak to the rank of *wazir,* he surrendered to him his personal seal saying, "I have given you charge over the flock, taking away the yoke from my neck and giving it to you. Therefore, rule according to what you deem right. Employ whomsoever you want and dismiss whomsoever you want. Deal in all matters as you see fit." [1]

The *wazir* was also in charge of supervising the functions of the *diwans,* "special departments," instituted to handle the various services in the state administration. For instance, there was the *diwan* of taxation responsible for replenishing the treasury, the *diwan* of the army in charge of administering all the military affairs of the empire, the *diwan* of archives in which documents and decrees issued by the caliphs were preserved, and several others. These *diwans* had branches throughout the empire in which officials kept records of official documents and correspondence pertaining to their work. At first the records were kept in the local languages of each section of the empire; but after the reign of Abd al-Malik (685-705) these records gradually began to be recorded in Arabic. By the tenth century, Arabic is believed to have replaced local vernaculars in Iraq, Syria, Palestine, Egypt, and North Africa.

Nevertheless, the *wazir* during the Abbasid regime did not always enjoy security and unlimited authority; on the contrary, because of

[1]Al-Tabari, *Tarikh,* Volume 10, p. 50.

plots and intrigues, the caliphs often blamed their *wazirs* for all their own troubles and not only dismissed them, but also imprisoned them, confiscated their properties, and on many occasions put them to death. The debacle of the Barmakid family during al-Rashid's reign was a frightening example of the unpredictability of the caliph's attitudes toward their ministers; many officials reportedly refused the rank when it was offered to them.

Office of the Hajib

The office of the *hajib*, "bodyguard," was first instituted by Caliph Mu'awiya to protect himself against the threats of the Kharijite sect. However, other caliphs followed his example and added more prestige to their personal bodyguards, who gradually became commanders over special military units known as palace guards. The *hajibs* soon began to exercise considerable authority in the administration of state affairs chiefly because they were closest to the person of the caliph and also because of their unique position of being able to choose the individuals who could gain entrance to the caliph's presence. It is reported that Caliph Abd al-Malik once said to his bodyguard, "I have made you in charge of my door. Only three persons should enter without your permission, the one who calls for prayer since he is the representative of God, the mailman by virtue of what he carries, and the waiter who brings my food."

Office of the Katib

Another public official who was almost as close to the person of the caliph as was the *hajib*, was the *katib*, "secretary." The office of the *katib* was instituted in the Islamic state as early as the time of Muhammad himself, who reportedly employed secretaries to record Qur'anic utterances as well as personal messages and other official documents such as the Treaty of Hudaybiyya. Islamic annals list Ali ibn Abi Talib, Zayd ibn Thabit, Mu'awiya ibn Abi Sufyan, and Mughira ibn Shu'ba as having been employed at one time or another as secretaries to the Prophet. Abu Bakr is believed to have employed Uthman as his secretary, and Umar chose Zayd ibn Thabit. When Uthman assumed the caliphate, he reportedly employed Marwan ibn al-Hakam, the fourth Umayyad caliph, as his secretary; Ali, however, chose a noted man of letters called Abd-Allah ibn Rafi'.

During both the Umayyad and Abbasid caliphates, the number of secretaries employed in the court of the caliph at any one time rose from one to at least five persons as each *katib* specialized in one of the main functions of the state. Among the most famous *katibs* in Islamic history was Abd al-Hamid, secretary to Marwan II (744-750) of the Umayyad dynasty; he was noted for his elegant flowing style. Another famous *katib* was Ibn al-Amid, secretary to Nuh I (942-954) of the Samanid dynasty, whose style was known for its beautiful rhymes.

Although the caliphs' secretaries could have become fertile soil for plots and intrigues, Islamic annals do not report troubles fomented by the *katibs*. Perhaps this was because they were usually chosen from among the best educated classes in the empire, and may have regarded their scholarly training so highly that they did not stoop to slander and gossip.

The Police Service

The police service was first instituted in the Arab Empire during the Abbasid caliphate. The need for it arose when verdicts handed down by local judges were not readily enforced. Accordingly, a number of officials were chosen in every city to see that legal verdicts were carried out; these officials became known as *shurta*, "police." As the scope of their service expanded to include an all-night vigil over their respective districts, their ranks and duties became further organized, leading to the creation of the high-ranking office of chief of police.

The police service further expanded to include the function of arresting and trying violators of public laws. This new function allowed police chiefs in every town and district to exercise considerable authority over the inhabitants – authority almost equal to that of the local governor or district supervisor. In the later Abbasid period several police chiefs were chosen as caliphs' bodyguards and sometimes ministers – an indication of the high prestige which they had attained by that time.

The Mail Service

The mail service was one of the most useful features of the Persian and Byzantine civilizations adopted by the Arabs. It was already in use in Egypt, Syria, Iraq, and Persia when the Arabs took over the rule in those countries. However, due to internal quarrels and disputes within the Islamic domain, the mail service assumed a much greater importance during the various periods of the Arab Empire than it had previously held elsewhere. As a matter of fact, during the Abbasid period, the mail became more of an intelligence agency than a public service. The Abbasid caliphs greatly improved the mail routes from Baghdad to Qayrawan and built more resting stations along the way, reducing the distances run by carrier horses or mules to between three and six miles. The mail service was so efficient, especially during the Buwayhid regime, that fresh vegetables and fruits were reportedly transported to Baghdad from other countries without decay.

One of the chief duties of the mail officials was to report regularly about the status of taxation in the provinces, the behavior of the governors, the condition of the army, and many other details that might interest the caliph. As mentioned above, the mail officials had the right to enter directly into the presence of the caliph without the permission of the bodyguard – an indication of the great importance which the caliphs attached to the mail service. For this reason, great care was taken in scrutinizing and choosing high postal officials. To attest to their unflinching devotion to the ruling caliph they were asked to take an oath of allegiance. In spite of these precautions, instances of treason on the part of the mail officials have been reported in Islamic annals, chief of which was their aid in the flight of Idris from Madina to North Africa in 785.

SOCIAL LEVELS AND TAXATION

Muslims and non-Muslims

Three official documents served as bases for regulating relations between Muslims and non-Muslims: (1) the Constitution of Madina proclaimed in 622, (2) the capitulation of Jerusalem in 638, and (3) the capitulation of Alexandria in 642. In these three documents the Muslims allowed non-Muslim scripturaries (Christians and Jews) to dwell among them on condition they paid a poll tax, or *jizya*, averaging about two dinars per person per year. Unbelievers and infidels, however, were not tolerated within the boundaries of the household of Islam. The Jews and Christians agreed to pay the prescribed *jizya* in return for peaceful coexistence with the Muslims. However, after the conquest of Syria and Iraq, Umar decreed that non-Muslims could not live in Arabia Proper even if they paid the poll tax. He therefore requested the Christians of Najran and the Jews of Khaybar to depart peacefully to southern Syria. Since that time, non-Muslims (other than those invited by the state) have never been allowed to establish residence in the Arabian Peninsula.

One article repeated in all three documents mentioned above became especially important in connection with conversions to Islam. This article exempted scripturaries from paying the *jizya*, "poll tax," if they accepted Islam as their religion. As it turned out, many scripturaries, especially Christians, were converted to Islam presumably on their own initiative and with no other pressure than their desire to obtain tax exemption. Nevertheless, all indications reveal that these conversions were made on an individual basis; a few instances of mass conversions have been reported, such as the case of a few thousand Egyptians who became Muslims in order to avoid massacre threatened by the Fatimid Caliph al-Hakim (996-1020).

At any rate, individual conversions are believed to have continued until by the twelfth century the number of Muslims outside Arabia approximately equaled that of the non-Muslims. By the fourteenth century, Muslims had become a majority in the Middle East. Christians and other non-Islamic groups were then a minority within the Islamic domain.

Arabs and Non-Arabs

The Arabs, or to be exact, the original dwellers of Arabia, constituted the core of the Islamic forces that defeated the armies of Persia and Byzantium and occupied most of their possessions in the Middle East. Emerging from a tribal social environment, they suddenly came in contact with sedentary populations with a much higher level of culture than their own. Caliph Umar, under whom the Arabs first expanded their empire, ordered his Arab forces to establish their own cities and live apart from the native inhabitants, who were allowed to pursue their own way of life. Several Arab tribes moved to these cities and a number of other locations, undoubtedly continuing to live as tribes. Since they were not allowed to take land from its original owners, the state distributed to them yearly allowances, known as *ata'at*, apportioned to each tribe according to its prestige and the number of its members. These *ata'at* continued to be given to the Arabs from the state treasury till they were abolished by Caliph al-Mu'tasim (833-842), who introduced Turkish mercenaries from Transoxiana to replace his own Arab warriors.

Before al-Mu'tasim's reign, the Arabs paid no taxes mainly because they supplied the fighting corps upon which rested the security of the empire. The non-Arabs who became converted to Islam were asked to join one of the Arab tribes and become its clients, or *mawali*. Having left their own communities, these clients became Arabicized and began to live as Arabs. This meant that as the Muslim population increased either by additions from Arabia or by conversions, the Arab way of life prevailed throughout the Arab Empire. There is no doubt that the Arabs adopted many material features of the cultures of their neighbors, the non-Arabs; but they led a life that may be considered in the main their own.

During the Umayyad regime, society in the Arab Empire may be divided into the following four groups: (1) the Arabs, who constituted the ruling elite, (2) the clients, who became Arabicized by conversions, (3) the scriptuaries, who kept to themselves, tilling the soil and paying taxes, and (4) the slaves, who were taken as prisoners of war. However, during the Abbasid regime the distinction between Arab Muslims and non-Arab Muslims was eliminated, causing the society to be divided into two main groups: (1) the fast-growing Muslim population, and (2) the fast-declining non-Muslim population (by that time slaves did not constitute an appreciable portion of the population).

Government and People in the Arab Empire

The government of the Arab Empire during the various administrations that ruled from Damascus, Baghdad, or regional capitals was in general authoritative and absolute. The caliphs and the various powers that later on controlled them ruled over the Islamic domain with unqualified authority; they could increase taxes, declare war, confiscate property, and jail suspects without consulting any council or receiving a mandate from the people other than the usual pledge of allegiance. However, this did not mean that the Arab Empire was totally a police state; on the contrary, the masses in the empire were usually left free to pursue their normal activities of life provided they paid their taxes and abstained from interfering in politics or participating in factional intrigues. Those who became involved in politics by siding with an opposition movement were usually subjected to arrest, confiscation of property, and execution without trial. This ruthless attitude on the part of the authorities forced many opposition movements to go underground, undermining the security of the empire; the Kharijites, the Shi'ites, and a few other political groups may be cited as examples.

The taxes required by the central government varied according to the social and religious standing of each group in the society. They may be divided roughly into the following types: (1) *jizya,* "poll tax," (2) *kharaj,* "land tax," (3) *ushur,* "trade tax," and (4) *zakat,* "religious tax." The *jizya,* "poll tax," was required from the scriptuaries (Christians and Jews) commonly known as *dhimmis,* who had been tolerated in the household of Islam. It ranged from half a dinar to three dinars per person per year apportioned according to the individual's financial status. Later on, as the number of *dhimmis* diminished by conversions and other causes, the *jizya* was increased and became intolerable at certain times.

The *kharaj,* "land tax," was levied upon owners of taxable lands regardless of whether the owners were Muslims or non-Muslims. Taxable lands included those which were not seized by conquests from their original owners; in case those owners were later on converted to Islam, or in case Muslims secured ownership of these lands by any means, Muslim owners of taxable lands were also required to pay *kharaj.* Lands seized by conquest and distributed among Arab owners were not usually taxable.

The *ushur,* "trade tax," was levied upon merchants who imported merchandise from outside the household of Islam; this tax was set at one-tenth of the value of the merchandise. The *zakat,* "religious tax," was a duty upon all Muslims. At first it was voluntary, but when some rulers of the Arab Empire desired to replenish the treasury, they ordered all Muslims to pay *zakat* ranging from one-fortieth to one-tenth of the increase in their cattle and planted products. Theoretically, this tax, considered one of the religious duties of Islam, was to be spent by the state for welfare and charitable purposes.

It may be of some interest to note here two other sources of income during the expansion of the Islamic state, namely, *fay',* "booty," and *ghanima,* "spoils of war." The *fay'* included properties acquired by Muslims without actual combat, while the *ghanima* represented all properties gained as a result of war. The particular army responsible for acquiring either booty or spoils of war was allowed to retain four-fifths of its total value, remitting one-fifth to the central government.

CHAPTER 41

ISLAMIC SECTS

BEGINNING OF SECTARIANISM

After the Murder of Uthman

It may be recalled that following the assassination of Uthman (third orthodox caliph), the Islamic world split into two camps, those who supported Mu'awiya, Uthman's distant cousin, and the supporters of Ali, the Prophet's cousin. This split represented, on a large scale, the original rift within the Quraysh tribe between the clan of Umayya and that of Hashim, to which Mu'awiya and Ali belonged respectively. Civil war broke out between the two contending camps and ended only after both sides agreed to arbitration, a customary procedure among the Arabs to secure justice.

As soon as Ali accepted arbitration his supporters split into two groups: (1) the Kharijites, who criticized him for yielding his authority to the outcome of arbitration, and (2) the Shi'ites, who supported him completely. In any case, arbitration failed, because of a trick by Mu'awiya's representative, leaving the Islamic domain divided into three main political groups: (1) the Umayyads, who supported Mu'awiya's claims, (2) the Shi'ites, who supported Ali's claims, and (3) the Kharijites, who supported neither and advocated general elections by which Muslims could elect a new caliph.

After the Murder of Ali

To achieve their goals, the Kharijites sent out assassins to kill both Ali and Mu'awiya in order to relieve the Islamic society (according to Kharijite interpretation) from their harmful rule. The assassin assigned to kill Ali succeeded, while his companion in Damascus failed. Mu'awiya was acclaimed caliph in both Syria and Iraq as Ali's supporters were still recovering from the shock of losing their leader.

Since politics and religion usually were interrelated in the Islamic community, the three political factions that emerged after the murder of Uthman and the failure of arbitration between Ali and Mu'awiya soon developed into religio-political sects as each tried to establish its claims on religious grounds. The Shi'ites produced several traditions attributed to Muhammad in which the Prophet granted greater authority to his cousin Ali than to other companions. The Kharijites produced other traditions revealing that Muhammad wanted the leader of his community to be the best qualified among them. The Umayyads, however, developed into a religious sect known as the Murji'ites, which advocated the postponement of passing judgment against any caliph till the day of judgment. The Murji'ites supported the Umayyad caliphs in spite of the brutal atrocities they committed against the Prophet's household and against the two holy cities of Makka and Madina. As the Umayyad regime gained momentum, especially after the reign of Abd al-Malik, the Murji'ite sect lost its *raison d'être* and disbanded, leaving two opposition sects, the Kharijites and the Shi'ites, battling for survival.

THE KHARIJITES

Ali and the Kharijites

As soon as Ali accepted arbitration to settle his dispute with Mu'awiya, after the battle of Siffin in 657, the Kharijites accused him of abusing the high office of the caliphate and subjecting it to human judgment. Islamic annals report that Ali tried to reason with the Kharijites and show them that he had submitted the matter of the caliphate not to human judgment but rather to God's judgment as revealed in the Qur'an, insisting that his concession was not a sign of weakness but of strength inasmuch as he was thoroughly confident of his position. However, all his efforts were in vain; the Kharijites united against him and demanded his resignation. Ali had no alternative but to pacify Mu'awiya's camp, at least temporarily, and turn his attention to the emerging threat among his own followers.

The Kharijites, numbering about 4000 warriors, gathered near Nahrawan, where Ali's supporters (the Shi'ites) besieged them in

658. Ali dispatched a final appeal to the Kharijites to halt their resistance, rejoin his camp, and fight their common enemy, the Umayyads. They reportedly rejected his appeal, attacking in derogatory terms the personality of the caliph himself. Upon Ali's orders, his followers attacked the Kharijite rebels, inflicting upon them a decisive defeat in which 1400 men were reportedly killed while the rest fled eastward. In 661, however, Ali himself was murdered by a Kharijite assassin, enabling Mu'awiya to achieve his ultimate goal of becoming caliph.

The Umayyads and the Kharijites

The Kharijites who escaped to Persia after the battle of Nahrawan resumed their propaganda against Mu'awiya's rule. They invited the inhabitants of Kufa and Basra, already dissatisfied since their region had become subservient to Damascus, to join them in fighting the Umayyads in Syria. Doubting the loyalty of the Iraqis to his regime and fearing their alliance with the Kharijites, Mu'awiya appointed his adopted brother Ziyad as governor of Iraq. Ziyad delivered fiery speeches in both Basra and Kufa in which he threatened the Shi'ites of Iraq with complete annihilation if they even thought of rebellion. These threats by Ziyad, a warrior known for his ruthlessness, caused the Shi'ites to hold their peace and the Kharijites to go underground.

During the early years of Abd al-Malik's reign, the situation in Iraq was rather confused. Ibn Zubayr officially proclaimed an independent caliphate in Hijaz, while Basra and Kufa gained independence. At this point, the Kharijites emerged, seeking some advantage in the midst of disturbances; however, a warrior named Muhallab was dispatched against them by the interim government of Basra. Muhallab pursued the Kharijites into Persia, where he continued to fight them relentlessly till Abd al-Malik consolidated his rule over Iraq.

By that time, the Kharijites had split into several groups, chief of which were the Azraqites, followers of Azraq, who had been badly defeated by Muhallab. Later on, Abd al-Malik empowered Hajjaj to destroy other Kharijite groups inside Persia. Hajjaj managed to inflict several defeats, but could not completely exterminate the numerous underground cells. Umar II, known for his piety and forgiveness, tolerated the Kharijites, and because of the caliph's personal goodness, the Kharijites caused no troubles. When Hisham assumed the caliphate some of the Kharijites who had fled to North Africa instigated the Berbers to revolt against the Umayyads in 738. This rebellion was soon suppressed by Handhala, Hisham's capable commander in Egypt.

The Kharijites made their last bid for power during the reign of Marwan II (744-750). Taking advantage of the Umayyads' internal quarrels in Damascus after the murder of Walid II, they regrouped under the leadership of Dahhak and captured Kufa in 745. While Marwan II was busy consolidating his rule in Damascus, the Kharijites under

Dahhak proceeded northward in an effort to subjugate the rest of Iraq. However, in a swift move, Marwan II led his armies against the Kharijites and defeated them near Nasibin in 747; Dahhak himself was killed and his supporters dispersed. Less than two years later a group of Kharijites attempted to seize control in Hijaz, but in 748 Marwan II defeated them in the battle of Wadi al-Qura. Ironically, Marwan II, who brought an end to the Kharijite movement in 748, was himself defeated two years later by the Abbasid forces, which brought an end to the Umayyad regime that had been the main target of the Kharijites during their ninety years of relentless struggle.

Main Beliefs of the Kharijites

As a religio-political sect the Kharijites believed in the sanctity of the office of the caliph, considering the caliph God's representative on earth. They believed only in the caliphates of Abu Bakr and Umar and recognized as valid the early period of Uthman and that of Ali before he accepted arbitration. All other caliphs, in their estimation, were illegal and installed contrary to Islamic principles. Kharijite doctrines may be summarized as follows:

1. The caliphate should not be restricted to any tribe or clan; any Muslim regardless of his race or ethnic origin, could be nominated to the caliphate.

2. The caliph should be elected by the entire Muslim community.

3. Once elected, the caliph should not abdicate or withdraw from office.

4. If an elected caliph committed any impious act, he should be impeached and dismissed; if he resisted dismissal, his murder was permissible.

The Kharijites used the Qur'an as the basis of their doctrines. They used certain Qur'anic utterances about moral standards and developed from them degrees of religious piety. Contrary to orthodox Islam, the Kharijites believed that mere faith in God and the Prophet was insufficient to entitle a Muslim believer to paradise. Only when a believer reached a certain standard of piety could he claim to be worthy of eternal bliss. Certain impious actions, if committed by a Muslim, would render him on a par with infidels; further impious actions would make a Muslim believer, in Kharijite estimation, worse than an infidel. It has been reported that once when a Mu'-tazilite was captured by Kharijites, he pretended to be an infidel, hoping that this might save him from a worse fate than if he had confessed his real beliefs.

The Kharijites were as ruthless in persecuting their enemies as they were extreme in their religious views. Their astonishing inflexibility was perhaps due to their firm belief that they were God's own standard bearers on earth; as such they felt compelled to execute God's judgments (as they interpreted them) upon those they believed had deviated from the right path. Their fanaticism was accompanied by daring and self-sacrifice. Throughout their history they never sought riches or personal gain. This perhaps was the reason why they won so many adherents. The Kharijites were divided into several groups such as the Azraqites, the Najdites, the Ibadites, [1] etc., each of which emphasized a particular doctrine of piety. Islamic annals mention sporadic Kharijite activities during the Abbasid regime, but without any indication as to their significance.

THE SHI'ITES

Main Shi'ite Doctrines

The Shi'ites began as Ali's supporters against both the Kharijites and the Umayyads. After Ali's death in 661 and the abdication of his son Hasan, the Shi'ites supported Husayn as their imam. From that time on, Shi'ite imams were the descendants of Ali through his son Husayn.

The Shi'ites, who still live in great numbers at the present time, believe that Muhammad's rightful heir was his cousin Ali and that the imamate therefore has been restricted to the latter's descendants. To substantiate their contentions, they produce several traditional utterances purporting to be the Prophet's intentions to appoint Ali as his successor.

Some Shi'ites believe that the imams are infallible, being endowed with special divine characteristics. Accordingly, Ali and his descendants are believed to have been divinely appointed to lead the Muslim community in the way of Islam. Since they believe that God is unchanging, they also believe that his appointments are unchangeable. In other words, according to the Shi'ites, the imams have been God's appointed rulers over the Islamic community in spite of the fact that most of them never reached the high office of the caliphate.

Shi'ite Subdivisions

It may be recalled that twice during the Umayyad regime the Shi'ites attempted to establish their own imam as caliph in Kufa but failed. Instead, they had two more martyrs besides Ali to lament – Husayn, killed in 680 during Yazid's reign, and Zayd, Husayn's grandson, killed in 740 during Hisham's reign. After that time, the

[1] The Ibadites have survived till the present time in the region of Uman in eastern Arabia.

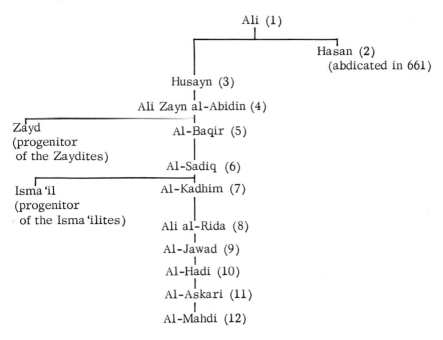

The First Twelve Imams of the Shi'ite Sect

Shi'ites dared not stage an open revolt against either the Umayyads or the Abbasids; however, they continued to use propaganda and tact to advance their cause. A favorable opportunity afforded itself when Ali al-Rida, the eighth imam, won al-Ma'mun's confidence shortly after 813, resulting in Ali's appointment by the Abbasid caliph as heir to the caliphate. However, Ali al-Rida died in 819 under mysterious circumstances during al-Ma'mun's trip back to Baghdad, and thus were dashed all Shi'ite hopes to install one of their imams as caliph.

Isma'il, eldest son of the sixth imam, al-Sadiq, died during his father's lifetime, allowing the younger son al-Kadhim to become the seventh imam immediately after his father's death. However, when al-Kadhim died, a group of Shi'ites supported Isma'il's son against those who supported Ali al-Rida, son of al-Kadhim. Followers of Isma'il's descendants established a new Shi'ite sect which became known later as the Isma'ilite sect. Others, who followed the regular line of Ali al-Rida, continued to support his descendants until the time of the twelfth imam, al-Mahdi, who reportedly entered a cave near Samarra in 879 and disappeared. Since nobody could find him there, his followers believed that he was taken to paradise and that he would appear at the end of time to restore peace and justice to the world. Shi'ites who continued to believe in the hidden imam, al-Mahdi, became known as the "Twelvers," sometimes referred to as "the Imamites"; their doctrines developed mainly around eschatology inasmuch as they continued to look forward to the coming of their expected "messiah."

It is believed that some Shi'ite Imamites became disillusioned in the continued absence of their imam and began looking for living imams. Accordingly, several Shi'ite splinter groups arose, each establishing its own doctrines and supporting one or another of Ali's descendants as imam. Chief of these groups was the Zaydite sect, which chose one of the descendants of the martyr Zayd, son of Ali Zayn al-Abidin, and established a new movement that has survived in Yaman to the present.

Other disillusioned Shi'ite Imamites joined the Isma'ilite faction, which was also splintered into several groups, chief of which were the Fatimids, who ruled in Egypt and North Africa in 909 – 1171, and the Qarmatians, who established themselves in Hijaz and southern Iraq for almost a century between 890 and 990. The Qarmatians undermined the security of the Arab Empire; they not only molested Sunnite pilgrims on their way to Makka, but also stole the Black Stone from the Ka'ba in 929 and hid it for over twenty years. Other Isma'ilites moved into India, where they survive as a Shi'ite sect under the leadership of their imam, the Agha Khan.

Regardless of variations in doctrine, all Shi'ites are fanatically devoted to the household of Ali, whom they venerate. His grave in Najaf and that of his son Husayn in Karbala are their most revered shrines and are visited yearly by thousands of Shi'ites, who solemnly meet to lament the murder of their imams.

THE SUNNITES

Sunnite Doctrines

Sunnite Muslims, known as traditionalists, are those who do not belong to any of the sects that emerged within the Islamic community. They never defined their own doctrines until they were challenged by other sects and forced to produce arguments to refute theological attacks. In other words, Sunnite doctrines emerged as a reaction to a number of assertions made by non-Sunnites. For example, the Sunnite doctrine about the non-createdness of the Qur'an emerged mainly as a rebuttal to the Mu'tazilite emphasis on its createdness.

Besides their belief in the uncreated and eternal character of the Qur'an, the Sunnites also believe in its miraculous revelation to Muhammad as clear evidence of his prophetic call. They also maintain that Muslim believers are always candidates for paradise as long as they maintain their faith in Islam; only apostasy excludes a Muslim from paradise. In other words, Sunnites believe that Islam does not allow for differentiation between a good Muslim and a bad Muslim; the maximum differentiation they allow is the existence of more or less pious Muslims.

Another important Sunnite doctrine that emerged as a reaction to some Shi'ite and mystic allegations was the belief in the absolute and transcendent nature of God. According to Sunnite belief, God is infinite and cannot be limited to a human form. The Sunnite belief in the absolute power of God led them to refuse to talk about God's justice since they maintained that God might, if he wills, punish a good person for no apparent cause and reward a sinner in spite of his evil. In other words, their belief in the absolute power of God made them fatalists, accepting without question or complaint whatever God would bring for or against them.

Since the Mu'tazilites were philosophers as well as theologians, their writings during the early Abbasid period were full of convincing arguments against Sunnite traditional concepts. The Sunnite theologians were forced either to defend their position or admit defeat. Two noted Sunnite theologians spoke eloquently in behalf of Islamic traditional doctrines, using philosophical arguments to refute heterodoxy and to substantiate Sunnite beliefs. These theologians were al-Ash'ari (873-935) and al-Ghazali (1058-1111). The latter, known to many non-Arabs as Algazel, gained a reputation among Sunnite Muslims as the greatest Muslim thinker after the Prophet Muhammad. He wrote a number of excellent books in defense of Islamic traditions. His masterpiece, *Ihya' Ulum al-Din,* may be translated as "Revival of the Sciences of Religion." In this book he refuted many allegations against Islamic traditions and produced philosophical arguments in support of orthodox Islam.

Sunnite Subdivisions

There were no substantial theological differences among the Sunnites. Their main divisions revolved mainly around their understanding and application of Islamic law and jurisprudence. Since most of the reigning caliphs were Sunnites, matters of law and jurisprudence were explained mostly by Sunnite jurists, who frequently faced cases for which no precedents had occurred in either the Qur'an or *hadith.* These jurists had to pass judgment and issue verdicts on several matters pertaining to everyday life; however, since orthodox theology limited them to traditional precedents, they were not totally free to use personal opinion much less innovate and introduce new laws – innovation in Islam was synonymous with apostasy. Accordingly, they resorted to supporting their personal opinions by analogy with traditional precedents. It is mainly on the scope and limitation of analogy that the Sunnites became divided into four schools of law, all of which have become authoritative within the Islamic community. These four schools of law are: (1) the Hanifites, (2) the Malikites, (3) the Shafi'ites, and (4) the Hanbalites.

The Hanifites, followers of Abu Hanifa of Iraq (d. 767), believed in the exercise of personal opinion and the application of liberal methods in the use of analogy. Their liberality sometimes verged on the border of casuistry when they stretched some precedents in order to make them applicable to particular situations.

The Malikites, followers of Malik of Hijaz (d. 796), claimed that any analogy was valid as long as it was based on a valid *hadith,* "an item of tradition." Thus, they were referred to as the Traditionalist School; nevertheless, their liberality in applying what they called "good *hadiths*" did not differ very much from the Hanifite school. In any case, the Malikites may be considered slightly more rigorous than the Hanifites in their choice of the traditions upon which they based their judgments.

On the other hand, the Shafi'ites, followers of al-Shafi'i (d. 820), maintained that only good analogy was valid in making juridical judgments. In other words, any outstretched parallelisms used by the other two schools of law were considered erroneous by the Shafi'ites and therefore unfit for use as precedents in Islamic jurisprudence. Al-Shafi'i himself composed a manual for Islamic law, in which he set forth rigorous principles by which analogy could be used.

The Hanbalites, followers of Ibn Hanbal (d. 855), were the most conservative of all schools of law. They disallowed completely the use of personal opinion based on analogy and permitted only Islamic traditions as the basis for all legal cases. Because of his emphasis upon tradition, Ibn Hanbal himself collected about 80,000 *hadiths,* that he considered valid for Islamic jurisprudence.

The great effort exerted by these four schools of law was known as *ijtihad,* or "personal endeavor." Toward the end of the ninth century, it was agreed by *ijma',* "consensus of opinion," to close the door of *ijtihad* and to open the door of *taqlid,* "imitation." Accordingly, Muslims everywhere were advised to become imitators–imitating the example of the Prophet, his traditions, and the precedents of the four schools of Islamic law, the only schools approved by Sunnite Muslims.

OTHER ISLAMIC SECTS

The Mu'tazilites

The beginning of the Mu'tazilite movement is still shrouded in mystery; however, it is probable that they began to emerge during the lengthy conflict between the Shi'ites and the Umayyads in which politics and religion often collided. The Mu'tazilites appear to have first advocated complete separation between religion and politics in order to keep religion above the violence and scandals that surrounded a number of caliphs.

Mu'tazilite leaders were theologians before they were philosophers; they organized their movement as a separate religious sect having its own set of doctrines and beliefs. The Mu'tazilites as a whole emphasized the following concepts:

1. The oneness of God.
2. Divine justice.
3. Divine punishment.
4. The state between the two states, i.e., the intermediate status of impious Muslims that would render them neither believers nor infidels.
5. Practical godliness.
6. The createdness of the Qur'an.

Their main task was to reveal God's justice toward man and to emphasize man's responsibility toward God. They maintained that God's justice would never allow him to treat pious and impious Muslims alike; and in order not to allow impious Muslims to reach the level of infidels, they introduced into Islamic theology the doctrine of the intermediate state of Muslim wrongdoers. In this intermediate state, impious Muslims would be given a chance to repent and be restored to the fold of pious Muslims; otherwise, they would never be permitted to enter paradise.

Whenever the Mu'tazilites were faced with explicit texts in the Qur'an contrary to their beliefs, they would explain them away as being the outward meaning of the Qur'an, or *dhahir*, which would require an inward meaning, revealed only to them, known as *batin*. This *dhahir* and *batin* interpretation of Qur'anic utterances, as the Mu'tazilites believed, would allow many innovations to creep into the corpus of Islamic religion. It is no wonder, therefore, that Sunnite Muslims have branded the Mu'tazilites, in spite of the latter's great philosophical achievements, as heretics and refused to accept their doctrines.

Besides the doctrine of the intermediate status of impious Muslims, which caused much controversy between Sunnites and Mu'tazilites, the doctrine of the createdness of the Qur'an not only produced differences and misunderstandings among Muslim believers, but also at one time rocked the whole Islamic structure to its foundations. This was the period (813-847) during which Caliph al-Ma'mun and his two successors espoused the Mu'tazilite doctrines and ordered Sunnite jurists and theologians dismissed and jailed. However, after a distressing period generally known as the period of inquisition, the Sunnites emerged strongly armed with their old traditions and turned the tide against the Mu'tazilites, who were driven underground during the reign of Caliph al-Mutawakkil (847-861).

The Sufis

The Sufis are the mystics of Islam. They derive their name from the Arabic word *suf*, meaning "wool," since many of them wore coarse woolen garments. Some historians have tried to explain the rise of mysticism in Islam as a direct influence of Christianity; others have attributed it to Zoroastrian and Buddhist influences. However, since Sufism, as a religious movement, had its own peculiar Islamic orientation, it may also be regarded as a natural development within Islam caused, like other mystical movements, by a deep desire in man to attain a closer relationship with the Supreme Being.

The Sufis believe that all Islamic duties of worship prescribed by the *ibadat* branch of religion are tangible means of bringing man closer to his creator. Once man reaches a stage in which direct communication with God is possible, rituals and other tangible duties cease to be important. The Sufis outlined a series of steps by which a sincere believer could attain direct communication with God: love of God, penitence, meditation, self-denial (until the individual felt his own nothingness), illumination, ecstasy, and unity with God.

Very few Sufis have claimed to have attained the final stage of complete unity with God. However, many of them have claimed to have gone through several of the initial stages, especially those of love of God, penitence, and meditation. A number of Sufis have left behind a wealth of verses describing eloquently their love of God. Others, who wanted to emphasize their penitence, led lives of poverty and austerity and became known as *faqirs*. Those who emphasized meditation would gather in large numbers and chant several verses of the Qur'an as well as other rhymes. These are known as "the dervishes," and their ceremony is called *dhikr;* their ceremonies are still practiced in rural areas of many Muslim countries today.

During the reign of Caliph al-Muqtadir (910-932), a certain Sufi named Hallaj claimed that he had reached the stage of complete unity with God. The following are some verses attributed to him:

I am whom I love, and whom I love I am; we are two souls in one body.

If you see me, you have seen Him, and if you see Him, you see both of us.

Many Sufis believed Hallaj's claim of having become one with God and began to worship him, believing that angels as well as *jinn* were under his control.

In any case, Hallaj was arrested in 914, tried, and found guilty of infidelity to Islam. He was then put to death and his corpse burned and thrown into the Tigris River. His followers later claimed that Hallaj was never killed, but it was his likeness that the Abbasids murdered.

CHAPTER 42

ISLAMIC SCHOLARSHIP

ARABIC LITERATURE

The Arabic Language

Arabic, originally the language of Hijaz and Najd, in Islamic times became the *lingua franca* of the Middle East Proper as well as North Africa. It is sometimes called North Arabic in contrast to South Arabic, which was the language of several kingdoms that emerged in Yaman before the rise of Islam. From a linguistic point of view, Arabic belongs to the Semitic family of languages, which includes Hebrew and Amharic as living examples. Languages such as Akkadian, Ugaritic, Phoenician, South Arabic, Aramaic, and to a certain degree Ancient Egyptian belonged to the same family, but have long since died out as spoken vernaculars.

One of the main characteristics of the Semitic family of languages, retained also in Arabic, is the root-pattern morphological construction. This means that Arabic word stems are usually constructed from roots, each of which usually consists of three consonants, and from patterns (mainly vocalic) with which the roots interdigitate. Roots supply the general semantic connotation of the word, while patterns supply its derivational meaning. For example, the stem *kātib*, "writer," is made up of the root *k t b*, meaning "the general idea of writing," plus the pattern *-ā - i -*, referring to "the doer of action." The root *k t b* may be interdigitated with other patterns, such as *- a - a -*, "action completed in the past," *ma - - ū -,* "recipient of action," and so on. The result of such interdigitation is the formation of other stems, such as *katab,* "he wrote," and *maktūb,* "written," etc. Other roots may interdigitate with the same patterns, giving parallel meanings. For example, the root *q t l,* "the idea of killing," becomes *qātil,* "killer"; *qatal,* "he killed"; and *maqtūl,* "killed person," and so on.

This particular feature of the Arabic morphology makes the language quite rythmic and pleasing to the ear. Moreover, its elaborate system of suffixation allows it to be as rhyming as it is rythmic, rendering it conducive to poetry. It is no wonder, therefore, that long before the Arabic script became fully developed, the Arabs composed, memorized, and recited thousands of poetic verses, which became a source of relief from their otherwise tedious desert life.

The development of Arabic literature may be viewed in terms of four periods of Islamic history: (1) the pre-Islamic period, (2) the early Islamic period, (3) the Umayyad period, and (4) the Abbasid period, also known as the classical period.

The Pre-Islamic Period

The predominant feature of Arabic literature during the pre-Islamic period was the abundance of poetic verses which the Arabs would memorize and recite on several occasions. To the Arabs, poetry was a sport as well as an entertainment; in essence, it was an expression of their emotions. It is reported that Arab poets used to meet in market places such as that of Ukaz, near Makka, not only to engage in religious debates, but also to compete in verse before hundreds of their admirers. After reciting their prepared poems, they would compete extemporaneously without pause, and whoever outlasted all the others was declared the champion of the season.

Pre-Islamic poems, known in Arabic as *qasidas,* had their own peculiar form quite unlike that of Western lyrics, ballads, or epics. Each *qasida* was composed of a number of verses, each of which was known as a *bayt,* usually containing an independent thought. Each *bayt* was divided into two sections separated by a juncture. The two sections of the first *bayt* of any *qasida* usually ended in the same rhyme, which was then repeated at the end of each succeeding verse. The number of verses in each *qasida* varied from a few to as many as a hundred. The verses depicted many features of desert life, such as chivalry, courage, hospitality, honor, eulogy, etc.

Seven of the pre-Islamic *qasidas* were reportedly selected from among many others and hung on the walls of the Ka'ba; hence they were called the *mu'allaqat,* meaning "suspended." The best of the *mu'allaqat* is probably that of Umru' al-Qays (d. 560), the last prince of the kingdom of Kinda in central Arabia, in which he eloquently described various themes such as the thick darkness of night, the speed of his horse, war, wine, and many other features of the desert life. Following is a translation of only four verses of this *mu'allaqa,* in which Umru 'al Qays expressed his feelings about love:

O, Fatima, be kind and stop your tease;
   if you think of breaking up with me, be gentle please.

You became conceited, knowing that your love is killing me
   and that whatever you ask, this I shall do.

You never shed tears except to thrust your arrows
   into the bosom of a heart already stricken with sorrows.

If any of my habits did cause you dismay
   let your clothes rub mine, and let anger rub away.

In addition to poetry, pre-Islamic literature includes many proverbs and maxims that were handed down from generation to generation
until they were recorded in the ninth century during the classical
period. They deal mainly with family discipline, preparation for warfare, and advice against cowardice. Following are some of the
pre-Islamic Arabic maxims:

Many men were killed by covetousness.

The tongue is more dangerous than a strong weapon.

The beginning of wisdom is counsel.

Free men fulfil their promises.

Your hand belongs to you even if it were paralyzed.

The Early Islamic Period

The most important source of Arabic literature during the early
Islamic period is undoubtedly the Qur'an. Its style, idiom, and vo-
cabulary dominated all other compositions in either poetry or prose.
Following is a transcription of a short *sura* of the Qur'an about the
oneness of God, introduced here in order to give the reader an idea
of the rhymed prose of the Qur'an:

1. qul huwa Allahu ahad
2. Allahu s -samad
3. lam yalid wa lam yulad
4. wa lam yakun lahu kufwan Ahad

It is translated as follows:

"Say: He, Allah, is One.
Allah is He on whom all depend.
He begets not, nor is He begotten;
And none is like Him."

Qur'an 112:1-4

Although early Islamic poetry lost most of its prestige in favor of the Qur'an, it continued to follow more or less the pre-Islamic pattern of style and format. A few pagan terms, however, became lost and were replaced by new Islamic terms such as *salat*, "prayer"; *zakat*, "alms"; *ansar*, "supporters"; *muhajirun*, "emigrants," and so on. Early Islamic prose developed considerably beyond the maxims and proverbs of pre-Islamic times, especially when several caliphs and army commanders learned the art of oratory and began to deliver public addresses during the Friday congregational meetings. These orations usually included praises to God and Muhammad, promises of assistance and support to Muslim adherents, and threats to their enemies. Following is an excerpt from a speech reportedly delivered by Caliph Umar, known for his piety and benevolence:

> . . . whoever recites the Qur'an, seeks God and what He has. However, some people recite the Qur'an and still covet the wealth of men. I urge you as you recite to seek after God and His works. I have known you while the Qur'an was being revealed and while the Prophet of God, may God bless him and give him peace, was among us. Now revelations stopped and the Prophet, peace be upon him, has departed; therefore I know you by what I tell you. Whoever among you does good, of him we shall think good and him we shall also praise. But whoever does evil to us, we shall think evil of him and ridicule him. . .[1]

The Umayyad Period

The political situation during the Umayyad period was clearly reflected in the Arabic literature of that time. The Umayyad caliphs encouraged poets to praise them and derogate their enemies. Since the Umayyads had many opponents in both Iraq and Hijaz, most of the poetry of this period was either panegyrical or invective as poets attempted to win the favor of the reigning caliph.

The most famous poets of this period were Farazdaq and Jarir. They were both descended from the Tamim tribe, and both died around the year 737. They introduced into the Arabic language new themes of sarcasm and satire so eloquently expressed that they became patterns followed by later poets. These two poets began their literary careers as satirists; however, as their fame spread throughout the Arab Empire, they competed in derogating each other. This unprecedented competition in both panegyric and satire continued between them for almost forty years, gaining wide publicity among the poets. Following are samples of Farazdaq's self-praise and Jarir's stinging sarcasm; all ending in the same rhyme:

[1]Translated from A.H. Zayyat, *History of Arabic Literature* (Cairo, 1955), p. 185.

Farazdaq: The creator of heaven built for us mansions whose foundations were laid for eternity.

Jarir: Be ashamed of yourself—the great creator of heaven built you a house in the lowest bottom of the chasm.

Farazdaq: All members of our household wear royal garments and never hesitate to wear their uniforms to the battleground.

Jarir: Do not mention royal garments, because you, next to Zubayr, are dirtier than a woman soiled in blood.[2]

Moreover, the early Islamic period produced other poets who excelled in composing love songs and flirtation poems, chief of whom was Umar ibn Abi Rabi'a (d. 720), who lived during the reign of Caliph Abd al-Malik and who composed most of his verses describing the beautiful women he used to watch during the pilgrimage season. Another noted poet of this period was al-Akhtal (d. 722), whose main theme was praise of the reigning caliphs and their supporters. Among his contemporaries, al-Akhtal possessed the most elegant and impressive style.

Prose also flourished during the Umayyad period and was most evident in public speeches delivered by the various governors during the Friday congregational meetings. A famous speech was given by Hajjaj in Kufa exhorting the Iraqi Arabs not to participate in any hostile acts against the Umayyad caliphs. Following is the translation of a part of Hajjaj's speech:

O, people of Iraq, by Allah, I am not the man to be bluffed or swayed by any breeze. I have been tested in understanding and examined in experience. The Commander of the Faithful, may God grant him long life, spread his jewels in his hands and found me to be the hardest of them all. He therefore threw me at you, because you have frequently sought sedition and followed the path of deception.

. . . You are like the inhabitants of a town which was once safe and secure, receiving wealth and prosperity from all directions. However, it denied God's blessing upon it, and therefore God allowed it to taste both hunger and terror. By God, I never say anything without meaning it, . . . after three days if I see a man loitering around after receiving his allowance, I shall surely strike off his head. . . .[3]

The Abbasid (Classical) Period

In the history of the Arab Empire, the Abbasid period stands out as the period in which the Arabs passed through a great cultural

[2] *Ibid.,* pp. 120, 121.

[3] *Ibid.,* pp. 194, 195.

revolution. The main features of this revolution may be described simply as the deference of Arabs to the secular cultures of non-Arab peoples whom they had already conquered and partially Arabicized. The Arabs gave the inhabitants of the Middle East both a new language and a new religion; in turn they received from them several highly developed patterns of culture, both material and intellectual. Undoubtedly, Arabic literature was a chief beneficiary of this significant merger which allowed new branches of knowledge to emerge suddenly. Among the new fields of scholarship during the classical period were philology, historiography, theology, jurisprudence, as well as philosophy and science.

Besides this cultural merger in the Middle East Proper during the Abbasid period, four other factors also contributed to the flourishing of Arabic literature during the classical period:

1. Introduction of papermaking techniques from China around the beginning of the ninth century.

2. Development of a new cursive Arabic script that was both easy and economical to use in comparison with the old and cumbersome Kufic script.

3. Standardization of classical Arabic—a factor that helped many Arab writers to produce grammatically correct literary compositions.

4. Translation of several noted Persian, Greek, and Syriac works into Arabic—a factor that opened new horizons of knowledge to Arab writers.

Perhaps the most significant feature of the Abbasid cultural revolution was the fact that Arab scholars began to write their works instead of having them memorized as their predecessors had done in earlier periods. The legacy of these classical writings includes hundreds of manuscripts, several of which are extant, representing encyclopedic works covering all phases of Islamic scholarship. Islamic historians today have not yet been able to complete a thorough examination of all the works left behind by their predecessors, who wrote prolifically during this era in which fine writing flourished. Only a few of these writers are mentioned here to give the reader some idea of the scope of Arabic literature during the classical period.

Studies in Arabic philology were reportedly launched by two schools of Arabic grammar: one in Basra headed by Sibawayh (d. 793), a noted Arabist whose book *al-Kitab* later became a guide for all succeeding grammars, and the other in Kufa headed by al-Kisa'i (d. 805), who sharply disagreed with Sibawayh on some details of Arabic grammar. These two schools became the foundations of Arabic grammar; succeeding grammarians either interpreted or embellished the famous works of Sibawayh and al-Kisa'i.

During the classical period, Arab poets, already urbanized, developed new styles and themes based on logic and refined metaphors to replace the unbridled imagination of their predecessors of the desert life. Among the leading Iraqi poets were: (1) Abu al-Atahiya (d. 827), who started out composing love songs and ended by writing several poems dealing with piety and wisdom; (2) Abu al-Nuwwas (d. 814), who distinguished himself as master of the metaphor, devoting most of his compositions to describing wine; (3) Ibn al-Rumi (d. 897), whose poems combined both logic and imagination with emphasis on sense rather than sound; and (4) Ibn al-Mu'tazz (d. 908), whose works describe the beauty of nature, festivities, and other social gatherings.

The following Syrian poets are noteworthy: (1) Abu Tammam (d. 845), known for his skill in expressing logic in poetry; (2) al-Buhturi (d. 897), whose works reflected both logic and eloquence; (3) al-Mutanabbi (d. 965), whose poems included many philosophical themes expressed in beautiful metaphors; and (4) Abu al-Ala (d.1057), the blind poet whose works reflected his deep insight into human behavior, as well as philosophy and wisdom.

Arabic prose during the classical period was mainly characterized by its rich expressions of courtesy, resulting perhaps from the fact that a number of Arabic prose writers were originally Persians acquainted with the royal courts. The most noted writers of this period were: (1) Ibn al-Muqaffa (d. 759), translator of the famous story *Kalila wa Dimna;* (2) al-Jahidh (d. 869), author of many encyclopedic works, chief of which was *al-Bayan wa al-Tabyin;* and (3) al-Hariri (d. 1122), author of a number of well-written selections called *maqamat,* whose style was quite poetic and full of rhymes. Another prose compilation, known in the Western world as *The Arabian Nights,* was first translated from Persian during the classical period under the name of *One Thousand and One Nights,* This compilation consists of numerous stories about a king, his *wazir,* and his daughter Shaharazad, who were greatly interested and sometimes involved in all sorts of stories of Indian, Persian, and Arabian origins. The stories of *The Arabian Nights* were finally completed in the post-Abbasid period and serve as a guide to the type of life and entertainment that prevailed in the various periods of Islamic history.

Arab historians included famous names such as Ibn Hisham (d. 838), who wrote about the life of the Prophet Muhammad, quoting from an earlier account attributed to Ibn Ishaq (d. 768); al-Baladhuri (d. 892), who wrote extensively about Islamic expansions; al-Tabari (d. 923), author of *Tarikh al-Umam wa al-Muluk;* and Ibn al-Athir (d. 1234), author of *al-Kamil fi al-Tarikh.*

Two noted works about Islamic jurisprudence are *Kitab al-Kharaj, The Book of Taxes,* written by Abu Yusuf (d. 798) and *al-Ahkam al-Sultaniyya, Islamic Legislations,* by al-Mawardi (d. 1058). Numerous Arabic poems ranging in time from the pre-Islamic period to the early Abbasid period are collected in the famous book of songs known as *Kitab al-Aghani,* compiled by al-Isfahani (d. 967). Several com-

mentaries on the Qur'an were also written during the classical period, chief of which were that of the noted historian al-Tabari (d. 923),
that of al-Zamakhshari (d. 1143), and that of al-Razi (d. 1209).

A noted reference work mainly about Islamic geography was
Muruj al-Dhahab, Gardens of Gold, compiled by al-Mas'udi (d. 956).
Other encyclopedic works include the two dictionaries of Yaqut
(d. 1229), one called *Mu'jam al Buldan, Dictionary of Countries,*
and the other *Mu'jam al Udaba, Dictionary of Writers.*

ISLAMIC PHILOSOPHY

Background of Islamic Philosophy

Perhaps the greatest contribution that the early Abbasid caliphs
made to Islamic scholarship was their encouragement of the translation of several noted Greek and Persian works into Arabic. One of
the pioneer translators named Hunayn (d. 873), a multilingual Syrian,
translated into Arabic a number of Greek scientific works. When
al-Rashid captured several Byzantine posts in Asia Minor, he reportedly carried back to Baghdad a number of Greek books, which he
ordered translated into Arabic. However, it was his son al-Ma'mun
who actually established an academy for learning in Baghdad and invited to it many scholars of various fields to pursue their work. He
reportedly imported from Constantinople several Greek manuscripts
and entrusted their translation into Arabic to a number of translators
under the leadership of a capable multilingual known as Ibn Luqa.

It is believed that by the time of al-Ma'mun, several works of
Aristotle and Plato, as well as a number of Neoplatonic books, had
been already translated into Arabic and made available to Arab
scholars. Since a few Neoplatonic concepts about God and his attributes seemed to agree with certain Islamic beliefs, Muslim theologians became greatly interested in Greek philosophy. However,
the main link between Islamic theology and philosophy was the Mu'tazilite scholars, who from their early beginning indicated their pref-
erence for rational thinking. It is therefore believed that when early
Islamic rationalism came into contact with Greek logic, Islamic
philosophy was born. Although some Muslim thinkers were acquainted with Greek philosophy, they developed their own ideas and shaped
their own philosophical concepts; albeit, they adopted from the Greeks
logic and reason that characterized their newly developed system of
rationalism. Muslim philosophers are divided into two groups: (1)
the liberals, who felt free to innovate new concepts in the corpus of
Islamic religion, and (2) the conservatives, who were faced with the
burden of using philosophical techniques in refuting the liberals'
innovations and upholding orthodox Islamic doctrines.

Liberal Abbasid Philosophers

The first original Islamic philosopher during the early Abbasid period is believed to have been al-Kindi (d. 870), who began his academic life by translating Greek books into Arabic. A deep interest in the material he was translating encouraged him to write something original. His main contribution to Islamic philosophy was his exposition of the compatibility between philosophy and revelation; in fact, he maintained that revelation was the source of logic and metaphysical concepts.

Two other noted Muslim philosophers after al-Kindi were al-Farabi (d. 950) and Ibn Sina (d. 1037), known in Western literature as Avicenna. Al-Farabi was greatly influenced by Plato's writings from which he developed a theory of civilian administration based on the concept of emanation of power from an absolute center, namely, God. Ibn Sina seems to have been influenced by both Aristotle and Plato; he quoted, commented on, and embellished many of their ideas in an attempt to introduce a rationale for prophetic revelations based on intellect rather than emotion. Ibn Sina is known to have been a prolific writer not only in philosophy but also in the natural sciences, especially medicine. His two most famous works are *Al-Qanun fi al-Tibb*, an encyclopedic medical work in fourteen volumes known as *The Canon of Medicine*, and *Kitab al-Shifa*, a philosophical source book in twelve volumes known as *The Book of Healing*.

Andalusian Liberal Philosophers

Islamic scholarship was not restricted to the eastern portion of the Islamic domain. In the west, and more specifically in Spain, Islamic theology and philosophy made remarkable progress. Among the first Spanish Islamic philosophers was Ibn Hazm (d. 1064), who greatly elaborated on the outward meaning of the Qur'an known as *dhahir* as contrasted to its inward significance known as *batin*. His main objective was directed against anthropomorphism in an effort to uphold the metaphysical essence of religion, emphasizing the importance and far-reaching scope of nontangible concepts.

After Ibn Hazm, a number of philosophers appeared in Spain, chief of whom were Ibn Bajja (d. 1138) and Ibn Tufayl (d. 1185), who emphasized the esoteric rather than the tangible concepts of religion.

One of Ibn Tufayl's students known as Ibn Rushd (d. 1198) – Averroes in Western literature – became one of the most revered philosophers, not only in the Islamic world, but also in Europe. He was a grandson of Ibn Rushd the jurist, recognized in the Islamic world as an outstanding legal scholar. Ibn Rushd the philosopher aimed always at harmonizing religion and philosophy. He expressed his religious views in his famous book entitled *Fasl al-Maqal*, which may be translated as *The Conclusion of Research*, in which he upheld the truthfulness of both revelation and logic and emphasized the necessity for establishing harmony between the two.

One of the great contributions of Ibn Rushd to Islamic philosophy was his answer to al-Ghazali's book *Refutation of Philosophy* in which the latter – a noted orthodox theologian and philosopher – eloquently repudiated the philosophical assertion that revelation and philosophy could be harmonized. In his answer, known as the *Refutation of the Refutation,* Ibn Rushd attempted to disprove al-Ghazali's thesis which all but branded philosophy as heretical. Although Ibn Rushd's thoughts were profound and logical, he apparently failed in carrying them through to the Islamic world. Soon after his death, philosophy was branded as heresy and liberal philosophers were no longer permitted to pursue their work, bringing a brilliant era of Islamic philosophy to an end.

Orthodox Philosophers

Most of the orthodox philosophers in Islamic history began as theologians who used logic and philosophical techniques to refute heterodoxy and uphold Islamic traditions. Foremost among these theologian-philosophers were al-Ash'ari (d. 935) and al-Ghazali (d. 1111). Al-Ash'ari began as a Mu'tazilite, but soon abandoned that sect and concentrated most of his efforts on refuting their unorthodox allegations. In so doing he founded a school of orthodox philosophy which defended Sunnite doctrines against intrusions and innovations. Al-Ash'ari used rationalism and logic to substantiate revelation, but he always held to the primacy of revelation.

The undisputed master of the orthodox school was al-Ghazali, known in Western literature as Algazel, who had been so revered by some Sunnite scholars that they called him the greatest Muslim after Muhammad. He was the first theologian to acquire a thorough knowledge of several philosophical writings, such as those of al-Farabi and Ibn Sina. Nevertheless, he disagreed sharply with them, and, using their methods and techniques, he wrote his famous book *The Refutation of Philosophy.* Later he must have passed through an intense mental struggle, trying to find religious fulfillment, for in 1095 he reportedly abandoned his work as a jurist and theologian in order to become a *sufi,* or "mystic." However, ten years later he returned to his theology, devoting the remaining years of his life to writing. Among his chief works are the *Deliverer from Error,* an autobiography describing his religious experiences, and *Revival of the Sciences of Religion,* in which he upheld the principles of orthodox theology.

NATURAL SCIENCES

The Arabs and Natural Sciences

The Abbasid regime was distinguished from that of the Umayyads perhaps most sharply by universalism which not only allowed non-Arabs to participate in the political affairs of the state, but also encouraged them to pursue scholarly research in both humanities and natural sciences. Since Arabic was the *lingua franca* of the Arab Empire, it became the language of research and scholarship, especially after the Abbasid caliphs had ordered scholarly works to be translated into Arabic, mostly from Greek, Persian, and Syriac.

In the fields of humanities such as theology, literature, jurisprudence, and philosophy, Muslim scholars almost monopolized the field; however, in the various fields of natural science non-Muslims participated in almost every field, conducting research and promoting knowledge with special emphasis on medicine, chemistry, and mathematics. In these three fields Islamic scholarship pooled together resources from three different cultures – Semitic, Greek, and Persian – resulting in an era of scientific achievement unequaled in the medieval period. In fact, a number of noted Arabic works in the above-mentioned fields contributed greatly to the advancement of science and technology during and after the European Renaissance.

Medicine

Medicine made great strides in the Arab Empire even before Greek medical works – especially those of Galen – were translated into Arabic. Both Umayyad and early Abbasid caliphs encouraged medical research by building many hospitals in the major cities of the empire and employing physicians of both Arab and non-Arab origins. During the late Abbasid period, Arabic medical science reached new heights as several medical books were written and made available for training new physicians.

Among the noted physicians of this period were Ibn Masawayh and Bukhtyashu', who lived before and during the reign of al-Wathiq (842-847); and Hunayn ibn Ishaq (d. 874), known to have been the first physician to translate Greek medical works into Arabic. Among the physicians who contributed greatly to medicine in the Arab Empire were al-Razi (d. 925), known in Western literature as Rhazes, and the philosopher-physician Ibn Sina (d. 1037), known as Avicenna. These two medical scholars wrote several books that included descriptions, remedies, and surgical advice for a good number of ailments varying from internal diseases to mental abnormalities. These books were later translated into Latin and served as basic works in European medicine for hundreds of years.

Besides dealing with internal medicine, Arabic physicians dealt also with eye diseases, dental ailments, obstetrics, mental disease, surgery, and pharmacology. They reportedly treated diseases such as pneumonia, measles, smallpox, and influenza. They are also reported to have been able to perform surgical operations including replacement of severed ears, tonsillectomy, mastectomy, surgical cases of difficult labor, and several other operations. Their remedies were mainly plant extracts, animal extracts, chemical compounds, alcohol, drugs, and other medicines.

Chemistry

Two main reasons motivated the Arabs' interest in scholarly research in chemistry. Beside the desire to develop chemical products
to serve as remedies for certain diseases, the Arabs were also interested in the pseudo-science of alchemy, which sought a formula for
transforming base metals into gold. Accordingly, Arab chemists
searched for new chemical compounds in the hope of making gold; however, instead they discovered such useful products as sulfuric acid,
nitric acid, sodium hydroxide, and silver nitrate. While experimenting
on their new products, they developed several useful laboratory techniques such as evaporization, condensation, filtration, distillation,
and crystallization.

Among the first Arab chemists was Jabir ibn Hayyan, known
in Western literature as Geber, who lived during the ninth century
and who reportedly was the first to discover the importance of
acids and alkalis in producing salts. To the present, modern chemists
use the term "alkali," which is derived from the Arabic term *al-
qalawi,* first used by Jabir. The word "chemistry" itself may be
traced back to the Arabic term *al-kimya,* used by the Arabs to describe this branch of natural science.

The Arabs composed several works on chemistry, chief among
which was Jabir's own book *al-Kimya,* which was translated into
Latin and used as a text for many years in European schools. Other
works on chemistry were written by the physicians al-Razi and Ibn
Sina, mentioned above.

Mathematics

The greatest Arabian breakthrough in mathematics occured when
the Arabs adopted the decimal system from the Hindus of India. With
the decimal system of counting, the Arabs also learned of the role
of zero (Arabic *sifr*) as a digit between the plus numbers and the minus
numbers. This discovery opened to Arab mathematicians wide horizons for solving many problems whose solutions otherwise would
have been difficult or impossible. In fact, arithmetic would have been
a backward science, had it been limited to Roman numerals and not
expressed in Arabic numerals.

Perhaps the greatest contribution of the Arabs to modern mathematics was "algebra," which was developed in the attempt to solve
equations. The Arabs solved first degree equations, but when they
tried second degree equations, they needed new techniques. Chief
of these techniques was called *al-jabr,* meaning "restoration," which
supplied symbols for the unknown items in mathematical problems.
The derivation of the English term "algebra" from the Arabic *al-
jabr* is easily seen.

The Arabs are believed to have initiated the science of trigonometry and discovered the usefulness of tangents and other relationships in the study of triangles. They also made progress in the analysis of squares, cubes, and reportedly distinguished for the first time the prime numerals, calling them "mute numerals."

Among the chief Muslim mathematicians were al-Khwarizmi (d. 850) and Umar al-Khayyam (d. 1123). Al-Khwarizmi was the father of algebra, and he made many mathematical discoveries that were used later as fundamentals for solving complicated equations. Umar al-Khayyam, who became well known to many Europeans as the author of the beautiful poems called *The Ruba'iyyat*, was in fact a mathematical genius. He developed al-Khwarizmi's methods and elevated mathematics to an even higher level than that attained by the Greeks.

Other Contributions

Other fields of science in which the Arabs distinguished themselves were astronomy, agriculture, navigation, and engineering. Muslim advances in these fields of science are believed to have contributed to the scientific progress achieved in Europe during and after the Renaissance. [4]

---

[4] Arabic scientific manuscripts are believed to have been introduced first to Palermo in Sicily and then to Naples in Italy about A.D. 1224. Other works were introduced to France from Spain about A.D. 1200. Some of these works were translated into Latin and became later on textbooks in a number of European institutions of learning.

CHAPTER 43

TRIBALISM AND SOCIETY

ISLAMIC REFORMS

Social Reforms

Islam introduced important social reforms to Arabia. Legislation against infanticide and slavery is believed to have given the Arabs a new understanding about the value of the individual, regardless of sex or background. Although the limitation to four wives may now seem repugnant to modern values, it was actually a great emancipation for women in Arabia, where polygamy had been unlimited, with no regard to blood relations among wives or to the ability of the husband to support them. Furthermore, Islam strengthened the marriage institution by insisting upon a written marriage contract drawn up before two witnesses, providing for a financial settlement for the wife in case of divorce. These reforms initiated by the Prophet Muhammad introduced greater social stability to a formerly nomadic and disorganized society.

Other Islamic reforms introduced into Arabia were several legislative acts greatly limiting such practices as adultery, usury, gambling, drinking alcoholic beverages, and eating the flesh of unslaughtered animals. Furthermore, Islam regulated trade by establishing officially stamped measures of weight and size in order to prevent cheating in business transactions. Many features of individual ownership were regulated, and several laws were passed against theft and property damage. Detailed regulations concerning inheritance governed almost all possible quarrels among close and distant relatives of any deceased individual. These regulations prevented many of the family feuds and conflicts that had afflicted Arab society after the death of wealthy persons.

Perhaps the most significant reform in Arabia attributed to Islam was its strong measures against pagan practices. These measures prohibited both idol worship and sorcery, gradually relieving the individual Arab of much fear whenever misfortune struck or sickness befell any member of his family. Although Islam, meaning "submission to the will of God," encouraged the Arabs to be fatalists, it nevertheless provided them with more dignified means for overcoming doubts, supplying them with both zeal and hope for a prosperous life both here and in paradise.

Political Reforms

Perhaps the most significant single religio-political institution which Islam introduced into Arabia was that of the Islamic *umma*. It appears that the ultimate goal of the Prophet had been always to unite the badly divided Arab tribes into one nation bound together by the strong bonds of religion. Since purely political institutions, in spite of their efficiency, would have never received the approval of all Arab tribes, Islam combined religion with politics, considering all believers as citizens of the newly established religio-political institution, called *al-umma al-islamiyya,* "the Islamic community." In other words, the united allegiance of the Arabs had to be channeled first toward supporting a religion that was believed to have received its authority from God before it could be directed toward supporting a political structure under the leadership of one man.

At any rate, in order to ensure the continued allegiance of the various Arab tribes to one leader, that leader was considered a *khalifa* (caliph), "successor of the Prophet," with authority theoretically obtained not from man, but from God, in spite of the fact that he was selected by his fellow men. The caliph in Islam officially ruled as an agent of God, the real owner of all power, whose divine authority was necessary to establish a political institution under which all Arabs would be united.

The concept of the *umma* succeeded in prevailing over the then-existing tribal system of government and bringing about, for the first time a sense of national existence among the Arabs in the peninsula. As soon as the Arabs began to transfer some of their loyalty from individual tribes to the newly established Islamic state, the cornerstone of the Arab Empire was laid; within a mere decade of the death of the Prophet, the Arabs were in control of the entire Middle East Proper.

SURVIVAL OF TRIBALISM

Islam and the Arab Tribes

In spite of the far-reaching laws and regulations introduced by Muhammad into Arab society, Islam did not succeed completely in transferring Arab loyalties from individual tribes to the newly established Islamic state. Individual Arab tribes were allowed to continue as sub-units possessing local authority within the larger structure of the Islamic state. The sudden death of Muhammad during the crucial period of the Arab transition from tribalism to "national existence" cut short the flow of authoritative legislation through revelation and the possibility of further laws to outlaw completely the survival of tribal authority within the Arab Empire. Before his death Muhammad had recognized the local authority of the Arab tribes and allowed them to perform certain official political and social functions within the Islamic state. When he died, these functions became part of the standardized Islamic heritage and were allowed to survive within the religio-political structure of Islam.

Political Recognition of the Tribes

In the Constitution of Madina drafted by Muhammad in 622, the concept of the *umma*, "Islamic community," was introduced for the first time. The Prophet then announced that Muslim believers of all tribes would be united by bonds of the Islamic religion and would thus constitute the Islamic *umma*. This was undoubtedly the first significant religio-political effort seriously attempting to unite the Arabs and establish their national existence. Nevertheless, the Constitution of Madina did not completely eliminate the political functions of the Arab tribes. Aside from asserting the unity of all Muslims under Islam, the Constitution of Madina allowed each tribe to be responsible for satisfying the obligations of its members, especially in connection with the payment of blood money. This political provision in the structure of the Islamic state at its inception stipulated that individual Muslims were accountable to their respective tribes in personal matters and to the Islamic *umma* in matters of religion and national security.

Furthermore, after the capture of Makka when more Arab tribes began to accept Islam and join the Islamic *umma*, Muhammad recognized their sense of identity as autonomous units by sending to each tribe an administrative representative to supervise collection of the religious taxes and to lead its members in congregational prayers. This meant that the central government of the Islamic state was dealing with its Muslim citizens not individually, but as tribes – a formal recognition of the tribe as a unit of authority. It becomes evident therefore that as Islam introduced to the Arabs a formula for unity, it included in that formula recognition of the continuation of tribal authority. It may be recalled that the acclamation of Muslim caliphs during the early Arab Empire required a pledge of allegiance sworn by chiefs of the Arab tribes to the newly elected caliph – a further indication that the tribes continued to exercise political authority within the empire.

Social Recognition of the Tribes

A traditional saying attributed to Muhammad himself and reported in the collections of Ibn Hanbal, a theologian known for his extreme care in collecting *hadith,* includes an admonition by the Prophet to one of his companions named Sa'ib, advising him to apply Arab pre-Islamic mores to the Islamic community.[1] Such an admonition on the part of Muhammad should not be surprising, for he himself lived in a tribal environment and learned to appreciate several ethical standards of the Arab tribes. As a matter of fact, the Qur'an itself is full of admonitions that clearly reflect the tribal element in some of Muhammad's religious utterances. The following verses are cited as samples:

> And if you fear a breach between the two, appoint a judge (arbiter) from his people and a judge (arbiter) from her people; if they both desire agreement, Allah will effect harmony between them . . . .

> And serve Allah . . . and be good to parents, and to the near of kin, and the orphans, and the needy, and the neighbour of (your) kin and the alien neighbour, and the companion in a journey and the wayfarer, and those whom your right hands posess. Surely Allah loves not him who is proud, boastful:[2]
>
> Qur'an 4:35, 36

and also:

> And kill not any one whom Allah has forbidden, except for a just cause. And whoever is slain unjustly, We have indeed given to his heir authority (to revenge), but let him not exceed the just limits of slaying; for he will be surely helped.[3]
>
> Qur'an 17:33

These verses indicate that besides the admonitions to show kindness to wayfarers and travelers (a clear reference to nomadic life), Muhammad seems to have formally recognized at least two

[1] Ibn Hanbal, *Musnad,* Volume 3, p. 425.

[2] Parentheses mine.

[3] Parentheses mine.

pre-Islamic social institutions and included them as a part of the social structure of Islam: the institution of arbitration, and the institution of blood revenge.

Arbitration, originally a pre-Islamic tribal institution established to bring peace and justice to feuding Arab tribes, continued to function within the Islamic society. A clear sample of its use by Muslims was the famous arbitration arrangement between Ali and Mu'awiya after the battle of Siffin in 657. Although this arbitration ended in failure, it demonstrated the great importance Muslims attached to an institution introduced from pre-Islamic times.

The verse in Qur'an 17:33 (about blood revenge) is valid enough to have allowed many Muslim believers throughout Islamic history to attach great significance to blood revenge, another pre-Islamic institution maintained in the social structure of Islam. In fact, after the murder of Caliph Uthman (644-656), blood revenge became a scourge that plagued Islamic society throughout both the Umayyad and Abbasid regimes.

Binding Force of Early Islamic Patterns

The relative remoteness of pre-Islamic times from the classical period of the Arab Empire, during which Islamic ethics became somewhat codified, may be brought up as an argument against the survival of tribal mores within the Islamic society. This argument may be strengthened by the fact that the Arabs had mixed with their non-Arab neighbors and learned from them new ethical values. Nevertheless, Islam as a religion, a social institution, and a political structure has always modeled its patterns on the instructions found in its two main sources, the Qur'an and the Traditions. Furthermore, during the ninth century, when, by consensus of the Islamic theologians, the door of interpretation, known as *ijtihad,* was closed, Muslims became known as traditionalists. The Arabic word for "traditionalist" is *muqallid,* which literally means "imitator." This indicates that orthodox Muslim believers, by virtue of their theology are "imitators" – imitators of earlier patterns of culture made binding upon them by the force of their religion. Muslim believers are expected to look back to the time of their Prophet for guidance and inspiration.

ROLE OF TRIBALISM IN ISLAMIC CIVILIZATION

Flow of Culture

While Muslims were expanding their rule into the Middle East Proper and adjacent areas, nomadic Arabs migrated in great numbers from Arabia and settled in other wealthier and more prosperous regions within the Arab Empire. However, as these Arab emigrants began to settle outside Arabia, they were not allowed to mix with the non-Arab inhabitants of the captured territories. As mentioned above,[4] Caliph Umar (634-644) is reported to have ordered the Arabs to build new settlements for themselves, in which they would lead their own way of life apart from the rest of the population. Apparently Umar had taken into consideration the differences between the Arab nomadic way of life and the sedentary habits of the conquered peoples, and therefore, in an effort to preserve the material cultures of the captured areas, he decided to keep the Arabs apart from the original inhabitants of these areas. These Arabs moved into these new cities as tribes and lived there as such for many succeeding generations. It is reported that during the Arabic classical period, many individual Arabs took great pride in tracing their tribal genealogies, referring to their tribal designation rather than their place of birth.

From the religious and social points of view,[5] the Arabs adopted very little from the peoples around them. However, materially speaking, they absorbed almost every feature of the luxury and prosperity that characterized the Persians and Byzantines. They built large houses and cooked elegant foods; they learned the art of entertainment and banquets, utilizing the talents of many slave singers and dancers; they wore silk clothes and adorned themselves with jewels and gold. In its material aspects, culture flowed rapidly from non-Arabs to Arabs. On the other hand, in the social and religious spheres, the direction was almost reversed; the non-Arabs, who were steadily converted to Islam, left their own communities and joined Arab tribes as *mawali*, "clients." Since these conversions took place mostly on the individual level, converts were soon absorbed by the Arab population and became fairly Arabicized. This process continued for many years till around the tenth century when Muslims began to gain numerical ascendancy over non-Muslims.

At a certain time during the history of the Arab Empire the Islamic population seems to have reached a level of homogeneity in which differentiation between Arab Muslims and non-Arab Muslims was greatly reduced. At that time, the Arab nomadic society lost many of its distinguishing desert features and became urbanized. As a result, a new Arabic society emerged in which all Muslims (both Arabs and non-Arabs) constituted, broadly speaking, one integrated culture having two main substrata — one Arabian (on the religious and social levels) and the other Persian-Byzantine (on the material level). Through the religio-social Arabian substratum, several tribal patterns of culture were allowed to survive within the newly emerging society. Among the legacies bequeathed to the Islamic society during the empire period by pre-Islamic tribal patterns of culture were extremes of behavior, clannish prestige and

[4] See p. 334.

[5] It may be said that indirectly the material culture of the countries occupied by Muslim armies influenced many features of the Arab social life.

blood revenge, personality cult in leadership, dual allegiance, and factionalism.

Extremes of Behavior

Because of the adverse living conditions in their original desert home, the Arab nomads developed certain extreme and often contradictory characteristics, which later on became distinctive features in their everyday life. The Arabs are known to be very hospitable whenever guests or travelers visit their homes. Their extreme hospitality has been manifested on several occasions when some of them reportedly have gone to great financial expense in order to make their guests happy and comfortable. At the same time, the Arabs may be also very hostile at the slightest doubt or suspicion. Extreme and ambivalent behavior such as hostility and hospitality, suspicion and trust, antagonism and amiability, malevolence and benevolence, and perhaps arrogance and servility exhibited simultaneously by the same people may be considered as tribal legacies that have survived mainly from father to son into Islamic times.

Clannish Prestige and Blood Revenge

Clannish prestige and blood revenge are two characteristics peculiar to the nomadic life of Arabia that also survived into Islamic times and became distinctive features of the Islamic society. Much of the political history of the Arab Empire was greatly influenced by the many quarrels and disputes among the leaders of the Islamic state caused mainly by conflicts involving clan prestige and by the obligation of blood revenge. The murder of Husayn at Karbala and the ensuing wars with the Umayyads and the Hashimites are vivid samples of these tribal legacies. Even today many modern Arabs continue to attach great importance to the prestige of their respective households, refusing to allow marriages between families that are considered to be of lesser prestige (and for no other reason). Other Arabs, especially in remote rural areas, still refuse to allow local law-enforcing agents to prosecute a murderer, in order to allow the next of kin of the murdered person to take revenge at his own convenience.

Personality Cult in Leadership

As for leadership, it is a well-known fact that the Arab tribes used to pledge allegiance to their own personal leaders known as *shaykhs*, who then would become, as it were, physical symbols of their own honor, prestige, and social status. This feature of tangibility in leadership, which also became one of the characteristics of Islamic society, allowed several groups of Muslims to support their respective feuding leaders, all of whom might be striving toward the same goal. In other words, it was not the goal itself that mattered, but the leader symbolizing the goal. This feature partially explains the many quarrels and disputes among several Muslim leaders within the Arab Empire, each of whom was supported by a segment of the population loyal to him personally rather than to the cause for which it was fighting. As a result of this feature of Islamic society, whenever a strong ruler took power, he would usually eliminate all potential rivals lest they succeed in rallying their supporters and thus foment further trouble. When a ruler was unable to get rid of all his rivals, mounting troubles would usually follow, leading to more fighting and bloodshed.

Dual Allegiance and Factionalism

Arab dual allegiance may be considered a direct development of certain traditional tribal tendencies by which the individual in Arab society owed allegiance first to his own household, then to his clan and tribe. When the Islamic state was established in 622, the Arabs were expected to pledge allegiance to the Islamic *umma*, "community," in addition to their allegiance to their respective clans and tribes. Thus as the Islamic state expanded and a major Arabicized community developed in the Middle East, members of this community became accustomed to the principle of "dual allegiance" by which they were expected to be loyal both to the Arab community as a whole and at the same time to their individual tribes, factions, or regions as the case might have been. In case of a clash between the goals of the unified community and those of its various factions, quarrels and rifts usually followed, leading to the ultimate weakness of the whole empire.

Arab factionalism may be considered a middle stage between tribalism and regionalism. During the urbanization process of the newly emerging Arab society in the empire period, as tribal boundaries expanded, Arab society became divided into several factions, each representing some earlier tribe or clan, or a newly developed local community within the empire. These factions required from their members the same loyalty which a tribe or a clan had earlier required from desert Bedouins. Accordingly, as factional loyalties began to supersede state loyalties, schisms beleaguered the community. These factional splits continued throughout almost the entire history of the Arab Empire till its downfall in 1258.

Ibn Khaldun, one of the most brilliant Arab historians, at the turn of the fifteenth century describes the tribal legacy of the Arabs as follows:

> In the passing of time, several generations separated the Arabs from the (religious origins) of their state. They neglected religion and forgot the principles of government,

returning to the (rules) of the desert and causing their factional loyalties to oppose the interests of the state, leading them to insubordination. They reverted to nomadism as they had been before, retaining nothing of the discipline of sovereignty except the memory of their descent from the caliph's line and genealogy. When the caliphate lost its power, (the Arabs) lost their political prestige, allowing non-Arabs to take over (their state). They then resettled in their own desert, forgetting that they had ever established sovereignty or maintained discipline.[6]

[6] Ibn Khaldun, *op. cit.*, p. 272.

IMPORTANT TERMS

Amil: Administrative supervisor of a province or a district within the Arab empire. He was appointed either by the caliph himself or the district governor.

Amir al-Mu'minin: "Commander of the Faithful." It was one of the titles of the reigning caliph.

Ata'at: Financial allowances granted to Arab tribes settling in the various sections of the Arab Empire. These allowances were considered compensations for their readiness to fight in defense of the empire.

Dar al-Islam: "Household of Islam." It represented all territories ruled by Muslims in the Middle East during the empire period.

Dervishes: A group of Muslim Sufis, "mystics," still existing today in rural areas of some Muslim countries. They believe in attaining ecstasy by rapidly chanting Qur'anic verses and religious formulas. Their chanting ritual is known as *dhikr.*

Dhikr: see *Dervishes.*

Dhimmis: A term used to refer to the Jews and Christians allowed to reside in *dar al-Islam.* They are sometimes called "scriptuaries."

Diwan: Administrative department of government in the Arab Empire. The several *diwans* were administered by the *wazir.*

Faqirs: A group of Muslim Sufis, "mystics," who believed in renouncing worldly wealth and pleasures in order to attain closeness with God.

Fay': Booty acquired by Muslims without actual combat.

Ghanima: Booty acquired by Muslims during combat.

Hajib: "Bodyguard." An office established in the courts of Muslim caliphs during the Umayyad regime to protect the person of the caliph and screen his visitors.

Hanbalites: An Islamic school of law which maintained extreme conservatism in applying rules of the Qur'an and Traditions.

Hanifites: An Islamic school of law which used personal opinion and liberal methods in jurisprudence.

Ijma': "Consensus of opinion." New laws and regulations in the Islamic state may be validated by the *ijma'* of all Muslim jurists.

Ijtihad: Right to use personal opinion or give added interpretations in Islamic jurisprudence. The door of *ijtihad* has been closed since the ninth century by the use of *ijma'*.

Imam: "Religious leader." According to Sunnite beliefs, an imam leads Muslims in congregational prayers. According to the Shi'ites, he is both the religious and political leader of the Islamic community.

Imamites: A subdivision of the Shi'ites; they supported the descendants of al-Kadhim, brother of Isma'il the seventh imam. Since their twelfth imam, al-Mahdi, reportedly disappeared, they believe that he is still living and that he will appear at the end of days to restore justice to the world. They are also called "Twelvers."

Isma'ilites: A subdivision of the Shi'ites; they support the line of Isma'il, brother of the seventh imam.

Jizya: "Poll tax." It was levied on *dhimmis* for being allowed to reside in the Islamic state and receive its protection.

Katib: "Secretary." It literally means "writer," or "recorder." The *katibs* were capable men of letters who excelled in Arabic prose.

Khalifa: "Caliph." It means "successor." The *khalifa* was a successor of the Prophet for the purpose of administering the Islamic state religiously, politically, and militarily.

Kharaj: "Land tax." It was required from owners of taxable lands, regardless of whether they were Muslims or non-Muslims.

Kharijites: An Islamic sect that branched from the Alids. They opposed Ali for submitting his case to arbitration.

Malikites: A school of law that started in Hijaz and emphasized the use of the Traditions in Islamic jurisprudence.

Mawali: "Clients." They were the non-Arabs who were converted to Islam during the early period of the empire and had to join themselves to Arab tribes as clients.

Mu'allaqat: Seven poems belonging to the pre-Islamic period, which reportedly were recorded and placed inside the Ka'ba.

Mu'tazilites: One of the Islamic sects that thrived during the Abbasid period. One of their main doctrines was their belief in the createdness of the Qur'an.

Qarmatians: A sub-group of the Isma'ilites. They resorted to violence in their attempt to achieve their Shi'ite goals.

Shafi'ites: An Islamic school of law which advocated a rational use of analogy in jurisprudence.

Shi'ites: A major sect in Islam which contends that Ali was the rightful successor of Muhammad and therefore his descendants should have been leaders of the Islamic state.

Shurta: "Police service." It was a service that developed during the Abbasid period to maintain security in towns and see that legal verdicts were carried out.

Sufis: "Muslim mystics." They believed in attaining closeness to God by renouncing worldly pleasures and emphasizing spiritual values.

Sunnites: "Traditionalists." They represent the orthodox Muslim population which did not align itself with any particular sect.

Taqlid: "Imitation." When the door of *ijtihad* was closed in the ninth century, Muslims were advised to imitate the revelations of the Prophet, his traditions, and the precedents set forth in the works of the four schools of law.

Twelvers: See Imamites.

Ushur: "Trade tax." It was required from merchants importing goods into the Islamic state.

Wali: Governor of a province or one of the administrative divisions of the Arab empire.

Wazir: "Minister." It was the office occupied by the administrative assistant of the caliph.

Zaydites: An offshoot of the Alids supporting the line of Zayd son of Ali Zayn al-Abidin. They still exist in Yaman.

SUPPLEMENTARY READINGS

ARBERRY, A.J., *Reason and Revelation in Islam* (London, 1957).
_____, *Aspects of Islamic Civilization* (London, 1964).
_____, *Sufism, An Account of the Mystics of Islam* (London, 1952).
ARNOLD, T.W., and A. GUILLAUME, *The Legacy of Islam* (London, 1931).
BAER, T.J.de, *The History of Philosophy in Islam* (London, 1961).
COULSON, N.J., *A History of Islamic Law* (Edinburgh, 1964).
DONALDSON, D.M., *The Shi'ite Religion* (London, 1933).
_____, *Studies in Muslim Ethics* (London, 1953).
FARIS, NABIH A., *The Arab Heritage* (Princeton, 1946).
GIBB, H.A.R., *Arabic Literature* (Oxford, 1963).
_____, *Studies on the Civilization of Islam* (Boston, 1962).
GRUNEBAUM, G.E., von, *Unity and Variety in Muslim Civilization* (Chicago, 1955).
_____, *Islam: Essays in the Nature and Growth of a Cultural Tradition* (Madison, Wisconsin, 1955).
ISSAWI, CHARLES, *An Arab Philosophy of History* (London, 1955).
JEFFREY, ARTHUR, *Reader on Islam* (The Hague, 1962).
KHADDURI, M., *Islamic Jurisprudence—Shafi'i's Risala* (Baltimore, 1964).
_____, *War and Peace in the Law of Islam* (Baltimore, 1961).
KHADDURI, M., and LIEBESNY, H., *Law in the Middle East* (Washington, 1955).
KHUDA-BAKHSH, S., *Contributions to the History of Islamic Civilizations* (Calcutta, 1929).
KRITZECK, JAMES, *Anthology of Islamic Literature* (New York, 1963).
LEVY, REUBEN, *The Social Structure of Islam* (Cambridge, 1957).
MACDONALD, D.B., *Aspects of Islam* (New York, 1911).
_____, *The Development of Muslim Theology, Jurisprudence, and Constitutional Theory* (London, 1903).
NICHOLSON, R.A., *A Literary History of the Arabs* (Cambridge, 1953).
O'LEARY, DE LACY, *How Greek Science Passed to the Arabs* (London, 1951).
SARTON, G., *Introduction to the History of Science* (Washington, 1927-1948).
SCHACHT, JOSEPH, *An Introduction to Islamic Law* (Oxford, 1964).
WATT, W.M., *Islamic Philosophy and Theology* (Edinburgh, 1962).
YOUNG, CUYLER T., *Near Eastern Culture and Society* (Princeton, 1951).

APPENDICES

Excerpts from the arbitration discussions undertaken to settle the dispute between Ali and Mu'awiya.
(Translated from al-Tabari, TARIKH, Vol. VI, pp. 38-40.)

The two arbiters met and Amr ibn al-As said, " O, Abu Musa (al-Ash'ari), don't you know that Uthman, may God be satisfied with him, was unjustly killed?" He (al-Ash'ari) said, "I do." (Ibn al-As said,) "Don't you know that Mu'awiya and his household are his nearest of kin?" He said, "Yes." He (Ibn al-As) said, "God, mighty and majestic is He, ordained that whosoever is unjustly killed, his next of kin will have authority (to revenge) on condition that he should not be excessive in murder and (in so doing) he would be justified. What prevents you then, O Abu Musa, from supporting Mu'awiya, who is Uthman's next of kin; and moreover his household belongs to Quraysh as you know. If you fear lest people say you preferred Mu'awiya for no good reason, you certainly can say that you found him to be the next of kin of the unjustly treated Uthman and the one in charge of avenging his blood. Moreover, he (Mu'awiya) is a good diplomat and a wise organizer, besides his being a brother to Umm Habiba, wife of the Prophet, may God bless him and give him peace. . . ." Abu Musa said, "O Amr (Ibn al-As), fear God, mighty and majestic is He, whatever you mentioned about Mu'awiya's honor (is acceptable), yet this matter cannot be decided on the merits of honor, or else Abraha ibn al-Sabbah would have been selected. This matter con-

373

cerns people of religion and greatness. Furthermore, if I have the
right to select the greatest of Quraysh, I would select Ali ibn Abi
Talib. As for what you mentioned about Mu'awiya's being the next of
kin to Uthman, may God be satisfied with him, this is what you say,
but I do not like to give him this privilege. . . ."

. . . Amr said to him, "What is your opinion?" He (Ash'ari)
said, "My opinion is to depose both men and submit the whole matter
to the counsel of the Muslims. Let the Muslims choose for themselves
whomsoever they like." Amr said to him, "My opinion is like yours."
When they went out to the people who were gathering outside, Abu
Musa said (to Amr), "Tell them that we have already agreed."

. . . Abu Musa then stepped forward and after giving praise to God,
mighty and majestic is He, said "O people, we have discussed the
matter of this *umma* and found that the best solution to heal its
rift, as both of us have agreed, is to depose both Ali and Mu'awiya
and let the people settle the matter and select whomsoever they like.
I (therefore) announce the deposition of both Ali and Mu'awiya and
submit the matter to you to choose whomsoever you like as your
leader." He then sat down. Amr ibn al-As then stood up in his place,
and after giving praise to God he said, "This man (Ash'ari) has just
said what you have heard and deposed his friend (Ali). I do also
depose his friend just as he has done. But I establish my friend
Mu'awiya since he is the next of kin to Uthman son of Affan, may God
be satisfied with him, and the person in charge of avenging his blood.
Furthermore, he is the most worthy of all people for this post."

(The record goes on to say that a quarrel between Amr's friends
and Ash'ari's men followed after which each group left as arbitration
completely collapsed.)

APPENDIX 2

After the murder of Marwan II.
(Translated from al-Mas'udi, MURUJ AL-DHAHAB (Cairo, 1928),
Vol. II, pp. 206, 207.)

When Amir severed Marwan's head and captured his soldiers,
he entered the church where Marwan had been hiding, sat on his
chair, and ate of his food. Marwan's eldest daughter, known as Umm
Marwan, went to him and said, "O, Amir, destiny (literally, time)
which caused Marwan to descend from his chair and permitted you
to sit in his place, eat his food, capture his authority, and rule in
his regime, is also capable of changing that which you have
obtained."

Thereupon, Amir sent Marwan's daughters, his concubines, and
his slaves to Salih ibn Ali. When they entered into his presence,
Marwan's eldest daughter said, "O, Uncle of the Commander of the
Faithful, may God preserve for you (a portion) both in this world and
in the world to come. We are both your daughters and your nieces;

let us receive of your indulgence as much as you have received of our injustice." He said, " Accordingly we should not leave any of your men or women alive. Didn't your father kill recently my nephew Ibrahim . . . the Imam, in his prison in Harran? Didn't Hisham, son of Abd al-Malik, kill Zayd, son of Husayn, crucifying him in Kufa; and didn't he also kill Zayd's wife in Hira through Yusuf ibn Umar al-Thaqafi? Didn't Walid, son of Yazid, kill Yahya, son of Zayd, and crucify him in Khurasan? Didn't Ubayd Allah ibn Ziyad kill Maslama, son of Aqil son of Abu Talib, in Kufa? Didn't Yazid, son of Mu'awiya, kill Husayn, son of Ali, through Umar, son of Sa'd, together with other members of his household who died before his eyes? Didn't he take captives some of the women of the Prophet's household, may God bless him and give him peace, bringing them to the presence of Yazid, who, before their arrival had received Husayn's head atop a spear after it was paraded in the districts and cities of Syria and brought to Yazid in Damascus, as if it were a head of an infidel? Didn't he then cause the women of the Prophet's household, may God bless him and give him peace, to stand like captives to be looked over by the brutal soldiers of the Syrian army, who wanted him to deliver to them the women of the Prophet's household, may God bless him and give him peace . . .? What is it then that you left for us to consider for justice?" She then said,"O, Uncle of the Commander of the Faithful, we seek your pardon." He said, "As for pardon, I grant it; if you like, I shall give you as a wife to al-Fadl, son of Salih, son of Ali, and give your sister to his brother Abd-Allah, son of Salih." She said, "O, uncle of the Commander of the Faithful, is it now a time for weddings? Let us go to Harran." He said, "Let it be so, God willing." They were then allowed to go to Harran. As they entered they wailed with loud cries the death of Marwan, tearing their garments and shrieking loudly till the whole encampment was shaken by their weeping for Marwan.

APPENDIX 3

Letter from Muhammad the Pure Soul to Caliph Abu Ja'far al-Mansur answering the Caliph's request to give up his claim and accept amnesty.
(Translated from al-Tabari, TARIKH, Vol. IX, pp. 210-211.)

In the name of God, the merciful, the compassionate . . . I offer you amnesty like that which you offered me. The right (to rule) is ours; you have claimed it through us, reached it through our supporters, and acquired it through our prestige. Our father Ali was both guardian and imam; how then could you inherit him while his descendants are still living? You know that none ever claimed this right, who could also claim any prestige and honor similar to ours through our predecessors. We are not the descendants of evildoers, profligates, or careless individuals. None of Hashim clan could ever claim such closeness (to the Prophet), benevolence, or favor as we do. We are the descendants of the mother (in-law) of the messenger of God, may God bless him and give him peace, through Fatima, daughter of Amr in pre-Islamic times. God has chosen us; our father is one of the prophets, namely, Muhammad, may God bless him and give him peace. Our lineage goes back to the first convert to Islam, Ali, and to the best of wives, the flawless Khadija, first to perform prayer toward the *qibla*.

Our lineage also goes back to the best (of women), Fatima, mistress of all women in paradise; of those born in Islam we belong to Hasan and Husayn, masters of all young men in paradise. Hashim begat Ali twice (through both parents), and Abd al-Muttalib begat Hasan twice. The messenger of God, may God bless him and give him peace, begat me also twice through Hasan and Husayn. I claim therefore a clear and distinct lineage in the Hashim household; non-Arabs did not mix in my lineage, and my maternal progenitors have been always Arab mothers. God has been always choosing for me my parents from pre-Islamic times till Islam, including also those who became destined to hell (unbeliever ancestors in pre-Islamic times). Accordingly, I am son of the best of all people in paradise and of the least to be tormented in hellfire: I am son of the best of the pious and son of the best of the wicked, son of the best people in paradise and son of the best of the people of fire.

Therefore, God is witness to what I say, if you submit to me and respond to my call, I shall guarantee the safety of your life and property; I shall forgive you for whatever you did except in matters of violating one of the oracles of God or one of the rights of either a Muslim or a person with a covenant. You know what should be done in such cases. I assure you that I shall keep my word and honor my promise. You have given me a promise of safety (safe conduct) similar to that which you have given to others before me. What kind of safety have you promised to give me? Is it one like that given to Ibn Hubayra, or that given to your uncle Abd-Allah, son of Ali, or that given to Abu Muslim?

(Al-Tabari does not record any further closing remarks.)

APPENDIX 4

Answer of Caliph al-Mansur to the letter of Muhammad the Pure Soul in which the latter emphasized his right to the caliphate due to the prestige and honor of his lineage.
(Translated from al-Tabari, TARIKH, Vol. IX, pp. 211-213).

In the name of God, the merciful, the compassionate. I was informed of what you said and I also read your letter. If you have put most of your glory in your relationships to women, (you should know) that only mobs and disreputable persons do so. God never allowed women to equal uncles and fathers, or any paternal relative or guardian; on the contrary, God allowed an uncle (to receive honor) similar to that of a father. . . .

When God sent forth Muhammad, peace be upon him, he had four uncles. God, mighty and majestic is He, told him, ''Warn your household, the nearest of your kin.'' (Qur'an 26: 214). He then warned them (his uncles) and called them to believe. However, two accepted his call, one of whom was my father and two rejected him, one of whom was your father. . . . You have claimed that you are the son of the least tormented of persons in hellfire and the son of the best of the wicked. There are no degrees in unbelief, and in the torment of hellfire there is nothing that could be called the least or easiest. Moreover, there is no best among the wicked and a believer in God should not glory in hellfire. . . .

As for your glory in Fatima, mother of Ali, and the fact that Hashim begat him twice, and in Fatima, mother of Hasan, and the fact that Abd al-Muttalib begat him twice, and in the fact that the Prophet, may God bless him and give him peace, begat you twice, (you should know) that the pride of all first and last, the messenger of God himself, may God bless him and give him peace, was not born of Hashim except only once and was not born of Abd al-Muttalib except also once. . . .

Furthermore, members of your household are the descendants of his (the Prophet's) daughter. Although it is a close relationship, yet it does not allow inheritance, neither in rulership nor in the imamate. How could you then claim inheritance through it? Your father tried hard to claim it, but no sooner was (his argument) produced in the morning, than it became sick by noon and was buried by night. . .; and besides, tradition itself, upon which Muslims do not disagree, prescribes that neither the maternal grandfather nor the maternal uncle or aunt is entitled to inheritance. . . .

Moreover, Hasan sold his claim to Mu'awiya for money and went to Hijaz, surrendering his support to Mu'awiya, allowing the high office to go to individuals other than its proper claimants, and receiving money that did not belong to him. At any rate, if you (your household) had ever any claim to it (the caliphate), you have already sold it and cashed its price. . . . You then rose against the Umayyads, who killed you, hanged you on palm trees, burned you in fire, and exiled you into far away places. . . until we rose against them and avenged your blood, causing you to inherit their lands and homes because we honored and preferred your lineage. You are now taking all this against us. . . .

You know that none was left to inherit Abd al-Muttalib after Muhammad, may God bless him and give him peace, except him (al-Abbas). He became his (Muhammad's) heir by virtue of his being

his uncle. Several of the sons of Hashim tried to inherit this privilege and none succeeded except his own sons. Accordingly, . . .
the Prophet's inheritance became his, the caliphate became restricted
to his sons; no honor or favor (of the Prophet) in both Islamic and pre-
Islamic times and in both this world and the world to come could be
inherited by anybody except al-Abbas and his heirs. . . .

How then can you boast over us, while we helped you (materially)
during this period of unbelief, redeemed you from captivity . . . inherited against you the seal of all prophets, and took revenge for you
while you could not do anything for yourselves?

Peace be upon you and God's compassion.

APPENDIX 5

Traditional story of the death of Harun al-Rashid.
(Translated from al-Tabari, TARIKH, Vol. X, pp. 110, 111.)

It has been reported that Jibril ibn Bukhtyashu' (court physician)
said:

"I was with al-Rashid in Raqqa and was the first one to enter
into his presence every morning to find out how he spent the night.
He used to describe to me many of his secret details and often talk
about the stories of his concubines, what he did during his evening
parties, the amount of wine he drank, and the length of time he stayed.
Then he used to ask me about the news of the people and their conditions. One morning I entered into his presence and greeted him.
However, as soon as he lifted up his face, I discovered that he was
frowning, engrossed in thought, and distressed. I stayed with him
longer during that morning, but he still was unmoved. After some
time, I approached him and said, 'Sir, may God allow me to bear your
sorrow, what is your condition? If it is a disease tell me, perhaps
I have a remedy; or if a tragedy befell some of your loved ones,
this cannot be helped except by yielding (to the will of God). Accordingly distress will not benefit at all; and besides royal courts cannot
be immune to tragedies. I am the first person to whom you should
divulge your secrets and obtain relief through counsel.' He then
said, 'Alas, Jibril, my distress and trouble are not caused by anything
of what you mentioned, but by a vision which I saw last night and which
greatly disturbed me.' I said, ' Commander of the Faithful, you have
relieved me of much worry.' Then I approached him, kissed his
feet, and said, 'Did your vision cause all this distress? Perhaps it
was due to some imagination, intestinal gases, hallucinations or mere
nonsensical dreams.' After this he said, 'I shall relate it to you. I
saw as if I were sitting on my chair, and behold an arm and a hand
were stretched beneath me, which I could recognize but could not
remember to whom they belonged. The hand was carrying red soil.
A voice which I heard but whose source I could not see then told me
that that was the soil in which I should be buried. When I asked about

the whereabouts of this soil, the voice mentioned that it was in Tus. Thereupon the hand disappeared, the voice hushed, and I awoke.' I said, 'Sir, this is rather a confused vision; perhaps when you slept your thoughts wandered around Khurasan and your wars there and you began to think about some of its conflicting reports.' He said, 'That is true.' I said, 'For this reason your thoughts were somewhat confused, resulting in this vision; accordingly, do not let it disturb you, may God allow me to bear your sorrows. Let pleasure take away this distress from your heart and do not let it cause you any discomfort.' "

He (Bukhtyashu') continued his report saying:

"I continued to cheer him up with all kinds of means until he became comforted and relaxed. He then ordered the preparation of the kind of (food) he likes and continued his pursuit of happiness. Many days passed during which he, as well as all of us, forgot that vision and none of us thought much of it. However, it was destined that he (al-Rashid) should go to Khurasan for a time. . . When he began his journey, sickness overtook him and his condition became more serious till we reached Tus, where we lodged in the house of a certain al-Junayd ibn Abd al-Rahman at his farm known as Sanabadh. While he (al-Rashid) remained sick there near a garden in the palace, he remembered the vision. He then tried to stand up, rising and falling several times, until we all rushed to him asking him, 'Sir, what is the matter and what has happened?' He said, 'O Jibril, do you remember my vision in Raqqa about Tus?' Then he motioned with his head for a certain man (called) Masrur saying, 'Bring me a sample of the soil of that garden.' Masrur went and brought some soil in his hand, while his sleeves were rolled up. When he looked at him he said, 'By God this is the arm which I saw in my vision, and by God this is the hand itself, and by God this is the same red soil. I surely was not deluded.' He began to weep and cry, and after three days he passed away and was buried in that particular garden."

APPENDIX 6

Sample of the interrogations during the inquisition ordered by al-Ma'mun against jurists and theologians who continued to uphold the position of the uncreatedness of the Qur'an.
(Translated from al-Tabari, TARIKH, Vol. X, pp. 287, 288.)

Ishaq ibn Ibrahim invited to his presence a group of jurists, governors, and theologians (a list of names is given including the name of Ibn Hanbal), and read to them al-Ma'mun's letter twice so that all of them would clearly understand it. He then said to Bishr ibn al-Walid, "What do you think about the Qur'an?" He (Bishr) answered, "You already know my position which I have already stated to the Commander of the Faithful several times." He said, "The order (for investigation) has been renewed by this letter of the

Commander of the Faithful." He (Bishr) answered, "I maintain that the Qur'an is the word of God." He said, "I did not ask you this question, I asked you, 'Is it created?' " He answered, "God is the creator of all things." He asked, "Is the Qur'an considered a thing?" He answered, "It is a thing." He asked, "Is it created?" He answered, "It is not a creator." He said, "I did not ask you about this. Is it created?" He answered, "There is nothing better than what I said, and I have promised the Commander of the Faithful not to talk more about it; and therefore I have nothing more to add." Thereupon Ishaq ibn Ibrahim took a paper that was in his hands, read it to him and asked him to testify. He read, "I testify that there is no God but Allah, one and single; nothing was before Him and nothing after Him; and none of His creations should be likened unto Him, neither by metaphor nor by substance." He (Bishr) said, "I do (testify)."

Then he turned to Ibn Hanbal and asked him, "What do you say about the Qur'an?" He answered, "It is the word of God." He asked, "Is it created?" He answered, "It is the word of God. I have nothing to add to this." He (Ishaq) then tested him according to the document, and when he reached the statement, "Nothing is like Him, neither in metaphor nor substance," he stopped. . . . Ishaq then asked Ibn Hanbal, "What is meant by saying, hearer and seer?" He answered, "It is as has been described." He asked, "What does this mean?" He answered, "I do not know, it is as has been described."

He (Ishaq) then called them (the theologians) one by one, and they all testified that the Qur'an was the word of God except the following group: (nine are listed). (One of them named) Ibn al-Buka the senior said, "The Qur'an is made because God, may He be exalted, said, 'We have made it an Arabic Qur'an.' " . . . Ishaq then reiterated, "What is made is also created." He said, "Yes." He (Ishaq) asked, "Is the Qur'an then created?" He answered, "I do not say created, but made." He (Ishaq) then recorded his testimony. . . .

He also recorded the testimonies of the whole group one by one and sent his report to al-Ma'mun.

APPENDIX 7

Excerpts from Ibn Khaldun's remarks on Arab tribal legacies. (Translated from TARIKH AL-ALLAMAH IBN KHALDUN, Vol. I, (Beirut, 1956), pp. 269-271.)

The Arabs cannot attain sovereignty (solidarity under one rule) without religious motivation by either revelation, guardianships, or a significant religious influence on the whole community. The reason for this lies in the fact that they are composed of nomadic peoples possessing traits that render them unwilling to accept leadership one from another. This is due to the toughness, pride, insubordina- tion, and rivalry for leadership; seldom did their aims meet around one target. However, under the influence of religion maintained by either revelation or guardianship (of revelation), the motivation comes from within and acts as a hindrance to pride and rivalry among them, making them easier to unite and to lead. Religion (in this case) serves as a force to destroy toughness, pride, insubordination, and all acts of envy and competition. Accordingly, if a prophet or religious guardian could encourage them to do the will of God, abstain from evil, and learn good, he would be able to unite them for truth's sake, form them into a society, and obtain for them sovereignty. They (the Arabs) are fast to respond to truth and enlightenment, mainly because their nature is still raw and away from crookedness and innate evil, except for their nomadism which is (relatively) easier to treat since primitive peoples are more inclined to accept reform than (others) upon whom bad desires and evil traits have already been strongly impressed. As it is mentioned in the Traditions, every new baby is born innately innocent. . . .

(Nevertheless) Among other peoples, the Arabs are the hardest to respond to (the discipline of) sovereignty, the reason for this being the fact that they are the most accustomed to nomadism among nations. They are also more used to poverty and more capable of enduring austerity (than other peoples) because they became used to deprivation and possessing little to live on. This in turn caused them to be independent in character and hard to subordinate. Since their leader needs their loyalties for defense purposes, he is forced to treat them nicely and avoid their antagonism lest the balance of their sub-loyalties should become disturbed, leading to his and their destruction alike. Sovereignty and authority (among Arabs) require that the political leader should be firm and determined, otherwise his policies would utterly fail. . . .

(On the other hand), the Arabs may accept the discipline of sovereignty after a complete change in their character. This begins with religion, which removes their (insubordination) and creates within them motivation that would help them realize the benefits of solidarity for the purpose of defense as we have mentioned above. This has been eventually achieved for them through religion which had already established for them political (precedents) through religious laws and regulations in conformity with culture both outwardly and inwardly. Caliphs then succeeded each other and were able to strengthen their rule and increase their authority.

APPENDIX 8

Names and Dates of the Abbasid Caliphs

1.	Abu al-Abbas	750 - 754
2.	Al-Mansur	754 - 775
3.	Al-Mahdi	775 - 785
4.	Al-Hadi	785 - 786
5.	Al-Rashid	786 - 809

6.	Al-Amin	809 - 813
7.	Al-Ma'mun	813 - 833
8.	Al-Mu'tasim	833 - 842
9.	Al-Wathiq	842 - 847
10.	Al-Mutawakkil	847 - 861
11.	Al-Muntasir	861 - 862
12.	Al-Musta'sim	862 - 866
13.	Al-Mu'tazz	866 - 869
14.	Al-Muhtadi	869 - 870
15.	Al-Mu'tamid	870 - 892
16.	Al-Mu'tadid	892 - 902
17.	Al-Muktafi	902 - 910
18.	Al-Muqtadir	910 - 932
19.	Al-Qahir	932 - 934
20.	Al-Radi	934 - 940
21.	Al-Muttaqi	940 - 944
22.	Al-Mustakfi	944 - 946
23.	Al-Muti'	946 - 974
24.	Al-Ta'i'	974 - 991
25.	Al-Qadir	991 - 1031
26.	Al-Qa'im	1031 - 1075
27.	Al-Muqtadir	1075 - 1094
28.	Al-Mustadhhir	1094 - 1118
29.	Al-Mustarshid	1118 - 1135
30.	Al-Rashid	1135 - 1136
31.	Al-Muktafi	1136 - 1160
32.	Al-Mustanjid	1160 - 1170
33.	Al-Mustadi'	1170 - 1180
34.	Al-Nasir	1180 - 1225
35.	Al-Dhahir	1225 - 1226
36.	Al-Mustansir	1226 - 1242
37.	Al-Musta'sim	1242 - 1258

APPENDIX 9

Umayyad Amirs and Caliphs in Spain

1.	Abd al-Rahman I	756 - 788
2.	Hisham I	788 - 796
3.	Al-Hakam I	796 - 822
4.	Abd al-Rahman II	822 - 852
5.	Muhammad I	852 - 886
6.	Al-Mundhir	886 - 888
7.	Abd-Allah	888 - 912
8.	Abd al-Rahman III	912 - 961
9.	Al-Hakam II	961 - 976
10.	Hisham II	976 - 1009 and 1010 - 1013
11.	Muhammad II	1009 and 1010

12.	Sulayman	1009 - 1010 and 1013 - 1016
13.	Ali (Hammud dynasty)	1016 - 1018
14.	Abd al-Rahman IV	1018
15.	Al-Qasim (Hammud dynasty)	1018 - 1021 and 1022
16.	Yahya (Hammud dynasty)	1021 - 1022 and 1025 - 1027
17.	Abd al-Rahman V	1023 - 1024
18.	Muhammad III	1024 - 1025
19.	Ilisham III	1027 - 1031
20.	Regional rulers	1031 - 1090

APPENDIX 10

Names and Dates of the Fatimid Caliphs

1.	Ubayd Allah	909 - 934
2.	Al-Qa'im	934 - 945
3.	Al-Mansur	945 - 952
4.	Al-Mu'izz	952 - 975
		(moved to Egypt in 973)
5.	Al-Aziz	975 - 996
6.	Al-Hakim	996 - 1020
7.	Al-Dhahir	1020 - 1035
8.	Al-Mustansir	1035 - 1094
9.	Al-Musta'li	1094 - 1101
10.	Al-Amin	1101 - 1130
11.	Al-Hafidh	1130 - 1149
12.	Al-Dhafir	1149 - 1154
13.	Al-Fa'iz	1154 - 1160
14.	Al-Adid	1160 - 1171

TABLE OF IMPORTANT DATES

272	Fall of Palmyra
275	Abyssinians attack South Arabia
374	South Arabians regain independence
525	Abyssinians reoccupy South Arabia
571	War between the Abyssinians and South Arabians
	Also the year of the Elephant in which Muhammad was born
619	Death of Khadija, Muhammad's first wife
622	Year of the *hijra* in which Muhammad immigrated to Madina

624	Battle of Badr
625	Battle of Uhud
627	Expedition of the Trench
628	Truce of Hudaybiyya
629, 630	Muslim defeat at Mu'ta
630	Capture of Makka
632	Muhammad's death
632 - 661	The orthodox caliphate
633	Victory over the Arab apostates
634	Battle of Ajnadayn
636	Battle of Yarmuk
637	Battle of Qadisiyya
639	March against Egypt
642	Battle of Nihawand – Surrender of Alexandria
644	Assassination of Umar
649	Beginning of naval wars against Byzantium
656	Assassination of Uthman, battle of the Camel
657	Battle of Siffin
658	Arbitration between Ali and Mu'awiya
661	Assassination of Ali
661 - 750	The Umayyad dynasty
670	Uqba conquers North Africa
680	Massacre of Karbala in which Husayn was murdered
682	Uqba reconquers North Africa
683	Sack of Madina and bombardment of Makka by Umayyad troops
684	Battle of Marj Rahit
685	Battle of Warda, rise of Muhktar in Iraq
687	Defeat and murder of Mukhtar at the hands of Mus'ab's troops
691	Defeat and murder of Mus'ab at the hands of Umayyad troops
692	Second bombardment of Makka
695	Capture of Carthage
698	Hassan reconquers North Africa
705	Musa ibn Nusayr appointed commander of Arab troops in North Africa
707	Conquest of Transoxiana
708	Conquest of the Indian borders
711	Conquest of Spain
717	Siege of Constantinople
728	Rebellion of Khurasan against Caliph Hisham
732	Arab defeat at the battle of Tours and Poitiers
739	Suppression of the Coptic rebellion against Hisham
740	Murder of Zayd, son of Ali Zayn al-Abidin. Suppression of the rebellion of North Africa against Hisham
744	Assassination of Caliph Walid II, Death of Caliph Yazid III, Defeat of Caliph Ibrahim by Marwan's troops
747	Battle of Nasibin between Marwan II and the Kharijites

749	Abbasids capture Kufa and proclaim Abu al-Abbas as their caliph
750	Battle of the Zab and end of the Umayyad dynasty
754	Al-Mansur proclaimed caliph
756 - 1090	Rule of the Umayyad dynasty in Spain
762	Murder of Muhammad the Pure Soul in Madina
785	Murder of Husayn the Alid in Hijaz and flight of Idris to al-Maghrib
786	Al-Rashid's reign begins
788 - 922	The Idrisid dynasty
797	Empress Irene usurps the throne of Byzantium
800 - 909	The Aghlabid dynasty
803	Debacle of the Barmakids
804	Al-Rashid's wars with Byzantium begin
809	Civil war between al-Amin and al-Ma'mun
811	Al-Ma'mun's forces capture Hamadan
813	Al-Ma'mun's forces capture Baghdad
819	Al-Ma'mun's return to Baghdad
	Death of Ali al-Rida the Shi'ite
820 - 872	The Tahirid dynasty
820	Nasr's rebellion in northern Iraq
830	The Copts' rebellion in Egypt
	Babek the Khurramite receives help from Byzantines against Arab rule
835	*Zatt* people (gypsies) sent to Asia Minor
836	Introduction of the Turkish mercenaries and founding of Samarra
837	Defeat of the Khurramites
838	Defeat of Emperor Theophilus of Byzantium
839	The Mazyar-Afshin revolt crushed
845	Turkish mercenaries suppress a revolt in Hijaz
861	Al-Mutawakkil assassinated by Turkish mercenaries
868 - 905	The Tulunid dynasty
870 - 872	Negro rebellion in Iraq
872 - 910	The Saffarid dynasty
909 - 973	The Fatimids in Qayrawan
910 - 999	The Samanid dynasty
931 - 1003	The Hamdanids in Mosul and Aleppo
935 - 969	The Ikhshidid dynasty
945	The Buwayhids capture Baghdad
973 - 1171	The Fatimids in Cairo
999 - 1186	The Ghaznavid dynasty
1004	The Ghaznavids capture Punjab
1026	The Ghaznavids cross the Ganges River
1055	Tughril Beg defeats the Buwayhids
1060	Basasiri's revolt suppressed
1062 - 1145	The Murabit dynasty
1090	The Murabits cross over to Spain
1097	Beginning of the Crusade wars

1127 - 1182   The Atabegs of Mosul
1135   Caliph al-Mustarshid's revolt against the Seljuqs sup-
               pressed
1145 - 1225   The Muwahhid dynasty
1148   Crusaders besiege Damascus
1166   Seljuqs enter Egypt
1171 - 1260   The Ayyubid dynasty
1180   Beginning of rule of the Khwarizm shahs
1187   Salah al-Din captures Jerusalem from the Crusaders
1192   Agreement between Salah al-Din and Richard the Lion-
               hearted
1195   Battle of Badajoz
1212   Battle of Las Navas de Tolosa
1220   The Mongols attack the region of Khwarizm
1228   The Crusaders allowed to occupy Jerusalem
1244   Al-Salih the Ayyubid recaptures Jerusalem
1258   The Mongols under Hulagu sack Baghdad
1260   Baybars defeats the Mongols at the battle of Ayn Jalut

INDEX

*al-Abbas, son of Ibn Tulun, 300, 307
al-Abbas, the Prophet's uncle, 106, 111, 121, 130, 202, 231
his descendants, 223
Abbasid caliphs, names and dates, 381, 382
Abbasids, 293, 318
consolidation of regime, 223
emblem of, 220
first ten caliphs, 223
open revolt, 219
reasons for decline, 263, 264
secret organization, 218
underground movement, 201, 202
under Seljuqs, 276
war with Umayyads, 219-221
Abd-Allah, Abbasid commander, 221-223, 226-228, 265
Abd-Allah, Muhammad's father, 69
Abd al-Malik, 210, 330
against Kharijites, 179
defeats Ibn Zubayr, 178, 179
his problems, 174
negotiates with Byzantium, 175, 177

reforms, 180
Abd al-Mu'min, 304
Abd al-Rahman I, 199, 318
consolidates rule, 233, 234, 265, 290, 291
escapes massacre, 222
flight to Spain, 232, 289, 290
Abd al-Rahman III, 293, 295
Abraham, the patriarch, 5
Abrogation, 91, 92
Abu Abd-Allah, 302, 310
Abu al-Abbas, 265
acclaimed caliph, 221
brutality, 224
dealings with revolutions, 225-227
inaugural speech, 215, 216
moves to Kufa, 220
Abu al-Ala, 353
Abu al-Atahiya, 353
Abu Bakr, 107, 143, 325, 326
advice to Arab troops, 138
organizes Islamic expansion, 140
selection to caliphate, 135-137
Abu al-Fawaris, 310
Abu Hanifa, 231, 240, 343

*"Al" is the definite article prefix in Arabic and has been discounted in alphabetizing this index.